Bellwether

UNIVERSITY *of* VIRGINIA
CENTER *for* POLITICS

This work was made possible by the UVA Center for Politics.

Bellwether

Virginia's Political Transformation, 2006–2020

David J. Toscano

HAMILTON BOOKS
AN IMPRINT OF
ROWMAN & LITTLEFIELD
Lanham • Boulder • New York • London

Published by Hamilton Books
An imprint of The Rowman & Littlefield Publishing Group, Inc.
4501 Forbes Boulevard, Suite 200, Lanham, Maryland 20706
www.rowman.com

86-90 Paul Street, London EC2A 4NE, United Kingdom

British Library Cataloguing in Publication Information Available

Library of Congress Cataloging-in-Publication Data

Names: Toscano, David J., 1950- author.
Title: Bellwether : Virginia's political transformation, 2006-2020 / David
    J. Toscano.
Description: Lanham, Maryland : Hamilton Books, 2022. | Includes
    bibliographical references and index. | Summary: "Bellwether tells the
    story of how the reliably Republican state of Virginia was transformed
    into a Democratic stronghold between 2006 and 2020"—Provided by publisher.
Identifiers: LCCN 2022001357 (print) | LCCN 2022001358 (ebook) | ISBN
    9780761873228 (paperback) | ISBN 9780716873235 (epub)
Subjects: LCSH: Political parties—Virginia—History—21st century. |
    Elections—Virginia—History—21st century. | Political
    culture—Virginia—History—21st century. | Virginia—Politics and government—
    21st century.
Classification: LCC JK2295.V8 T67 2022 (print) | LCC JK2295.V8 (ebook) |
    DDC 324.209755–dc23/eng/20220213
LC record available at https://lccn.loc.gov/2022001357
LC ebook record available at https://lccn.loc.gov/2022001358

To those dedicated Virginia public servants
who have helped make the Commonwealth a special place.

Contents

List of Illustrations

Foreword

I was born in 1958. At that time, Virginia was allowing public schools to close rather than to comply with the commands of *Brown v. Board of Education*. Women could not attend many Virginia colleges. One of out every one hundred Virginia residents was an immigrant. And Virginia ranked thirty-fifth in the nation in personal per capita income.

As I write these words in 2021, Virginia is a diverse and forward-looking state. Our K-12 schools and higher education system are often ranked among the nation's best. One out of every eight Virginians is an immigrant. The state ranks thirteenth in personal per capita income. We elected the nation's first African American governor in 1989, and our politics has gone from regressive and exclusionary to progressive and welcoming.

It has been the joy of my life to work with so many over the years to accomplish what I believe is the most significant political and economic transformation of any state in the Union during this period.

David Toscano is a friend who served in our General Assembly during the key moments of this transformation. After serving in local government in Charlottesville, he was elected to the Virginia legislature the same year as I became Virginia's 70th Governor. And his fourteen years of service, including as Democratic Leader during the years that the party went from a tiny minority to a majority, were an important element of Virginia's success.

This book tells the story of the transformation. More importantly, it points out how far we still have to go and offers ideas about a new Virginia Way that will accelerate the gains of recent years.

Our progress has not created the society of equals that Jefferson articulated—far from it. But it does offer hope that we need not despair of achieving that vision. I thank my friend for challenging us to increase our efforts in that direction.

U.S. Senator Tim Kaine of Virginia
July 13, 2021

Foreword

Acknowledgments

When I was first elected to the Virginia House of Delegates in 2005, I never envisaged writing a book like this; I was just happy to be the delegate from Charlottesville, occupying the seat once held by Thomas Jefferson in the oldest democratic assembly in the western world. But as I contemplated stepping down from my position as House Minority Leader in 2019, I thought more about the dramatic change that had occurred in Virginia over the last two decades. A state that was reliably Republican in 2000 had been transformed into one where Democrats in 2021 controlled the House of Delegates and the State Senate, and where every major statewide office was occupied by a Democrat. And I had been in the middle of much of this dramatic change. There were stories to tell, and my perspective might be useful in explaining what occurred. Hence, this book.

Few authors work from a blank slate, and I certainly did not. There were so many who helped me with this project, providing historical context, the inside scoop, and insightful analysis. I was happy to borrow from all of them, and hopefully provide credit where it is due. But in the end, this book is only one person's view, and I take full responsibility for it.

I am indebted to so many historical analyses, only some of which can be listed here. Frank B. Atkinson's *The Dynamic Dominion: Realignment and the Rise of Two-Party Competition in Virginia, 1945–1980*, and his *Virginia in the Vanguard: Political Leadership in the 400-Year-Old Cradle of American Democracy, 1981–2006*, a work that ends in the year that this book begins, provide great examples of scholarly analysis combined with political acuity. Albert C. Pollard's *Outsider Looking In: An Outsider's View of the Inner Workings of Virginia Politics and Policy* (2010); and *Notes from the Sausage Factory* (2005), edited by Barnie Day and Becky Dale, both use vignettes to illustrate historical points. Jeff Thomas's *Virginia Politics & Government in a New Century: The Price of Power* (2016); and his *The Virginia Way: Democracy and Power after 2016* (2019) are revealing exposes of present-day scandals that raise important issues about the role of money in politics. *Points of Personal Privilege* is an interesting compendium of perspectives written by past and present Virginia State Senators and Lieutenant Governors.

It is difficult to discuss Virginia without reference to our past, and wonderful historians have assisted me in understanding it. Ed Ayers, Brent Tarter, recently deceased Ron Heinemann, Elizabeth Varon, and David Johnson all provided key background about our history, especially Douglas Southall Freeman and the origins of the so-called Virginia Way. Other scholars also provided penetrating insights, including A. E. B "Dick" Howard, Daniel Palazzolo, Carl Tobias, Richard Schragger, and Alan Greenblatt at *Governing* Magazine.

I received encouragement from many observers of Virginia politics. I am deeply indebted to Larry Sabato at the University of Virginia's Center for Politics, not only for his scholarship and analyses of Virginia politics, but also for his insistence that a book like this ought to be published. Jeff Schapiro, Bob Gibson, Paul Reagan, and L. F. Payne read portions of the manuscript and provided great comments. Richard Cranwell, Dwayne Yancey, Michael Martz, and Gordon C. Morse shared stories.

Tremendous assistance was graciously extended by Paul Reagan, chief of staff for Governor Terry McAuliffe, Larry Roberts, former counsel to Governor Tim Kaine and now head of the Sorensen Institute for Political Leadership, Robert "Bob" D. Holsworth, longtime policy professor and consultant, and Frank B. Atkinson. Each read the entire manuscript and proved incredibly helpful with my prose as well as my perspective.

As a member of the Virginia General Assembly, you learn that actions often occur without you being in the room. Senate committees are acting independently of House groups, and countless meetings occur where you are not present. Consequently, you have to rely on your colleagues for their recollection of what happened. I was fortunate to know so many members that are friends upon whom I could rely. It is impossible to thank them all, but some stand out. Thank you to Mark Sickles, who was always available to discuss politics and policy. My seatmate during my time as Leader, the irrepressible Alfonso Lopez, was the source of much intelligence, and was always helpful to me on the House floor by feeding me information that I could use in debate. Eileen Filler-Corn, now Speaker, was an invaluable ally throughout my tenure. Vivian Watts helped me understand complex bills, and people like Dave Marsden, Dick Saslaw, Ward Armstrong, and Bob Brink supplied not only great insight but also the more-than-occasional laugh. In most recent years, Rip Sullivan provided penetrating analyses and Delores McQuinn was a source of spiritual strength. The list would be longer if my editors had only permitted it.

I am especially grateful to the former Speaker of the House, Bill Howell, who gave me more time to discuss events than I either deserved or was required. Chris Peace provided a glimpse into internal Republican battles. Dave Albo was, as usual, both enjoyable and forthright in our conversations. My state Senator, Creigh Deeds, provided wonderful support through the years.

I could not have written this without insight derived from the executive branch. Former Governor Bob McDonnell was incredibly giving of his time when he did not need to be. For all that happened to the former governor, he never recoiled from sharing his perspective, and I have greater appreciation for how he has rebuilt his life. Though I took office after now-Senator Mark Warner left the governorship, his accomplishments while facing a General Assembly dominated by Republicans were impressive, and his reflections valuable. Tim Kaine and Terry McAuliffe were always willing to talk and share stories about successes and failures; since I was Leader during McAuliffe's first term, I worked with him more closely and was privy to private moments ladened with insight. Governor Ralph Northam was forthright in discussing his dramatic term.

Staff members from various administrations and government departments were extremely helpful, including Aubrey Lane, Brian Moran, Lillian Peake, Norm Oliver, Clyde Cristman, Todd Haymore, Angela Navarro, Rick Holcomb, Shannon Valentine, Carlos Hopkins, Brad Komar, and Brian and Holly Coy. So too were House and Senate Clerk's offices, including Suzette Denslow, Jeff Finch, Paul Nardo, and Susan Schaar. Our Division of Legislative Services and our House and Senate committee staffs are always helpful and generally nonpartisan. People like Tony Maggio and David Conmy provided specific help to this volume, but we should celebrate the professionalism of all of our public servants as one key to explain why Virginia is special.

I am grateful to members of the Virginia lobbying core, most notably Myles Louria, Whitt Clement, and Don Hall, for providing stories about the legislators and the process.

Numerous academics helped in explaining economic data and demographic trends, including Robert McNabb of Old Dominion University, and Hamilton Lombard of the Weldon Cooper Center at the University of Virginia. Nick Kessler provided help with maps and graphs, and David Poole from Virginia Public Access Project (VPAP) was always willing to answer questions. Advocates such as Lori Haas, Dubby Wynne, Gil Harrington, and Lisa Smith revealed stories about their efforts at change.

Over the years, I have had great people work with and for me—Carmen Bingham, Erin Monaghan, Jenny Hogan, Sarah Buckley, Jane Dittmar, David Brown, Jim Nix, Makala Gray, Trent Armitage, Trevor Southerland,

Katie Baker, and Naomi Miller—all of whom have helped immensely and will hopefully testify on my behalf if any of the stories I relate here come to be criticized. Kudos to Elizabeth McMartin for her graphic design skills in producing the cover.

Thanks to Nadine Zimmerli and Erin Monaghan for editing some of my early and occasionally rambling drafts. My deep appreciation goes to the editors and staff at Hamilton Books and Rowman and Littlefield, most notably Brooke Bures and Sam Brawand, consummate professionals who were willing to take confusing portions of this manuscript and translate them into engaging prose.

I would not have been in the position writing this book without the thousands who voted for me over 26 years. I have represented some of the best and brightest in the Commonwealth, and hopefully some of their insights have rubbed off on me. Finally, I want to thank my family, Nancy and Matthew, who put up with what seemed at times to be an obsession. I love them and can never repay them for their support over the many years.

History is usually told from the outside looking in. Analysts examine documents and may occasionally even talk to people involved. This book is a perspective from the inside looking out and is told through the lens of my own experience. The last two decades of Virginia politics and policy are fascinating. I hope this volume is a contribution to their understanding.

Charlottesville, Virginia
June 15, 2021

Introduction

Harbinger of Change

When fifty-nine-year-old Delegate Ken Melvin took the floor of the Virginia House of Delegates on January 19, 2009, I had just completed my third year in the state's General Assembly, and he had just finished his twenty-third. An African American from Portsmouth, Melvin had gifts that many of us envied; when he spoke, people listened. His ability to affect legislative outcomes during debate was so respected that colleagues referred to him as "the terminator." The delegate began his speech slowly and softly, as he had done so many times during his two decades in the House, setting the stage for the crescendo we all anticipated. Explaining how this day was important because Barack H. Obama was about to be inaugurated as the first African American President of the United States, Melvin spoke about how Virginia had changed since he arrived in Richmond, and how blacks in the General Assembly enjoyed greater influence than at any time since Reconstruction.

Melvin then vividly described the scene in his home on November 4, 2008, the night of Obama's election. His brother and his two adult sons had joined the delegate in his living room, and all watched anxiously as the results came in. When the media reported that Obama had carried Virginia, it was clear he would be the next President. His sons jumped up and down with joy, but Melvin and his brother remained seated, quietly sobbing as television screen flashed "OBAMA ELECTED FIRST BLACK PRESIDENT." His children were dumbfounded by the reactions of their elders, and asked the brothers "why are you crying?" Melvin's brother told them that he feared "they would take it away." "Who is 'they'?" asked his sons. "Who is going to take it away? He was ahead in the polls. He was the best person. He should have won."

Melvin proceeded to share with House members how that election night had changed his view of the United States of America. The country had been forever altered, and Melvin felt that the racial prism from which he had seen the world had now become different from his descendants. He expressed the belief held by so many African Americans of his generation. "For most of my life," he said, "I thought I loved America more than America loved me." Melvin had come to believe that race and history mattered so much that Obama could never win. His sons did not view the election that way. For them, race and history would not prevent "the best man" from winning the presidency. When Melvin finished his speech, he received a standing ovation, and more than a few members on both sides of the aisle wiped an emotional tear from their eyes.

Melvin's speech captured the feelings of the time and convinced me that for all the partisan arguments I had heard in the Virginia House of Delegates, there was always a sense that we were involved in something special. There was an optimism that if we worked together, much positive could be accomplished. Some have called this "the Virginia Way," the notion that Virginia's unique combination of civility, respect for the business environment, and political collaboration produced results that made the Commonwealth the envy of many other states. Others explained it as a type of Virginia exceptionalism. In short, we always practiced politics differently (and better) in Virginia.

For a person who grew up in New York state, was educated at a small liberal arts institution (Colgate University) and received my advanced academic training in Boston (Boston College), this notion that Virginia was special took considerable time to get used to. I had always viewed the South as somewhat backward and racist, as a place that you might want to visit but where you would never choose to live. Arriving as a young academic in Charlottesville in 1981, I certainly experienced my share of culture shock and witnessed racial injustice first-hand, particularly when I became an attorney defending indigent clients. But, over time, for all of its faults, I came to see Charlottesville as a terrific place to live. I had the good fortune to be elected to City Council in 1990, and to be selected Mayor in 1994.

Until serving in public office, my encounters with policy and politics were largely intellectual and gleaned from books rather than from experience. But that changed as I came to understand that politics was the art of the possible and the key to success was "getting into the room" where decisions are made. My twelve years as a local elected official made me keenly aware of how much state policy affected local communities. And when an opening for the delegate's seat once held by Thomas Jefferson appeared in 2005, I sought the Democratic nomination, won the contest, and prevailed in the general election. It was a time of Republican ascendency, President George W. Bush, and the Gulf War. For the next fourteen years, I would be in the unique position of participating in the legislative process of an assembly with a 400-year history.

With Obama's election on November 4, 2008, America changed, and Virginia changed with it. Not only did the state select an African American president, but the Commonwealth of Virginia also voted for the Democratic candidate for the first time since Lyndon B. Johnson prevailed against Barry Goldwater in 1964. While most of us did not realize it at the time, this was a key watershed event in Virginia's political transformation from what was a reliably Republican state at the beginning of the twenty-first century to one that has now voted for Democrats in each presidential election since 2008. In addition, the Commonwealth chose Democrats in four of last five gubernatorial elections prior to 2021, selected Democrats to serve as U.S. Senators since 2009, and, in 2019, elected blue majorities in both the Virginia House of Delegates and the state Senate.

The first Obama election was a sign of the political changes that would envelope the Commonwealth over the next decade, as the political complexion of the state changed from red to purple to blue. It was not, of course, the only time Virginia experienced a milestone that ushered in change not predicted at the time. There is always a cyclical character to politics as attitudes and fashions change. And Virginia has had its own twists and turns. The career of populist Henry E. Howell, Jr., for example, shook the establishment in ways not fully understood by those of us who did not live here at the time, with his emphasis on civil rights, economic fairness, and "keeping the big boys honest."[1] Howell, who served as lieutenant governor from 1971 to 1974, pushed, but failed three times in his efforts to win the governorship.

And over the last three decades, some statewide races have proved more significant than others. Charles "Chuck" Robb's victory in 1981 began a string of three successive democratic victories in gubernatorial races, including L. Douglas Wilder's historic win in 1989. George Allen's success in 1993 heralded a conservative resurgence that carried forward into James "Jim" Gilmore's administration, and helped build a seemingly indestructible Republican majority in the House of Delegates. Both Mark R. Warner and Timothy M. Kaine won the governorship but had to face at least one chamber of the General Assembly generally resistant to their approaches. Hence, when Obama carried the state, Democrats greeted it as a potential harbinger of things to come. For me, I was just fortunate to be a witness to this history as it unfolded.

A PURPLE STATE

Virginia's politics between 2002 and 2020 could be viewed as a time of Republican hegemony punctuated by periodic sprints to the political center. The House of Delegates was dominated by conservative lawmakers for much of this time. Legislators embraced the culture wars with a vengeance, pushing measures to further restrict abortion, expand gun rights, and enact policies viewed as anti-immigrant and antigay. After the GOP gained power early in this century, they remained focused on maintaining their power. They passed a redistricting bill in 2011 (ultimately ruled to be unconstitutional) designed to protect their incumbents and target certain Democrats. They enacted measures to make it more difficult for people to vote. And they mostly had their way. Occasionally, the so-called *sensible center* would assert itself to pass a reasonable budget, or occasionally to enact major change, examples being Warner's tax reform package of 2004, Governor Robert F. "Bob" McDonnell's 2013 transportation bill, and even Medicaid expansion in 2018. In most cases, the only forces standing in the way of conservative initiatives were Democratic governors and the occasional opposition from the Senate, which until recently included a group of Republicans who could derail the more controversial House measures.

But major changes were on the way. Virginia's population was diversifying, as larger numbers of persons born in foreign nations or other states came to live in the Commonwealth. The African American vote was becoming increasingly significant in statewide races. Educational levels were rising, especially in Northern Virginia (NoVa), where so much of the population was residing. And the state was beginning to experience the nationalization of politics at all levels that it had avoided for most of its recent history. The Commonwealth conducts its statewide elections in the off-years, when no federal contests are on the ballot. For that reason, the political polarization and gridlock present in Washington, DC and in some other state capitals seemed less apparent in Richmond. But, for a variety of reasons, that began to change in the 2010s. Media coverage of state government declined dramatically, leading many news consumers little choice but to view politics from a national perspective. And the very thing that appeared to inoculate Virginia from national divisions—its off-year elections—now became a source of weakness. Only New Jersey and Virginia now conduct their statewide elections in the off-year, making them the locations for national donors who seek to make their mark. Add to that the state's lax campaign financing laws, and a perfect environment exists for the nationalization of Virginia politics. No longer would political races be won or lost primarily on the basis a candidate's position on a set of issues unique to Virginia voters, but instead on whether they were a Republican or a Democrat. The Donald J. Trump presidency only accelerated this process. A state that was reliably red was moving more quickly to blue than perhaps any other state in the Nation.

A 2017 EARTHQUAKE AND THE 2019 TRIFECTA

The November 2017 election dramatically changed the political dynamics in the Commonwealth, when Democrats picked up a shocking fifteen seats in the House of Delegates and came within a *coin toss* of gaining the majority. As the Democratic leader in the House since 2011, I had been engaged in every element to these races for years. And our efforts to build our numbers were finally proving successful. It now appeared that Democratic electoral wins would not be limited to statewide elections, but the party might actually regain control of the legislature. Two years later, it happened! A number of dynamics—changing demographics, the federal court's drawing of new legislative districts, and anti-Trump sentiment—propelled the Democrats to majority status in both the House and the Senate. The party now enjoyed a political trifecta, controlling the executive and both legislative Bodies. They seized the moment and went bold, repealing a number of Republican measures adopted over the last twenty years and enacting big changes of their own. In just two years, Democrats took action to make voting easier by repealing the photo ID requirement previously enacted by the GOP and by expanding early voting. They increased the minimum wage and passed the Equal Rights Amendment (ERA). They enacted sweeping climate change legislation, nondiscrimination measures, and criminal justice reform, including the repeal of the death penalty. The only thing slowing these efforts was the COVID-19 pandemic, which imposed budget constraints on spending plans while providing a subtle brake to any efforts at imposing too many changes on businesses.

Initially, Democrats insisted that they would retain the longstanding bipartisan approach that positioned the Commonwealth as the "best state for business." But the rhetoric and proposals of some of the newer members made the business sector nervous, prompting some to wonder whether a paradigm shift was in the making. The pace of policy change was breathtaking, and it marked the greatest progressive advance in recent Virginia history. Whether the Democrats could continue their political domination would await the results of 2021 statewide campaign, but, for the moment, Virginia Democrats were in the driver's seat. What this will mean for "the Virginia Way" in the future remains an open question.

THE CHARLOTTESVILLE BACKDROP

This book is written in Charlottesville, Virginia, my home for more than forty years, and where I got my start in politics. Charlottesville claims to be in the South, but not of it, as if it can avoid its own experience with segregation.

People forget that the city closed its schools in the 1960s rather than integrate. Or that its zoning patterns contributed to segregated neighborhoods, and that, under the guise of urban renewal, the city razed the neighborhood of Vinegar Hill, destroying black-owned businesses and displacing residents. Charlottesville is a university town that boasts its educational attainment and liberal politics. It is a special place, large enough to enjoy the amenities of city life but small enough that an individual or small groups can really make a difference. Yet, for all of its education, wealth, and prosperity, it is a city with pockets of severe poverty; over one-half of its public-school children qualify for the free lunch program.[2] Fissures of class and race are evident, as they are in all of Virginia. Until 1980, city government was controlled by Republicans or conservative Democrats, usually drawn from the business community. But since my election to City Council in 1990, it has become one of the most reliably Democratic cities in the Commonwealth.

My election to the Virginia House of Delegates in 2005 came after the retirement of the beloved Mitchell Van Yahres, who had stepped down after twenty-four years of service. The experience was totally different from my time in local government. I was in the minority, and the politics in Richmond were more conservative than mine, both within the Democratic ranks, and certainly within the Republican Caucus. Like many first term representatives, I had big decisions to make. Would I be a firebrand or a conciliator, a partisan or a collaborator? Would the focus be agitation or legislation? These choices were no different than the ones faced by most new representatives. And it was easy to see how legislators, in order to be effective, would change their emphases over time. There is always a delicate balance between policy you hope to enact—and that which you can pass. And a fine line between preserving your relationships and vocally calling out what one perceives to be injustice and unfairness. This book is about the personalities and perspectives of many players on the stage of state politics, and how they succeed or fail in making policy that guides the Commonwealth. It is about who was in the room at the time, the choices they made, and how their decisions have shaped the Virginia and influenced the Nation.

***

Charlottesville has always occupied a unique place in this country, being the home of Jefferson, and the site of one of the oldest and most distinguished universities in the country. Unfortunately, many Americans now remember the city for the mayhem and murder that occurred in the August 2017 "Unite the Right" assault of white supremacists on this community. On two steamy days, hatred and racism descended on our town in a dramatic surfacing of a movement that had remained largely dormant for years, and which was strengthened by the rhetoric from the White House during the Trump administration. That event plunged this community into deep soul searching about both our past and our future. The Commonwealth of Virginia was no exception. In our early history, Virginia was viewed as the source of revolutionary ideas and the state of presidents. As our Nation matured, Virginia found itself on the wrong side of history, taking up arms to defend slavery. Following the Civil War, the Commonwealth enjoyed a brief period where it had the potential to shape Reconstruction in a way to involve African Americans and whites in common cause, but those efforts collapsed under a conservative backlash, and plunged Virginia into another period of white supremacy that remained largely intact until the 1954 *Brown v. Board of Education*,[3] the lunch counter sit-ins, and the Civil Rights legislation of the 1960s. Today, the Commonwealth's unique history places it in a key position to shape the future of America.

OUR ROADMAP

The creation of America has always meant entering "the room" of politics and policymaking—to participate, advocate, and educate. For many, this means electoral politics, and chapter 1 describes some of the events that brought me to local, and then to state government. Different experiences—from City Councilor to Mayor to Delegate to Democratic House Leader—all provide different lessons about how policy is made. But the key message is this—the Cardinal Rule of politics is that "decisions are made by those people in the room at the time."

Chapter 2 examines the notion that Virginia is an exceptional state, both in how it views itself and in how others see it. The Commonwealth ranks highly on many measures of life quality, but, as the case with most states, can suffer from an exalted view of its accomplishments. The Commonwealth cannot escape the stain of slavery and its aftermath. Race is pervasive in the history and politics of all states, but in Virginia it takes center stage, whether this involves the state's leadership in the Civil War, its Jim Crow initiatives, or the construction of *massive resistance* to school desegregation. But our history also tells other stories of resistance and of hope. One finds this history in the biracial coalition who seized control of state government in 1881,[4] only to be repelled by the conservative backlash several years later. We see it through the eyes of former school children in Farmville, the town in Prince Edward County which occupied a central role as one of the legal contestants in *Brown v. Board of Education*. We celebrate the audacious election of L. Douglas Wilder, the grandson of slaves, to be this Nation's first elected

African American Governor in 1989. And we examine it in the responses to the recent blackface controversy involving Governor Ralph S. Northam.

Chapter 3 begins a discussion of the continuing significance of race in the Commonwealth, starting with recent controversies involving Governor Northam and then-Lieutenant Governor Justin E. Fairfax. Chapter 4 explores the origins of the "Virginia Way." Many Virginians do not realize that the phrase that was first used as a justification for segregation. The concept has been transformed over the decades into what now serves as a euphemism for the notion of "Virginia exceptionalism." One finds similar concepts in every state, but "the Virginia Way" has recently taken on a character much larger and more positive than its actual origins would justify.

A state cannot become great without addressing the historical impact of race relations on its policy. Chapter 5 discusses how Virginia has been affected by shifts in its demographic mix and cultural values. The population characteristics of the state have changed dramatically in the last twenty years—especially in NoVa—and that has fueled major political change. But throughout this disruption, there is also continuity, both in terms of our state's approaches to policy and to the institutions within which such change occurs. Chapter 6 explains how elections affect policy in the Commonwealth, and explores the dynamic between money, politics, and policy.

Public policy is made by people. Chapters 7 and 8 describe some of the personalities who have occupied center stage in Richmond in the last two decades. These include governors, attorneys general, and, of course, legislators. In my experience, most public servants at the state level are serving for the right reasons. They may feel strongly about an issue or a series of issues. They may simply be compelled to serve their friends and neighbors. Or both! Certainly, few expect to get rich in the job. They sacrifice time at their day job and with their family. And no matter how popular, they will hear people yell at them for various reasons and at times for little reason. It is not easy, but, for all its challenges, public service is the best job in the world. For if you do it well, you can assist people who need help and construct policy that works for future generations.

The issues of the Commonwealth may have changed over the last two decades, but some of the dynamics are not that different, whether they involve friction between the executive and the legislative branches, or even between the Virginia House of Delegates and the state Senate. In addition to the officeholders, state politics involves many groups and individuals who argue for one policy or another. These include everyday citizens, who influence legislation in countless ways, either as individuals or as members of groups, and lobbyists, who are frequently criticized but without whom a citizen legislature would find it difficult to function. These "Advocates" are discussed in chapter 9.

Like the Nation, Virginia's political fissures frequently take on the character of a culture war, and those dynamics, whether they involve immigration, abortion, or guns, are described in chapter 10. Similarly, the polarization in the country has found its way to Richmond, and parties frequently pass laws simply because they are in the majority; chapter 11 discusses how the majority party dictates certain policies simply *because they can*. Chapter 12 provides insights not only into the electoral process, but also what happens when there is a massive political change—like the Blue Wave elections that washed over Virginia between 2017 and 2019. It includes the examination of a key piece of the political process—redistricting—and shows the importance of this process in explaining the political composition of the legislature. In 2020, the voters amended the Virginia Constitution to establish a "bipartisan" redistricting commission, and time will tell whether the public will view this new process as more legitimate than the previous approach that, in most cases, was an exercise in raw political power.

Chapter 13 examines not only how Democrats won control of the legislative apparatus in the 2019 election, but also how they decided to *go bold* in 2020 and 2021, passing the most progressive agenda the Commonwealth has ever seen. Though the pandemic and its budgetary impacts delayed many of the costliest initiatives, the state has embarked on a number of changes that will affect Commonwealth residents for decades.

Many pundits are now struggling with how to define the Commonwealth politically. As recently as 2015, the state was viewed as a moderately conservative *purple* state. But with Trump in the White House and the demographic changes making their mark, the state had become so Democratic by 2020 that neither party invested much in the Presidential race. It has been a remarkable change, and one that few predicted would be so dramatic and occur so quickly. Nonetheless, it is difficult to predict the future twists and turns of political fortunes. Will the progressive legislation passed in 2020 and 2021 prompt a backlash? Will a new President lead to a reduction of Democratic energy that will raise Republican opportunity in the 2021 statewide elections? And how will the 2021 redistricting affect who will run for office and who will prevail?

The Conclusion offers perspective on some of the long-term major issues facing the Commonwealth. Many of these are similar to the challenges of other states; others are unique to Virginia. How these disputes are resolved will be determined by many factors and forces. The economy will influence the investments that the Commonwealth will be able to make in the years ahead. Voters will certainly be key; once they put their energy behind certain people or ideas, their impact is undeniable. And their chances to influence policy are frequent. As we say in Virginia, every year is another election— and yet another chance to determine which players will determine the policy priorities of the Commonwealth, and how those initiatives will be viewed in the national context. Finally, how policymakers conduct themselves will have a tremendous impact on the ability to get things done. There is grave concern that the partisan gridlock and divide that is so omnipresent in Washington, DC is now finding its way into state politics. In Virginia, we argue that we govern ourselves very differently than in DC. We supposedly get things done in a unique way—a Virginia way—that allows us to escape the vitriol and dysfunction of Washington. But upon closer examination of the trends over the last decade, one cannot avoid being concerned about the future of civil discourse. At issue is the extent to which the Commonwealth can serve as a bellwether for the rest of the Nation, and whether it can be a model for how state lawmakers can construct thoughtful policies to serve the constituents they represent. It begins with "the cardinal rule of politics"—that decisions are made by those "in the room at the time."

NOTES

1. Margaret Edds, "Remembering Henry Howell 'Keeping the Big Boys Honest' Is What He Loved Best," *Virginian-Pilot* (Opinion), July 13, 1997, J5, https://scholar. lib.vt.edu/VA-news/VA-Pilot/issues/1997/vp970713/07110021.htm (accessed May 31, 2021).

2. Katherine Knott, "Charlottesville School Lunch Program Gets a Healthy-Sized Grant," *Daily Progress*, November 28, 2020, https://dailyprogress.com/news/local /education/charlottesville-school-lunch-program-gets-a-healthy-sized-grant/article _0b741cc2-2f7b-11eb-a02a-db53b5016f34.html (accessed May 31, 2021).

3. *Brown v. Board of Education of Topeka.* 347 U.S. 483 (1954). https://supreme. justia.com/cases/federal/us/347/483/ (accessed April 22, 2021).

4. For several years in the early 1880s, Virginia was actually governed by a biracial coalition. Prominent in the group was William E. Cameron, who served as Governor from 1882 to 1886 and William "Billy" Mahone, a colorful former Confederate general who had formed the "Readjuster Party" in hopes of leading the state out of Reconstruction. Blacks had been elected in significant numbers to the House of Delegates in the late 1870s and early 1880s. Educational and other reforms were passed during the time, including the creation of the first of Virginia's black colleges, which eventually became known as Virginia State University. The power of the Readjusters was short-lived; by 1883 it had largely fallen victim to a conservative backlash, as Democrats swept two-thirds of the General Assembly seats in that fall's election. See Jane Dailey, *Before Jim Crow: The Politics of Race in Postemancipation Virginia* (Chapel Hill and London: University of North Carolina Press, 2000); Ronald L. Heinemann, John G. Kolp, Anthony S. Parent, Jr., and William G. Shade, *Old Dominion, New Commonwealth: A History of Virginia, 1607–2007* (Charlottesville: University of Virginia Press, 2007); and George Harrison Gilliam, "Building a

Modern South: Political Economy in Nineteenth-Century Virginia," unpublished Ph.D. diss., Corcoran Department of History, University of Virginia, 2013, https:// doi.org/10.18130/V39639

Abbreviations

AAA	Bond Rating (Highest); Triple-A
ABC	Alcohol Beverage Commission, Virginia
ACA	*Patient Protection and Affordable Care Act*
ACEEE	American Council for an Energy Efficient Economy
ACP	Atlantic Coast Pipeline
ACS	American Community Survey, U.S. Census Bureau
AFL-CIO	American Federation of Labor and Congress of Industrial Organizations
AG	Attorney General
APCO	Appalachian Power
ARTS	Medicaid Addiction and Recovery Treatment Services
BPOL	Business, Professional, and Occupational License
CBD	Cannabidiol
CDC	U.S. Centers for Disease Control and Prevention
CED	Committee for Economic Development
CIRCLE	Center for Information & Research on Civic Learning and Engagement
CLG	Commission on Local Government, Virginia
COVID-19	Coronavirus 2019 Pandemic
CTB	Commonwealth Transportation Board, Virginia
DACA	Deferred Action for Childhood Arrivals
DAGA	Democratic Attorneys General Association
DHCD	Department of Housing and Community Development, Virginia
DHS	U.S. Department of Homeland Security
DMAS	Department of Medicaid Assistance Services, Virginia
DNA	Deoxyribonucleic Acid
DOJ	U.S. Department of Justice
DRPT	Virginia Department of Rail and Public Transportation
EPA	U.S. Environmental Protection Agency
ERA	Equal Rights Amendment
ERPO	Extreme Risk Protection Order
EVMS	Eastern Virginia Medical School
FATA	*Virginia Fraud Against Taxpayers Act*

FRED	Federal Reserve Bank of St. Louis
GOP	Grant Old Party; Republican Party
HBCU	Historically Black Colleges and Universities
HD	House District, Virginia
HEW	U.S. Department of Health, Education, and Welfare
HQ2	Amazon's number two headquarters in Arlington County, Virginia
ICE	U.S. Immigration and Customs Enforcement
IOU	Investor-Owned Utilities
JFK	John F. Kennedy
JLARC	Joint Legislative Audit and Review Commission, State of Virginia
KKK	Ku Klux Klan
LBJ	Lyndon Baines Johnson
LCV	League of Conservation Voters, Virginia
LIS	Legislative Information System, Virginia
MEPAV	Municipal Electric Power Association of Virginia
MIRC	Medicaid Innovation and Reform Commission, Virginia
NAACP	National Association for the Advancement of Colored People
NAAG	National Association of State Attorneys General
NARA	U.S. National Archives and Records Administration
NAS	U.S. Naval Air Station
NAWJ	National Association of Women Judges
NCSL	National Conference of State Legislatures
NDRC	National Democratic Redistricting Committee
NILC	National Immigration Law Center
NLC	National League of Cities
NORML	National Organization for the Reform of Marijuana Laws
NoVa	Northern Virginia
NRA	National Rifle Association
PAC	Political Action Committee
RAGA	Republican Attorneys General Association
RFP	Request for Proposals
RGGI	Regional Greenhouse Gas Initiative

ROVA	Rest of the state of Virginia, excluding Norther Virginia (NoVa)
SCC	State Corporation Commission, Virginia
SCHEV	State Council of Higher Education for Virginia
SELC	Southern Environmental Law Center
SOQ	Standards of Quality
UVA	University of Virginia
VACo	Virginia Association of Counties
VADA	Virginia Auto Dealers Association
VCDL	Virginia Citizens Defense League
VCEA	*Virginia Clean Energy Act*
VCU	Virginia Commonwealth University
VEDP	Virginia Economic Development Partnership
VEPCO	Virginia Electric Power Company
VHHA	Virginia Hospital & Healthcare Association
VLBC	Virginia Legislative Black Caucus
VMI	Virginia Military Institute
VML	Virginia Municipal League
VPAP	Virginia Public Access Project
VPLC	Virginia Poverty Law Center

Chapter 1

The Cardinal Rule

No one else was in
The room where it happened . . . .
No one really knows how
The game is played.
The art of the trade,
How the sausage gets made.
We just assume that it happens.
But no one else is in
The room where it happens . . . .
No one really knows how the
Parties get to yes.
The pieces that are sacrificed in
Ev'ry game of chess.
We just assume that it happens.
But no one else is in
The room where it happens.

—Lin-Manuel Miranda, from the musical *Hamilton*[1]

When I was growing up, I never remotely thought I would live much of my life in Virginia. Like many other Virginians, I am a transplant from another place. I came to Charlottesville in 1981 as a progressive academic from New York and Massachusetts, twenty-seven years after *Brown v. Board of Education* (1954)[2] and the subsequent decision by Virginia to close most of the state's public schools rather than integrate. My wife Nancy and I had come to visit my in-laws, who had just retired in Charlottesville. My father-in-law had been a school administrator in the city until he was encouraged to leave in 1966 after pushing too hard and too fast for integration. Despite this poor treatment, he and his wife had always wanted to return, and moved to the city two weeks before we arrived. My wife and I had no intention of remaining in Virginia, until I was offered a job teaching sociology at the University of Virginia (UVA) and Nancy landed a position at the University

Press. We stayed, but not without the need for a major adjustment in how we viewed the world.

As I traveled around my new community, I noticed several things that were jarring. I walked into libraries and would see large paintings of Robert E. Lee rather than the portraits of Abraham Lincoln that adorned similar buildings in the North. My first experience in finding housing was remarkable in how the landlord, without any prompting, exclaimed, "don't worry, people don't rent to those kinds of people around here." There were few black elected officials. And Confederate monuments were everywhere.

`As a Northerner, Charlottesville and UVA took some getting used to. The university dripped in tradition. UVA has an honor code which mandates "no lying, cheating, or stealing," with a student-run enforcement system that requires expulsion upon conviction. I learned quickly from the department secretary that faculty members were called "Mister" instead of "Doctor," unless, of course, you were either a physician or, for some strange reason, a professor in the School of Education. And one should never use the word "campus"; it was always the "Grounds." The reason for this vernacular was clear; "Mr. Jefferson would have wanted it that way." In the early 1980s, the Jefferson luster had not yet been tarnished by the Sally Hemings revelations. He was revered, and most locals either ignored or excused his reliance on slavery and his failure to reconcile the powerful words of the Declaration of Independence[3] with his personal ownership of human beings.

My first foray into electoral politics came in 1982, when I went against tradition and ran for the U.S. Congress as a liberal in the conservative 7th District in Virginia. My leftist orientation and environmental politics did not mesh well with the local Democratic committees, which had commenced— but not yet completed—severing ties with the conservative Byrd machine.[4] At the time, Democrats and Republicans seemed only marginally different; they both appeared to be controlled by corporate interests and were prisoners of uninspired politics. I felt we needed a third party, and embraced what was called the Citizens Party, whose presidential candidate in 1980 was the famous environmentalist Barry Commoner. I was selected to be the candidate by a small group of approximately ten activists, nothing like the cauldron of primary fights by which major party candidates are now chosen. My opponents were the longtime Republican incumbent, J. Kenneth Robinson and Lindsay G. Dorrier Jr., a kindly Democrat who made the mistake of describing himself as a "boll weevil" Democrat, which some viewed as code for a "Byrd Democrat." With that one statement, he alienated the progressive wing of the Democratic Party and gave me the opportunity to gain some traction in Charlottesville, even though my campaign had little idea what it was doing.

My candidacy was all about ideas, and I was not afraid to embrace controversial positions, arguing that military spending was bad for the economy, proposing a nuclear freeze, supporting worker rights, and even once suggesting that we choose U.S. Supreme Court justices by direct election. I traveled the district in search of free media and ran on a budget of $10,000, mostly funded by rock concerts and selling some of our wedding gifts at yard sales. When the votes were counted, I emerged with 11 percent of the vote in Charlottesville, not bad for someone who was new to the area. I became both the darling of the Left and an anathema to the local Democratic Party establishment.

The campaign further fueled my interest in politics and in policy. But I quickly realized that my ability to "get into the room" was severely comprised if I remained an outsider. I made overtures to the local Democrats and fortunately for me, leaders like future Mayor Tom Vandever and City Treasurer Jennifer Brown thought I was worth being given a chance. By then, I had entered law school at UVA and was planning to remain in Charlottesville after my graduation in 1985. Soon thereafter, I was appointed to a city board, the now-defunct Charlottesville Social Development Commission, and plunged headfirst into race relations and the emerging movement to have local governments divest their retirement portfolio of stocks in businesses that had interests in apartheid South Africa. Charlottesville became the first Southern city to divest, and I was learning the "cardinal rule of politics."

GETTING INTO THE ROOM

I ran for City Council in 1990 to be a voice for the voiceless. I narrowly won the Democratic nomination in an upset, landing a slot on the two-person ticket for the open slots on the Council. At this phase in Charlottesville's political history, however, being a Democrat was no assurance of winning the general election. The smart money was on my Democratic running mate, Kay Slaughter, and the loveable Republican incumbent Darden Towe, a fifty-five-year-old Charlottesville native and insurance agent who had played Santa Claus to countless youngsters and organizations.

But the political demographics in the city were changing rapidly, and Towe and his supporters never realized it until it was too late. I outworked him, knocking on door after door, and following up contacts with personal notes and letters. In relatively small turnout races like these, door-to-door campaigning makes all the difference, and unless the political demographics are too stacked against you, the person who works the hardest will often prevail. Even Towe's last-minute attack on me as a socialist failed because my door knocking had inoculated me from the criticism. On election night, I was behind until the last precinct reported, and then eked out a seventy-nine-vote margin. I was finally in the room.

Newly elected local officials quickly discover that they have less control than they thought. In Virginia as in many other states, some of the challenges for local electeds are rooted in the Dillon Rule, the legal construct by which localities are prohibited from acting in certain areas unless given authority by the state to do so. I would frequently argue that the city could do many positive things, if only it were not constrained by the Dillon Rule. On Council, I also learned how dramatically the state can impact local priorities based on the policies it enacts. While Mayor in the mid-nineties, I became embroiled in the debate initiated by Governor Jim Gilmore's attempt to repeal Virginia's car tax, a personal property tax levied on vehicle ownership. Since the tax was levied at the local level, state repeal would create a huge hole in the city's budget. While many in the legislature were not enthused by the proposal, a partial repeal was eventually passed, and that decision created problems for the city's ability to fund critical programs. The adverse fiscal impact of Gilmore's partial repeal proved to be so great that the legislature was forced, following Democrat Mark Warner's election as the Commonwealth's 69th Governor, to raise taxes to balance the budget and prevent a potential reduction in Virginia's sterling bond ratings.[5] This experience clearly revealed the significance of state policies to the success of local communities. It also illustrated that the people "in the room at the time" can have a tremendous impact on the decisions that affect so many who remain outside. I carried these lessons for twelve years in local government, and for the fourteen years I served in Richmond.

INITIATION INTO THE LARGER ROOM

My first election to the Virginia House of Delegates was never in doubt; I easily bested my Republican opponent, winning 75 percent of the vote. I soon discovered that the Virginia General Assembly is a much larger room than Charlottesville City Council. In a city of five elected officials, all you needed was three votes to pass any measure. This occasionally seemed insurmountable, but now feels quaint after serving in the General Assembly where, to get anything done, you need the support of at least fifty-one members of one Body, twenty-one in the other, and may even need to surmount a possible gubernatorial veto. This was undeniably a far more complicated task than persuading two other members of a five-person council to help accomplish a goal.

In addition, my immediate constituency had doubled in size (80,000 vs. 40,000), and I was now involved in making policy for a state of 8 million persons. There was much that I did not know and had to learn—about regions like Southside, Hampton Roads, southwest Virginia, and Northern Virginia

(NoVa). The issues were more complex, and the advocates came from totally different perspectives than the ones with which I was most familiar.

The initiation of new Delegates involves getting to know the Virginia Capitol building, an imposing place steeped in history. With a design based on drawings that Jefferson sent from Paris in 1785, it dripped with grandeur and tradition, some of it a reminder of days of division embodied in the Civil War. It is impossible to forget the first time you enter the House Chamber, and how it feels when you sit at a century-old desk and recall some of the members who preceded you—Jefferson, James Madison, Patrick Henry, James Monroe. In a room off the grand chamber of the House of Delegates is the Old Chamber, much smaller in size, where the House met from 1788 until the major expansion of the Capitol was completed in 1904. Many historical events occurred in this room. In December 1791, the House voted to ratify the proposed Bill of Rights.[6] In 1807, Aaron Burr was acquitted of treason in a trial presided over by U.S. Supreme Court Chief Justice John Marshall. And in 1861, Robert E. Lee accepted his commission to command Virginia's military forces a few days after the state voted to secede from the Union. Some of the original desks remain in that room, and they were surrounded, until very recently, by busts of people who once crusaded for the destruction of the Union, including two non-Virginians: Confederate president Jefferson Davis and vice-president Alexander Stephens. A large statute of Lee stood at the entrance to the room until its removal in 2020.[7]

As you leave the Old Chamber and proceed into the Rotunda, you encounter a magnificent Carrera marble statue of George Washington. Commissioned by the General Assembly in 1784, and designed by Jean-Antoine Houdon, a French sculptor recommended by Jefferson and Benjamin Franklin. The 6 feet 2 inches tall sculpture stood in stark contrast to the smaller one of Lee in the Old Chamber and illustrates further the contradictions of the Old Dominion.[8] When I first took my seat on the House floor in January 2006, I entered this history and tradition in a new way.

Even before a vote is cast, Delegates are also introduced to the norms, rules, and values of the House of Delegates. One of my initial encounters with the traditions of the House involved securing an office in the General Assembly office building. As Delegate-elect, I contacted House Clerk Bruce Jamerson and asked for the same office as my predecessor, Mitchell Van Yahres (a corner office with a spectacular view of the Capitol). Upon hearing my initial request, Jamerson calmly and coolly said, "Mr. Toscano, I can assure you of two things. First, you will have an office, and second, it will have a window." Since invoking Van Yahres as an argument for a good office had failed, I then pulled the Jefferson card. "Mr. Jamerson," I said, "I have the seat that was once held by Thomas Jefferson. Should I not receive an office reflective of that honor?" Jamerson again responded with a sly smile and a dry hint of sarcasm. "Mr. Toscano," he reiterated, "you will have an office, and it will have a window." Eventually, I received an office—with a window—in a remote section of the building. It had a view, not of the Capitol, but of Richmond's City Hall and the offices of its newly-elected Mayor and former Governor, L. Douglas Wilder. As a freshman, I had entered the room of the General Assembly, but my initiation made it clear that new members are not accorded immediate legitimacy; one had to earn it.

Within several weeks of being sworn in, I recognized that there are different ways to "get into the room" and influence policy. Robert A. Caro, the preeminent biographer of Lyndon Baines Johnson (LBJ), once detailed the former president's approach when he was first elected to Congress. Johnson would simply wait outside the men's room so he would have the opportunity to meet most of the members with whom he would serve.[9] I did not follow LBJ's example. Instead, I decided to establish my credentials by choosing some issues that were relatively non-controversial and finding ways to work with the other side to accomplish things. In a tradition-bound institution like the Virginia House of Delegates, you were encouraged to learn the system and wait your term. At the time, first termers were advised against giving stirring speeches on the House floor during its "morning hour," where Delegates would take turns regaling the Body about one issue or another, or during debate on key bills. The speeches might prove to be great oratory, but they did little to influence votes and often alienated other members for no good reason. In my first session, a very bright and articulate Delegate gave a fiery speech on an issue that I have since forgotten. From that point, he was labeled as a showboat, was never able to get much done, and was gone after several sessions. Today, many newly-elected representatives see their roles differently; they feel that they were elected to "shake things up," and if that means speaking often before the Body, so be it.

As a new Delegate, I deferred to the tradition at the time, and remained quiet on the House floor. But as the session was coming to an end, I considered dipping my feet into the water. The issue involved the subject of eminent domain, the legal concept by which a person's property could be taken for "just compensation" by the state for a public use like schools, parks, roads, or utility lines. An extremely complex but important issue, the public generally paid little mind to it—until they thought it might affect them. In 2005, the issue became controversial because of a U.S. Supreme Court case holding that, under Connecticut law, the private property of a person could be taken not for a public use, but instead for a private development.[10]

In the controversy that followed the Court's decision, both ends of the political spectrum began to demagogue the issue and argued that Virginia's laws needed changing. In actuality, the Commonwealth's eminent domain law was very protective of private property and did not remotely resemble

Connecticut's. But feeling the need to respond to the Court's decision, the legislature created a working group of stakeholders, including local governments and utilities, to come up with a new law that could address the *Kelo v. City of New London* (2005) case while ensuring the building of public infrastructure would not be unduly restricted. In time, the stakeholder group reached a compromise, and the bill reflecting it came to the House floor for possible passage.

In a moment of freshman naivete, I thought this might be a great opportunity to stand up and talk about the importance of a compromise on a significant issue. I was so glad I did not. The debate turned contentious, the compromise came under attack, and the bill was voted down in large measure due to a speech by Delegate by Johnny Joannou, a Democrat from Portsmouth. Joannou was not the most eloquent speaker, but he was closely allied with the majority Republican Caucus, frequently providing them intelligence about Democratic legislative strategy. For his efforts over the years, Republicans awarded him one of the coveted seats on the House Appropriations Committee. He was usually one of the conferees who worked on the final State budget.[11] Joannou was also a strong advocate of private property rights, and his speech on the bill turned enough Republicans against the bill to defeat it. Eventually, a new bill was passed, but I had learned a lesson about when a junior legislator should take the floor and when to remain seated.

I learned quickly that the major work of the assembly is done in committee. Consequently, I decided to focus on concrete issues before the major committee to which I had been appointed, the House Courts of Justice Committee. A major rewrite of Virginia's adoption law was before us, and there were very few Delegates who had any background in this area of the law or who had a personal interest in the subject. Since I had both, I became engaged in revising the entire legislation, and worked closely with the various patrons to get it passed through the House and the Senate. My involvement and expertise were rewarded when I was appointed as a conferee to work through the final details reconciling the House and Senate versions of the legislation—even though I was neither a patron of the bill nor in the majority. This was unusual for a newcomer, and it helped me establish bipartisan credibility, both in the committee and in the House as a whole.

From that point forward, my colleagues tended to trust my opinion on adoption bills and family law matters, and my view could frequently determine the outcome of specific legislation. While it was sometimes uncomfortable having that degree of influence, I was more than happy to use it. When it came to lawmaking, policy and personality often intertwine, and building trust and relationships can have a large impact on the success of legislation.

This was not the conceptual framework advanced in academic books about policymaking but instead the practical process of legislating.

TRAINS AND CHANGE

Only after being elected did I realize that my long-past predecessor Thomas Jefferson was just one of the unique things about representing the 57th District. Many of my colleagues in the House constantly worried about their next campaign (a Delegate's term is just two years) and envied my representation of such a great place—its beauty, history, and increasingly solid Democratic leanings. Based in Charlottesville, my district was solidly blue, and gold-plated for a Democrat like me, so long as I remained true to progressive values. The only way that I was likely to lose an election was in a primary contest (something which no one even attempted until 2017). But being a Delegate meant little if I got nothing accomplished. Because Democrats were then the minority party in the House, I had to find ways to enlist Republicans to be successful.

I also discovered early that making change was not necessarily about just passing bills. Instead, it could occur by finding the best way to leverage your position and relationships. This became apparent early in my tenure, when several of my colleagues and I convinced then-Governor Tim Kaine that the Commonwealth should invest state monies to expand and to improve Amtrak passenger train service between Charlottesville and Washington.

Today, Charlottesville residents enjoy the option of taking a daily train to and from DC. Its reasonably priced fare and its reliable service now seems commonplace, but in 2008, that was not the case. Charlottesville had long been served by Amtrak, but only via often-unreliable long-distance trains that ran either between New Orleans or Chicago and Washington. Studies conducted by the Virginia Department of Rail and Public Transportation (DRPT) showed substantial demand for additional and more reliable service, but, despite the efforts of citizen advocacy from places like Charlottesville, where former City Councilor Meredith Richards and others had been writing letters for years, this was not likely to happen without an investment of state monies. And the state's budget was contracting because of the Great Recession of 2007–2008.

This challenge did not deter Shannon Valentine, then the Democrat Delegate from Lynchburg and the future Virginia Secretary of Transportation in the administration of Governor Ralph S. Northam. Lynchburg was on the same train line as Charlottesville, and Valentine's constituents wanted better service as much as mine. Though both of us were new Delegates, we decided to push for the expansion, with Valentine taking the lead.

We knew that convincing Kaine and former Secretary of Transportation Pierce Homer to include major funding for this new daily train service that would run from Lynchburg, in Valentine's district, through Charlottesville (my district) to the Nation's capital would be a minor miracle. First, Congress was threatening to force states to assume responsibility for funding Amtrak's regional intercity rail routes or risk losing them altogether. Virginia already had several routes that could be affected, and even rail advocates had to admit the difficulty of arguing for a new route when monies might be needed to shore up the existing service. In addition, the national economy had just taken a nosedive, and Virginia's budget was extremely stressed. Kaine had the unfortunate bad luck of presiding over the worst state economic conditions since the Great Depression (1929–1939) and would need to cut billions out of the state budget before his term would end. Why would he agree to support funding of a new train when schools might need to be cut? Although he agreed to meet with Valentine and me in his office to discuss the train, I was not optimistic. We had our work cut out for us.

Delegate Valentine understood the intersection between policy and politics. Politely relentless in pressing the Governor, she knew the effort was important not only for the Commonwealth, but also for her red-leaning district, where the Chamber of Commerce had advocated for better rail for more than a decade. The Governor wanted to help, but he knew this could not be done solely by three Democrats. He challenged us to find Republicans to sign on to the effort; if we got them, he said, he would find the money. We—mostly Valentine—went about the task. Within a week, we were able to convince three of our Republican colleagues, Rob Bell of Albemarle, Ed Scott of Culpeper, and William Fralin Jr. of Roanoke, to join us on a letter to the Governor in support of the project. The Governor delivered, and, on October 1, 2009, a three-year pilot project of state-sponsored Amtrak service commenced. In the first month, ridership doubled expectations, and the three-year pilot was so successful that it was extended without objection. In November 2017, the Lynchburg-Washington route was extended further southwest to Roanoke, the first time in thirty-eight years that the city with deep historical ties to the railroad industry, has been served by passenger rail. This route continues to be one of the strongest performers in the entire Amtrak system. And its creation it proved the cardinal rule—decisions are made by those in the room at the time.

RACE STILL MATTERS

For much of the twentieth century, African Americans were largely excluded from the rooms of policymaking. Fortunately, this has changed, even if not as quickly as many would prefer.[12] As an elected official in Virginia, it is impossible to escape its past. And so much of the state's history revolves around race. For some, Virginia's struggles are detailed, even if forgotten, in the written word; for others, they are etched deeply into the depths of our souls. Though many of our debates have centered on policies that either exacerbate or address the problems of the past, others are about symbols, the physical manifestations of an oppressive history. Richmond has occupied center stage in these recent arguments, but Charlottesville was one of the first communities where these debates turned violent. I will never forget first seeing the massive bronze statues of Robert E. Lee and Stonewall Jackson prominently displayed in two downtown parks in Charlottesville. Their size and placement seemed strange; after all, the Confederacy had lost the war, and Lee and Jackson might easily be viewed as traitors to their country. Nonetheless, the statues were imposing. Both Lee and Jackson were posed on horseback and positioned on huge pedestals. The statues harkened back to the Beaux Arts period of urban design, where large structures occupied prominent places in public parks. They were erected in the 1920s, much later than most of the other Confederate statuary built in this country. But their imagery was no less significant.

Between 1981 and 2015, I heard little about the statues; they were simply part of the landscape and most people never much thought about what they symbolized or their oppressive nature. I walked by them almost every single day, either on the way to the Albemarle County Circuit Court, itself a building of historical significance given that Jefferson, Madison, and Monroe all practiced law at the site, or as I headed toward the Charlottesville downtown pedestrian mall, one of the most beautiful, energetic, and successful public spaces in the country.

Festivals of all kinds would occur in these parks over the years, including an annual event to celebrate Gay Pride Month, where a multicolored array of balloons would be strung from one side of the Lee statue over its head to the other, like a rainbow, as if to clearly illustrate the contrast between this century and the last. To be sure, the public knew that Lee and Jackson were Confederate generals and that they fought for the continuation of slavery. But the historical context within which most of these statues were erected, their role of perpetuating the myth of the "southern lost cause," and their outward projection of white supremacy, remained largely unknown or ignored. That all began to change in spring 2017, shortly after the Charlottesville City Council voted three to two for their removal.

Prompted by the council decision, the Ku Klux Klan (KKK) called for a rally in early July to protest. More ominous, however, was the announcement of another demonstration planned for August under the banner of what came to be called "Unite the Right," a loose network of nationalist and white supremacist groups from across the country. Many communities had become used to KKK rallies; in most cases, these involved a small number of protesters who would assemble in white hoods at a certain site in the company of a phalanx of police officers designed to protect them from the counter demonstrations that inevitably occurred. These events were typically small and of short duration.

It quickly became clear that the Unite the Right rally would be fundamentally different, both in size and in scope. When hundreds assembled on the evening of August 11, 2017, in front of the Rotunda at UVA carrying tiki torches and chanting "Jews will not replace us," the Nation saw a level of hate not witnessed in years. And the mayhem and the death of Heather Heyer on the following day only confirmed that impression. If the statues were not viewed as symbols of white supremacy prior to that date, they certainly were after. Statues that formerly seemed physically impressive were now understood as *oppressive*, as citizens across the country began to understand them in historical context. The Unite the Right violence focused attention on race relations in this country and sparked a massive change in public attitudes on the subject.

The murder of George Floyd in May 2020 crystallized another problem affecting communities of color—police brutality—and accelerated the demand for an improvement in race relations. While President Barack Obama's election in 2008 changed this Nation, it also prompted a backlash that appeared, in part, to be racially motivated. President Donald J. Trump's false "birtherism" assertions simply fueled the white supremacist sentiment that was growing, and which threatened the positive attitudinal changes in race relations over the last several decades. More and more examples of police brutality were being reported—and recorded, an outgrowth of the proliferation of cellphones and their video capabilities. Confederate monuments and statues emerged as key symbols in the debate, and while some argued that taking them down would not resolve the systemic problems facing the country, the demands for their removal were heard far and wide. Numerous cities, including Richmond and New Orleans, eventually unleashed the construction cranes on these icons of Confederate idolatry. For three years, I carried bills that would permit Charlottesville to remove the statutes. Republicans defeated them. The legislation was finally passed in 2020, and in July 2021, the city removed those monuments to the "lost cause."

Floyd's murder generated a torrent of protest, and while the vast majority of this was nonviolent, there was nonetheless numerous examples of property destruction. While Charlottesville escaped the rioting in 2020, Richmond did not. And it was upsetting to see that city, which had undergone a steady improvement over the last several decades, endure looting, property destruction, and street clashes between citizens and police. As the protests unfolded, a common topic of conversation focused on what was happening in Virginia and across the land. Several of my constituents could not understand why people would desecrate monuments and destroy property. "It is depressing," one of them said. "Don't they have better things to do? And doesn't it hurt the country?" She had a point. Driving down Broad Street, the main Richmond thoroughfare, to the sight of countless graffiti-marked, boarded-up storefronts and closed businesses brought home the dual impacts of COVID-19 and racial strife. The downtown police station resembled a barricaded embassy in a hostile land, as it was surrounded by massive concrete bollards blocking the street in both directions. Seeing this was both depressing and disturbing. Something clearly had to change.

Similar objections were raised to the toppling of the Jefferson Davis statue from its 65-foot pedestal on Richmond's Monument Avenue. I was quick to respond that Davis was a traitor to this Nation. He and others like him wanted to destroy the United States of America so that they could preserve the Southern way of life, which had, at its center, the ownership of human beings for exploitation. Unlike Lee, Davis was neither a Virginian nor a military man, and therefore could not lay claim to the largely discredited notion of being a humble servant in the service of the Old Dominion. Putting aside the issue of property destruction, an approach that I do not embrace, it was surprising that Davis, who had been perched high above Richmond since 1907, had not been pulled off his pedestal a long time ago.

Richmond is only 72 miles from Charlottesville, but sometimes it feels light years away. And not always in a good way. When I joined the House of Delegates in 2006, the area around the impressive Capitol building was not always perceived as a place where you would walk alone at night, and the Capital police would make themselves available to transport Delegates and Senators to their lodgings if committee meetings went too late. Broad Street, the main thoroughfare through downtown, had many boarded-up buildings and had just seen the closing of two major department stores—Thalheimers and Miller & Rhoads—the last gasp of the suburban exodus that had gripped the city for decades. In 2004, the crime rate caused one publication to rank the city as the fifth "most dangerous place" in America.[13]

During my fourteen years as a Virginia Delegate, the city, like many other cities across the Nation, underwent a type of renaissance. People began moving back from the suburbs. Restaurants sprouted. A new courthouse and more housing were built downtown. By 2012, Virginia's Capitol had dropped out of the dangerousness ratings altogether and by 2019, it had cut its murder rate by one-half. Although still beset by pockets of severe poverty, the city was seeing more investment downtown. Virginia Commonwealth University (VCU) continued its expansion east toward the Capitol. Condominiums appeared along the river and in other parts of downtown. The arts and entertainment scene were hopping, and Richmond began to show up on several national lists as hot place to visit and a good destination for millennials. Serious problems remained, but Richmond appeared to be on the rise. The riots that followed Floyd's killing disrupted this progress. Hopefully, this will be short-lived. Richmond is the Capitol city, and its physical presentation as well as its underlying social and economic conditions will undoubtedly affect how the public views the state.

IN THE ROOM AT THE TIME

It is important to be "in the room" of policymaking. But elected leaders and public officials also operate within the economic, historical, and cultural factors that have helped shaped a state's development. There are the unique formal and informal norms and rules of each individual state. Its Constitution, statutes, and political culture all provide the guardrails within which policymakers operate. And, as the COVID-19 pandemic illustrates, unpredictable events can intervene to overwhelm policy plans that took countless hours and tremendous energy to develop. These factors work together to create the special mix that determines how states—including Virginia—operate and how successful they are in serving their citizens.

The Commonwealth's story is exceedingly complex, and replete with examples of extraordinary triumphs, devastating tragedies, and systemic outrages of racial oppression. We celebrate the founding of the Nation's first permanent settlement at Jamestown, condemn the carnage of the Civil War, mourn the victims of eugenics, celebrate the victories over "massive resistance," and struggle to understand the tragedy of the Virginia Tech massacre. We search for explanations about how and why Charlottesville and Virginia could be the point of mobilization of white supremacy, as we continue to confront the Virginia version of what the Swedish economist Gunnar Myrdal described as our "American Dilemma,"[14] the challenge of living up to the aspirational words of our founding documents. And while Virginia frequently performs better economically than other states, we sometimes fail to recognize that the benefits are unequally distributed by geography and by race.

Serving in a state house may not bring the same level of public attention as being in the U.S. Congress, but a state legislator is more likely to influence the success or failure of local communities than a representative in Washington. Because of this, state lawmakers can come to view their state as special—even exceptional. Many have asserted that claim for Virginia. That is the focus of the next chapter.

NOTES

1. Lin-Manuel Miranda, "The Room Where It Happens" from "Hamilton: An American Musical." In *Hamilton: The Revolution*, ed. Jeremy McCarter (New York: Grand Central Publishing, 2016), 186–87.

2. *Brown v. Board of Education of Topeka*, 347 U.S. 483 (1954), https://supreme.justia.com/cases/federal/us/347/483/ (accessed April 22, 2021).

3. See U.S. Declaration of Independence, *National Archives*, July 4, 1776, https://www.archives.gov/founding-docs/declaration-transcript (accessed June 8, 2021).

4. The "Byrd Machine" is the phrase used to describe the informal political organization led by former Governor and U.S. Senator Harry F. Byrd (1887–1966) and his son, Former U.S. Senator, Harry F. Byrd, Jr. (1914–2013). The machine dominated Virginia politics through its control of the Democratic Party for much of the twentieth century and was known for its fiscal conservatism and opposition to racial integration.

5. Virginia prides itself on consistently receiving Triple-A bond ratings (AAA) from the independent rating agencies, a mark of fiscal prudence and stewardship. These ratings also allow the Commonwealth to borrow money at the lowest possible rates.

6. Ratified by Virginia December 15, 1791, see U.S. Bill of Rights, September 25, 1789, *National Archives*, https://www.archives.gov/founding-docs/bill-of-rights (accessed June 8, 2021).

7. In July 2020, the new Speaker of the Virginia House of Delegates, Eileen Filler-Corn (D), ordered the removal of some of the Confederate busts and the large statute of Robert E. Lee from the Capitol's Old House Chamber. See Gregory N. Schneider, "Confederate Memorials Quietly Removed from Virginia Capitol Overnight," *Washington Post*, July 24, 2020, https://www.washingtonpost.com/local/virginia-politics/confederate-memorials-quietly-removed-from-virginia-capitol-overnight/2020/07/24/8d2a0dee-cced-11ea-bc6a-6841b28d9093_story.html (accessed April 22, 2021).

8. In his will, George Washington (1732–1799) gave instructions to free his slaves, but only upon the death of his wife; even one of the staunchest defenders of liberty was dependent on and entangled in America's most troubling institution, in life and beyond. See Washington, "A Decision to Free His Slaves," *George Washington's Mount Vernon*, n.d., https://www.mountvernon.org/george-washington/slavery/washingtons-1799-will/ (accessed April 22, 2021). The term "Old Dominion" arose early in Virginia's history as a reflection of its status as Great Britain's first colony in the new world that was directly run by the Crown through a governor. Beyond that, King Charles II purportedly gave it the title of "dominion" partly to express appreciation for the colony's initial loyalty to the Crown during the English Civil War of the 1640s. A decade following the execution by the Parliamentarians of his father, Charles I, Charles II was able to regain the throne. He subsequently acknowledged a gift from the colony as being from the "Dominion of Virginia." Library of Virginia, "Questions About Virginia," 2019, https://www.lva.virginia.gov/faq/va.asp (accessed June 15, 2021).

9. Robert A. Caro, *The Years of Lyndon Johnson: The Path to Power* (New York: Alfred A. Knopf, 1982).

10. *Kelo v. City of New London*, 545 U.S. 469 (2005), https://supreme.justia.com/cases/federal/us/545/469/ (accessed April 22, 2021).

11. For much of my time in the House of Delegates, Johnny Joannou was the *only* House Democrat appointed to that very important conference. Eventually, his collaboration with the Republicans led another Democrat, Steve Heretick, to successfully challenge him in 2017.

12. As of January 2021, less than 10 percent of the approximately 7,500 state legislators nationwide were African Americans (only thirteen of these were Republicans), an increase from 9 percent in 2015 and from 2 percent in 1971. Maryland has the largest African American contingent, at 29 percent, and several deep south states—Georgia, Louisiana, Mississippi, and South Carolina—each have more than 25 percent of their Bodies composed of African Americans. See Carl Smith, "Blacks in State Legislatures: A State-by-State Map," *Governing*, January 13, 2021, https://www.governing.com/now/Blacks-in-State-Legislatures-A-State-by-State-Map.html (accessed April 22, 2021). In 2021, twenty-two of 140 House and Senate legislators in Virginia were African American, up from seventeen in 2006, my first session.

13. Dionne Waugh, "Richmond Drops Out of Top 25 Most Dangerous Cities," *Richmond Times Dispatch*, November 20, 2007, updated September 18, 2019, https://richmond.com/richmond-drops-out-of-top-25-most-dangerous-cities/article_87a75bb7-0f1a-5948-b520-62aac1ce880f.html (accessed April 22, 2021).

14. Gunnar Myrdal, *An American Dilemma: The Negro Problem and Modern Democracy* (New York: Harper & Brothers, 1944).

Chapter 2

˙ Virginia Exceptionalism

How many Virginians does it take to change a light bulb? Five. One to turn the new bulb and four to talk about how much better the old one was.

—Old Virginia Adage

Each one of our American states considers itself *exceptional* in one way or another. Think of Missouri, nicknamed the "show me state" because of its healthy skepticism and a commonsense approach to life. Delaware is special because it is the first state in the Nation. Massachusetts asserts (incorrectly) that its citizens are descendants of the first permanent English-speaking colonial settlement (actually, that honor belongs to Virginia). Ask Alabamians about what makes their state exceptional, and they might mention a football team that has won eighteen national championships. Kentucky celebrates the Derby; Louisiana has Mardi Gras; and Arizona claims the Grand Canyon. But, with all these claims, it is hard to beat the accolades accorded to the Commonwealth of Virginia.

To be sure, the term "exceptionalism" is infused with political meaning and can be used in the services of multiple ends, some of which harken back to a time of Jim Crow and overt racial oppression. In Virginia, the exceptionalism argument has focused both on our early history, and about our special way of governing which some call "the Virginia Way," a phrase whose origins are problematic but one that has since come to convey an approach to government that values fiscal responsibility, support for business, and civil discourse.

Again, and again, the Commonwealth has occupied center stage in the democratic experiment that we call America. On a small island near what we now call Jamestown, settlers arrived in 1607, thirteen years prior to the landing of the Mayflower. This was followed by the creation of the first representative Body in 1619, an assembly which still exists today as the Virginia House of Delegates. Virginia colonists were key in organizing resistance to

17

the British in the 1760s and 1770s that ultimately led to American independence. A Virginian, George Washington, headed the Continental army. And it was Virginians like George Mason, George Wythe, Thomas Jefferson, and James Madison who provided much of the intellectual firepower necessary to build a new nation, defining citizens' rights and responsibilities through such powerful writings as the Virginia Declaration of Rights, the Declaration of Independence, the Constitution of the United States, and the Bill of Rights. Seven of the first dozen U.S. Presidents were born in Virginia.

With a history like this, it would be hard for the Commonwealth not to view itself as anything but exceptional. But the Old Dominion's narrative has a dark underside as well. For all its exceptionalist trappings, Virginia was a key part of the "iron triangle" of the Atlantic slave trade. It was the epicenter of the Civil War, serving as the capital of the Confederacy and the site of devastating carnage and the ultimate surrender of the army of Robert E. Lee (yes, another Virginian) at Appomattox. And it was in Virginia were many of the templates of racial oppression, embodied in the provisions of the 1902 Constitution, the *Racial Integrity Act of 1924*, the Eugenics movement of the early twentieth century, and numerous other Jim Crow statutes, were constructed, refined, and spread to other states.

The paradox of a democratic nation existing alongside a system of racial oppression was in full bloom in the Commonwealth prior to the Civil War. Virginia had more slaves at the beginning of the conflict than any other state.[1] It was one of the states that undermined Reconstruction efforts to bring political, social, and economic rights to African Americans after the War. Initially, the Commonwealth bowed to the pressure from the North and extended some degree of political rights to African Americans. Blacks were allowed to vote and were elected to the General Assembly. In the early 1880s, they had assembled a limited degree of political influence, even participating in a biracial coalition that governed the state for several years in the 1880s.[2] But the hope of political equality was brought to an abrupt end with the collapse of Reconstruction. Whites reasserted control of the state legislature and passed a series of measures that effectively disenfranchised black voters and destroyed the vestiges of their political influence. The Commonwealth's Constitution of 1902 and *Racial Integrity Act of 1924* became models for other Southern states as they marched toward further institutionalization and strengthening of white supremacy. Virginia was the intellectual headquarters of the Eugenics movement, from which Fascist European dictators in the 1930s borrowed many concepts. Political leaders in the Commonwealth were those who developed the strategy of opposing school desegregation— "massive resistance."

Throughout this history, however, many Virginians also fought for progress. The Commonwealth has been the home of countless individuals who would use the language of the Declaration of Independence and the words of the U.S. Constitution to fight for civil rights and destroy barriers to equality, people like Maggie Lena Walker, Barbara Rose Johns, attorneys Spottswood W. Robinson III and Oliver Hill, Mildred and Richard Loving (and their attorney and later Virginia Delegate Bernard S. Cohen), Wyatt Tee Walker, Governor L. Douglas Wilder, and Virginia state Senator Henry L. Marsh III. In the process, they proved themselves exceptional, and created a counter-narrative that promised hope and provided inspiration in the face of Virginia's history of racial oppression. They fought back using their ingenuity, direct action, the courts, and the vote. Maggie Walker achieved national prominence as the first African American woman to charter a bank in the United States; she also ran a newspaper and was instrumental in forming the National Association for the Advancement of Colored People (NAACP) in the state.[3] At the age of sixteen years, Barbara Johns led a student strike in her Farmville high school that eventually led to the student-initiated filing of *Davis v. Prince Edward County* (1952),[4] which was consolidated into *Brown v. Board of Education*,[5] the landmark 1954 U.S. Supreme Court decision declaring the unconstitutionality of "separate but equal" public schools. Her portrait now hangs in the Governor's Mansion in Richmond, and she is prominently displayed in the Virginia Civil Rights monument located on the grounds of the state Capitol.

The Commonwealth generated several successful lawsuits in the civil rights arena. Robinson and Hill handled countless cases that expanded legal rights for African Americans.[6] Legal action brought by the Lovings against Virginia's legal prohibitions of interracial marriage resulted in the U.S. Supreme Court decision declaring those laws to be unconstitutional in the Commonwealth and in seventeen other states.[7] Marsh, the African American civil rights attorney who served in the Virginia Senate from 1991 to 2014, described the Commonwealth's role in this way. "The rest of the Southern states were . . . watching Virginia to see what would happen . . . We had to rise to the occasion. We had the strongest group of civil rights and NAACP fighters of any state in the union because that's where they chose to make a stand."[8] In fact, the NAACP filed more lawsuits in Virginia than in any other state. Barrier after barrier continued to fall, but Virginia truly regained its place as one of the most significant states in the Nation when, in 1989, Wilder, the grandson of slaves, became the first elected African American Governor in U.S. history.[9] These were exceptional accomplishments, and for those interested in racial justice, Virginia had become a state that truly mattered.

RANKINGS BOOST THE COMMONWEALTH

Virginians point to our history as a sign of our uniqueness and importance. But state leaders also use the Commonwealth's rankings to tout our exceptionalism. Today, the state places highly in a number of categories that are celebrated by elected officials and citizens alike. The state's Gross Domestic Product ranks thirteenth among the states, just below North Carolina and above Michigan.[10] A 2018 report published by *USA Today* ranked Virginia as the eleventh "Best State to Live in America"; Massachusetts placed first and Mississippi last.[11] *U.S. News & World Report* placed Virginia as the "20th best" state in the Nation in 2018 (Iowa was ranked number first). In 2019, the Commonwealth had jumped to number seven (with Washington ranked first).[12]

But of all the ratings celebrated in the Commonwealth, the ones that have received the most attention over the years involve business climate and fiscal responsibility. For the last decade, Virginia has consistently finished in the top ten of all the states in CNBC's rating of the best states for business. The Commonwealth ranked number one in two consecutive surveys(2019 and 2021),[13] a rating consistently celebrated by elected officials. In the last decade, Virginia has also earned accolades for being the "best managed state in the nation,"[14] and has achieved the highest bond rating Triple-A (AAA), the gold standard by which states measure fiscal responsibility, by the bond rating agencies *in every year* since 1938, longer than any other state.[15]

As a practical matter, the stellar bond rating has saved taxpayers substantial monies, since it allows the Commonwealth to borrow at lower interest rates to fund capital projects. Beyond that, however, it gives the Old Dominion bragging rights for fiscal responsibility that few other states can match.[16] Virginia Governors and the legislature are scared to death that the state would lose this rating on their watch. And that concern continues to have an impact on decision-making, especially when it comes to the state budget. In 2004, for example, a major tax increase was sold to Virginia residents and legislators based on concerns that the bond rating might otherwise be lowered. Concerned again in 2018 about the views of the bond rating agencies, the legislature set aside extra money in a special savings account over and above what was deposited in the multimillion-dollar Rainy Day fund rather than spend it. This savings account was among the first revenue sources tapped to make up for the budget shortfall due to the COVID-19 impacts.

The Commonwealth also does well in educational rankings. The University of Virginia (UVA) is traditionally ranked among the top five public universities in the Nation,[17] and the 2019 *U.S. News & World Report* Best High Schools rankings placed Virginia as eighth best of all the states. Almost one-third of its high schools rank in the top 25 percent nationwide.[18] The educational attainment level of Virginia residents consistently places the state in the top ten, and the Commonwealth's ranks in top five states for the percentage of residents with professional or graduate degrees, and is the sixth most educated state in the Nation.[19] Our system of public universities is top notch, including liberal arts powerhouse William & Mary, founded by royal charter in 1693, making it the second oldest college or university in the United States. We also benefit from tech dynamo Virginia Polytechnic Institute and State University (Virginia Tech), rapidly expanding George Mason University, our historically black colleges and universities (HBCUs), and others that distinguish themselves in so many ways. Higher education, while it has its challenges, is something to celebrate in Virginia.

RANKINGS AND POLITICS

While Virginia consistently ranks in the top half of all states in most national rankings, it has nonetheless come under fire in several well publicized reports. A 2015 report on *The Health of State Democracies*, issued by the Center for American Progress Action Fund, labeled Virginia as the least "democratic" state in the country, due largely to its voter identification laws and its campaign finance provisions that allow unlimited contributions.[20] Similarly, Oxfam ranked the Commonwealth dead last among the states and DC in its 2018 report on *The Best States to Work Index: A Guide to Labor Policy in US States*.[21]

To illustrate how these rankings can become fodder for politics, the Oxfam study was frequently cited by Democrats seeking changes in labor policies. Business groups, however, pushed back, suggesting the report's methodology was fundamentally flawed. The Oxfam rankings so rankled the pro-business group, Virginia FREE, that its executive director, former Virginia Delegate Christopher B. Saxman, devoted an entire newsletter to building a case for how good Virginia is for workers.[22]

One should be careful before drawing too many conclusions based on rankings, and even more cautious in arguing that these are solely due to policy and political decisions. Oxfam gave low marks to Virginia for its work environment, but the state consistently ranks among the "best states to do business in the nation." Why? Some, myself included, celebrate the state's highly educated workforce as the key factor, and employ this argument as a rationale for more state investment in education and workforce development. Others suggest that the high rankings are due to relatively low taxes or the fact that the Commonwealth is a "right-to-work" state; this leads to a different policy approach that emphasizes maintaining taxes at their present level or even cutting them.[23] These debates inevitably are reflected in legislative policymaking and political campaigns.

Rankings can also mask major differences among different Virginia regions, and in socioeconomic, racial, and ethnic groups. Among the most dramatic differences involve the economic disparities between Northern Virginia (NoVa) and the rest of the state (what some call ROVA). Loudoun County boasted the highest median household income in 2018 for the entire Nation at $140,000 while Arlington and Fairfax followed close behind at $122,394 and $122,227 respectively, substantially more than the median household income for the entire state of Virginia, which recent U.S. Census data placed at $72,577.[24]

NoVa's success is based largely on its ability to tap federal spending and its location as a center of technological innovation. The area is the home to the largest concentrations of data centers in the Nation and remains the world's largest hub for internet traffic.[25] And this was before Amazon placed its giant new HQ2 headquarters in Arlington County. As one travels south in Virginia, however, it is another story. The Blacksburg metro area, which is wealthier than its neighbors to the south, reported median household income at $50,313 in 2018, a decline of almost 7 percent over the three years previous.[26] Scott County in the far southwest, reported median household income of $ 39,144.[27] In fact, the $112,367 disparity in median household incomes between Loudoun and Dickenson counties is the largest difference that existed between two counties in any state in the country in 2019. In that year, the top three largest differences in median household incomes between counties were in Virginia.[28] Exceptional as the state may be for economic activity, the benefits have not been evenly distributed across the Commonwealth.

Virginia is a sprawling state, and communities like Fairfax and Arlington in the north are separated from places like Bristol and Grundy in the southwestern portion of the state, not only by hundreds of miles but also, occasionally, by what can appear to be hundreds of years. The former's orientation is to Washington, DC, and points north; the latter relates more to rural communities to the south and west running up the spine of the Appalachian Mountains. Travel by car between Richmond and Bristol is 324 miles and takes about five hours. Traveling to DC would be another two hours. Bristol is actually *closer* to the capitals of six other states (West Virginia, Tennessee, Kentucky, North Carolina, South Carolina, and Georgia) than it is to Richmond. And perhaps is culturally more like them.

Virginia's differences are also clear in the area of educational attainment. In Arlington County, for example, over 80 percent of the population between the age of twenty-five and sixty-four years has at least an associate degree. By contrast, only 25.5 percent of Wise County residents have this certification, and in Sussex, in southside Virginia, less than 20 percent have earned this qualification.[29] Not surprisingly, the degree gap between whites and African Americans and Hispanics, like in most states, is dramatic. Nationally, the gap between whites and African Americans is about sixteen points. In Virginia, while a larger percentage of African American residents (35.4 percent) have an associate degree than the national average, the gap between whites and blacks is actually higher (17.9 percent).[30] And we know that factors such as educational attainment have a major impact on income equality, an increasing concern nationally and in the Commonwealth.

In some cases, looking at ratings over time provides the best indication of the degree to which a state is making progress. And clearly, the Commonwealth has shown dramatic improvement in some areas. In 1970, for example, Virginia ranked fortieth among the states in life expectancy at 70.08 years, just under the national average, and worse than southern counterparts like Florida, Arkansas, Tennessee, and Kentucky. By 2014, however, life expectancy in the state had risen to 79 years, exceeding the national average (78.9 years), and moving it up in the rankings to twenty-fourth. In those forty-four years, Virginia had moved far beyond most of its southern counterparts in this ranking. A similar change has occurred in infant mortality. In 1967, Virginia ranked fortieth among the states at 24.3 deaths for every 1,000 live births.[31] By 2017, however, the state had improved, not just in its national ranking, to the twenty-fifth spot, but also in its actual numbers (5.9 deaths per 1,000 live births), a tremendous accomplishment during a period where its southern counterparts like North Carolina continued to be ranked in the forties.[32] Independent of policy changes, the best way to explain these improvements is the increasing prosperity of the state over the last fifty years.

Tracking historical performance of these data is critically important to an understanding of where the state is going. Until recently, the Commonwealth maintained a commission called the Council on Virginia's Future, that tracked the Commonwealth's historical performance on a series of measures. The group was disbanded several years ago, and the state's Joint Legislative Audit and Review Commission (JLARC) now provides similar data to those interested.[33]

Figure 2.1 provides data of where the Old Dominion has ranked on several measures between 2005, when I was first elected to the Assembly, and 2020, when I retired. There is a striking consistency to the Commonwealth's performance over time. What emerges is a state that, given its relative wealth, has been relatively frugal compared to others, spending less on programs such as Medicaid, and more conservative than you might expect in its educational investments. It is also a state that celebrates its support for business and is now in a better position to do so following Amazon decision to locate HQ2 in the Commonwealth.

How Virginia Compares 2005 – 2020

Measure	2005 Ranking		Virginia Ranking Change	2018-'20 Ranking*	
	Virginia	#1 State		Virginia	#1 State
Population[1]	12	CA	■	12	CA
Percentage change in population[1]	11	NV	▼	18	UT
Per capita personal income[1]	7	CT	▼	12[4]	CT
Annual unemployment rate[2]	47	MI/HI	▲	42[4]	AK/HI
State & local taxes as percentage of personal income[1]	45	NY	▲	32	AK
Per capita local taxes[1]	17	NY	■	17[3]	NY
Per capita state taxes[1]	26	VT	▼	30[3]	VT
Per capita state expenditures[1]	40	AK	▲	29	AK
Per capita general fund expenditures[1]	25	DE	▲	23[4]	AK
Bond ratings[1] (includes all states rated AAA)	1	DE/GA/ MD/MO/ UT	■	1	DE/FL/GA/ IA/IN/MD/ MO/NC/SD TN/UT
Per capita Medicaid expenditures[1]	48	NY	▲	37[4]	NY
Percentage of population under age 65 with health insurance[1]	21	MN	▼	24[4]	MA
State & local funding per pupil, K through 12[1]	22	NJ	▼	27[3]	NY
State funding per pupil, K through 12[1]	42	HI	▲	40[3]	VT
Average salary of K–12 teachers in public schools[1]	27	CT	▼	32[3]	NY
Average annual in-state tuition & fees at public 4-year institutions[1]	18	VT/FL	▲	8	VT/WY

[1] Higher ranking = higher number   [2] Higher ranking = lower unemployment rate   [3] 2018 data   [4] 2019 data
*2020 ranking except where specified.

Figure 2.1. How Virginia Compares, 2005–2020

AMAZON CHOOSES THE COMMONWEALTH

On a crisp September day in 2017, Virginia Governor Terry McAuliffe and his Secretary of Commerce and Trade, Todd Haymore, had just departed from Richmond in the state helicopter to promote yet another economic development opportunity, this time in Roanoke. Quickly moving above the Virginia countryside, the chuf, chuf, chuf of the whirling rotor blades made it almost impossible to have a conversation, especially in the absence of headphones, which neither McAuliffe nor Haymore had donned for the short trip. Suddenly, a message arrived on the Governor's phone. Amazon had just announced a Request for Proposals (RFP) to locate a massive expansion of their operation. "Let's get this chopper down," the Governor shouted above the din for everyone to hear. "We've got to fly to Seattle ASAP to meet with Bezos—right away." The Governor understood the significance immediately. This project, which came to be known as HQ2, could be a game changer for Virginia, bringing millions of dollars and thousands of jobs to the Commonwealth. McAuliffe knew that this could be the mother of all deals. It would permanently cement Virginia's reputation as being open for business and the Governor's legacy as a key architect of what he was calling "the new Virginia economy."

The Governor knew the state had to work fast; the initial deadline for submittals was one month from the announcement. The chopper landed shortly thereafter, and the Commonwealth's chief salesperson switched into an even higher gear of activity than that we were accustomed to seeing. He immediately empowered Virginia Economic Development Partnership (VEDP) President and CEO Stephen Moret and others to launch what would become the largest single economic development recruitment effort ever undertaken by the Commonwealth. McAuliffe and his team knew that Virginia could not offer the financial incentives of other states. But they saw the potential of putting together a package to capitalize on the state's uniqueness. Haymore recognized that the state would need help, and pushed to hire McKinsey & Company, the large international consulting firm, to advise on the state's pitch. This itself was a gamble; their costs would likely total between $2 and $3 million, a sum not immediately available for such an undertaking.

The VEDP could cover some of the costs, and the Governor's contingency fund could pay for others. But McAuliffe would have to raise money from other sources to make this happen. The state needed partners, and Haymore was charged with going after them.

Haymore decided that higher education would be a primary target, and his first call was to Elizabeth Hooper, his friend and the government affairs officer for Virginia Tech. Hooper understood the game and posed the key questions immediately. "Todd," she said, "how much is this 'participation' going to cost me? And who else have you asked?" Haymore demurred, saying only that it might involve "the low six figures . . . . And we have to know soon." Virginia Tech had been looking for opportunities to expand its footprint into NoVa and its President, Tim Sands, was not only entrepreneurial but he also trusted Hooper, who was able to gain his quick support. But it would come with a price. "We are in," said Hooper in her return call to Haymore, "but we want to lead—and we want to be at the table." With that, Virginia Tech became a critical player in development of the proposal, and potentially a great beneficiary of Amazon's move to Virginia.

McAuliffe left office in January 2018, and few initially gave Virginia much of a chance. But Ralph Northam worked hard to convince Amazon of the merits of the Commonwealth. Most understood that a package that did not rely extensively on financial incentives would have to be "exceptional" to draw the company's attention. And it was! Local governments stepped up to back the Commonwealth's pledge to beef up tech education in K-12. The state offered to produce up to 17,500 new computer science degrees, and to invest in a new innovation campus of Virginia Tech to generate master's graduates. NoVa was hip and was able to sell the region as a bustling set of communities where the so-called creative class[34] of well educated, creative, and young persons provided energy that attracts new talent. State legislature leaders committed to appropriating the monies necessary for key infrastructural requirements.

Moret, brought to the state from Louisiana in 2016 to re-energize the Commonwealth's economic development initiatives, argued that Virginia's proposal stood out as the only one that made education the centerpiece of its plan.[35] In the end, the decision was never really about financial incentives. Some states, most notably New Jersey and Maryland, offered much higher packages—$7–$8.5 billion respectively. But as Amazon's Vice President of Public Policy Brian Huseman, remarked, "tech talent was the biggest driving factor for us. Both tech talent on day one, but also tech talent in the future."[36] Some observers called Virginia's winning of the Amazon competition "exceptional"; others have termed it "unique." But whatever the label, Moret made it clear that the Commonwealth "wanted to win this in a Virginia way."[37] On November 13, 2018, Amazon announced it had selected NoVa as one of the two communities (Brooklyn was the other) for HQ2.

The HQ2 story is, in some ways, emblematic of "the Virginia way" of doing things. First, while the state is consistently viewed as cultivating a strong business climate, it has not aggressively used financial incentives to recruit and to retain companies. Second, the Commonwealth continues to tout its workforce, educational institutions, and infrastructure as its selling points. And finally, Commonwealth leaders tend to work together on business ventures, independent of party or administrations. While the McAuliffe team helped generate the proposal, the Northam administration carried it forward, cultivated the company, and sealed the deal. Despite some criticism from affordable housing advocates, Democrats and Republicans were both very supportive of the deal, and the company experienced little of the pushback that was so strong in Brooklyn that Amazon altered its plans to expand there. When the funding package arrived in the General Assembly, it was easily passed, yet another example of a broad consensus across party lines to support business activity and economic opportunity. To the extent there is a "Virginia way" supportive of business, it was successful in recruiting Amazon.

A TRADITION OF CIVILITY

The notion that the Commonwealth is exceptional is about more than about its early history, some important national rankings, or its support for business. Over the years, the state's leaders have also constructed a narrative of Virginia as a model state for political discourse and civil decision-making, a place where leaders, unlike their Washington counterparts, work together to get things done. This notion has frequently been described as "the Virginia Way," an aspirational phrase that embodies civility, cooperation, and finding common ground in decision-making. Though its origins, examined in chapter 4, were formerly associated with racial subjugation in Virginia's past, the traits with which it has been most associated—civility, cooperation, and respect for business—has been evident in Virginia's leaders for years on both sides of the aisle.

One positive example of the Virginia way could be found in the working relationship between Timothy M. Kaine and Robert F. "Bob" McDonnell while both served in statewide office. Republican McDonnell was elected Attorney General (AG) in the same year as Democrat Kaine won the governorship. Both Roman Catholics, they had extensive governmental experience prior to winning their offices, Kaine as Mayor of Richmond and Lieutenant Governor, and McDonnell in the House of Delegates. Their politics, however, were very different. Kaine instincts were demonstrably more liberal than his campaign for governor suggested, and McDonnell's conservative bona fides were never questioned, even as he occasionally campaigned as moderate.

Kaine was influenced by his service as a missionary in Honduras and the social justice aspects of Catholicism. McDonnell was shaped by more conservative tenets of the Catholic church and had also been influenced by his friend from Virginia Beach, televangelist Pat Robertson. Nonetheless, they developed a cordial and respectful working relationship, both believing in the importance of public service and that civil discourse among statewide elected officials served the Commonwealth better than continuous pitched battles.

The Kaine-McDonnell public relationship began in rocky fashion. In the waning days of his administration, Governor Mark Warner issued an executive order adding sexual orientation to the state's antidiscrimination policy and Kaine issued a similar order almost immediately upon taking the office. Some legislators were offended by this action, and one, Bob Marshall of Prince William, asked, as any Delegate or Senator can do, for an opinion from McDonnell, the new AG, about whether Kaine's order was legal. McDonnell responded with a statement that the new Governor had exceeded his legal authority. Kaine's office fired back, stating that he was "flabbergasted"[38]; the new officeholders were now engaged in a very public flap.

Shortly after this public dispute, Kaine and McDonnell engaged in back-channel efforts to develop a better working relationship. William C. "Bill" Mims, then an Assistant AG and confidant of McDonnell, and later to become a Virginia Supreme Court Justice, worked with Larry Roberts, Kaine's counsel and political advisor, on protocols to improve communication.[39] As a result, they reached an informal agreement designed to temper public criticism of each other on key issues until they could better understand each other's views and motivations. They both knew there would be disagreements, but each felt it important that one not "blindside" the other. This was significant at the time; nationally, many Republican states AGs were engaged in frequent battles with the Obama administration, and continued to emphasize differences in policies between the national Democrats and the GOP.

This process was complicated by McDonnell's ambitions for national office. He had strong views about a variety of issues important to the Republican base. One of these was immigration. McDonnell wanted to push state and local governments to embrace a controversial program called "287(g)"[40] that conservatives across the country were advocating. But he knew that Kaine, a strong ally of President Obama, would not approve state participation in the program. Each thought their own position would benefit the state, but both recognized that the issue was extremely volatile and highly divisive. Instead of fanning those flames, Kaine sent his top advisors to the AG's office to engage McDonnell and his team in a genuine policy discussion on the issue. Going to McDonnell's office was a sign of respect extended to the AG by the new Governor. And McDonnell reciprocated; as he put it, "the Governor was my client. We decided, for the sake of the Commonwealth, that we would not criticize the other publicly without the courtesy of giving the other advance notice."[41] As expected, Kaine remained firmly against Virginia joining the program but understood that McDonnell would remain publicly in support of it. Both offices released detailed policy positions that reflected their desire to disagree professionally and based on policy rather than personality. Ultimately, McDonnell requested 287(g) authority for Virginia when he became Governor, but the request was denied by the Obama Administration.

Similarly, and while not required to do so, Kaine would often inform McDonnell, whose office was responsible for defending death penalty appeals, in advance about decisions he was making in the administration of the sanction. While both were Catholics, they differed in their views about the ultimate sanction. Carrying out executions was always difficult for Kaine. His faith led him to oppose the death penalty even as he promised that he would carry out the law. And that is what he did. Eleven inmates were executed during his term; he commuted only one death sentence. Kaine did, however, take steps to slow Virginia's reliance on the death penalty. In 2008, when the U.S. Supreme Court accepted a case challenging the imposition of lethal injection, Kaine suspended executions until the court ruled the procedure to be constitutional.[42] And Kaine vetoed several measures to expand the death penalty; as one who has always objected to the administration of this punishment, I fully supported these actions.[43] McDonnell's public statements on Kaine's death penalty actions were pointed but measured. One can speculate about whether McDonnell's comments about Kaine's actions were less strident than they might otherwise have been had the communication between the two not occurred. Clearly, this arrangement was not simply about their personalities, but also a product of the Virginia political culture at the time. This version of "the Virginia Way" was on full display.

While Kaine and McDonnell continued to have public differences, they were largely unveiled as policy disputes rather than personal attacks. This working relationship paid dividends as the Commonwealth responded to the Virginia Tech shootings in April 2007, the largest school shooting in our Nation's history. Kaine's reaction to the tragedy was among his finest moments. While a strong supporter of gun safety measures, he did not politicize the tragedy. And neither did McDonnell, who was in Blacksburg with him, and delivered a prayer at the service. Tucker Martin, then a press secretary for the state's Republican AG, complimented Kaine on his words and actions. "Say what you will about someone's political positions," he said. "In a moment of crisis, you learn about their character, and I think that moment spoke volumes for Gov. Kaine." Shortly thereafter, the two leaders appeared at a joint press conference where Kaine issued an executive Order closing a loophole that had made it easier for the shooter to purchase a weapon.[44]

There were even times when McDonnell offered some behind-the-scenes assistance to the Democratic Governor. In 2006, the House and Senate deadlocked on a budget, and the state faced the prospect that for the first time in its history, the fiscal year might commence with no appropriations bill in place. Kaine had publicly implied that he would assert his authority to keep the government open and to spend money to do so beginning July 1, even without a budget, feeling that this assertion of executive power would put pressure on the recalcitrant legislature to act. McDonnell issued an AG's opinion asserting that the Governor lacked the constitutional authority to continue spending. Ironically, this increased the pressure on the legislature—not Kaine, as the General Assembly became increasingly concerned about the prospect of a government shutdown. The pressure was successful, and the budget was passed and signed on June 30—the last possible day to avert a potential state shutdown and possible constitutional crisis.

EXCEPTIONALISM AND FISCAL PRUDENCE

The "Virginia as exceptional" narrative is also rooted in the fiscal responsibility exercised historically by lawmakers, their generally thoughtful approach to policymaking, and special elements of the Commonwealth's governmental structure that sets it apart for other states. The Commonwealth is the only state where governors cannot succeed themselves, the only state with independent cities,[45] one of only several states where the elections for state House and Senate, and major statewide offices are conducted in odd-numbered years, and one of few that permit unlimited campaign contributions. To be sure, these characteristics make Virginia unique. But they are not necessarily exceptional. In fact, some argue that these unique characteristics create inefficiencies and disadvantage urban areas of the state.

Historically, there have been instances where the ethos of fiscal responsibility has been sidelined in the service of political expediency. Such an example is found in the decision of the state to repeal the car tax in 1998. In each of my fourteen years of service, our budgeting process was adversely affected by the loss of revenue caused by that decision.

Virginians, especially in the northern part of the state, had complained about the personal property tax on motor vehicles for years, many feeling that there was little they could do about it except to suffer in personal silence and pay the bill. The fact that the tax came due in many jurisdictions shortly before Election Day made it an appealing target for political opportunists who wanted to capitalize on voter discontent about the tax. Thus, in 1997, Republican AG Jim Gilmore seized upon the concern to win his race for governor against two-term Lieutenant Governor Donald S. Beyer Jr. Gilmore devised a catchy proposal and phrase, "no car tax," and rode it to victory in the gubernatorial election.

Gilmore's idea changed state tax policy in major ways. Still controversial to this day, this initiative nicely illustrates the complex interplay between politics, policies, and personalities. It was a political masterstroke; the phrase was simple and pithy, and Gilmore won with 56 percent of the vote, including substantial majorities in NoVa, where the tax had the most bite. As policy, it was more problematic, especially in a state known for conservative budgeting and for which maintaining its Triple-A (AAA) bond rating was an article of faith. The fundamental problem with repealing the car tax involved the state's localities. The tax was not even a state tax; it was collected locally and used to fund city and county budgets. Because of this, repealing the tax would create huge deficits in cities and counties.

Facing stiff opposition at the local level, Gilmore and state lawmakers devised a convoluted plan. They would eliminate the tax, but then replace revenues lost by local governments through large transfers of state monies. This solved the problem for localities but created a huge challenge for the state. The budget was no longer in balance, and the money necessary to fund the repeal had to come from other sources. The challenge was more difficult because Gilmore had wildly underestimated the costs of full repeal, and legislators now saw that enacting the entire plan could throw the state budget into disarray.

Gilmore's challenge was further exacerbated by his problematic interpersonal relationships with prominent members of the legislature, including those of his own party. The Virginia Senate was controlled at the time by a group of budgetary moderates who prided themselves on fiscal responsibility, including Finance Committee Chair John H. Chichester. Many of them were leery about providing major tax breaks when the future was uncertain. Funding the repeal would force initial state budget cuts of $1.2 billion during a time when revenues were stagnant. And stewards of the budget knew the amount would only increase in the future.

The 1998 legislative session broke down over the issue, with the result that the budget could not be passed by the traditional sixty-day deadline, a first for the Commonwealth.[46] But Gilmore kept fighting. The Assembly eventually passed a budget which included partial car tax relief, not what the Governor wanted but all that he could get; the price tag was capped at $950 million per year, and the next Governor, Democrat Warner, was left to deal with the budgetary problems which resulted from Gilmore's plan.

Gilmore's car tax relief made other pressing issues—particularly transportation—even more difficult to solve. When I entered the General Assembly in 2006, Virginia had not raised any major additional monies for transportation since the 1986 plan advanced by former Governor Gerald Lee Baliles. The legislature had been grappling for years with how to address increasing demands for roads in NoVa and Hampton Roads. Anyone traveling in those areas recognized that the infrastructure was crumbling, and the road network was overwhelmed. Tim Kaine won the governor's race in 2005 in part because of his promise to address the issue. Some of his proposals addressed problems of suburban sprawl but, as is so often the case, many other solutions would require additional monies, and there are only so many ways to raise it. Since the legislature was largely controlled by representatives from rural areas, where traffic was not viewed as a significant problem, and by Republicans who had taken a pledge never to raise taxes, efforts to increase the gas or other taxes had failed year after year. Kaine proposed several different initiatives, but most involved raising taxes. Almost in desperation, the Republicans in 2007 developed a proposal that they—and Governor Kaine—would come to regret.

The new approach would place the burden of fixing roads on those who committed traffic offenses by adding additional fees to the fines already imposed on offenders for violations for which they were convicted. Labeled "abusive driver fees," Republicans pushed the idea as an innovative solution consistent with Virginia exceptionalism. The plan would raise new revenue in two ways. First, courts would levy an additional fee on all misdemeanors and felony convictions committed while operating a motor vehicle. A conviction for speeding, for example, would require the transgressor to pay a fee over and above the usual fine. Second, the state could also impose a fee on a driver who had eight or more demerit points, even if he or she had not been convicted of a misdemeanor or felony. It was estimated that over 130,000 Virginians could be affected solely because of demerit points, even if they had never committed a criminal traffic offense.[47] Instead of passing the new policy as a bill, it was inserted it into the biennial budget to make it more difficult to vote against. It was projected to generate nearly $65 million annually, not nearly enough to meet the need (which was estimated in the billions), but something to which they could point in an election year as an innovative attempt to have "bad drivers" pay for roads that benefit "good drivers."

Instead of gaining accolades for finding money for transportation without raising taxes, however, the measure created a political firestorm. First, many drivers who had not thought of themselves as "bad drivers" became, under the terms of the legislation, subject to the abusive driver fee. Second, the amount of the additional fees was itself a problem. A conviction for speeding at 20 mph over the speed limit not only could bring a fine but a hefty "abusive driver fee" as high as $350. What really incensed Virginians, however, was something that few legislators realized was in the bill when it was passed. Under the new arrangement, there was no practical or legal way to compel payment of the fees from nonresidents who were guilty of the same offense as those committed by Virginians. All over the Commonwealth, Virginians were asking, "why should I pay these fees if Marylanders who do the same thing in our state do not have to do so?" The fire had been lit; over 100,000 people signed an online petition demanding the law's immediate repeal.[48] Lawmakers responded. Governor Kaine joined Republican legislative leaders in promising they would repeal the abusive driver fee during the next legislative session. The General Assembly quickly did so when it returned for the 2008 session.[49] Whether legislators would have avoided this policy blunder if they had heeded the advice of experts in the field is anyone's guess. What was clear, however, is that lawmakers never considered the appropriateness of the remedy in resolving the problem. The plan was rational in that it raised revenues, but it was never perceived as reasonable by the public. Such dissonance creates problems in making policy.

All states have pride, and Virginia has more of it than most. Most understand the importance of not allowing this confidence to cloud realistic analyses of a state's politics and policies. Nonetheless, the creation of an exceptionalist narrative has its advantages, mainly for how it produces an aspirational pull toward conforming actions to the image. We know, for example, that the assertion in our Declaration of Independence that "all men are created equal" did not apply to all men—or to any women.[50] But the words established a marker against which future behavior could be measured. And it continues to inspire countless citizens to fight to achieve its professed goals. The Commonwealth has struggled historically to conform our policies to the principles of the Declaration, and this challenge recently took on new meaning in the aftermath of Governor Ralph Northam's confrontation with photographs from his distant past and the massive changes occurring in the Nation as the result of murder of George Floyd. As the Commonwealth continues to change and evolve, newer conceptualizations of Virginia exceptionalism and the Virginia way will undoubtedly emerge, only to be measured against the expectations of its residents.

NOTES

1. Amber Pariona, "Which U.S. States Had the Most Slaves at The Start of The Civil War?" *World Atlas*, September 28, 2018, https://www.worldatlas.com/articles /which-u-s-states-had-the-most-slaves-at-the-start-of-the-civil-war.html (accessed June 1, 2021).

2. See Jane Dailey, *Before Jim Crow: The Politics of Race in Postemancipation Virginia* (Chapel Hill and London: University of North Carolina Press, 2000); Ronald L. Heinemann, John G. Kolp, Anthony S. Parent, Jr., and William G. Shade, *Old Dominion, New Commonwealth: A History of Virginia, 1607–2007* (Charlottesville: University of Virginia Press, 2007); and George Harrison Gilliam, "Building a Modern South: Political Economy in Nineteenth-Century Virginia," unpublished Ph.D. diss., Corcoran Department of History, University of Virginia, 2013, https:// doi.org/10.18130/V39639.

3. John Hope Franklin and Alfred A, Moss Jr., *From Slavery to Freedom: A History of Negro Americans*, 6th ed. (New York: Alfred A. Knopf, 1988); and Muriel Branch and Dorothy Rice, *Miss Maggie: A Biography of Maggie Lena Walker* (Richmond, VA: Marlborough House, 1984).

4. *Davis v. County School Board of Prince Edward County*, 103 F. Supp. 337 (ED Va. 1952), https://law.justia.com/cases/federal/district-courts/FSupp/103/337 /1469032/ (accessed June 1, 2021). The case was remarkable, partly because it was initiated by students over the fears of many adults in the community, and amazing when considering the political dynamics of the time. See Taylor Branch, *Parting the Waters: America in the King Years, 1954–63* (New York: Simon & Schuster, 1988).

5. *Brown v. Board of Education of Topeka*, 347 U.S. 483 (1954), https://supreme.justia.com/cases/federal/us/347/483/ (accessed April 22, 2021).

6. Margaret Edds, *We Face the Dawn: Oliver Hill, Spottswood Robinson, and the Legal Team That Dismantled Jim Crow* (Charlottesville: University of Virginia Press, 2018).

7. *Loving v. Virginia*, 388 U.S. 1 (1967), https://supreme.justia.com/cases/federal/us/388/1/ (accessed June 1, 2021).

8. Virginia Museum of History and Culture, "Civil Rights Movement in Virginia," n.d.,__https://www.virginiahistory.org/collections-and-resources/virginia-history-explorer/civil-rights-movement-virginia (accessed June 2, 2021). See Henry L. Marsh III, *The Memoirs of Hon. Henry L. Marsh III, Civil Rights Champion, Public Servant, Lawyer*, ed. Jonathan K. Stubbs and Danielle Wingfield-Smith (Jonesboro, AR: GrantHouse Publishers, 2018).

9. L. Douglas Wilder, *Son of Virginia: A Life in America's Political Arena* (Guilford, CT: Lyons Press, imprint of Rowman & Littlefield, 2015).

10. World Population Review, "GDP by State," 2020, https://worldpopulationreview.com/state-rankings/gdp-by-state (accessed June 2, 2021).

11. Cheyenne Buckingham and Grant Suneson, "Where Is the Best Place to Live in America? All 50 States Ranked," *USA Today*, November 6, 2018,_https://www.usatoday.com/story/travel/destinations/2018/11/06/americas-best-states-live-ranked/38375051/ (accessed June 2, 2021), original article published "America's Best States to Live In," *247wallst*, November 2, 2018, https://247wallst.com/special-report/2018/11/02/americas-best-states-to-live-in-3/ (accessed June 2, 2021).

12. U.S. News & World Report, "Best States Rankings," *U.S. News & World Report*,_https://www.usnews.com/news/best-states/rankings (accessed June 19, 2019).

13. CNBC.com Staff, "America's Top States for Business 2018," *CNBC*, July 10, 2018,_https://www.cnbc.com/2018/07/10/americas-top-states-for-business-2018.html (accessed June 2, 2021); Scott Cohn, "Virginia is back as America's Top State for Business in 2021,"*CNBC*, July 13, 2021, https://www.cnbc.com/2021/07/13/virginia-is-back-as-americas-top-state-for-business.html (accessed August 1, 2021); and Scott Cohn, "Amazon Had It Right: Virginia is America's Top State for Business in 2019," *CNBC*, July 10, 2019, updated July 12, 2019, https://www.cnbc.com/2019/07/09/virginia-is-americas-top-state-for-business-in-2019.html (accessed June 2, 2021).

14. Government Technology, "Report Card Evaluates How States Manage Public Resources," *gt*, March 4, 2008, updated July 27, 2020, https://www.govtech.com/policy-management/Report-Card-Evaluates-How-States-Manage.html (accessed June 2, 2021).

15. In 2017, only twelve states enjoyed Triple A ratings from all three rating agencies; this allows them to borrow money at lower rates in the market, saving taxpayers substantial money. See Pew Charitable Trusts, "Rainy Day Funds and State Credit Ratings: How Well-designed Policies and Timely Use Can Protect Against Downgrades,"*pewtrusts.org*, May 2017, https://www.pewtrusts.org/~/media/assets/2017/05/statesfiscalhealth_creditratingsreport.pdf (accessed June 2, 2021).

16. The Mercatus Center at George Mason University, known for its conservative public policy approaches, recently ranked Virginia as fourth best among the fifty

states in terms of "service level solvency," which it defined as the level of taxes, revenues, and spending, in comparison to personal income, in Eileen Norcross and Olivia Gonzalez, "Ranking the States by Fiscal Condition: 2018 Edition," Mercatus Research, Mercatus Center at George Mason University, Arlington, Virginia, October 2018, https://www.mercatus.org/system/files/norcross-fiscal-rankings-2018-mercatus -research-v1.pdf (accessed June 2, 2021).

17. *Smart Asset*, a financial advising periodical, consistently ranks the Commonwealth of Virginia as among the best states for higher education; in 2019, it was rated the "best state for higher education," in Derek Miller, "Top States for Higher Education – 2019 Edition," *Smart Asset*, March 05, 2019, https://smartasset. com/checking-account/top-states-for-higher-education-2019 (accessed June 2, 2021).

18. U.S. News & World Report, "How States Compare in the 2019 Best High Schools Rankings," *U.S. News & World Report*, April 29, 2019, https://www.usnews. com/education/best-high-schools/articles/how-states-compare.

19. Adam McCann, "Most & Least Educated States in America," *WalletHub*, January 20, 2020, updated February 16, 2021, https://wallethub.com/edu/e/most -educated-states/31075/ (accessed June 2, 2021).

20. Lauren Harmon, Charles Posner, Michele L. Jawando, and Matt Dhaiti, *The Health of State Democracies* (Washington, DC: Center for American Progress Action Fund, 2015),_https://www.americanprogressaction.org/issues/courts/reports/2015/07 /07/116570/the-health-of-state-democracies/ (accessed June 2, 2021). This conclusion was made prior to major voting law changes enacted by Democrats when they took control of the legislature in 2020.

21. Oxfam America, *The Best States to Work Index: A Guide to Labor Policy in US States* (research report) (Washington, DC: Oxfam America, 2018), https:// policy-practice.oxfamamerica.org/static/media/files/Best_States_to_Work_Index.pdf (accessed June 20, 2021).

22. By Virginia FREE's tally, Virginia is the sixth (#6) best state for workers, based on the assemblage of rankings from other sources catalogued at Virginia FREE, "Table 1: Best State for Workers," *vafree.org*, August 23, 2019, https: //files.constantcontact.com/005ceb5f201/f415139e-f39d-4946-a3c0-1b4773b3f3c0. pdf (accessed June 2, 2021). The organization's analysis ended with determination to move up, because "being #6 might be good enough for most states, but this is the Commonwealth of Virginia and we have standards. Being #1 is the standard." See Chris Saxman to Virginia FREE email newsletter subscription list, "Interesting Poll and State Rankings," October 16, 2019. Saxman ranked Virginia number six for work- ers; Minnesota, Utah, and Massachusetts placed numbers one, two, and three, https: //files.constantcontact.com/005ceb5f201/f415139e-f39d-4946-a3c0-1b4773b3f3c0. pdf (accessed June 2, 2021). Of the top ten states ranked by Saxman, three, Virginia, Utah, and Iowa, are right-to-work states. See also National Right to Work Committee (2021), https://nrtwc.org/, and six (Minnesota, Virginia, Vermont, Connecticut, New Hampshire, and Washington) are Dillon Rule states.

23. Among the groups taking this view is the Thomas Jefferson Institute for Public Policy (2021), https://www.thomasjeffersoninst.org/.

24. David Hodes, "This Is the State of the Salary in Northern Virginia," *Northern Virginia Magazine*, December 9, 2019, https://northernvirginiamag.com/culture /culture-features/2019/12/09/this-is-the-state-of-the-salary-in-northern-virginia/ (accessed June 2, 2021).

25. Jeff Clabaugh, "Northern Virginia Remains the 'King of the Cloud,'" *WTOP News*, September 8, 2020, https://wtop.com/business-finance/2020/09/northern -virginia-remains-the-king-of-the-cloud/ (accessed June 2, 2021).

26. U.S. Census Bureau, "American Community Survey (ACS)" (2019), https:// www.census.gov/programs-surveys/acs/ (accessed June 2, 2021).

27. U.S. Census Bureau, "American Community Survey (ACS)" (2019).

28. U.S. Census Bureau, "Median Household Income (in 2019 Inflation Adjusted Dollars) by County," prepared by Social Explorer, https://www.socialexplorer.com /17707f1ed3/view (accessed April 25, 2021).

29. Part of this reason for the difference in educational attainment is because the county is home to a major correctional facility.

30. See Lumina Foundation, "A Stronger Nation," 2021, https://www. luminafoundation.org/stronger-nation/report/2021/#state/VA (accessed June 2, 2021).

31. U.S. Department of Health, Education, and Welfare (HEW), *Vital Statistics of the United States 1967. Volume II–Mortality, Part A* (Washington, DC: GPO, 1969), https://www.cdc.gov/nchs/data/vsus/mort67_2a.pdf (accessed June 2, 2021).

32. Virginia, Joint Legislative Audit and Review Commission (JLARC), "Virginia Compared to the Other States," updated January 16, 2020, http://jlarc.virginia.gov/ va-compared-1.asp (accessed June 2, 2021). The 2021 report shows a large increase in the Commonwealth's ranking for number of people under sixty-five with health insurance (from 31st in the nation in 2018 to 24th in 2019). Part of this improvement can be attributed to the state's Medicaid expansion in 2018. Virginia, Joint Legislative Audit and Review Commission (JLARC), "Virginia Compared to the Other States," 2021 Edition, http://jlarc.virginia.gov/pdfs/other/Virginia%20Compared%202021 -FULL%20REPORT-FINAL-web.pdf (accessed June 23, 2021).

33. At least nine other states that produce similar compendiums: Georgia, Hawaii, Iowa, Minnesota, Nebraska, North Carolina, Ohio, Texas, and Washington.

34. Richard Florida, *The Rise of the Creative Class: And How It's Transforming Work, Leisure, and Everyday Life* (New York: Basic Books, 2002).

35. Luke Mullins, "The Real Story of How Virginia Won Amazon's at HQ2," *Washingtonian*, June 16, 2019, https://www.washingtonian.com/2019/06/16/the-real -story-of-how-virginia-won-amazon-hq2/ (accessed June 2, 2021).

36. Scott Cohn, "Amazon Reveals the Truth on Why It Nixed New York and Chose Virginia for Its HQ2," *CNBC*, July 10, 2019, https://www.cnbc.com/2019/07 /10/amazon-reveals-the-truth-on-why-it-nixed-ny-and-chose-virginia-for-hq2.html (accessed June 2, 2021).

37. Richard Levick, "Amazon Goes to Virginia: How Long-Term Thinking Won the HQ2 Prize," *Forbes*, April 15, 2019, https://www.forbes.com/sites/richardlevick /2019/04/15/amazon-goes-to-virginia-how-long-term-thinking-won-the-hq2-prize/ ?sh=3fc23f91264c (accessed June 2, 2021).

38. Christina Nuckols, "McDonnell Rules Kaine Out of Order on Gay-discrimination Ban," *Virginian-Pilot*, February 25, 2006, https://www.pilotonline.com/news/article _04196d73-5d8d-5f88-a6f4-ec2f83250d06.html (accessed June 2, 2021). Although their legal reasoning is often cited in court opinions, Attorney General Opinions under Virginia law do not carry the force of law, and only reflect the legal views of the office at the time of their issuance. When McDonnell succeeded Kaine in 2010, he refused to issue a similar Order. The issuance of these executive orders by Virginia Democratic Governors upon their inauguration became commonplace, with McAuliffe and Northam both signing these statements as the first acts of their administrations. When Democrats took control of the Assembly in 2020, they passed legislation codifying the protections as part of state law.

39. In March 2010, Mims was appointed by the General Assembly to be a Justice of the Virginia Supreme Court.

40. Section 287(g) is named for that portion of the *Immigration and Nationality Act* (INA) that allows the Department of Homeland Security (DHS) to enter into formal written agreements with state or local police departments and deputize selected state and local law enforcement officers to perform the functions of federal immigration agents. The program has been controversial because it imposes costs on state and local government and can lead to deportation of undocumented persons who have been detained for what activists view as relatively minor offenses. See U.S. Immigration and Customs Enforcement (ICE), "Delegation of Immigration Authority Section 287(g)," in *Illegal Immigration Reform and Immigrant Responsibility Act of 1996, Immigration and Nationality Act*, https://www.ice.gov/identify-and-arrest/287g (accessed June 2, 2021).

41. Governor Robert F. McDonnell, interview by author by telephone and email, January 30, 2020 and January 5, 2021.

42. Sheryl Gay Stolberg and Thomas Kaplan, "On Death Penalty Cases, Tim Kaine Revealed Inner Conflict," *New York Times*, July 23, 2016, https://www.nytimes. com/2016/07/24/us/politics/tim-kaine-death-penalty.html (accessed June 2, 2021). In 2005, Kaine's opponent in the gubernatorial race, former Attorney General Jerry Kilgore, ran a series of campaign ads alleging that "Tim Kaine says Adolf Hitler doesn't qualify for the death penalty." Many observers suggest that the ads backfired against the Republican candidate.

43. Despite the large Republican majorities in the House, Democrats were often able to sustain Kaine vetoes against expansion. See Michael Hardy and Jeff E. Schapiro, "Assembly Overrides, Upholds Kaine Vetoes on Death Penalty," *Richmond Times-Dispatch*, April 5, 2007, https://richmond.com/news/article_fd7a512f-95ae -5a75-b91a-0e618d4eb7ab.html (accessed June 2, 2021).

44. Kaine also convened a major task force to investigate the incident and make policy recommendations to the state, many of which were adopted. See Virginia Polytechnic Institute and State University [Virginia Tech], "Mass Shootings at Virginia Tech," April 16, 2007, report of the Virginia Tech Review Panel Presented to Timothy M. Kaine, Governor Commonwealth of Virginia, August 2007, https://rems. ed.gov/docs/MassShootingsatVirginiaTech.pdf (accessed June 2, 2021). The records of the hearings of the Panel can be found in the collection at the Library of Virginia,

"A Guide to the Records of the Virginia Tech Review Panel, 2007–2009," http://ead. lib.virginia.edu/vivaxtf/view?docId=lva/vi00999.xml (accessed June 2, 2021). The men continued to hold very different views on gun safety but worked together during this difficult period.

45. There are several other independent cities in the Nation, notably Baltimore, Maryland, Carson City, Nevada, and St. Louis, Missouri, and numerous other cities that have significant elements of home rule, but Virginia's system is unique in separating cities from counties.

46. Frank B. Atkinson, *Virginia in the Vanguard: Political Leadership in the 400-Year-Old Cradle of American Democracy, 1981–2006* (Lanham, MD: Rowman & Littlefield, 2006), 244.

47. Virginia Joint Legislative Audit and Review Committee, "Interim Review of the Results of Abusive Driver Fees in Virginia and Other States," report to Joint Commission on Transportation Accountability, December 5, 2007, http://jlarc. virginia.gov/pdfs/reports/Rpt_2007_driver_fees.pdf (accessed June 2, 2021).

48. Tim Craig, "Va. Driver Fees Now Election Weapon," *Washington Post*, July 17, 2007, http://www.washingtonpost.com/wp-dyn/content/article/2007/07/16/ AR2007071601934.html (accessed June 2, 2021).

49. Bob Lewis, "Virginia Senate Passes Repeal of Abusive Driver Fees," *Insurance Journal*, February 1, 2008, https://www.insurancejournal.com/news/east/2008/02/01 /86924.htm (accessed June 2, 2021).

50. U.S. Declaration of Independence, *National Archives*, July 4, 1776, https:// www.archives.gov/founding-docs/declaration-transcript (accessed June 8, 2021).

Chapter 3

Race Matters

The grainy black and white photo that flashed across the Twitter feed late Friday, February 1, 2019, seemed incomprehensible; the picture purported to show mild-mannered, decent pediatric neurosurgeon and Virginia Governor Ralph S. Northam photographed in blackface next to another man dressed in the white-hooded terroristic garb of the KKK. The photo had been taken thirty-five years earlier and was displayed prominently on the Governor's medical school yearbook page. The year was 1984, not 1954, and the picture was not of a teenager, but instead a twenty-five-year-old medical student. Most experienced politicians thought immediately that if Northam was in the photo, there was little chance his governorship could survive. The next year would show, however, the power of civil rights activist Bryan Stevenson's recent assertion that "Each of us is more than the worst thing we've ever done." [1]

The disclosure came at an inopportune moment. Northam was coming off the worst week of his term. In the aftermath of a major misstep by a first-term Democratic Delegate while explaining a bill which Republicans portrayed as giving women unfettered access to third trimester abortions in the state, Northam implied during a radio interview that infants born with deformities might even be allowed to die at the time of delivery if their parents concluded that this was the best option.

Though the Governor quickly attempted to clarify his remarks, the political damage was not easily repaired. He and the Delegate were unfairly accused of supporting infanticide, a claim that generated threats against the legislator and supercharged the conservative Republican base at a time when they seemed despondent after losing badly in the 2017 statewide and General Assembly elections.

The blackface / KKK uniform photo emerged from a right-wing website, which had obtained it from a source upset by the abortion controversy.

Whatever the source of the photo, it was met with shock and outrage. How could this be? This was not the Ralph Northam that Virginians had come to know and respect as a person who had served his country admirably as a U.S. Army doctor during Operation Desert Storm and spent countless hours providing free medical care to thousands in his community and in southwest Virginia at the annual Remote Area Medical clinic. It was not the Ralph Northam who, as a pediatric neurosurgeon, counted many children and families of color among his patients. Or the Ralph Northam who was a reasoned advocate for reproductive health rights and better health outcomes for women and for children. And this certainly was not the Ralph Northam who came to Charlottesville after August 2017 to grieve with us after the racist and anti-semiticrioting and to say, "never again."

The initial response from the Governor's Office that evening seemed to confirm the authenticity of the yearbook photo, and the Governor began meeting with his aides to discuss various options, none of which were very attractive. In a video statement issued later that evening, he stated that he was in the picture, but said that he was "not sure" whether his face was the one covered in black paint or under the symbolic KKK hood. This would prove to be a terrible communications error. Even supporters were left scratching their heads as to why he would not know who he was in the photo.

Only later would the Governor deny that he was in the photo at all. He explained that his early mistaken acceptance of responsibility for the photo was driven by his guilt that it appeared on his page of the medical school yearbook. Northam asserted that he had not authorized use of the photo or seen the final version of the yearbook before it was published. Insiders were aware that the First Lady Pam Northam, his girlfriend during medical school, had adamantly denied from the start that the Governor was in the photo, and argued that he should not apologize or accept responsibility.

Almost immediately after release of the photo, Northam began calling members of the Virginia Legislative Black Caucus (VLBC) to discuss the press reports. In the 2019 election, the caucus had increased its membership to twenty-three, the largest number of people of color in the House since Reconstruction, and seven more than when I took office in 2006. The caucus had become a very powerful force within the General Assembly. During the evening of February 1, Northam met with VLBC members several times. Reports from their first meeting indicated that the Governor did not immediately recognize the photo. In response to a question from one Delegate asking, "which one are you?" Northam responded, "I don't know."[2] The fact that the photo was on his personal yearbook page incensed several in the meeting, who asserted that he needed to "own it." Northam then reportedly acknowledged the photo included him, apologized profusely, and proclaimed his commitment to racial healing. During this first meeting, he was not asked to resign, and some VLBC members even insisted that he should stay, apologize, and use the opportunity to educate the public about the evils of racism and the need for racial justice.

To many in the public, Northam's explanation did not make sense. How could he not know about the photo in the first place? If he was in the photo, how could he be confused about whether he was in the hood or blackface? How involved, if at all, was he in choosing the photo for placement on his yearbook page? Could he have really forgotten that the photos in the year-book were on his page at all? Why was such an offensive term, "coonman," prominently displayed next to his photo in the Virginia Military Institute yearbook of several years prior, and suggested as his possible nickname?[3]

The political damage was swift. Almost immediately, calls began for resignation. Former Governor Terry McAuliffe, who had himself recruited Northam to run for office, was one of the first, and Attorney General (AG) Mark Herring followed shortly thereafter, as the chorus of Virginia and national leaders began clamoring for the Governor to step down. Democrats in the Virginia House debated what to do. Having stepped down as House Democratic Leader in December, I deferred to others about communicating with the Governor's office and had heard nothing from either him or his staff. In hindsight, I should have given the Governor the benefit of the doubt until assembling more facts and argued that everyone should wait 24 hours before proceeding to judgment. This was, in fact, what Senate Democratic Leader Dick Saslaw initially had done, stating that this was not the Ralph Northam he knew, and the photo, if he was in it at all, had been taken thirty-five years ago.

An emergency meeting of the entire House Democratic Caucus was called for late that Friday night to decide what to do. It was clear from the begin-ning that the caucus was inclined to defer to the VLBC on a matter with deep racial implications. But then things got more complicated. Prior to the House Caucus meeting, a smaller group of African American legislators had returned to the Governor's mansion. This group, composed of younger and newer members of the Assembly, wanted resignation, and represented during the phone call that entire caucus that VLBC now wanted Northam to step down. Based on this assertion, the Virginia state House Democratic Caucus immediately issued a public demand for the Governor's resignation. The Senate Democratic Caucus joined in shortly thereafter, and the floodgates were now fully opened.

A torrent of criticism poured in from across the country, with prominent Democrats calling on the Governor to resign. U.S. House Speaker Nancy Pelosi, Democratic National Committee Chair Tom Perez, and almost every single 2020 presidential candidate joined the chorus, as did political pundits and editorial pages. U.S. Senators Mark Warner and Tim Kaine delayed issuing an immediate demand for resignation, probably out of respect for a fellow Virginia Governor. Their call would wait until later Saturday, after an uncomfortable press conference by the Governor. Warner and Kaine then joined U.S. Representative Bobby Scott in issuing a joint statement asking for Northam's resignation. Early Saturday morning, I released my own statement requesting resignation. After hearing more details about that Friday evening's events, I came to regret it.

What many did not know at the time was that despite public perceptions, the VLBC, though clearly outraged by the photo and by Northam's response to it, was divided about whether he should resign. In a meeting with the Governor early that Friday evening, several members, including Delegate Delores McQuinn of Henrico/Richmond, suggested that Northam remain on the job. "It is not a time for retreat," she suggested to the Governor, "but a time to teach. You are in a unique position to speak to others with influence. If you leave now, you will be forgotten and will have lost an important opportunity to make change."[4] No formal vote was ever taken by the VLBC to demand resignation.

One wonders how events would have unfolded had everyone waited until the next morning to consider their respective positions. But things move fast in a Twitter-speed news environment, and legislators in an election year were especially worried about what could happen if they were insufficiently rapid in their condemnation. This kind of "quick reaction syndrome" is increasingly occurring in the era of social media and the twenty-four-hour news cycle, and it is unfortunate because people feel compelled to act without enough information. And that action can determine how the story is told. Northam had thought that some of his friends might stick with him in the crisis; he was wrong.

Although not clear at the time, many of us had all fallen victims to "Groupthink." The concept, made famous by social scientist Irving Janis, who tried to explain a number of disastrous policy decisions such as the Bay of Pigs invasion of Cuba by the John F. Kennedy administration in the early 1960s, describes a psychological phenomenon that occurs when the desire for harmony or conformity within a group results in an irrational or dysfunctional decision-making outcome.[5] Group members attempt to minimize conflict and reach a consensus decision without critical evaluation of alternative viewpoints from the outside. The House Democratic Caucus had chosen to defer to the VLBC, believing it to unified. Beneath the surface, however, there were divisions in the VLBC. One group of primarily younger members born years after the Civil Rights movement, were more strident and outspoken in support of resignation. They had witnessed recent efforts to suppress voting, police brutality, and a reemergence of white supremacist groups, and felt that this was the time to seize the mantle of leadership. It was understandable that they would desire to brandish their civil rights bona fides. The older members, many of whom had fought similar battles in the past, were more cautious and inclined to give Northam some additional time. Perhaps we all should have waited a day; it may or may not have made any difference. What was clear, however, is that as the result of our statements and others, Northam was now being buffeted by forces largely out of his control.

Most pundits did not believe the Governor would survive the weekend. To complicate matters, in the Saturday afternoon news conference televised live to the Nation, the Governor stood in the Executive Mansion, stated that there was "no way" he was in the photo, and vowed to serve out his term. The Internet exploded; the Governor's performance only incensed those who had previously called for resignation. For those who knew the Governor, his change in course was perplexing at best, and even more troubling at worst. Critics argued that he was either lying about being in the photograph or clueless in his Friday evening explanation, neither being a good omen for a governorship that was now in existential crisis. Why would he admit to something so significant on Friday only to dramatically change his mind less than twenty-four hours later?

The national commentators, many of whom knew nothing about Northam or Virginia, had a field day, tarring Northam with the broad strokes of "racist," and, in some instances, even discussing impeachment. Northam's Virginia allies cringed in mixed feelings of dismay, outrage, and sorrow, and my colleagues felt that his press conference performance had sealed his fate. Many believed it would only be a matter of time.[6]

Republican Party leadership were playing their cards very close to the vest, feeling that the less they said the better, following the old adage that if an opponent is suffering from self-inflicted damage, let it continue. After all, the media were doing a pretty good job of creating chaos and Democrats had turned on their own. Republicans also remembered that they had stood by former Governor Bob McDonnell as he faced calls for resignation due to corruption charges and did not want to open themselves to charges of hypocrisy.

I was convinced that Republicans were holding off because to do otherwise would open them up to charges of racial insensitivity of their own. They remembered George Allen's "macaca moment," when the former Governor uttered racially inflammatory statements on the campaign trail that went viral and not only doomed his 2006 U.S. Senate re-election bid but also destroyed what appeared, at the time, to be an inevitable march toward the presidency. And any charges of racism aimed at Northam would draw a counterattack directed at them for their silence in the face of Donald J. Trump's actions and statements, whether they involved his racist "birther" arguments, his demagoguery in the 1989 Central Park jogger case,[7] or his comments in the aftermath of Charlottesville 2017 that suggested some members of the white nationalist invaders were "good people."[8] They would play on this field at their peril.

Public sentiment of Northam's actions turned against the previously popular Governor; a poll taken right after the scandal hit found more voters disapproved (44 percent) of the Governors performance than approved (43 percent). Perhaps more significantly, seventy-three percent of respondents did not believe the Governor's version of events.[9]

THE TURMOIL INCREASES: ALLEGATIONS AGAINST THE LIEUTENANT GOVERNOR

Political fortunes, however, can shift in an instant.

On the Monday following Northam's Saturday press conference, information began to circulate detailing an allegation of Dr. Vanessa Tyson, an African American associate professor of politics at Scripps College in California, that Lieutenant Governor Justin Fairfax forced her to have oral sex in a hotel room in Boston during the Democratic National Convention in 2004. The news rocked Virginia's Capitol and shifted attention away from the Governor's problems.

Rumors had floated for some time about "other women" in the life of the Lieutenant Governor, who was now married and the father of two young children. One might chalk up such unsubstantiated stories to racial tropes that can follow around powerful black men. But this new report seemed different. Fairfax responded there had been "consent," and claimed that it is rarely clear what precisely happens when an intimate encounter happens behind closed doors with no one else is around. Nonetheless, Tyson's explanation seemed plausible, and the media reported that credible persons would support her story. Numerous individuals and groups now joined a new chorus calling for his resignation as well.[10]

Democrats were clearly caught in a dilemma. So many had opposed Brett Kavanaugh's elevation to the U.S. Supreme Court in response to allegations of sexual misconduct as a young man that it would appear hypocritical to stand on the sidelines in the face of comparable allegations made against a Democrat. At the same time, the #MeToo movement was exerting a powerful influence on the Democratic Party and its activist base. Many Democrats felt they had no choice but to call for the Lieutenant Governor's resignation. The condemnations of Fairfax were strong and swift; no one would be able to say that Democrats were not clear in their opposition to sexual assault.

As if things were not chaotic enough, on Wednesday, February 6, AG Mark Herring issued a statement revealing that decades earlier, when he was nineteen years old, he had dressed in costume imitating the African American rapper Kurtis Blow at an undergraduate fraternity party. There were no photos, only Herring's admission. In a well-crafted statement that helped minimize the political fallout, he took full responsibility and suggested that he might himself need to resign. Some viewed Herring's statement as hypocritical, the AG having called on Northam to quit because of his transgression. But the political climate had now become so chaotic that many gave him a pass.

The next explosion came just forty-eight hours later, when the *Washington Post* (which had decided not to publish Tyson's allegation two years earlier) reported a second accusation against Fairfax. Fairfax's new accuser alleged that he had raped her in 2000 while the two were undergraduates at Duke University. Although he again responded that this was a consensual encounter, the accusation generated more calls for his resignation; one Democratic Delegate even drafted an impeachment resolution.

While Governor Northam was facing political problems, the allegations against Fairfax, if true, constituted crimes. The stakes were now higher than ever, and the Lieutenant Governor now seemed much more in peril than the Governor. Fairfax continued to profess his innocence, but then proceeded to commit his own political missteps. The day after Dr. Tyson's allegations surfaced on the Internet, he subtly suggested that perhaps Governor Northam or Richmond's African American Mayor, Levar Stoney (then a potential challenger to Fairfax's gubernatorial ambitions), had played a role in leaking her claims to the website that published them. Fairfax called for an FBI investigation, something that would not typically be possible since these were not federal crimes.[11] Reports surfaced that Fairfax had engaged in expletive-laced criticisms of one of the women during a closed-door meeting of Democrats. The Nation was now so focused on him that when stories broke that the Republican Leader in the Virginia Senate, Thomas K. "Tommy" Norment Jr., had served as editor of a high school yearbook that was full of racist photos and comments, people hardly blinked their eyes.

Ironically, the Fairfax scandal increased the likelihood that Northam would stay in office. There was no way the legislature could force the Governor to resign. Impeachment for his actions, however reprehensible they were if proven, was not legally justified. Beyond that, many were concerned about elevating the Lieutenant Governor to the higher position considering the serious criminal allegations made against him. The alternative, if both Northam and Fairfax resigned, would be an AG (Mark Herring) who had also admitted to wearing blackface in college and had his own political fence-mending to do.

The prospect of losing prominent statewide Democrats was not appealing to those who had worked so hard to get them elected in 2017. In addition, the line of succession would have made Republican House Speaker Kirk Cox the Governor *if* Northam, Fairfax, and Herring all left office.

Events were now aligning to provide Northam with an opportunity for survival. He indicated that he would fight for his job and for redemption. At the same time, different activists within the Democratic Party were trying to determine what to do. Some felt that easing the pressure on Northam to resign while demanding the Lieutenant Governor's resignation would mean that a prominent African American (Fairfax) could lose his office while a white politician (Northam) remained. Such an outcome would likely raise concerns among many in the base of African American voters who provide strong support to the Democratic Party and provided the margin of victory in many Virginia statewide races. Not acting against Fairfax, however, would mean that another strong component of the nascent Democratic majority in Virginia—progressive women—would question the Party's commitment to equality and to safety for women.

As all these events were unfolding, the legislature was in session, and members from both parties continued to go about the business of governing. There was a budget to pass and a bill with major tax implications to consider. With the Governor largely hobbled by the allegations, Republicans had increased bargaining power on these issues. Nonetheless, Virginia governors have considerable power and Northam could exercise it if he remained in office.

In the weeks following the photo disclosure, Northam retreated from public view but remained active behind the scenes, determining which measures he would veto and how he could alter the state's budget to better reflect his priorities. As the General Assembly adjourned in late February 2019, the legislature was not able to do much of anything to affect Northam's decisions to remain in office or his pledge to work on racial equity throughout the rest of his term.[12]

At the same time, efforts began to determine whether Northam was in the photo at all. Some of these occurred behind the scenes, while others were more public. Eastern Virginia Medical School (EVMS), Northam's medical school, hired McGuireWoods LLP to investigate the photo and the school's role in publishing it in the yearbook. This inquiry, which took four months and cost over $300,000, included detailed interviews with the Governor himself and several staff members.[13] The investigative team even conducted sophisticated photographic analysis to determine the height of the people in the images.

During the inquiry, rumors began circulating that one of the persons in the photo had been identified, but it was said that Northam, who felt that his reputation had been ruined by the allegations, was reluctant to identify the person out of concern that a former classmate, most likely a prominent physician, might meet the same fate. Some suggestions emerged that one of the persons was actually a woman. The McGuireWoods report was unable to confirm or refute the rumors. The report was also similarly unable to determine the origin of the photo and who placed it on the yearbook page.[14] The

Governor continued his denials that he was in the photo and went about the business of governing.

As the Governor was quietly trying to repair his image, Justin Fairfax came out fighting. Having previously called for an FBI investigation, he "doubled down" in a late February adjournment day speech in the Senate, warning the Body against "political lynchings." The imagery was shocking and evoked memories of Justice Clarence Thomas, who, during his U.S. Supreme Court confirmation hearings in 1991, accused supporters of attorney and Professor Anita Hill of attempts at a "high tech lynching" designed to put an "uppity" black male in his place. The parallels were unmistakable and troubling. Fairfax had now taken the issue to another level and more clearly injected race into the ongoing turmoil.

One hour earlier, on the other side of the Capitol building, Republicans were playing their own political cards when Rob Bell of Albemarle, Chairman of the House Courts of Justice Committee, challenged Democrats to join with him in convening a meeting to hear from the women who had accused Fairfax. Bell never used the words "investigation" or "impeachment," but they were clearly on people's minds. House Republican leadership had been toying with the Democrats for several days with nondescript and vague requests to convene a bipartisan panel to investigate the Fairfax allegations. When pressed for details and a written plan, Republicans offered nothing, instead demanding a simple "yes or no" answer as to whether Democrats would participate.

Democrats were justifiably concerned; not only was this political dynamite that could further divide the party, but also no one was quite sure about the goal of such hearings, or, more significantly, the rules under which they would take place. Republicans, however, were salivating at the potential opportunity to criticize Democrats for an alleged failure to side with women, in hopes that the GOP delegates could deflect attention away from their rejection of the Equal Rights Amendment (ERA) and their continuing efforts to reduce reproductive choice. They claimed Democrats were attempting to block the efforts of the women to tell their story, and announced that if Democrats did not join them, they would conduct an inquiry on their own.

The Republican strategy of going it alone never made much political sense. First, it was not clear that Dr. Vanessa Tyson, the first woman to come forward, would appear even if Republicans organized their own hearing. Tyson had indicated from the beginning that she was not interested in participating in a "political circus," and that the prospect of a group of white men asking sexually charged questions of an African American woman about an African American man certainly seemed likely to devolve into one. Such hearings posed a huge political risk to the Republicans; such a partisan spectacle might mobilize more African Americans to vote in an off-year election, especially

if the Republicans chose to investigate Fairfax but ignore two white men—
Northam and Herring—who had engaged in serious affronts to decency. In
addition, without Tyson's testimony, the inquiry would appear even more like
a show, thereby raising more questions about its real purpose.

There were other reasons for Republicans to be leery of conducting their
own inquiry. The committee would have no power to issue subpoenas to persons outside of Virginia. Hence, the only person subject to subpoena would
be Fairfax, and no one knew what position he might take. There would be
serious issues involving due process, especially if a criminal investigation
was happening at the same time in either Massachusetts or North Carolina—
investigations Fairfax had requested without success—where the events
allegedly occurred. Would holding a hearing of any kind compromise such
ongoing criminal cases, and if it might, would that be fair to the women?

Finally, most lawyers looking at the case felt that impeachment of Fairfax
was extremely problematic, even if the allegations against him were true.
The language on impeachment in the Virginia Constitution suggested that the
remedy was available only if the Lieutenant Governor had committed crimes
against the Commonwealth.[15] While many believed that Fairfax's political
career was over, they did not think that the behavior, even if proved at a
criminal trial, was impeachable. The Republicans were playing with political
fire, even though it was not clear that they realized it.

Throughout the summer and fall of 2019, Fairfax continued to profess his
innocence, but few appeared to be listening. In a last-ditch effort to clear
his name, and perhaps to resurrect his dashed hopes to run for Governor, he
filed a $400 million lawsuit against CBS for defamation, again asserting that
the claims against him were false.[16] Ultimately, Fairfax sought vindication
by seeking the Democratic nomination for Governor in 2021; he finished a
distant fourth.

Northam, not eligible to run for re-election under the Virginia Constitution,
took a different approach. He quietly began attending small and large gatherings of African Americans in an unofficial capacity and meeting with different leaders around the state to listen to critics and attempt to rebuild his
image. The events of the next several months illustrated the force of quiet
leadership and the power of political redemption.

JAMESTOWN PROTESTS AND
REDEMPTION AT FORT MONROE

In July 2019, Virginia recognized the 400th anniversary of the establishment
of American representative government at Jamestown and the first landing of
enslaved Africans at Point Comfort in what is now Hampton, Virginia.

The Commonwealth has consistently asserted its claim to be the location of the first permanent English settlement in the Nation and birthplace of the longest continuous legislative Body in the Western Hemisphere, facts celebrated as examples of the state's exceptionalism. Until recently, however, the slavery component of Virginia's history has largely been de-emphasized or ignored on commemorative occasions.

The 2019 commemoration was designed to be different. At its center was an acknowledgment that enslaved Africans were part of the texture of colonial Virginia from its early days. Organizers of the commemoration had already scheduled events with this theme in mind, but the Northam scandal subjected the planning to additional scrutiny. And when President Trump, fresh off a tweetstorm where he suggested that four congressional members of color should "go back to where they came from," decided to attend the events in Jamestown, racial issues took center stage.[17]

The VLBC organized a boycott of the President's visit, going so far as to state that those who attended were complicit with racism.[18] As a result, few African Americans attended the Jamestown event, and many Democrats stayed away as well.

Although Northam and the commemoration committee had extended the President a ceremonial invitation to attend Jamestown many months prior to the event, few thought that Trump would go. With Trump's announcement that he would attend, Northam made sure that he would leave the scene before the President's arrival. Instead, the Governor attended a church service to open the day, made brief remarks, and was whisked off to another event. President Trump arrived to little fanfare, but when a newly-elected state delegate rose from his chair to interrupt the President's speech, unveiling a sign with the words "Deport Hate" and "Reunite My Family,"[19] the commemoration that had been planned for years as an effort to draw attention to both our exceptionalism and our oppression of black Virginians had become a polarized spectacle.

Northam continued his efforts to secure redemption several weeks later, when the commemoration of the anniversary of the first arrival of enslaved Africans in America took place at Fort Monroe in Hampton. Calling slavery an atrocity, Northam had earlier ordered the removal of the letters "Jefferson Davis Memorial Park" from the iron gate leading into the site, something he had advocated four months earlier.[20] Speaking to a racially diverse crowd on that hot day in August 2019, Northam made clear his sentiments: "If we're serious about righting the wrong that began here at this place, we need to do more than talk. We need to take action." The crowd erupted into applause and gave the Governor a standing ovation.[21] Perhaps Northam might be able to put the blackface incident behind him after all.[22]

The Governor's approval / disapproval numbers improved in the fall; by early October, he reached a 47/29 favorable split,[23] and Democratic takeovers of the U.S. House and U.S. Senate in the November 2019 election proved that the issue, which many had believed in February would loom large in the fall contests, had little impact on General Assembly elections.

Northam did in fact put actions behind his words. He created a Director of Diversity, Equity and Inclusion, an entirely new position in state government.[24] He initiated a Commission on African American History Education to upgrade Virginia's education standards to ensure they were "inclusive of African American history."[25] His 2020 budget included new funding to attack maternal mortality among people of color and new investments in historically black colleges and universities (HBCUs).[26] The Governor initiated a process to replace a bust of Robert E. Lee at the U.S. Capitol that had been there since 1909, eliminated the Lee-Jackson state holiday,[27] and, following George Floyd's murder in Minneapolis in May 2020, authorized the removal of the massive statue of Robert E. Lee that had dominated the entrance to Richmond's Monument Avenue for over one hundred years. He pitched his support for the legalization of marijuana and for the repeal of the death penalty in terms of racial justice.

Northam's actions solidified his strong support among African Americans across the state, who had, notwithstanding the scandal, given him higher ratings than white Virginians. What finally redeemed Northam, however, was his response to COVID-19; in an April 2020 poll, 76 percent of Virginians approved of his handling of the pandemic.[28] By late October, Northam's job approval rating had jumped to 56 percent, up thirteen percentage points from what was reported in the wake of the blackface scandal.[29] Many challenges remained for the Governor, but it appeared that the adverse impact of the scandal had largely dissipated. Nonetheless, these events changed Northam. "Things happen for a reason," the Governor explained. "Although I did not understand it at the time, this would give me an opportunity that few in my position would ever have—to discuss race in ways that had not been done in decades and to assist in making the changes that are so needed in the Commonwealth and the Nation. Painful as it sometimes was, I would like to think it also made me a better person in the process."[30]

Virginia, like much of the Nation, is undergoing a massive re-examination of race relations. This involves not just the clearly oppressive elements of slavery and of past injustices, but also the dynamics of present inequality and forces that are sometimes more difficult to understand and to confront. Part of that investigation in Virginia means looking anew at how the Commonwealth has operated and exploring more fully the precise nature of what some call "the Virginia Way."

NOTES

1. Bryan Stevenson, *Just Mercy: A Story of Justice and Redemption*. New York: (Spiegel and Grau, 2014).

2. McGuireWoods LLP, "Report to Eastern Virginia Medical School," *Eastern Virginia Medical School*, May 21, 2019, 15, https://www.evms.edu/media/evms _public/departments/diversity_office/final-evms-report-with-exhibits.pdf (accessed June 2, 2021).

3. On its face, the term "coonman" appeared to be a racially pejorative term applied to actions taken or attitudes that were purportedly held by Governor Ralph S. Northam. Yet, other reasonable conclusions could have been drawn. One was that Northam, who grew up on the rural Eastern Shore of Virginia, was being teased for his rural upbringing in an area where raccoon or "coon" hunting was common (See Democratic Political Initiative, "There Are Three Reasons Ralph Northam Might Be Called Coon Man," *Medium*, February 4, 2019, https://medium.com/@NewsHillbilly /there-are-three-reasons-ralph-northam-might-be-called-coon-man-44b2e82498ae [accessed June 2, 2021]). Another was that Northam, a product of public schools, had considerable numbers of African American friends and was being criticized for it. As for the use of term "blackface," it not only occurred frequently in the South but was common in the North as well during much of American history. See Eric Lott, *Love & Theft: Blackface Minstrelsy and the American Working Class*, 20th Anniversary ed. (New York: Oxford University Press, 2013).

4. Delegate Delores McQuinn, interview by author by telephone, November 18, 2020.

5. Irving L. Janis, *Groupthink: Psychological Studies of Policy Decisions and Fiascoes*. 2nd ed. (Boston: Houghton Mifflin, 1982).

6. Northam was not the only Governor that became embroiled in a blackface scandal. In August 2019, reports emerged that Republican Governor Kay Ivey of Alabama had dressed up in blackface during a 1967 college skit. She apologized but refused to resign. The media attention was minimal as compared to the Northam story. Reis Thebault, "Alabama's Republican Governor Apologizes for Wearing Blackface in College, Refuses to Resign," *Washington Post*, August 30, 2019, https://www. washingtonpost.com/politics/2019/08/30/alabamas-republican-governor-apologizes -wearing-blackface-college-refuses-resign/ (accessed June 2, 2021).

7. Patrick Ryan, "Ava DuVernay Lets Trump 'Speak for Himself' in Central Park Five Series 'When They See Us,'" *USA Today*, June 3, 2019, https://www.usatoday. com/story/life/tv/2019/06/03/looking-back-trumps-involvement-1989-central-park -five-case/1212335001/ (accessed June 2, 2021).

8. This was unfolding several months before Donald J. Trump's racially charged comments directed at four first-term U.S. Congresswomen of color, known as the "Squad," urging them to go back to where they came from, suggesting they were not loyal to the United States, and ignoring that all but one had been born in the United States.

9. Peter Jamison and Scott Clement, "Virginians Are Split on Governor's Fate Amid Blackface Scandal, Poll Shows," *Washington Post*, February 9, 2019, https: //www.washingtonpost.com/local/virginia-politics/virginians-split-on-governors

-fate-amid-blackface-scandal-poll-shows/2019/02/09/93002e84-2bc1-11e9-b011
-d8500644dc98_story.html (accessed June 2, 2021).

10. In the strangest of political twists, Vanessa Tyson hired the attorneys who represented Christine Blasey Ford during the Justice Brett Kavanaugh hearings—and Lieutenant Governor Justin Fairfax hired Kavanaugh's lawyers.

11. Here is one example where nuance can be lost in a crisis. Fairfax had reason to ask for the FBI to investigate. The FBI investigated when he received a top-secret security clearance as a federal prosecutor, and he simply asked them to reopen those investigations. The FBI responded by saying that it could investigate, but only if his clearance was still active. Unfortunately for Fairfax, his clearance had expired shortly before Tyson came forward.

12. Gregory S. Schneider, "Va. Gov. Ralph Northam Says He Wants to Focus Rest of His Term on Racial Equity," *Washington Post*, February 9, 2019, https://www.washingtonpost.com/local/virginia-politics/va-gov-ralph-northam-says-he-wants-to-focus-rest-of-his-term-on-racial-equity/2019/02/09/2a739b20-2c76-11e9-984d-9b8fba003e81_story.html (accessed June 2, 2021).

13. McGuireWoods LLP, "Report to Eastern Virginia Medical School."

14. The language of the report's conclusion was itself intriguing: "we could not conclusively determine the identity of either individual depicted in the Photograph." Did that mean that there was some evidence pointing to people other than the Governor in the photo, but that no one would corroborate it for the record? (McGuireWoods LLP, "Report to Eastern Virginia Medical School," 2).

15. Virginia, *Constitution of Virginia*, Article IV. Legislature, Section 17. Impeachment, https://law.lis.virginia.gov/constitution/article4/section17/ (accessed June 2, 2021).

16. Patrick Wilson, "Justin Fairfax Files Defamation Lawsuit Against CBS News," *Richmond Times-Dispatch*, September 12, 2019, https://www.richmond.com/news/virginia/government-politics/justin-fairfax-files-defamation-lawsuit-against-cbs-news/article_bb364dd8-0be4-54d4-bcc0-c761404f2917.html (accessed June 2, 2021). The complaint included allegations that Richmond Mayor Levar Stoney, an ally of former Governor Terry McAuliffe and a person who many pundits perceived to be one of Fairfax's major rivals for the Democratic gubernatorial nomination, was part of a conspiracy to damage Fairfax politically. Stoney, of course, denied the claim, branding it as "offensive," but the dirty laundry was now in full view, as the rivalry between two prominent African American politicians took on a distinctly personal nature. Fairfax continued his efforts to clear his name into 2020, but CBS showed its willingness to fully litigate the claim, alleging that the Lieutenant Governor was simply using the lawsuit to "disparage" and "attack" the two women who accused him. The court ultimately dismissed Fairfax's case. See Graham Moomaw, "CBS Calls Lt. Gov. Justin Fairfax's Defamation Suit a Ploy to 'Attack' Accusers," *Virginia Mercury*, November 2, 2019, https://www.virginiamercury.com/2019/11/02/cbs-calls-lt-gov-justin-fairfaxs-defamation-suit-a-ploy-to-attack-accusers/ (accessed June 2, 2021).

17. Gregory S. Schneider, "Trump Will Speak at Jamestown Event Marking 400 Years of Representative Government," *Washington Post*, July 26, 2019, https://www.washingtonpost.com/local/virginia-politics/trump-will-speak-at-jamestown-event

-marking-400-years-of-representative-government/2019/07/26/9320b69c-b003-11e9 -a0c9-6d2d7818f3da_story.html (accessed June 2, 2021).

18. Gregory S. Schneider, "Black Va. Legislators to Skip Jamestown Because of Trump, Say Those Who Attend are 'Complicit' in Racism," *Washington Post*, July 29, 2019, https://beta.washingtonpost.com/local/virginia-politics/black-lawmakers-skip -jamestown-because-of-trump-say-those-who-attend-are-complicit-in-racism/2019 /07/29/e30a7f3e-b211-11e9-8949-5f36ff92706e_story.html (accessed June 2, 2021).

19. Ibraheem S. Samirah, "Why I Disrupted Trump's Speech at Jamestown," *Atlantic*, August 2, 2019, https://www.theatlantic.com/ideas/archive/2019/08/why-i -disrupted-the-presidents-speech-at-jamestown/595366/ (accessed June 2, 2021)

20. The inscription had been erected in the 1950s to recognize that the President of the Confederacy was imprisoned for a time at Fort Monroe, which had remained in Union control throughout the Civil War.

21. Gregory S. Schneider, "Virginia Marks the Dawn of American Slavery in 1619 with Solemn Speeches and Songs," *Washington Post*, August 24, 2019, https://www. washingtonpost.com/local/virginia-politics/virginia-marks-the-dawn-of-american -slavery-in-1619-with-solemn-ceremonies-speeches-songs/2019/08/24/adbc84ae -c66f-11e9-9986-1fb3e4397be4_story.html (accessed June 2, 2021)

22. See the Conclusion of this book for an exposition of Northam's efforts, largely successful, to address racial issues in a very different way. See also WAPO Editorial Board, "Opinion: How Ralph Northam Came Back from the Political Dead," *Washington Post*, December 27, 2019, https://www.washingtonpost.com/opinions/ how-ralph-northam-came-back-from-the-political-dead/2019/12/27/941e4a46-282b -11ea-b2ca-2e72667c1741_story.html (accessed June 2, 2021).

23. Laura Vozzella, Gregory S. Schneider and Emily Guskin, "Poll Shows Virginia Gov. Ralph Northam's Approval Rating Improves Nine Months After Blackface Scandal," *Washington Post*, October 3, 2019, https://www.washingtonpost. com/local/virginia-politics/poll-shows-virginia-gov-ralph-northams-approval-rating -improves-months-after-blackface-scandal/2019/10/03/2d340ede-e473-11e9-a331 -2df12d56a80b_story.html (accessed June 2, 2021).

24. Gregory S. Schneider, "Northam Names First Diversity Chief for Virginia State Government, *Washington Post*, September 9, 2019, https://www.washingtonpost. com/local/virginia-politics/northam-names-first-ever-diversity-chief-for-virginia -state-government/2019/09/09/a5476cd4-d318-11e9-86ac-0f250cc91758_story.html (accessed June 2, 2021).

25. Virginia, Office of the Governor, Executive Order Number Thirty-Nine (2019): Establishment of the Commission on African American History Education in the Commonwealth, https://www.governor.virginia.gov/media/governorvirginiagov /executive-actions/EO-39-Establishment-of-the-Commission-on-African-American -History-Education-in-the-Commonwealth.pdf (accessed June 2, 2021). See also Mechelle Hankerson, "A Governor-Appointed Commission Begins Work on Improving black History Education in Virginia," *Virginia Mercury*, October 29, 2019, https: //www.virginiamercury.com/2019/10/29/a-governor-appointed-commission-begins -work-on-improving-teaching-of-black-history-in-virginia/ (accessed June 2, 2021).

26. Roger Chesley, "Governor's Support of HBCUs Laudable, Though Financial, Other Struggles Continue," *Virginia Mercury*, January 6, 2020, https://www.virginiamercury.com/2020/01/06/guvs-support-of-hbcus-laudable-though-financial-other-struggles-continue/ (accessed June 2, 2021).

27. Each state is granted two statues at the U.S. Capitol designed to celebrate key persons or events in that state's history. Virginia's other statue is of Washington. See Robert Zullo, "Governor's Office Seeks Legislation to Replace Lee Statue at U.S. Capitol," *Virginia Mercury*, December 23, 2019, https://www.virginiamercury.com/2019/12/23/governors-office-will-push-for-removal-of-lee-statue-at-u-s-capitol/ (accessed June 2, 2021).

28. Justin Mattingly, "76percent of Virginians Approve of Northam's Response to Pandemic, VCU Poll," *Roanoke Times*, April 14, 2020, https://www.roanoke.com/news/local/76-of-virginians-approve-of-northams-response-to-pandemic-vcu-poll-says/article_1e6ec8e5-409e-54e6-80d2-78cd160b1cb9.html (accessed June 2, 2021).

29. Gregory S. Schneider, Laura Vozzella, Emily Guskin, and Alauna Safarpour, "Post-Schar School Poll: Majority of Virginia Voters Approve of Northam's Job Performance," *Washington Post*, October 23, 2020, https://www.washingtonpost.com/local/virginia-politics/northam-job-approval-poll/2020/10/22/1e6e7bc8-13c5-11eb-ad6f-36c93e6e94fb_story.html (accessed June 2, 2021).

30. Governor Ralph S. Northam, interview by author in person, Richmond, Virginia, June 14, 2021.

Chapter 4

Reckoning with "The Virginia Way"

The Virginia Way . . . would dispose the Negroes to cooperate in the right sort of residential separation, by consent.

—Douglas Southall Freeman, editor, *Richmond New Leader*, 1930.[1]

Early in the 2018 legislative session, Delegate Delores McQuinn sat quietly in her seat in the House chamber. But behind her quiet demeanor, she was seething, having just heard a Republican colleague launch into yet another criticism of the "Democrat"[2] Party that attempted to blame it for the racial problems we have today. But as is typical for the Delegate, she gathered her thoughts while holding her fire. Democrats asked for a recess, and she helped engineer a thoughtful but firm response to the attack.

McQuinn was elected to the House of Delegates to represent parts of the City of Richmond, Henrico County, and Chesterfield County in 2009 after a long career in local public service which began as a Richmond school board member in 1992, and continued for almost seventeen years, including several terms on the Richmond City Council. She was a person of faith, actively engaged as a minister in her local church, and deeply rooted in her community. Born in the same year as the *Brown v. Board of Education of Topeka* (1954) decision,[3] McQuinn had to endure Virginia's state policy of massive resistance as she commenced her schooling. She was constantly searching for better ways of telling the story of race in America and led the way in finding monies to identify the remains of the deceased in unmarked black cemeteries in Richmond, an initiative I also took up for Charlottesville. After several of us had failed in efforts to give localities control over Confederate statuary in their communities, McQuinn was able to pass the bill to do so in 2020. When she spoke about race, people listened.

McQuinn was deeply troubled by Governor Ralph S. Northam's scandal, but viewed it more broadly than a problem simply for the Governor. "It's not by chance that God pulled back the covers in Virginia, the capital of the Confederacy." "We must acknowledge it," she continued in a speech at Virginia Union University. "The only way we can get beyond it is to acknowledge."[4] In other words, while holding people accountable for their transgressions, we needed to probe deeper and to look at more systemic and institutional origins and aspects of racism. McQuinn never asked for Northam to resign, suggesting instead that he should seize the moment and use his position to promote racial healing and equity. "In your position, you have an opportunity to reach so many people," McQuinn told Northam; "you can get into the Board rooms of companies, and speak to thousands both about the past, and what needs to be done. If you leave, you will miss the opportunity. You should seize it."[5] That is what Northam proceeded to do; in the process, he would come to grips with what was once known as "the Virginia Way."

Several recent Virginian leaders have used the phrase "the Virginia Way" to describe what sets the Commonwealth apart from other states. In November 2012, for example, newly elected U.S. Senator Tim Kaine used it immediately after a tough election. "This is the time," he said, "to find common solutions to our nation's common problems . . . . That is the Virginia way."[6] Governor Bob McDonnell, in his 2014 State of the Commonwealth address, stated, "In this Capitol, we debated passionately and civilly, we worked together, we shared the credit. We adhered to the 'Virginia Way' and our democracy is better for it."[7] Similarly, Governor Terry McAuliffe, in his 2014 inaugural speech, argued that the Commonwealth is "the national model for fiscal discipline because our leaders—leaders like Governor Doug Wilder—decided long ago to put the common good ahead of short-term politics. That's the Virginia way—it's a tradition that we should be proud of [and] that must be sustained through constant work by leaders who choose progress over ideology."[8] Not to be outdone, Governor Northam expressed a similar sentiment in his 2018 "State of the Commonwealth Address": "Virginia has led the nation by example. The Virginia Way charges us to put people ahead of politics, and to leave this place better than we found it."[9] My General Assembly colleagues have heard me argue on countless occasions to embrace a position because it is consistent with "the Virginia Way." Had I known the historical basis of the term, I doubt that I would have employed it in that fashion.

The "Virginia Way" has not always meant cooperation and civility. Instead, it springs from a problematic past. The term was first used in the writings Douglas Southall Freeman (1886–1953) in the 1920s and 1930s, during a time when politics, government, and the social order in the Commonwealth were controlled by the "Byrd machine," so-named for its creator, Harry F. Byrd Sr. (1887–1966). Committed to maintaining "separate but equal" facilities, Freeman, the influential editor of the *Richmond News Leader*, embraced a paternalistic view of race relations. Freeman argued that if whites were civil in their dealings with blacks, affording them a limited degree of equal opportunity, African Americans would more likely maintain a separation of the races "based on consent." This approach collapsed during the Civil Rights movement and "massive resistance." White segregationists showed their willingness to subjugate blacks, with violence as necessary. And African Americans were no longer willing to maintain the facade of "separate but equal." The notion of Virginia civility and respect, however, lived on, especially in how lawmakers made policy in Richmond. By the mid 2010s, the concept took on a character totally different than in the time of Freeman and Byrd.

Byrd and Freeman were giants of their times. Byrd was the politician, a son of a successful apple grower in the northern Shenandoah Valley. He assumed control of his father's newspaper, the *Winchester Star*, in 1903 and launched his political career in 1915 by winning a seat in the Virginia State Senate at the age of twenty-eight. He became Governor in 1926 and was then appointed to the U.S. Senate in 1933, where he served until his retirement in 1965. Byrd was the architect of an organization known as the Byrd machine, a group which largely controlled Virginia politics into the second half of the twentieth century. His legacy is equated with oligarchy, massive resistance, and Democratic politics, and was synonymous with rock-ribbed, old-school conservatism until his death in 1966.

Freeman, the lesser known of the two, was nonetheless tremendously influential within Virginia elites. Born in 1886, he had a flair for the written word and penned countless articles and books during his career. During his thirty-five-year stint as editor of the now-defunct *Richmond News Leader*, Freeman established himself as a thought leader, especially among white elites in the Commonwealth.[10] As such, he crossed paths frequently with Byrd, agreeing with Virginia's most powerful politician on fiscal matters and on the role of government, but remaining distrustful of the machine politics of the day and some of its views about race relations. A Pulitzer Prize-winning author of a two-volume biography of Robert E. Lee, Freeman's writings also provided intellectual undergirding to the "lost cause" imagery that emerged after the Civil War and remained prominent during his time.[11] This narrative asserted that Virginians were noble and heroic in their fight to protect the Commonwealth from Yankee invaders and the so-called War of Northern Aggression. And in Freeman's eyes and the eyes of most white Virginians at the time, Lee was the noblest of them all.

For Freeman, the "Virginia Way" related to the Commonwealth's conduct in race relations. At its core, the Virginia way embodied civility in public matters while maintaining a paternalistic relationship with blacks. This genteel racism was the foundation of white supremacy in the Commonwealth during these decades, providing a stark contrast to other states in the South, where overt terrorizing of the African American population was more commonplace.[12] That is not to say that racial violence did not occur in Virginia, but contemporaries claimed that it was neither the predominant nor the preferred means of enforcing segregation. A more subtle approach was in vogue.

Writing in a February 9, 1926 editorial, Freeman argued that

> beyond the broad fundamentals of no intermarriage, separation of the races is not to be assured by sweeping statutes, but by some public sentiment . . . . Virginia has her racial sore spots that call for treatment—careful, intelligent and in some instants drastic treatment—but overall, she has obtained very satisfactory results by avoiding needless racial law-making, and by applying her own methods of adjustment in her own way. That Virginia way is not one of contention, but of understanding, not the making of humiliating laws, but the establishment of just, acceptable usage.[13]

Freeman frequently referenced the "Virginia Way" as the approach to use when considering "racial legislation . . . before the General Assembly.[14] The "Virginia Way," he argued, "has always been the way of tolerance and of understanding," not "the way of headlong law-making, but of careful, friendly and intelligent inquiry." This careful, pragmatic approach "would dispose the Negroes to cooperate in the right sort of residential separation by consent." If "the racial question . . . is to be worked out," he explained, "both races must be stimulated to strengthen their racial integrity."[15]

Freeman continuously looked for ways to distinguish the Old Dominion and its approach to race relations from states to its south, where he argued that African Americans were controlled more by threats and intimidation. Freeman was not shy about condemning mob violence and the Ku Klux Klan (KKK), stating that it was not the "The Virginia Way" "to put on masks, to hide identity in a mob, to hang some wretch in the dark of the moon, and then shrink away in blood guiltiness."[16] The Virginia Way took on the characteristics of "noblesse oblige," where the upper classes and elites would govern by practicing a genteel brand of paternalism. When applied to race, his focus was on preserving order by "managing conflict" rather than by coercion and intimidation. His was a more nuanced support that more vociferous segregationists frequently criticized. Today, the tendency is to judge him by contemporary standards rather than by locating him within the period that he lived.[17]

Freeman's paternalism is further evident in an article he penned for the *Nation* in 1924 titled "Virginia: A Gentle Dominion." "The Virginia Negro," he said, is "the blue blood of his race," and, in Virginia, "the two races could live side by side . . . and have no strife."[18] In his view, racial hierarchy should be maintained by custom, not by violence or even by certain laws. For example, Freeman opposed legalized residential segregation, including an ordinance imposing the practice in Richmond, and suggesting that it would ultimately be struck down by the courts.

In contrast to Freeman's somewhat detached paternalism, Byrd operated in the political trenches, and was not shy about playing the race card when it suited his needs. While he tepidly supported Virginia's Anti-Lynching Law of 1928,[19] Byrd rarely criticized legislative measures proposed by segregationist politicians. Passage of Anti-Lynching Law was heralded by white elites as an example of how managed race relations could work, but it did little to address the everyday concerns of blacks. In fact, while fewer blacks were lynched in Virginia than in any other state, mobs killed at least seventy blacks by this method between 1880 and 1930.[20]

Byrd understood the political climate of the day and the power of the "lost cause" imagery that had been fueled not just by the writings of Southern historians but also by the visual presence through the construction of imposing monuments to the "heroic" efforts of Confederate generals and leaders erected throughout the South. The monuments were not, as many believed, constructed in the aftermath of the Civil War. Rather, they were erected in the aftermath of Reconstruction and into the early twentieth century to demonstrate the power of white supremacy across the South.

In Richmond, imposing statues of Robert E. Lee, J. E. B. Stuart, Stonewall Jackson, and even Confederate President Jefferson Davis were built on pedestals on what was to become the most prominent residential street in the city, Monument Avenue. The monuments were later graced on each side by mansions that evoked the so-called glory days of the past, and the boulevard became a major symbol of the former Confederate capital. In Charlottesville, large statues of Robert E. Lee and Stonewall Jackson were installed in two downtown parks in 1921 and 1924, and the Lee statue became the flashpoint for the infamous August 2017 "Unite the Right" rally in Charlottesville.[21] In July, 2021, they were removed.

The power of the "lost cause" narrative was not lost on Byrd. During his 1925 gubernatorial campaign, he argued, in an allusion to Reconstruction days, that Virginia should "never again enthrone the Negro as arbiter of our political destiny by giving him the balance of power."[22] And his policies reflected his view of keeping blacks (and poor whites, for that matter) in their place. Evidence of this is found in the Commonwealth's paltry investments in public education that could have served as a pathway to opportunity for blacks and poor whites. In 1928, Virginia ranked nineteenth of all the states in wealth, but only forty-fifth out of forty-eight states in education spending.[23] Moreover, state and local spending on black schools was about one-quarter that of white institutions.[24] Byrd proposed little to address this disparity, and most Virginians were simply comfortable with maintaining the status quo. In fact, when some black advocates proposed some additional investments in black public schools, even the most progressive whites responded that such black demands were "too radical for us."[25]

Byrd was first and foremost an institutionalist and guarantor of white elites and social order. If he could do it with racial paternalism, he would. If he needed to mix in an unhealthy dose of racial demagoguery, he would do that as well. And this "Virginia Way" continued—until *Brown v. Board of Education* turned the world of Harry Byrd and other segregationists upside down.

THE END OF PATERNALISM

Despite the earthquake it created, *Brown v. Board of Education* did not appear from nowhere; civil rights activists and lawyers had carefully orchestrated a legal campaign over many years that led to the decision. In the late 1930s and 1940s, and especially following World War II, blacks mounted numerous legal challenges to state-sanctioned discrimination and had engaged the lawyers of the National Association for the Advancement of Colored People (NAACP), including Virginians Oliver Hill and Spottswood W. Robinson III, to help.[26] A number of these cases also involved Virginians. Thirteen years before Rosa Parks' refusal to sit in the back of a Montgomery, Alabama bus ignited a massive boycott that brought national attention to the emerging Civil Rights movement, a Virginian, Sarah Davis of Norfolk, had become embroiled in a similar event. Davis did not plan a protest, but when she boarded a city bus on a June day in 1943, the only open seat was in the front between two whites. The driver told her to move, but she had no place to go, and whites in the back were never asked if they would exchange their seats for hers. She was arrested, convicted, and fined, and then appealed her case to the Virginia Supreme Court.[27] The court ruled that Davis was discriminated against because she was not provided another opportunity for a seat; it refused, however, to declare Virginia's common carrier statute mandating segregated seating as unconstitutional.[28]

The Davis case did not establish constitutional precedent, but other Virginia cases did.[29] And with every win, civil rights lawyers came closer to their most important goal—dismantling segregation in public schools. By the end of the 1940s, lawsuits had been filed involving one-half of Virginia's 125 school divisions.[30] It was Robinson who filed the federal lawsuit that became *Davis v. County School Board of Prince Edward County*, which ultimately merged into the *Brown v. Board of Education* case before the United States Supreme

Court. The state that had served as the Capital of the Confederacy was now the scene of some of the most significant legal challenges to segregation.

Ultimately, neither "separation by consent" nor paternalistic approaches would be able to withstand the pressure that was building for equality, but the old structure would not change without a fight. As legal crusaders continued to probe for the next opportunity to advance the cause in Virginia, their assertiveness dismayed white elites such as Freeman and Virginius Dabney, the influential editor of *Richmond Times-Dispatch*, who said in 1943 that "any effort to force the abolition of segregation, over the protest of a strongly hostile white South, is bound to do far more harm than good."[31]

By 1948, Freeman had realized that white elites had not really lived up to their part of the "separation by consent" bargain; it appeared more and more as a facade, and as a genteel justification for the system of white superiority. "Whites," he wrote, "must be prepared to pay for their insistence on separate schools and separate transportation. The equality must be real, and if real, it will be expensive."[32] In the same piece, he warned that the white South would "obstruct to the utmost" any attempt to fundamentally desegregate communities.[33] Freeman's admonition was proved true by events; Byrd and his machine would not raise the money necessary to build a truly "separate but equal" commonwealth.[34] Instead, they would choose to obstruct desegregation for over a decade with a strategy that came to be known as "massive resistance."

Civil Rights advocates continued pushing for equality, rejecting the paternalistic justification of segregation. "In Virginia," civil rights lawyer Oliver Hill once explained, "the powers that be were a little more sophisticated than they were in the deeper South, and they'd always apparently been. And as a consequence, you didn't have as much physical violence in Virginia as you had in the deeper South . . . [but] Virginia and the whole South were police states. There isn't a question about that. Negroes didn't serve on juries; they didn't serve on grand juries or petit juries. You saw no blacks in places like City Hall or public buildings, unless, except, maybe an elevator operator or janitor. And that's the way it was."[35]

For members of the white elite who had hoped that African Americans would acquiesce to "separation by consent" or agree to separate but essentially unequal facilities, *Brown v. Board of Education* would prove devastating. By the time of the Brown decision, a new generation of African American leaders had asserted themselves. Battle lines would now be drawn between ardent segregationists and those who sought a more inclusive society. *Brown v. Board of Education* would prove the death knell of the paternalistic approach to race relations. No one was left to argue for "the Virginia Way," Freeman having died in 1953. The paternalistic approach was no longer possible to maintain, having been undermined by both rampant segregationists and the Civil Rights activists of the time.

James J. Kilpatrick succeeded Freeman as editor of the *Richmond News Leader* and championed a more determined form of segregation. Words like "nullification" and "interposition" became the embodiment of the Kilpatrick resistance to the federal courts' insistence on desegregation. Byrd, who initially favored a more moderate response to *Brown v. Board of Education* than the most ardent segregationists, eventually determined that his political power would best be served by leading a newly energized conservative and populist opposition to desegregation. At its extreme, Byrd and the segregationists decided they would rather close schools than have white and black children be educated together. "If we can organize the Southern States for massive resistance to this order [*Brown v. Board of Education*]," Byrd asserted, "the rest of the country will realize that racial integration is not going to be accepted in the South."[36] Calling potential school integration "the gravest crisis since the War Between the States," Byrd purportedly called for laws to be enforced "by the white people of this country" to undermine the enforcement of *Brown v. Board of Education*.[37]

In 1956, the legislature passed a law that forced the Governor to close any school that enrolled a black student.[38] Federal judges, however, were not willing to go along with this defiance of the U.S. Supreme Court. In September 1958, federal Judge John Paul ordered Warren County, which had no black high school, to desegregate its all-white school. In response, Governor J. Lindsay Almond closed the school. Shortly thereafter, Almond took similar action against schools in Charlottesville and Norfolk, and 13,000 students were locked out in the process. The school closure law remained in effect until struck down when federal courts, on January 19, 1959, ruled, not unexpectedly, that this law violated the Fourteenth Amendment to the U.S. Constitution.[39]

In an interesting twist, on the same day, the Virginia state Supreme Court held that the 1956 law also violated the Virginia Constitution and its requirement that "the state must support . . . free public schools."[40] The legal underpinnings of segregation—and the paternalistic elements of the Virginia Way—were collapsing under the weight of a steady stream of federal court decisions, many of which originated in Virginia.

Some of these cases emerged from the direct action by Virginia activists committed to desegregation. On February 22, 1960, thirty-four students from Virginia Union University entered the famous "Richmond Room" restaurant at Thalhimers Department Store in downtown Richmond, sat down at the whites-only lunch counter, and demanded to be served. When they failed to leave, they were arrested, charged with trespass, and eventually convicted. Among the protesters was a future member of the House of Delegates,

Mamye BaCote. The convictions were overturned by the U.S. Supreme Court in 1963.[41] Other segregation laws began falling as well. Courtroom segregation was ended in 1963,[42] "freedom-of-choice" school plans created to avoid desegregation in public schools were struck down in 1968,[43] and, in the *Loving v. Virginia* (1967) case, three centuries of laws prohibiting interracial marriage in Virginia were ruled unconstitutional.[44] The twentieth-century version of the Virginia Way based on racial "segregation by consent" was essentially dead.[45]

RE-EXAMINATION AND ACTION

With the end of massive resistance, Virginia began making halting strides toward addressing racial inequality. The progress was not as fast nor as smooth as many desired, but attitudes were changing in many parts of the state, the most dramatic examples of which were the election of L. Douglas Wilder as governor and the selection of President Barack Obama to be the beneficiary of Virginia's electoral votes. Nonetheless, massive inequities remained, and events such as the 2017 white supremacist "Unite the White" rally prompted many to wonder how far we actually had come. And when George Floyd became yet another in a series of deaths of black persons at the hands of police officers in May 2020, we all knew that a more serious and extensive re-examination of race relations was in order.

It has now been fifty years since the National Advisory Commission on Civil Disorders, better known as the Kerner Report, cited gross racial inequities in America.[46] And while many argue that African Americans are, in many ways, better off in many ways than they were in 1968, substantial inequalities remain, and there are important areas where African Americans have lost ground. According to the Economic Policy Institute and other analysts, the mixed results look like this:[47]

1. The percentage of African Americans living in poverty has declined substantially since the 1968 report, but blacks remain disproportionately poorer than whites. The poverty rate for African Americans in Virginia is 18.3 percent, compared to 8.8 percent for white Virginians.
2. Substantial improvements have occurred in wages, incomes, and wealth of African Americans since 1968, but black workers still make only 82.5 cents of every dollar earned by white workers. Since 1970, the income gap between black and non-black Virginians has remained fairly consistent, with the exception of those in both groups who are college educated. Nonetheless, blacks with college degrees still earn only about 90 percent as much as whites with similar education.[48]

3. Black unemployment remains roughly twice that of whites, and the homeownership rate remains about the same as it was fifty years ago, about 40 percent. In one-third of Virginia counties, the homeownership rate for black Virginians is lower today than it was in 1940, including in some of its largest counties, such as Chesterfield and Fairfax.[49]
4. African Americans remain disproportionately affected by gun violence in the United States. Researchers at the U.S. Centers for Disease Control and Prevention (CDC) recently reported that black men experienced twenty-seven more firearm homicides per 100,000 people than white men (29.12 for black men vs. 2.1 for white men). The numbers for Virginia were 18.65 for blacks compared to 1.76 for whites.[50]
5. African Americans today are better educated than they were in 1968, but they still lag whites in overall attainment. In 1968, just over one-half of all African Americans had a high school diploma; by 2018, that had risen to 90 percent. African Americans are also twice as likely to have a college degree as they were in 1968.[51]

Racial attitudes among certain groups, especially millennials, are dramatically more tolerant and inclusive than in past generations. In 1972, for example, just one out of three whites supported laws that prohibited homeowners from refusing to sell to a person of a different race. By the early 1990s, this had grown to about two out of three, and increased to 71 percent by 2014.[52]

The inequality has been felt in communities of color for years. But it took a dramatic event—the killing of George Floyd—to galvanize change in ways not seen in decades. And Virginia policymakers readily embraced the challenge. While few Virginia legislators were willing to embrace the "defund the police" mantra of street demonstrators, they were nonetheless committed to making major change. Democrats had deferred addressing many of these issues during the General Assembly's 2020 regular session to remain united and avoid controversy. But Floyd's murder changed everything. Governor Northam called a special session to address COVID-19 and criminal justice for late August, and it went on until November. Changes in the budget were relatively easy, but disagreements emerged about what criminal justice reform measures should be passed immediately and what ideas required further study to avoid unintended adverse consequences.

House Democrats, viewing themselves as more progressive than their Senate counterparts, spoke frequently of "seizing the moment." Bills were introduced to restore parole, which had been abolished during Governor George Allen's administration in the 1990s, restrict police from using tear gas to break up demonstrations, allow the automatic expungement of criminal records,[53] and even cut police budgets, a proposal that would play into the conservative narrative that Democrats wanted to "defund the police." Much of this agenda was being driven by the Virginia Legislative Black Caucus (VLBC), which presented its agenda in late June and pushed it throughout the special session.[54]

Senate Democrats had their own plan that, while serious, nonetheless appeared more cautious than House proposals. Efforts to restore parole, for example, were deemed too complicated for what was supposed to be a short special session, and Senators attempted to steer clear of controversial issues such as abolishing qualified immunity for police to make it easier for citizens to sue officers. Since the House passed so many bills, however, the Senate would have to address them.

Discussing race inevitably prompts controversy, and the special session revealed strong divisions within the Democratic House caucus, and between the House and the Senate. In the House, some of the more moderate Democrats, who had been elected in swing districts during the "wave elections" of 2017 and 2019, were leery about passing too many reforms too quickly. It was the success of these moderates in winning their elections that allowed Democrats to take control in 2020, and some of them were now feeling that they were being put at risk politically by moving too quickly on some of these issues. At the same time, the VLBC was now larger than at any time since Reconstruction and were not shy about expressing the frustration that blacks were too often told to wait on reforms. Some in the group were not averse to labelling a failure to vote with them as racially insensitive. Balancing these competing interests was complicated by the pandemic, which caused many of the House meetings and Democratic Caucus meetings to be by Zoom and/or conference calls. Discussing race is difficult enough in person; doing it in these ways was fraught with the potential of misunderstanding.

For the VLBC, the urgency of action was palpable. Black America had been "told" for years what they needed to do to improve their situation and avoid policy brutality. For many, their view was now summarized by the statement, "we have tried everything you have suggested that we do, and we are still being shot; most of it has not worked." To paraphrase Martin Luther King, Jr., Virginia was confronted with "the fierce urgency of now," and it was up to the elected leaders to push change as quickly as they could.

The aftermath of Richmond Democrat Delegate Jeff Bourne's bill to remove protections for police who might be sued for brutality (the legal term is "qualified immunity") illustrated this dynamic. The measure received serious criticism during the committee process, and the Senate signaled that the measure would be defeated in their Body. Nonetheless, Bourne wanted a floor vote in the House, and he got it. With several Democratic defections, the measure was initially defeated on the House floor on a forty-seven to forty-eight vote, only to be resurrected the next day on a "motion to reconsider."

Following the initial vote, Delegate Ibraheem Samirah, who frequently billed himself as among the most progressive members of the House and who gained notoriety for disrupting Donald Trump's speech at Jamestown in 2019, was directly criticized by Bourne for his negative vote and "foolish clown show." Another delegate accused him of "grandstanding," and former Charlottesville City Councilor Wes Bellamy criticized him for engaging in a "stunt" that "the oppressor always does."[55] The exchanges revealed little about the substantive merits of the bill, just that you are "either with us or against us." Fissures among Democrats (amid a total lack of Republican support) were being exposed very publicly.

Several the more progressive measures passed by the House were eventually defeated by the Senate, further creating consternation among some House moderates who had already voted for bills that would not become law but would nonetheless be used against them in their next campaign. Nonetheless, the following measures were adopted:

1. A limitation on police uses of chokeholds;
2. A new requirement to force officers to intervene if another is using excessive force;
3. Authorization for some localities to establish civilian review boards; and
4. State authority to decertify officers who violate certain rules even if not convicted of lawbreaking.[56]

In addition, lawmakers authorized the removal of Harry Byrd's statue from Capitol grounds because of his prominence in "massive resistance. Speaker of the House Eileen Filler-Corn removed the Robert E. Lee statue from the Virginia Capitol and the Governor Northam pulled the statue of Robert E. Lee from the U.S. Capitol. Virginia became the first Southern state to declare racism to be "public health crisis."[57] The Commonwealth has now made permanent its Commission on Environmental Justice, now named the Virginia Council on Environmental Justice.[58] And Virginia recently created a scholarship program designed to help descendants of enslaved laborers who helped to build our universities.[59]

What will the next generation of leaders in the Commonwealth learn from reckoning with the traditional Virginia Way? The racially oppressive elements are easy to reject. But will Virginia still pride itself on a moderation in tone even as Progressives push a bold agenda and polarization remains apparent? Can inequity be addressed without rancor and pitched battles? Is there room in the Commonwealth for a modern and inclusive "Virginia Way" that will reject its racial history but still embrace positive elements of civil discourse and collaborative decision-making? Ultimately, the future, if any, of the Virginia Way will be determined by new leadership who will craft approaches to address our serious problems, racial inequality being but one. Glenn Youngkin's 2021 win notwithstanding, recent elections suggest that Virginia residents have become more progressive in their views, and leaders will undoubtedly need to respond. How this will translate not only into policies of the Commonwealth but the processes by which they are enacted remains to be determined.

NOTES

1. Douglas Southall Freeman, "Separation by Consent," *Richmond News Leader* (editorial), May 20, 1930, quoted in J. Douglas Smith, *Managing White Supremacy: Race, Politics, and Citizenship in Jim Crow Virginia*, new ed. (Chapel Hill: University of North Carolina Press, 2002), 4.

2. It has always been a mystery to me why some Republicans continue to use the term "the Democrat Party," as a mark of disrespect. Speaking that way does not change any votes and will not force any Democrats to redefine themselves. Yet, the custom exists. Putting aside for the moment the fact that "Democrat" is a noun rather than an adjective, some trace the use of the phrase back to the 1940s, when it would occasionally appear in Republican circles. U.S. Senator Joseph McCarthy used it in the 1950s, but it never really took hold until Republicans, under Speaker of the U.S. House of Representatives Newt Gingrich, employed the term to needle and to redefine his opponents. President George W. Bush used it periodically, and President Donald J. Trump turned the intended insult into an art form. To put it simply, "Democrat Party" is not the party's name, and most Republicans know it.

3. *Brown v. Board of Education of Topeka*, 347 U.S. 483 (1954), https://supreme.justia.com/cases/federal/us/347/483/ (accessed April 22, 2021).

4. Delores McQuinn, quoted in Justin Mattingly, "'If you sin, you must pay for the sin'—Al Sharpton Calls for Northam's Resignation at Virginia Union Event," *Richmond Times-Dispatch*, February 7, 2019, https://www.richmond.com/news /local/government-politics/if-you-sin-you-must-pay-for-the-sin-al-sharpton-calls -for-northams-resignation/article_ed070853-dd41-5640-97ff-0052fafda89c.html (accessed June 2, 2021).

5. Delegate Delores McQuinn, interview by author by telephone, November 18, 2020.

6. Ben Pershing, Laura Vozzella, and Errin Haines, "Kaine Wins Virginia Senate Race," *Washington Post*, November 7, 2012, https://www.washingtonpost.com/local /virginia-politics/virginia-senate-race-a-marathon-between-allen-kaine/2012/11/06 /06a938bc-27af-11e2-b2a0-ae18d6159439_story.html (June 2, 2021). And during his 2014 U.S. Senate race, Mark Warner lavished praise on his predecessor, Republican U.S. Senator John Warner, and embraced the Virginia Way: "There is something special about the Virginia Way, and John Warner has represented that every day of his public service," quoted in Jenna Portnoy and Rachel Weiner, "Incumbent Warner Pulls Out All the Stops as Va. Senate Race Tightens," *Washington Post*, November 1, 2014, https://www.washingtonpost.com/local/virginia-politics/incumbent-warner

-pulls-out-all-the-stops-as-va-senate-race-tightens/2014/11/01/f55129b4-5f9f-11e4
-9f3a-7e28799e0549_story.html (accessed June 2, 2021).

7. Governor Bob McDonnell, "Full Text: McDonnell's State of the Commonwealth Address," *Washington Post*, January 8, 2014, https://www.washingtonpost.com/local /virginia-politics/full-text-mcdonnells-state-of-the-commonwealth-address/2014/01 /08/fd129256-78b8-11e3-af7f-13bf0e9965f6_story.html (accessed June 2, 2021).

8. Governor Terry McAuliffe, "Full Text: Virginia Gov. Terry McAuliffe's Inaugural Address," *Washington Post*, January 11, 2014, https://www.washingtonpost.com/ local/virginia-politics/full-text-virginia-gov-terry-mcauliffes-inaugural-address/2014 /01/11/f8a1c35e-7a0c-11e3-af7f-13bf0e9965f6_story.html (accessed June 2, 2021).

9. Virginia, Office of the Governor, "Governor Northam Delivers State of the Commonwealth Address," press release, January 9, 2018, https://www.governor. virginia.gov/newsroom/all-releases/2019/january/headline-837676-en.html (accessed June 2, 2021).

10. David E. Johnson, *Douglas Southall Freeman* (Gretna, LA: Pelican Publishing, 2002). See also Lauranett L. Lee and Suzanne Slye, "'The Virginia Way': Race, the 'Lost Cause,' & the Social Influence of Douglas Southall Freeman," University of Richmond Inclusive History Project, January 2021, https://president.richmond.edu/ inclusive-history/freeman/report/Douglas-Southall-Freeman-Final-Report-20210216. pdf (accessed June 2, 2021).

11. Almost immediately after the war, the phrase "Lost Cause" began to be used to describe the "noble" struggle of the Confederacy. Edward A. Pollard's 1866 book, *The Lost Cause: A New Southern History of the War of the Confederates* (New York: E. B. Treat), glorified the Confederacy and slavery. See, for example, Elizabeth A. Varon, "UVA and the History of Race: The Lost Cause Through Judge Duke's Eyes," *UVA Today*, September 4, 2019, https://news.virginia.edu/content/uva-and-history -race-lost-cause-through-judge-dukes-eyes (accessed June 2, 2021).

12. J. D. Smith, *Managing White Supremacy*.

13. Douglas Southall Freeman, "Not the Virginia Way," *Richmond News Leader* (editorial), February 9, 1926.

14. Douglas Southall Freeman, "In the Virginia Way," *Richmond News Leader* (editorial), February 26, 1926.

15. Douglas Southall Freeman, "Separation by Consent," *Richmond News Leader* (editorial), May 20, 1930.

16. Douglas Southall Freeman, "A Dark Disgrace to Virginia," *Richmond News Leader* (editorial), August 18, 1926.

17. Lee and Slye, "The Virginia Way."

18. Douglas Southall Freeman, "Virginia: A Gentle Dominion" in *These United States: Portraits of America from the 1920s*, ed. David H. Borus (Ithaca, NY: Cornell University Press, 1992), 374–81, 378–79.

19. Virginia, General Assembly, Anti-Lynching Law of 1928, signed by Governor Harry F. Byrd on March 14, 1928.

20. J. D. Smith, *Managing White Supremacy*, 156. This is not to say that the Ku Klux Klan (KKK) was not active in Virginia. In fact, the group paraded through cities such as Lynchburg and attracted members throughout Virginia. Smith estimated that

Klan membership in Norfolk numbered almost 10,000 (J. D. Smith, *Managing White Supremacy*, 73).

21. Much has been written about the Charlottesville statues, and many argue some differences between these and other "lost cause" statuary in the South. These statues were neither commissioned by nor erected by Confederate support groups such as the United Daughters of the Confederacy, or by local government; instead, they were funded solely by Paul Goodloe McIntire, a local philanthropist and, like many of his time, a segregationist.

22. Harry F. Byrd, quoted in J. D. Smith, *Managing White Supremacy*, 31–32.

23. Jill Ogline Titus, *Brown's Battleground: Students, Segregationists, and the Struggle for Justice in Prince Edward County, Virginia* (Chapel Hill: University of North Carolina Press, 2011), 15.

24. J. D. Smith, *Managing White Supremacy*, 133, 135.

25. J. D. Smith, *Managing White Supremacy*, 8, citing Virginius Dabney, "Too Radical for Us," *Richmond Times-Dispatch*, July 17, 1939.

26. A history of Oliver Hill and Spottswood Robinson is found in Margaret Edds, *We Face the Dawn: Oliver Hill, Spottswood Robinson, and the Legal Team That Dismantled Jim Crow* (Charlottesville: University of Virginia Press, 2018).

27. The Virginia General Assembly never mandated that blacks occupy the rear of street cars or buses. Separation of white and black passengers was required of common carriers, but how that would be accomplished was left to drivers or conductors. See, for example, Virginia, *The Code of Virginia, Volume 1* (Richmond, VA: David Bottom, 1919), Title 36, chap. 155, §§ 3978–3980, 1595–96 (streetcars); or Virginia, *The Code of Virginia* (Charlottesville, VA: Michie, 1942), Title 36, chap. 104, §4097, p. 1494 (motor busses).

28. *Davis, Sarah B. v. Commonwealth of Virginia*, 182 Va. 760 (1944), https://cite.case.law/va/182/760/ (accessed June 3, 2021).

29. In *Alston v. School Board of City of Norfolk*, 112 F.2d 992 (4th Cir. 1940), https://law.justia.com/cases/federal/appellate-courts/F2/112/992/1498702/ (accessed June 3, 2021), Hill and others convinced the Fourth Circuit Court of Appeals to hold that Norfolk's discriminatory pay scale for teachers violated the Fourteenth Amendment; the ruling stood when the U.S. Supreme Court declined to take the appeal. In *Morgan v. Virginia*, 328 U.S. 373 (1946), https://supreme.justia.com/cases/federal/us/328/373/ (accessed June 3, 2021), a case arising out of Middlesex County, the U.S. Supreme Court declared that Virginia's state law enforcing segregation on interstate buses was unconstitutional. Many of the earliest legal victories occurred in the interstate transportation area. See also Catherine A. Barnes, *Journey from Jim Crow: The Desegregation of Southern Transit* (New York: Columbia University Press, 1983).

30. Larissa Smith Fergeson, "Oliver W. Hill (1907–2007)," in *Encyclopedia Virginia*, updated on March 25, 2014, http://www.EncyclopediaVirginia.org/Hill_Oliver_W_1907-2007 (accessed June 3, 2021).

31. Virginius Dabney, quoted in J. D. Smith, *Managing White Supremacy*, 250. Dabney's views are further described in Virginius Dabney, *Virginia: The New Dominion* (Garden City, NY: Doubleday, 1971).

32. Douglas Southall Freeman, "Virginia and Civil Rights," *Richmond Times-Dispatch*, February 25, 1948, 12; quoted in J. D. Smith, *Managing White Supremacy*, supra. 291.

33. J. D. Smith, *Managing White Supremacy*, 292.

34. Also, in 1948, the Virginia General Assembly assumed control of public-school textbook content and production when it created a special commission. This Body, largely controlled by Harry F. Byrd since its inception, hired authors and edited manuscripts for three statewide textbooks called "Virginia: History, Geography and Government." These books rewrote the history of the Civil War and whitewashed Virginia's legacy of slavery. The texts often described slaves as happy, and rarely referred to them as property. The Civil War was described as a "Defense Against Invasion," See Rex Springston, "Happy Slaves? The Peculiar Story of Three Virginia School Textbooks," *Richmond Times-Dispatch*, April 14, 2018, http://www.richmond.com/discover-richmond/happy-slaves-the-peculiar-story-of-three-virginia-school-textbooks/article_47e79d49-eac8-575d-ac9d-1c6fce52328f.html (accessed June 3, 2021). This commission was abandoned in the 1960s, and many of the decisions about textbooks presently rest with local school boards, who must meet state guidelines as they choose textbooks. For additional reading on this subject, see *Understanding and Teaching American Slavery*, ed. Bethany Jay and Cynthia Lynn Lyerly (Madison: University of Wisconsin Press, 2016), and Brian Barnes, review of *Understanding and Teaching American Slavery*, ed. by Bethany Jay and Cynthia Lynn Lyerly, *Journal of Southern History* 83, no. 2 (2017): 490–92, https://doi.org/10.1353/soh.2017.0158. See also Francis Butler Simkins, Spotswood Hunnicut, and Sidman P. Poole, *Virginia: History, Government, Geography* (New York: Scribner's, 1957).

35. Oliver Hill, quoted in J. D. Smith, *Managing White Supremacy*, 3.

36. Byrd, *Richmond-Times-Dispatch*, February 25, 1956, quoted in J. Harvie Wilkinson III, *Harry Byrd and the Changing Face of Virginia Politics, 1945–1966* (Charlottesville: University Press of Virginia, 1968), 113.

37. Byrd, quoted in Ronald L. Heinemann, *Harry Byrd of Virginia* (Charlottesville: University Press of Virginia, 1996), 345.

38. Candace Epps-Robertson, "The Race to Erase *Brown v. Board of Education*: The Virginia Way and the Rhetoric of Massive Resistance," *Rhetoric Review* 35, no. 2 (2016): 108–20, https://doi.org/10.1080/07350198.2016.1142812

39. *James v. Almond*, 170 F. Supp. 331 (E.D. Va. 1959), https://law.justia.com/cases/federal/district-courts/FSupp/170/331/2360668/ (accessed June 3, 2021).

40. *Harrison v. Day*, 200 Va. 439, 106 S.E.2d 636 (1959), https://www.courtlistener.com/opinion/1328174/harrison-v-day/ (accessed June 3, 2021).

41. *Randolph v. Virginia*, 374 U.S. 97 (1963), https://supreme.justia.com/cases/federal/us/374/97/ (accessed June 3, 2021).

42. *Johnson v. Virginia*, 373 U.S. 61 (1963), https://supreme.justia.com/cases/federal/us/373/61/ (accessed June 3, 2021).

43. *Green v. County School Board of New Kent County*, 391 U.S. 430 (1968), https://supreme.justia.com/cases/federal/us/391/430/ (accessed June 3, 2021).

44. *Loving v. Virginia*, 388 U.S. 1 (1967), https://supreme.justia.com/cases/federal/us/388/1/ (accessed June 1, 2021). The lead attorney for the Lovings was Bernard S.

Cohen of Alexandria who went on to serve in the Virginia House of Delegates from 1980 to 1996.

45. Even in 2020, vestiges of segregation remained in Virginia law. For example, the legislature repealed a measure that had remained on the books—though not enforceable pursuant to court rulings—ever since September 29, 1956 stating that "Notwithstanding any other provision of law, no child shall be required to enroll in or attend any school wherein both white and colored children are enrolled." This repeal was a part of a series of code changes adopted as recommendations of Governor Northam's Commission to Examine Racial Inequity in Virginia Law. See Mechelle Hankerson, "Northam Establishes Commission to Examine Racial Inequity in State Laws," *Virginia Mercury*, June 4, 2019, https://www.virginiamercury.com/blog-va/ northam-establishes-commission-to-address-racial-inequity/ (accessed June 3, 2021).

46. Susan T. Gooden and Samuel L. Myers Jr., eds., "The Fiftieth Anniversary of the Kerner Commission Report," special issue, *RSF: The Russell Sage Foundation Journal of the Social Sciences* 4, no. 6 (2018), https://www.jstor.org/stable/10.7758 /rsf.4.issue-6; and Fred Harris and Alan Curtis, "The Unmet Promise of Equality," *New York Times*, February 28, 2018, https://www.nytimes.com/interactive/2018/02 /28/opinion/the-unmet-promise-of-equality.html (accessed June 3, 2021).

47. Janelle Jones, John Schmitt, and Valerie Wilson, "50 Years after the Kerner Commission: African Americans are Better off in Many Ways but Are Still Disadvantaged by Racial Inequality," *Economic Policy Institute*, Report, February 26, 2018, https://www.epi.org/publication/50-years-after-the-kerner-commission/ (accessed June 3, 2021).

48. Hamilton Lombard, "Inside the Income Gap for some Black Virginians," University of Virginia, Weldon Cooper Center, *StatChat*, July 31, 2020, http: //statchatva.org/2020/07/31/inside-the-income-gap-for-some-black-virginians/ (accessed June 3, 2021). The challenges of inequality are even more pronounced for single parent families. The median income for black Virginia families with two spouses present is less than 85 percent that of all families with two spouses present. Families with a single parent lag considerably. Single parent families have risen dramatically in Virginia between 1970 and 2018, but the percentage increase has been greater for African American Virginia families (from 29 to 47 percent) than for their white counterparts (12 to 19 percent).

49. Lombard, "Inside the Income Gap for some Black Virginians."

50. Jacqueline Howard, "The Disparities in How Black and White Men Die in Gun Violence, State by State," *CNN Health*, April 24, 2018, https://www.cnn.com/2018 /04/23/health/gun-deaths-in-men-by-state-study/index.html (accessed June 3, 2021). Suicide rates by gun are much higher for white males than African American males.

51. Jones, John Schmitt, and Valerie Wilson, "50 Years after the Kerner Commission."

52. Maria Krysan and Sarah Moberg, "Trends in Racial Attitudes," August 26, 2016, University of Illinois System, Institute of Government and Public Affairs Race and Inequality Initiative, http://igpa.uillinois.edu/programs/racial-attitudes.

53. Expungement is part of the "Clean Slate" movement nationally. Two states not known for being soft on crime, Pennsylvania and Utah, recently passed bills that

automatically expunges the records of those convicted of low-level (non-violent and non-sexual) offenses and who have been crime free for at least seven years. See Nila Bala, "Automatic Expungement Plan Would Offer a 'Clean Slate' with Bipartisan Support," *R Street*, July 27, 2020, https://www.rstreet.org/2020/07/27/automatic -expungement-plan-would-offer-a-clean-slate-with-bipartisan-support/ (accessed June 3, 2021).

54. Graham Moomaw, "From Banning Chokeholds to 'Divesting' from Police, Va. Black Caucus Rolls Out Reform Agenda," *Virginia Mercury*, June 24, 2020, https: //www.virginiamercury.com/blog-va/from-banning-chokeholds-to-divesting-from -police-va-black-caucus-rolls-out-broad-reform-agenda/ (accessed June 3, 2021).

55. "Former Charlottesville City Council Member Wes Bellamy Rips Del. Ibraheem Samirah: 'This stunt you pulled is exactly what the oppressor always does,'" *Blue Virginia Blog*, September 5, 2020, https://bluevirginia.us/2020/09/ former-charlottesville-city-council-member-wes-bellamy-rips-del-ibraheem-samirah -this-stunt-you-pulled-is-exactly-what-the-oppressor-always-does.

56. Laura Vozzella, "Ban on Chokeholds, No-knock Warrants Among Bills Northam Signed into Law," *Washington Post*, October 28, 2020, https://www. washingtonpost.com/local/virginia-politics/northam-signs-police-overhaul-bills /2020/10/28/7104c368-1926-11eb-befb-8864259bd2d8_story.html (accessed June 3, 2021). See also Ned Oliver, "Virginia Lawmakers Get Mixed Reviews on Police Reform Efforts," *Virginia Mercury*, October 20, 2020, https://www.virginiamercury. com/2020/10/20/virginia-lawmakers-get-mixed-reviews-on-police-reform-efforts/ (accessed June 3, 2021).

57. Bill Atkinson, "Virginia Is Set to Become First Southern State to Declare Racism a Public Health Crisis: What It Means and Why It Matters," *USA Today, The Progress -Index*, February 23, 2021, https://www.usatoday.com/story/news/nation/2021/02/23/ virginia-racism-public-health-crisis/4566908001/ (accessed June 3, 2021).

58. Sarah Vogelsong, "Governor Signs Bill Making Virginia Council on Environmental Justice Permanent," *Virginia Mercury*, March 20, 2020, https:// www.virginiamercury.com/blog-va/governor-signs-bill-making-virginia-council-on -environmental-justice-permanent/ (accessed June 3, 2021).

59. Jeroslyn Johnson, "Virginia Passes Law Requiring Universities to Create Scholarships for Descendants of Slaves," *Black Enterprise*, April 3, 2021, https: //www.blackenterprise.com/virginia-passes-law-requiring-universities-to-create -scholarships-for-descendants-of-slaves/ (accessed June 3, 2021). Though few discussed this as a "reparations" bill, it may be the first bill of its type to pass in the country.

Chapter 5

Disruption and Continuity

Change is the Only Constant in Life.

—Heraclitus of Ephesus

Virginia is no longer the state of Mills E. Godwin, Jr., who was elected to his first term as governor in 1965 in a state that was primarily rural and under the control of the Byrd machine. It is no longer the state that elected Democrat Chuck Robb in 1981, whose campaign slogan "For a Virginia Future Worthy of Her Past,"[1] would have undoubtedly provoked controversy if used today. And it is not even the same state that elected Mark Warner to be governor in 2001, who attempted to lead by appealing to "the sensible center."[2]

Rapid population growth, predominantly concentrated in Northern Virginia (NoVa), doomed the Byrd machine, and created more space for Republicans to emerge as a competitive political party in the late 1960s and early 1970s. In 1969, the Commonwealth elected, as its 61st Governor, a Republican, Linwood Holton, who was neither shy about competing for black votes in a state where candidates typically ignored them or in sending his children to integrated public schools. There were additional signs that the state was moving away from the influence of the Byrd. In 1967, Dr. William Ferguson Reid became the first African American elected to the House of Delegates since Reconstruction. And in 1969, L. Douglas Wilder became the first African American ever elected to the state Senate in almost one hundred years. Wilder almost immediately confronted "old Virginia" by proposing the retirement of the Commonwealth's state song, "Carry Me Back to Old Virginny," with its racist lyrics.[3] He failed in that effort, but in 1986 became Lieutenant Governor, and then, defining himself as part of the so-called New Mainstream, was chosen by the voters in 1989 to be the first African American elected Governor of any state. He did it with guile and guts, and clearly never followed "the Virginia Way" as it had been previously conceived.[4]

During the decades of the 1970s and 1980s, Virginia continued its hard-charging transformation from a primarily rural state with pockets of financial and military-related growth centered in Richmond and Hampton Roads into a New Dominion where economic interests were more diverse, and increasingly concentrated in NoVa.[5] More liberal and moderate elements of the Democratic Party emerged, ushered in by Chuck Robb's election as Governor in 1981, and capped by Wilder's victory in 1989. At the same time, the Republicans were stirring in a way not experienced since just after the Civil War, as they recruited new leaders, and began to win elections. From 1979 to 1989, GOP representation in the House of Delegates jumped from twenty-one to thirty-nine out of one hundred. Virginia business leaders recognized that economic forces were transforming the traditional Old Dominion before their eyes, and they were looking to politicians of all stripes to protect their interests.

"The Virginia Way" was rarely mentioned during this period, though prominent columnist Mary McGrory discussed it in a 1981 column explaining the rise of Chuck Robb and his appeal to Republicans, in light of his being the son-in-law of the "most liberal Democratic president of modern times, Lyndon B. Johnson." "The whole thing," said McGrory, "is a perfect illustration of 'the Virginia Way,' which is to reproduce as far as possible the atmosphere of Brigadoon, where time stands still, and ambiguity, mist and fog prevail."[6] McGrory did not realize it at the time, but a new Virginia Way was emerging, one which coupled support for business and fiscal conservatism with governance based on civility and on compromise. Virginia business leaders recognized that putting segregation behind them, and building a better educational system, would be the keys to the future. That is not to say that political campaigns no longer played the race card, or that legislative actions would be purged of racial considerations; it meant, however, that the imperatives of economic growth would come to dictate much more of the state's agenda than would the narrow confines of segregation.

The GOP kept chipping away at Democratic control until they became the state's governing party at the turn of the century. But the state kept changing. It became more diverse, both ethnically and culturally, as increasing numbers of new Americans came to reside in the Commonwealth. By 2020, these demographic trends were impacting the state in ways that few had anticipated just two decades earlier. And the political dynamic had also changed; a state that was reliably Republican in national and state elections had turned dramatically blue, as the Democrats returned to power in Richmond.

DEMOGRAPHICS AND DESTINY?

Between 1960 and 2000, the state's population increased from 3.97 million to 7.08 million, a 78 percent jump.[7] Fairfax County, home to just under 100,000 in 1950, almost tripled its population in the next ten years. By 2000, its residents approached 1,000,000,[8] and by 2010, the county's estimated population was over 1.15 million, making it more populous than eight states and the District of Columbia. Moreover, the county's population, and that of its neighbors, was more ethnically diverse, generally wealthier, and better educated than other state residents. Arlington, Loudoun, and Fairfax counties were now included among the wealthiest jurisdictions in the United States. Though certainly not monolithic in terms of wealth or political affiliation, the Asian population in NoVa also grew, especially in the last decade[9]; by 2018, Asian Americans in Fairfax County comprised over 20 percent of its population.[10] These massive population increases and its diversity made a difference to the political power of the county; of the one hundred Delegates in the Virginia House, seventeen now represent some portion of Fairfax.[11] The Fairfax delegation in the House now includes members of Korean descent, members who ancestors came from south Asia, and another Delegate who is a Vietnamese American.

Similar population growth occurred in the other counties in the northern part of Virginia, notably Arlington, Loudoun, and Prince William. In Prince William, the total population grew from 402,000 in 2010 to an estimated 470,335 as of July 2019; the Asian population increased there from 7.5 percent to 9.4 percent, and the Hispanic population jumped from 20.3 percent to 24.5 percent.[12] This had a huge impact politically. Prince William County had mostly elected Republican legislators until 2017, when five Republican incumbents were defeated by Democratic challengers, and two Latinas captured seats in the House of Delegates.

Similar changes were occurring in the Richmond suburbs. Chesterfield County, once a bastion of Republican strength, has seen major change in its population in the last twenty years, and with it, large shifts in voting patterns. Between 2000 and 2019, the county's percentage of African American population grew from 18 percent to 24.5 percent, and the Hispanic share rose from 3 percent to 9.5 percent.[13] In 2004, President George W. Bush carried the county by 34,399 votes. By 2008, the Republican margin in the presidential race had dropped to 12,103 votes. In 2020, Joseph R. Biden carried Chesterfield by more than 23,000 votes.[14]

These demographic shifts were also affecting state Delegate elections. In the state's 2011 redistricting, Republicans drew districts with such surgical precision that Democratic numbers in the General Assembly declined dramatically. What they had not counted on, however, were changes occurring in the demographic mix of the state. Democrats could see it coming and knew that it would eventually overwhelm the carefully drawn district boundaries and evidence itself at the polls. In 2013, the demographic shift was beginning to benefit Democratic candidates, as many challengers appeared poised to win key contests. The only thing that prevented a major increase in the number of seats won by Democrats that year was the botched rollout of the *Affordable Care Act* (ACA) *of 2010* website (healthcare.gov), which had the effect of dampening Democratic performance.[15] By 2017, however, the demographic transition helped fuel the wave by which Democrats took back fifteen seats, and almost gained the majority. In 2019, Republicans lost control of the Virginia House for the first time in twenty years.

And the composition of the Body changed as well. In 2010, the Virginia House of Delegates was 19 percent female, 12 percent African Americans, and 2 percent Asians.[16] By 2019, the first Latino woman had been elected to the Body, and 27 percent were now women.[17] Four percent were of Hispanic origin, 14 percent were African American, and two percent Asian, with most of the change occurring in the Democratic Caucus.[18]

Population growth is not uniformly distributed throughout the Commonwealth. Researchers report that 94 percent of growth in Virginia between 2010 and 2019 was concentrated in its three largest metro areas—Hampton Roads, Northern Virginia, and Richmond—while the population living outside metro areas declined by 3 percent during the period.[19] In the southern and southwestern portions of the state, the decline was especially dramatic. Pittsylvania County, located just north of the Virginia / North Carolina line, was once the most populous county in the state. Its 2018 population, however, was actually lower than in the 1930s.[20] Much of this change can be traced to the decline of tobacco, textiles, and furniture industries, a multi-year process. Danville, for example, had an unemployment rate of 3.5 percent in November 2000.[21] But then the shock hit. Dan River Mills, the mainstay of textile manufacturing and economic activity in the city, was largely shuttered by 2005. Once employing 14,000 persons, the factory fell victim to the Nation's massive deindustrialization.[22] By January 2009, Danville unemployment had risen to 15.3 percent.[23] Between 2000 and 2020, the city lost almost 20 percent of its population.[24]

In places like Buchanan and Dickenson counties in the far southwest, population loss is largely about the decline in coal, as natural gas emerged as a less costly and less polluting source of energy. Buchanan's population, which peaked in 1980 at 37,989 now totals 21,576; Dickenson's population has been declining from its peak of 23,393 in 1950 to its most recent figure of 14,516.[25] Figures 5.1, 5.2, and 5.3 illustrate the rapid population declines in the southwest coupled with increases in the north. The substantial population

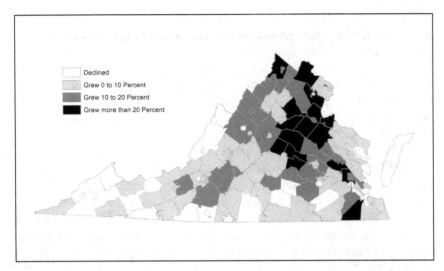

Figure 5.1. Virginia Population Change by County, 2000-2008

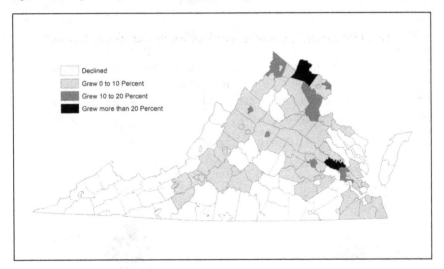

Figure 5.2. Virginia Population Change 2010-2018

loss in these primarily rural counties makes it difficult to generate much activity. And to make the economic situation even more challenging, younger people have been leaving these areas in substantial numbers, leaving a less educated, older, and poorer population behind.[26]

Although Virginia is not likely to see the large increases in population as it has in recent decades, shifts in concentrations are expected to continue.[27] The Weldon Cooper Center at the University of Virginia (UVA) projects that fifty-three of the state's 133 cities and counties will lose population by 2040, and that most of this will occur in south, southwest, and western Virginia, areas of the state that are most challenged economically.[28] Those areas are also getting older; more than 30 percent of the residents in rural counties are over the age of 65 years, double the statewide proportion. Seventy percent of the state's residents now live in the three largest metropolitan areas (NoVa, Hampton Roads, and greater Richmond); only 12 percent live in rural environs. These population trends are having a tremendous impact on the state and the localities where the change is occurring.

A decline in population usually means a loss of political power. When redistricting occurs again in 2022, more seats will be allocated to rapidly growing areas like Loudoun and Prince William counties. The tax base of many of the largely rural counties will continue to be challenged, making it more difficult to fund critical services for a population increasingly in need of them. The "urban-rural" divide, always prevalent in the Commonwealth, is likely to become more acute. Fairfax County, for example, not only has always viewed itself as the economic engine of the state but believes that the revenues its citizens and businesses generate for the state are providing massive subsidies to poorer localities in the south and southwestern regions of the state.[29] As NoVa acquires more political power, the region will have the votes to transfer more monies from the state budget to that region.[30]

Figure 5.4 shows the general movement of the center of Virginia for south to north between 1940 and 2020, projected out to 2040.[31] The state is now driven by urban and suburban centers, and it is showing up in the policies and politics of the Commonwealth.

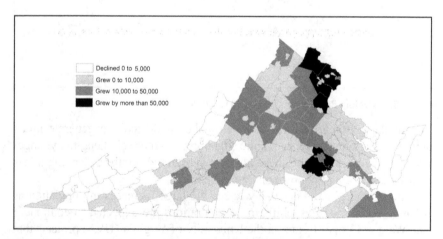

Figure 5.3. Virginia Population Change by County, 2000-2019

Figure 5.4. Virginia Population Center Movement, 1940–2040

POLITICAL REALIGNMENT?

When Timothy M. Kaine won the governorship in November 2005, it was the second straight election in which a non-native Virginian had taken the prize; his predecessor Mark Warner was born in Indiana. In fact, only two of the last six governors—Ralph S. Northam and Glenn Youngkin—were born in the state. To win the governorship, it is clearly no longer a requirement that you be born in the Commonwealth. One reason for this rests in the fact that so many residents actually hail from other states, a dramatic change from even two decades ago. In 1990, 54 percent of Virginia residents were born in the state; by 2014, that percentage had fallen to 49 percent. The top birth state for Virginia residents not born in the Commonwealth is now New York.[32] In addition, during this same period, the percentage of Virginians who

were born outside the United States increased from 6 percent to 13 percent.[33]
This is most pronounced in NoVa, where residents arrive from all over the
country, drawn by jobs in the Federal government and its auxiliary industries.
In NoVa, they are disproportionately more likely to have been born in the
Northeast or West Coast, or to be international immigrants; in many counties,
the percentage of native-born Virginians is less than 30 percent.[34]

By 2020, NoVa's population accounted for more than 36 percent of the
state's residents; Hampton Roads and Richmond were behind at 18 percent
and 17 percent, respectively. This means that the so-called Urban Crescent,
which stretches from NoVa down Interstate 95 to Richmond and then turns
southeast through the Peninsula to the Hampton Roads area, contains over 70
percent of the population of Virginia, a fact with tremendous implications for
the future of politics and policy in the Commonwealth. Following the next
census, NoVa may even gain one or two more seats in the Virginia House,
primarily at the expense of rural areas in the southwest.

The demographic data provide an overlay to political changes occurring in
the Commonwealth. In the last decade, the state's politics moved quickly from
purple to blue. Four of the five Governors elected between 2001 and 2017
were Democrats. The state's two Senators are Democrats and the state has
voted for the Democratic candidates for President in four consecutive elections through 2020. Democrats took control of both the House of Delegates
and the Senate in 2019. The demographic changes in the state have also generated dramatic differences in the political strategies of statewide candidates.
In the 2001 Virginia governor's race, for example, Mark Warner campaigned
extensively throughout rural parts of the state. And, as Figure 5.5 indicates, he
received substantial support from those areas. Tim Kaine's gubernatorial race
four years later employed a different strategy which focused on the Crescent.
Successful statewide Democrats have done the same ever since, and their
support from those parts of the state increased dramatically. In 2017, Ralph
Northam built a 271,000 vote margin in NoVA and carried the state by nine
percentage points. As Figure 5.6 shows, Bob McDonnell's 2009 victory was
the only interruption to this trend; in that election, he actually carried NoVA.

A diverse population has different needs that are reflected at the ballot
box and then in-state policy. When candidates campaign for votes in various
communities and promise to advocate for their interests, policies change. In
2020, for example, Democrats, who actively campaigned for Hispanic votes,
passed a series of measures that had been defeated by Republicans for years.
Virginia now permits "undocumented" persons to obtain driver's licenses
and now grants in-state tuition for Virginians born in the United States to
undocumented persons.

Though population change can affect state policymaking, one should be
careful before embracing the *demographics is destiny* argument. There is

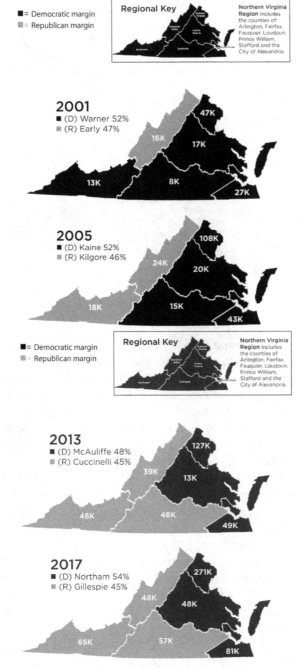

Figure 5.5. Virginia Governor—Party Vote Margins by Region 2001, 2005, 2013 and 2017

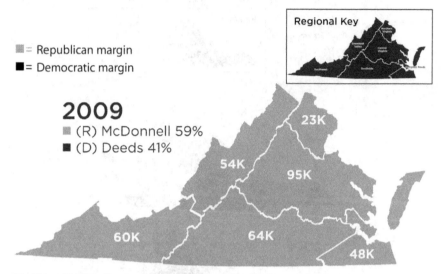

= Republican margin
= Democratic margin

2009
(R) McDonnell 59%
(D) Deeds 41%

Northern Virginia Region includes the counties of: Arlington, Fairfax, Fauquier, Loudoun, Prince William, Stafford and the City of Alexandria.

Figure 5.6. Virginia Governor—Party Vote Margins by Region 2009

little doubt that the Trump presidency generated considerable backlash in Virginia, and that this contributed to statewide Democratic gains during his term. It was no surprise that Ralph Northam's 2017 campaign referred to the former president as a "narcissistic maniac."But various ethnic groups have their own internal dynamics. Americans of Hispanic origin in Florida, with its large older anti-Castro Cuban population, are different politically than those of Puerto Rican origin in New York. Florida Democrats have consistently made the mistake of assuming that a growing Hispanic population in the state would bring greater success at the statewide level. That has not occurred. Trump easily carried the sunshine state, and it has been reliably red largely since the end of the Governor Lawton Chiles era in the late 1990s.[35] In short, changing demographics may allow parties to appeal to more groups in different ways, but they do not dictate a change in the political character of a state.

Virginia may be unique in that the changes in ethnicity are being coupled with an increase in educational attainment. The 2018 U.S. census data placed the Commonwealth seventh highest among all the states in overall educational attainment and sixth in the percentage of its population (38.8 percent) who possess a bachelor's degree or higher.[36] This is a large increase from the approximately 18 percent of Virginians who possessed at least a bachelor's in 2000, one of the largest increases of all of the fifty states for the period.[37] Many of those advanced degree holders are found in NoVa, where Democratic vote increased dramatically during the period.

Places where state Democrats have done better recently are correlated with high degrees of educational attainment. Prince William, Henrico, and Chesterfield counties now have over 40 percent of their populations with at least a bachelor's degree.[38] And Democratic performance has improved in these places in recent years. In 2006, for example, Tim Kaine lost Chesterfield County by 8,000 votes, then considered a victory for the Democrat. Terry McAuliffe lost the county in 2013 by a similar margin. But by 2017, the change was evident. Northam edged his opponent by 700 votes in 2017, and Biden won the county by over 20,000 votes three years later.[39]

TRADITIONS NONETHELESS REMAIN

For all of the political changes that have occurred in Virginia in recent years, the General Assembly attempts to maintain some traditions to limit the divisiveness that is prevalent in the Nation. These traditions have always had the effect of incorporating newer members into the institution and building camaraderie within the group. It is impossible to underestimate the role of these traditions, however silly they may appear to outsiders. For example, when Republicans controlled the Assembly, a small group of them created what was called "the sensitivity caucus," and proceeded to give out awards to various members of both parties at the end of session each year. This was a time when people could laugh at themselves and at each other, and a day that many members eagerly awaited each session. The group created different categories based on major debates or occurrences witnessed during the previous weeks. At the end of the thirty-minute presentation, the caucus also gave out the "pop up award," an honor reserved for that Delegate who spoke more often during floor debates than any other. It was both prized and dreaded, because it indicated that your colleagues recognized that you were speaking a lot, and perhaps more than they felt you should. One year, the sensitivity caucus awarded a rocking chair to Governor Tim Kaine, a gift that he grudgingly accepted but never really appreciated as it suggested that it was time for him to leave public life. In another year, the caucus gave Lee Carter, the self-proclaimed Democratic Socialist, a wooly winter hat complete with ear flaps that prominently displayed a communist star and which could easily have been worn by a Soviet in Siberia; the Delegate loved it. When the Democrats got close to the majority, they took their own turn at bestowing various awards, choosing to give winners a *blue* coffee cup with the words "Democratic Wave, 2017," emblazoned on it. While these awards would occasionally skirt the margins of tastefulness, they were largely done in good humor and had a way of humanizing colleagues with whom you were constantly engaged in partisan squabbles.

Another place where people were socialized into the group involved the roasting of new members upon passage of their first bill. It was a tradition where the members from the party of the new Delegate would ask a series of pointed and sometimes embarrassing questions about the measure. In most cases, these bills were innocuous, so the Delegate could often respond to the questions in a snarky and funny way without risk that the bill would be defeated. When the questions were finished and the vote was called, everyone would vote against the bill, only to have that vote reconsidered and the bill approved. It was all part of the initiation process.

These rites are important to the process of being socialized into the group. They have the tendency of breaking down artificial partisan barriers, and having people learn how best to consider legislation. Another place where this occurs is at large receptions sponsored by lobbyists and advocacy groups that are planned after the sessions every day. These events would often serve as environments where productive exchanges would occur, and potential resolutions emerged. They were bipartisan events, whether massive fetes sponsored by the agribusiness council or smaller and quirkier gatherings such as the "Wild Game" dinner, where legislators and others would feast on delicacies such as roast squirrel, possum stew, and groundhog chili. With the change in the ethics rules in 2016, the number of these receptions were reduced. In addition, there were subtle attempts by leadership to discourage partisan interaction. In this regard, the General Assembly became to resemble Congress, where bipartisan personal interaction would often take a back seat to politics. And as more bills are considered each year and the workload increases, there is less opportunity for these social events to occur. To further complicate matters, some of the Democratic House membership that arrived in 2018 was so opposed the role of lobbyists that they simply rejected opportunities to interact with them at all. During the COVID-19 pandemic, the House's decision to meet virtually ensured that these receptions would not take place. Instead, Delegates were treated to Zoom sessions that took on the appearance of a Hollywood Squares game show—without the humor. Over time, there is a risk that this reduced level of interpersonal contact between lawmakers will further heighten the partisan differences that already exist. There is value to these informal exchanges, but chances for them are only being reduced.

The increasing diversity of the state's population, coupled with resistance to the Trump presidency and the emergence of an activist progressive wing of the Democratic Party, may portend a political realignment in the Commonwealth. Although he says little about the demographic change affecting elections and the distribution of power, Jeff Thomas, in his recent book, *The Virginia Way: Democracy and Power After 2016*, argues that "Virginia's political class is facing the greatest upheaval since the days of Henry Howell, Jr.—and perhaps since Reconstruction."[40] Whether he is correct or not remains to be seen, but there is no doubt that the political class in the Commonwealth looks different than it did less than a decade ago. Today, both the House and the Senate are younger and include more people of color than in decades. For the first time in a century, less than 50 percent of the members of the General Assembly were born in Virginia.[41] When the Assembly convened in 2020, the House had thirty-eight new Delegates that were not serving in 2017, and forty-eight members had four years of service or less.[42] Many of the new faces had no experience in elective office, and some wanted to "shake things up." Some might even agree with Thomas's assertion that "the Virginia Way" is simply a "euphemism for corruption."[43] This criticism has some merit; Virginia's campaign financing system have elements of what some people call "pay to play." Such an arrangement undermines public confidence and can undermine the legitimacy of our system of governance.

NOTES

1. Ed Bruske, "Media Artists: Revealing the Statesmen In the Candidates," *Washington Post*, September 6, 1981, https://www.washingtonpost.com/archive/local/1981/09/06/media-artists-revealing-the-statesmen-in-the-candidates/91f6a23f-ad5b-4a4d-b5dd-0b351003da75/ (accessed June 3, 2021).

2. Mark R. Warner, "The Sensible Center," in *Notes from the Sausage Factory*, ed. Barnie Day and Becky Dale (Lawrenceville, VA: Brunswick, 2005), 288–89.

3. The story of the song, "Carry Me Back to Old Virginny," is itself fascinating, tinged as it is with overtly racist imagery. The song was written in 1878 by a college-educated, black man named James A. Bland, and adopted as the state's song by the Virginia General Assembly in 1940. Not only does the song include offensive words like "Darkey" and "Massa," but it tells an antihistorical and inaccurate story of a freed slave who seeks a return to the days prior to emancipation. In 1970, L. Douglas Wilder's bill sparked strong resistance and went nowhere. It took until 1997 for further action to be taken by the General Assembly, but instead of retiring the song, the legislature simply redefined it as "state song emeritus. Ned Oliver, "Why Is a Racist Minstrel Tune Still Recognized in Virginia Code as the 'State Song Emeritus?'" *Virginia Mercury*, February 20, 2019, https://www.virginiamercury.com/2019/02/20/why-is-a-racist-minstrel-tune-still-recognized-in-virginia-code-as-the-state-song-emeritus/ (accessed June 3, 2021). In 2015, the General Assembly approved two official state songs, "Sweet Virginia Breeze," by Robbin Thompson, and "Our Great Virginia," by Mike Greenly. Ironically, the second of these was composed by a New Yorker using the melody of the traditional song "Shenandoah," a song that actually refers to Missouri and not to the Old Dominion.

4. Dwayne Yancey, *When Hell Froze Over: The Untold Story of Doug Wilder, a Black Politician's Rise to Power in the South* (Dallas, TX: Taylor Publishing, with Roanoke Times, 1988).

5. Frank B. Atkinson, *The Dynamic Dominion: Realignment and the Rise of Two -Party Competition in Virginia, 1945–1980,* 2nd ed. (Lanham, MD: Rowman & Littlefield, 2006).

6. Mary McGrory, "Chuck Robb is Trying to Woo the Virginians," *Tampa Times,* October 1, 1981, https://tampabay.newspapers.com/clip/34645367/the_virginia_way _mary_mcgrory/ (accessed June 3, 2021).

7. U.S. Census Bureau, "Resident Population Data: 2010 Census," *U.S. Census 2010,* archived October 23, 2012, https://web.archive.org/web/20121023151158 /http://2010.census.gov/2010census/data/apportionment-pop-text.php (accessed June 3, 2021).

8. U.S. Census Bureau, "Census 2000 PHC-T-4. Ranking Tables for Counties: 1990 and 2000," https://www.census.gov/population/www/cen2000/briefs/phc-t4/tables/ tab02.pdf.

9. By 2019, Asian groups constituted approximately 6.9 percent of the Virginia population; U.S. Census Bureau, "QuickFacts: Virginia," Asian population estimate July 1, 2019, July 1, 2019, http://www.census.gov/quickfacts/va (accessed June 3, 2021).

10. U.S. Census Bureau, "QuickFacts: Fairfax County, Virginia," Asian population estimate July 1, 2019, https://www.census.gov/quickfacts/fairfaxcountyvirginia (accessed June 3, 2021).

11. Virginia, Fairfax County, "New Demographics Report Reveals Fairfax County Is Growing Older, Richer and More Diverse," report of Fairfax County, Virginia, February 6, 2020, https://www.fairfaxcounty.gov/news2/new-demographics-report -reveals-fairfax-county-is-growing-older-richer-and-more-diverse/.

12. U.S. Census Bureau, "QuickFacts: Prince William County, Virginia," Asian population estimate July 1, 2019, http://www.census.gov/quickfacts/ princewilliamcountyvirginia (accessed June 3, 2021), and U.S. Census Bureau, "Population of Prince William County, Virginia, Census 2010 and 2000 Interactive Map," *Census Viewer,* http://censusviewer.com/county/VA/Prince%20William (accessed June 3, 2021).

13. U.S. Census Bureau, "QuickFacts: Chesterfield County, Virginia," July 1, 2019, https://www.census.gov/quickfacts/chesterfieldcountyvirginia (accessed June 3, 2021); and U.S. Census Bureau, "Population of Chesterfield County, Virginia, Census 2010 and 2000 Interactive Map," *Census Viewer,* http://censusviewer.com/ county/VA/Chesterfield (accessed June 3, 2021).

14. Andrew Cain, "Biden's Wins in Chesterfield, Virginia Beach Extend Democrats' Dominance in Population Centers," *Richmond Times-Dispatch,* November 7, 2020, https://www.chesterfield.gov/802/Election-Results#/results/zBuD (accessed June 4, 2021).

15. U.S. Congress, *Patient Protection and Affordable Care Act* (ACA) *of 2010,* 124 Stat. 119, Pub. L. 111–148, 111 Cong., 2nd sess., March 23, 2010, https: //www.govinfo.gov/app/details/PLAW-111publ148/PLAW-111publ148 (accessed June 9, 2021).

16. Virginia, House of Delegates Clerks Office, "Advanced Member Search." House of Delegates Demographics, 2010, https://history.house.virginia.gov (accessed June 4, 2021).

17. Virginia Public Access Project (VPAP), "General Assembly: Legislators," *VPAP.org*, 2019, http://www.vpap.org/general-assembly/legislators/?display=gender (accessed June 4, 2021).

18. Virginia Public Access Project (VPAP), "General Assembly: Legislators." *VPAP.org*, 2019, https://www.vpap.org/general-assembly/legislators/?display=race (accessed June 4, 2021).

19. Hamilton Lombard, "Since 2010, Household Incomes Have Risen the Most in Rural Virginia," University of Virginia, Weldon Cooper Center, *StatChat*, May 7, 2019, http://statchatva.org/2019/05/07/since-2010-household-incomes-have-risen-the -most-in-rural-virginia/ (accessed June 4, 2021).

20. U.S. Census Bureau, "QuickFacts, Pittsylvania County, Virginia," July 1, 2019, https://www.census.gov/quickfacts/pittsylvaniacountyvirginia (accessed June 4, 2021).

21. U.S. Bureau of Labor Statistics, "Unemployment Rate in Danville, VA (MSA) [DANV251UR]," Federal Reserve Bank of St. Louis (FRED), 2021, https://fred. stlouisfed.org/series/DANV251UR (accessed December 21, 2020).

22. Timothy J. Minchin, "Dan River Mills," in *Encyclopedia Virginia*, updated on July 8, 2020, http://www.EncyclopediaVirginia.org/Dan_River_Mills (accessed June 4, 2021).

23. U.S. Bureau of Labor Statistics, "Unemployment Rate in Danville City, VA [VADANV0URN]," Federal Reserve Bank of St. Louis (FRED), https://fred. stlouisfed.org/series/VADANV0URN (accessed December 21, 2020).

24. World Population Review, "Danville Population, 2000–2020," 2020, https:// worldpopulationreview.com/us-cities/danville-va-population (accessed June 4, 2021).

25. Roanoke Times editors, "Editorial: Demography Reveals the True State of the Commonwealth," *Roanoke Times*, January 30, 2019, https://roanoke.com/opinion/ editorials/editorial-demography-reveals-the-true-state-of-the-commonwealth/article _1f2a466a-67a4-5c67-865e-f15952912682.html (accessed June 4, 2021).

26. Hamilton Lombard, *"Young Adult Migration Trends in Virginia,"* University of Virginia, Weldon Cooper Center, StatChat, August 9, 2016, http://statchatva.org/2016 /08/09/young-adult-migration-trends-in-virginia/ (accessed June 4, 2021).

27. Virginia grew rapidly at a rate of 13 percent in the last decade; this growth rate has declined dramatically in the last several years. Shonel Sen, "Population Projections Show that Virginia is Aging and Growing More Slowly," University of Virginia, Weldon Cooper Center, *StatChat*, July 1, 2019, http://statchatva.org/2019 /07/01/population-projections-show-that-virginia-is-aging-and-growing-more-slowly / (accessed June 4, 2021).

28. Emma North, "Population Expected to Shrink in Rural Virginia," *Virginia Mercury*, September 19, 2019, https://www.virginiamercury.com/blog-va/population -is-expected-to-shrink-in-rural-virginia/ (accessed June 4, 2021).

29. Both of these views are largely correct. It is not surprising to anyone that the county generates more revenue for the state than anyplace in the Commonwealth.

But few are aware that, because of how the state's school funding formula works, the county is essentially subsidizing the funding of rural school divisions.

30. As an example, the 2020 session saw the passing of a budget that provided a special stipend to teachers in Northern Virginia outside of the funding formula. This arrangement has been in existence for years, but 2020 was the first time in recent memory that the stipend had been increased.

31. Figure 5.4 is courtesy of Hamilton Lombard, Weldon Cooper Center at University of Virginia.

32. Gregor Aisch, Robert Gebeloff, and Kevin Quealy, "Where We Came From and Where We Went, State by State," *New York Times*, August 14, 2014, https://www.nytimes.com/interactive/2014/08/13/upshot/where-people-in-each-state-were-born.html (accessed June 4, 2021).

33. Aisch, Gebeloff, and Quealy, "Where We Came From."

34. U.S. Census Bureau, "QuickFacts, Fairfax County, Virginia."

35. Lawton Chiles was Governor until 1998. The only other Democrat after this period was U.S. Senator Bill Nelson, the former astronaut, who served as U.S. Senator of Florida from 2001 to 2019.

36. World Population Review, "Educational Attainment by State 2021," 2021, https://worldpopulationreview.com/state-rankings/educational-attainment-by-state (accessed June 5, 2021).

37. U.S. Department of Education, National Center for Education Statistics, "Educational Attainment of Persons 18 Years Old and Over, by State: Selected Years, 1994 through 2004," https://nces.ed.gov/programs/digest/d05/tables/dt05_011.asp (accessed June 5, 2021).

38. Index Mundi, "Virginia Educational Attainment—Persons 25 Years and Over—Percent Bachelor's Degree or Higher by County," 2014–2018, https://www.indexmundi.com/facts/united-states/quick-facts/virginia/percent-of-people-25-years-and-over-with-bachelors-degree-or-higher#chart (June 5, 2021).

39. Virginia, Chesterfield County, "2020 Chesterfield County Election Results," https://www.chesterfield.gov/802/Election-Results (accessed June 5, 2021).

40. Jeffrey Thomas, "The Virginia Way, Part 2 – New Threats to Old Powers," *Blue Virginia Blog*, August 2, 2019, https://bluevirginia.us/2019/08/the-virginia-way-part-2-new-threats-to-old-powers (accessed June 5, 2021); and Jeff Thomas, *The Virginia Way: Democracy and Power after 2016* (Charleston, SC: History Press, 2019).

41. The trend away from a "home grown " legislature has been underway for a while. In 2010, 56 percent of the members were born in the Commonwealth; by 2020, that number had declined to 48.6 percent. Virginia Public Access Project (VPAP). "General Assembly: Legislators," *VPAP.org*, 2020, https://www.vpap.org/general-assembly/legislators/?display=birth_state&session=28&chamber=both (accessed June 4, 2021).

42. VPAP, "Institutional Memory," December 16, 2019, http://www.vpap.org/general-assembly/legislators/ (accessed June 4, 2021). Only thirteen members had fifteen years or more experience.

43. Jeff Thomas, "'The Virginia Way' Is A Euphemism For Corruption," *Roanoke Times*, August 23, 2015, https://www.roanoke.com/opinion/commentary/thomas

-the-virginia-way-is-a-euphemism-for-corruption/article_dae6cdf1-e606-559c-b338 -30ad20ebb86e.html (accessed June 5, 2021). Thomas provocatively suggests that, without reform of the system, "Virginia will continue to be like Louisiana, but with more money."

Chapter 6

Pay to Play?

Politics has got so expensive that it takes a lot of money even to be defeated.

—Will Rogers, 1931.[1]

Throughout the twentieth century, Virginia was viewed as a relatively clean state where elected representatives, while conservative and supportive of business interests, rarely crossed the line into corrupt activity. At the same time, the argument that the state has been run by elites has been advanced by scholars for decades; the distinguished political scientist V.O. Key, Jr., for example, wrote in 1949 that Virginia's control by elites left the public with so few political choices that "by contrast, Mississippi is a hotbed of democracy."[2] Historian Brent Tarter argued that Virginia is a government "of the businessmen, by the businessmen, and for the businessmen,"[3] and that "outright graft was less common in Virginia because its politicians controlled public policy so thoroughly that they could just write the laws to directly benefit themselves."[4] In this view, corporate interests could avoid corruption to protect their interests simply because they controlled the levers of government. Their dominance was maintained through campaign contributions and an army of lobbyists who wrote and controlled legislation.[5] More recently, writers like Jeff Thomas have explicitly resurrected the term "corruption" to describe the Virginia system.[6]

While Virginia may compare favorably to other states when it comes to political scandal, the Commonwealth's image of clean politicians doing the people's business without taint of wrongdoing has taken a serious hit in the last fifteen years. In 2006, for example, one of the most powerful members of the House, Republican Phil Hamilton of Newport News, attempted to engineer a $40,000-a-year job for himself at Old Dominion University by inserting provisions in the state's appropriations act to fund it. He was convicted on federal corruption charges and spent almost eight years in prison.[7]

In 2017, scandal engulfed Republican Ron Villanueva of Virginia Beach, who had been celebrated as the first Filipino American elected to the Virginia General Assembly. Fond of quoting the Stars Wars mantra "may the force be with you," he was affable and seemed to enjoy considerable support both in his district, where he won re-election four times, and in his caucus, which appointed him to chair the House Transportation Committee. It was then discovered that he and his business partners had been defrauding the federal government for over a decade. He was indicted and lost his re-election bid to a newcomer in the 2017 Democratic wave. In 2019, Villanueva pleaded guilty to conspiracy to defraud the United States; he was sentenced to serve two and one-half years in prison.[8]

In addition to financial scandals, House of Delegates members have been involved in several other problematic incidents. In 2002, S. Vance Wilkins, Jr., then Speaker of the House and one of the architects of the Republicans' rise to power at the turn of the century, was forced to step down after the *Washington Post* reported that he had paid $100,000 in hush money to a woman to keep her quiet about "unwelcome sexual advances."[9] Delegate Rick Morris of Isle of Wight County left the Body after being charged with several counts of felony domestic abuse[10]; the charges were eventually dismissed. And then-Delegate Joe Morrissey of Henrico County resigned after reports emerged that he was involved sexually with an underage woman who worked as an intern at his law firm.[11] He was convicted of a misdemeanor and disbarred for a second time. Morrissey subsequently married the woman and was elected to the state Senate in 2019. He was pardoned Ralph Northam in 2021.

THE MCDONNELL SCANDAL

By far the biggest scandal of them all involved the 71st Governor of the Commonwealth, Robert F. McDonnell. McDonnell had risen through the ranks of party politics in Virginia, having first been elected to the House of Delegates in 1992, and gradually rising to Chair the powerful House Courts of Justice Committee. He ran and won a closely contested race for Attorney General in 2006, besting state Senator R. Creigh Deeds by less than one per-cent. In 2009, he was nominated for Governor and faced Deeds once again. This time, McDonnell sailed to a seventeen-point victory, campaigning on putting people back to work (*Bob's for Jobs*) after the Great Recession of 2008. He began to be viewed as a potential candidate for national office. He was personable, telegenic, and projected an image more moderate than others in his party. The national GOP elevated his stature by designating him to provide the Party's response to President Obama's 2010 State of the Union address.

Yet McDonnell could not elude a massive scandal of his own making. During his run for Governor in 2009, McDonnell met Jonnie R. Williams Sr. By McDonnell's own admission, the two became friends, and Williams's firm, Star Scientific, provided air travel valued in excess of $28,500 to McDonnell's 2009 campaign. Following the election, the company provided $80,000 in air travel to the Governor's political action committee (PAC) in 2010 and 2011. In 2011, Williams took the first lady, Maureen McDonnell, on a shopping trip in New York City, where he bought her expensive clothes and jewelry at three upscale stores.

A month later, Williams and Maureen McDonnell met privately at the Governor's Mansion, where the first lady supposedly asked him for a $50,000 loan for her business and help in covering $15,000 in catering costs for her daughter's wedding. Williams delivered, and so did Maureen McDonnell; she flew to Florida to pitch Star Scientific's new supplement "Anatabloc" to physicians, and publicly offered the Executive Mansion for the product's launch party. Upon hearing about the event, the Governor's aides tried to stop it. They were overruled, and the party occurred, the Governor in attendance. With a portion of the $50,000 received from Williams, Ms. McDonnell purchased 6,000 shares of Star Scientific stock.

In addition, the Governor himself began opening doors for Williams. The corporate executive gained a meeting with the state's Secretary of Health and Human Resources William A. "Bill" Hazel Jr. and attempted to enlist the University of Virginia (UVA) in applying for a grant from the Virginia Tobacco Region Revitalization Commission. None of these efforts bore fruit. Star Scientific representatives also met with Sara Wilson, the state's top human resource officer, in hopes of convincing her to include the company's product for reimbursement under the state health policy. She said no.

The gifts kept coming. Williams bought several rounds of golf for McDonnell's sons. He purchased a $6,500 Rolex watch inscribed with the words "71st Governor of Virginia," which Maureen presented to the Governor as Christmas present. In March 2012, Williams wrote a $50,000 check from his trust to MoBo Real Estate Partners, a corporation owned by McDonnell and his sister. Later, McDonnell attempted to characterize this, and a subsequent $20,000 check from Williams, as loans. The Governor failed to discuss ownership of the stock on his financial disclosure forms as required under state law, or the alleged loans on an application he made for a bank loan.

The first public inkling of the extent of McDonnell's relationship with Williams was detailed in a *Washington Post* article published in March 2013, following the adjournment of that year's legislative session.[12] McDonnell denied that anything inappropriate had occurred, but the revelations continued in a series of explosive news articles throughout the summer and fall. Legislators generally avoided criticizing the Governor, but they were embarrassed for the state and concerned about the political fallout. Unlike the demands for Governor Northam to resign in response to the "blackface" scandal in 2019 and Republican proposals to investigate the allegations against Lieutenant Governor Fairfax in the same year, neither party initially proposed any action against McDonnell. Perhaps A. Donald McEachin, then a Democratic State Senator from Richmond and now a U.S. Congressman, best expressed the common sentiment: "He has always come across in dealing with him, on a political level and personal level, as someone who is squeaky clean. Regrettably, it's appearing that that's not the case."[13] Questions were also raised about then-Attorney General Ken Cuccinelli, who also owned Star Scientific stock.[14]

Ten days after completing his term as Governor in January 2014, McDonnell and his wife were indicted on fourteen counts of federal corruption for receiving improper gifts and loans from Williams. The indictment occurred at the beginning of the legislative session, and the news rocked the Capitol. Even as they issued the obligatory "a person is innocent until proven guilty" statements, Republicans remained concerned about the political ramifications of the story. Terry McAuliffe had just been sworn in as the 72nd Governor of the Commonwealth and, with McDonnell now gone, the likelihood of the General Assembly taking action against McDonnell, even if it could, was minimal.

The federal trial, which began in August 2014, took more than a month. McDonnell mounted a number of defenses, including placing some of the blame on his wife (and co-defendant). The jury never bought it, and in September 2014, he was convicted of eleven counts and his wife found guilty of seven.[15] McDonnell, the first Virginia governor to be indicted or convicted of a felony, was sentenced in January 2015 to two years in prison, followed by two years of supervised release; his wife received a 366-day sentence. The McDonnell's appealed the convictions, and mobilized substantial support in his efforts. Six former Virginia attorneys general and 77 former AGs from across the country, the majority of whom were Democrats, filed amicus briefs arguing that the convictions should be overturned, and asserting that the verdict represented a "breathtaking expansion of public-corruption law (that) would likely chill federal officials' interactions with the people they serve and thus damage their ability to effectively perform their duties." The United States Supreme Court agreed, and in June 2016, unanimously overturned the verdicts and returned the case to the lower court. The court did not dispute the facts, but held that the actions were not an "official acts" and therefore not subject to the law for which the governor was prosecuted.[16] Less than three months later, the Obama Justice Department announced that they would not prosecute the case again, and the charges against the former governor and his wife were dismissed. He remains actively engaged in teaching, real estate development, and is writing a book on his years in public life.

After years of turmoil, including the end of his marriage and almost $27 million in legal bills, Governor McDonnell emerged with a reputation that was forever tarnished. And so too was the image of Virginia as a relatively clean state that operated according to "the Virginia Way," which had now come to mean governmental integrity, fiscal responsibility, and political compromise. Notwithstanding McDonnell's legal victory, legislators felt ethical reforms were necessary to restore some modicum of trust in state elected officials.

ETHICS AND LOBBYISTS

Criticism of the role of lobbyists and campaign contributions in politics is neither new nor unique to the Commonwealth. But the McDonnell scandal cast a bright light on practices to which too many lawmakers had become accustomed, particularly the acceptance of "gifts" of substantial value. Like most state legislatures, the Virginia General Assembly is composed of citizens who have other jobs or roles in their communities; they are not in session year-round and do not have an extensive staff apparatus similar to the U.S. Congress. They are paid little. State lawmakers typically have only one legislative aide and may occasionally add a second as a temporary assistant during the legislative session. These limitations leave legislators somewhat dependent upon lobbyists for information to assist them in assessing the various pros and cons of particular pieces of legislation, particularly those that are complex.

The lobbying corps has expanded in Richmond over the years, in part because legislation itself has become more complex. Lobbyists come in all forms and represent all types of interests, from the utilities and insurance industry to farmers, loggers, dentists, and even midwives. Good lobbyists understand the nuances of legislation and the pros and cons of their clients' proposals. Moreover, they realize the importance of integrity and trust; a good lobbyist understands that if they were to consciously misrepresent a position to a lawmaker, it might destroy a good working relationship and damage their reputation around the Capitol—forever. Nonetheless, there is good reason for lawmakers and lobbyists to be concerned about appearances; for citizens to have confidence in the system, they must feel that big money and influence are not overriding the legislator's allegiance to their constituents.

The McDonnell scandal brought heightened public scrutiny to the role of money in politics, and other instances surfaced that raised concerns. Press reports documented how Dominion Energy funded trips for legislators to the

Masters golf tournament and paid to entertain legislators in luxury boxes at Washington Redskins' football games.[17] One group of lobbyists paid for a multithousand dollar hunting trip for a prominent Senator and other representatives.[18] And Virginia Uranium, a company actively seeking to repeal the several-decades-old prohibition on uranium mining in the Commonwealth, funded several trips to France in 2011 for over a dozen Democratic and Republican lawmakers to visit a closed and reclaimed mine in the southwestern part of the country, sandwiched between several days in Paris for "lectures and briefings."[19]

Who wouldn't enjoy these excursions? To be sure, certain trips can be justified in order to examine possible initiatives in other states that might work in Virginia. But these instances seemed excessive and created the impression that few legislators sought to cultivate. I never attended any of these and would often quip on the campaign trail that "I need help with my putting stroke, but never thought it appropriate to have Dominion fly me to the Masters for a lesson."

In response to the McDonnell scandal and gifts like those already described, Governor McAuliffe imposed a gift limitation on his staff. The General Assembly then convened a special ethics panel in 2015. Over the next two years, the panel recommended, and the General Assembly passed, a number of new ethics laws. With the exception of certain exemptions, Virginia state legislators and executive officials, and their immediate families, could no longer solicit or accept a single gift or combination of gifts exceeding $100 during any calendar year from any lobbyist or their clients.

The 2015 actions were celebrated by both Governor McAuliffe, who called it a "victory for transparency and accountability,"[20] and by the Republican sponsor of the legislation, Delegate C. Todd Gilbert of Shenandoah, who asserted that by enacting the reform bill, the General Assembly had "solved all major problems that the public wanted us to solve."[21] Nonetheless, many believed that our reform efforts were relatively tepid. And while the Assembly created the Virginia Conflict of Interest and Ethics Advisory Council, it had little teeth or enforcement power compared to similar bodies in states such as Massachusetts, South Carolina, and Pennsylvania.

As is the case with much legislation, the ethics bill was a balancing act, seeking to reconcile competing interests. Legislators were sensitive to the public outcry in the aftermath of the McDonnell scandal. At the same time, however, there was a major concern that the legislature would either create new laws that could become "traps for the unwary" or used as political weaponry. Finally, while laws can prevent the most egregious transgressions, "at some point," as Democratic Senate Leader Dick Saslaw said, "you just can't legislate good ethics."[22] Critics continue to rail against the Virginia law, and cite the state's "D" grade for transparency and accountability from the State

Integrity Investigation report in 2015 as evidence. What critics often failed to note, however, was that only three states received a grade higher than "D+," and that the Commonwealth was actually ranked sixteenth best of all the states.[23]

THE WILD, WILD WEST OF CAMPAIGN FINANCE

The 2015 reforms never attacked the major channel of influence for corporate and outside donor groups, that is, campaign contributions. When it comes to campaign finance, Virginia is the wild, wild west; the Commonwealth is one of only eleven states that impose no limits on political contributions for state races.[24] Numerous reform efforts to cap the contributions have failed. In 2019, I proposed both limiting contributions to $10,000 per cycle per candidate and enacting prohibitions against regulated entities such as utilities from contributing directly to political campaigns.[25] Neither proposal received a serious hearing. Delegate Marcus Simon had, for years, proposed a bill that would prohibit Delegates and Senators from using campaign funds for personal benefit. For many, it seems outrageous that an elected representative could use campaign funds to pay their personal expenses. Yet year after year, the measure failed. In 2021, Simon finally succeeded in passing this reform in the House, albeit with some exceptions to allow for the payment of childcare while campaigning, only to have it derailed in the Senate. Virginia remained a national outlier in this area.

The 2019 campaign cycle brought a major uptick in money flowing into Virginia campaign coffers; both the Senate and House could potentially (and did) flip to the Democrats, and donors realized that much was at stake. The cost of winning a seat with a yearly salary between $17,600 (in the House) and $18,000 (in the Senate) kept rising as well. In the Richmond area, Delegate Debra Rodman spent $3.124 million in an unsuccessful bid to unseat state Senator Siobhan Dunnavant, a Republican from Henrico County, who spent some $2.672 million herself. In the adjacent district, Democrat Ghazala Hashmi ousted state Senator Glen Sturtevant, in a race where over $5 million was spent between the candidates.[26] In my first election cycle as Democratic Leader in 2013, spending for the entire House totaled just over $26.1 million; in 2019, it was almost $68 million.[27] These amounts are significantly higher than in most states with citizen part-time legislatures.[28]

Critics of Virginia's campaign finance laws believe they encourage "political corruption."[29] They argue that when corporations and wealthy individuals make large contributions, the candidates become beholden to those special interests. In Virginia, Dominion Energy has become the poster child for this argument and those who want finance reform. Dominion is the largest electric utility in Virginia, serving 2.2 million residential and more than 250,000 commercial and industrial customers. In the 2016–2017 fundraising cycle for Virginia House of Delegates candidates, the utility gave $750,257 to legislative candidates, caucuses, and leadership committees, with $340,043, or 37.8 percent, given to Democrats and $559,769, or 62.2 percent, to Republicans.[30] In 2019 alone, when control of the House and the Senate were both in the balance, the energy giant donated over $1 million to races. Unlike earlier years, the donations actually were slightly larger for Democrats than for their GOP counterparts. Campaign finance reports showed that the energy giant donated $580,000 to state Senate races, with the majority ($303,000) going to Democrats, and gave $428,000 to House races, $235,000 of which flowed to Democrats. Other large contributors included Dominion critic Michael Bills and his wife Sonjia Smith, who donated almost $1 million during the cycle to House and Senate races (mostly to Democrats), a number of business interests, various progressive environmental, labor, and prochoice groups, and even a conservative Midwest financier, Richard Uihlein, who gave $500,000 to Delegate Nick Frietas.[31]

Most legislators bristle at the accusations that campaign contributions bring political influence, if only because it suggests they can "be bought." Although members of the public take the view that lawmakers are overly influenced by money in politics, I have never heard a lobbyist suggest that a legislator vote in a certain way because of a campaign contribution (I have, however, heard individual contributors argue for certain votes). Occasionally, an individual might make an off-hand comment like "remember who brought you to the dance," but most lawmakers find such comments offensive. Virginia legislators cannot raise money while they are in session; for either a legislator or a lobbyist to even mention a campaign contribution during session is an ethics violation that is sanctionable. Most lobbyists understand that, and are respectful when legislators tell them that they cannot support their client's position on an issue or a legislative matter.

Business interests are usually the ones criticized for large campaign contributions. But they are not alone in plowing big money into campaigns and parties. In the 2016–2017 fundraising cycle, the Virginia League of Conservation Voters, or Virginia LCV, (a group whose values and positions I have historically supported) gave over $3 million to candidates for state office—and all but $3,500 of this went to Democrats.[32] Planned Parenthood, Win Virginia (a group of Northern Virginia Democratic donors), Everytown (a gun safety group), and various national and state labor groups provide financial and logistical support for progressive candidates, primarily Democrats. For lawmakers to claim that corporate interests expect a response consistent with their views, but other interests do not, is simply naive. All major campaign contributions raise ethical issues of how much influence they induce, but the good news is that most legislators attempt to "wall themselves off" from impropriety. As one colleague said, "when the election is over, and I am in session, I do not care who gave me what."

It has not escaped notice that when big issues are under consideration, interest groups make major contributions. When there was a debate about whether to repeal the moratorium on uranium mining, the industry gave substantially to House and Senate candidates.[33] When casino gambling was being considered, interests supporting the initiative donated handsomely; between 2018 and 2020, the industry contributed almost $3 million to Virginia campaigns.[34] The same will likely occur as the Commonwealth continues the terms and conditions of legalizing marijuana.

In some instances, campaign money can appear to be tied to a certain action requested of the candidate. One such case involves the advocacy group called "Clean Virginia." Funded predominantly by former Goldman Sachs vice president and present hedge fund manager Michael Bills from Charlottesville, the group had clear and laudable goals: fight climate change and transition to a renewable energy economy. The group was a strident opponent of Dominion Energy, a company they argued was a barrier to these changes. As a condition of his initial contributions, Bills asked legislators to take a pledge that they would not accept any money from utilities regulated by the state, their executives, or their employees.[35] If a candidate refused money from state-regulated utilities, he or she would be given money from the group.

While many Democrats supported the clean energy goals of the organization, the "pledge" appeared perilously close to the classic "quid pro quo" or "pay to play" approach that so many critics of campaign finance laws criticized. A number of legislators, myself included, refused to take the pledge. While my campaign committee had earlier stopped accepting Dominion contributions, I informed Clean Virginia that I would not take its contributions either; it just did not feel right. I was not alone; Speaker Eileen Filler-Corn also refused to take the pledge, as did a number of members of the Virginia Legislative Black Caucus (VLBC). In 2019, Clean Virginia gave $255,000 to House and Senate candidates.[36]

In 2020 and 2021, the group increased their involvement. Bills himself gave $ 3 million to Clean Virginia in early 2021, and the organization dispensed $720,000 and $100,000 respectively to two primary candidates for Governor, Jennifer Carroll Foy and Jennifer McClellan. Another $525,000 went to Attorney General candidate Jay Jones, who was attempting to oust two-term incumbent Mark Herring in the Democratic primary in 2021. Similarly, Smith was active, giving $500,000 to Carroll Foy and another $100,000 to Jones.[37] When Lieutenant Governor candidate Hala Ayala accepted $100,000 from Dominion Energy, Clean Virginia immediately spent $125,000 to oppose her.[38]

Bills and Smith consistently invested in Democratic candidates challenging incumbents who were viewed to be aligned with McAuliffe. The duo collectively gave $125,000 to Alexsis Rodgers in her failed attempt to oust Richmond Mayor Levar Stoney, an ally of McAuliffe. Prior to my retirement, Smith donated over $100,000 to Sally Hudson in an effort to oust me; Hudson now refers to Smith as "my mentor." This was followed by major contributions to the primary opponent to Senator Saslaw.[39]

Concerns about "quid pro quo" or "pay to play" seemingly had little impact on the voters, but the group prompted controversy after it was disclosed that they had given two separate contributions in 2019 and in 2020 totaling $10,000 to Amanda Chase, a Senator who sought the Republican nod for governor in 2021 and was known as one of the most conservative and combative members of the Senate.[40] Chase had become known for her controversial statements, and some of her comments generated criticism in both Democratic and Republican circles as racially insensitive.[41] Her statements became so outrageous that she was even censured by a bipartisan vote of the state Senate in 2021.[42] After the contributions were disclosed, Clean Virginia issued a statement that they would no longer give to the Senator. But the occurrence again raised the "quid pro quo" issue. Chase was not known as a leader in the fight against climate change; the only reason that Clean Virginia donated to her campaign, appeared to be her commitment not to take Dominion money. Some progressive elements of the party even publicly asked whether it was "Time to Clean Up 'Clean Virginia.'"[43]

Once Democrats took control of the General Assembly, Bills and Smith became even more aggressive in trying to install legislators to their liking. They were reportedly behind the failed attempt by Lashrecse Aird to defeat Filler-Corn for Speaker in 2020. In the 2021 primary season, Smith invested in a primary challenger to House Appropriations Chair and VLBC member Luke Torian. After the challenger failed to qualify for the ballot, Smith, Clean Virginia, and a newly-formed auxiliary PAC, Commonwealth Forward, focused their campaign largesse on challengers to Democratic incumbents Candi King and Steve Heretick, both of whom had rebuffed efforts to take the anti-Dominion pledge.[44] The group provided Heretick's opponent with $554,000 of the $600,000 he raised for the race.[45] And they showered King's opponent with a staggering $735,000—for a primary she ended up losing by a two to one margin.[46] Bills and Smith contributed $4 million and $1.8 million respectively between 2020 and April 2021, almost exclusively to Democrats. By contrast, Dominion's giving was placed at $2.3 million, with Republicans receiving about one-third of the funds.[47]

In the June 2021 Democratic primary, most all of these Bills / Smith / Clean Virginia investments failed. McAuliffe decisively won the primary against Carroll Foy and McClellan, Ayala won her race convincingly, and Herring easily bested his opponent. Heretick was defeated, but his loss was due largely to his voting record and corruption allegations that had dogged him for years.

Some legislators freely admit their interest in protecting business interests. Longtime Democratic Senate Leader Saslaw, for example, once stated "Go ask Dominion, go ask any of these companies, beer and wine wholesalers, banks, the development community—every one of them will tell you, they will tell you I am the most probusiness Senator."[48] As a result of his ties to Dominion, Saslaw, who has a strong record supporting educational investments, women's rights, equal opportunity, and health care access, became a target in the 2019 Democratic primary, challenged by a relatively unknown candidate who campaigned as a progressive outsider.[49] Saslaw, after spending a bit more than $1.4 million, barely survived, and now jokingly calls himself "landslide Saslaw."

For all of the criticism that the Virginia General Assembly is an arm of business interests, a review of policy decisions in the last decade suggests that the business class does not always get its way. For years, Virginia business fought for greater investments in highway construction and maintenance (some even supported a tax increase) but were stymied again and again by the very people presumed to be their allies—conservative Republicans—who were unwilling to raise the revenue necessary to address this problem.

Similarly, major hospitals and insurance business interests supported Medicaid expansion for five years before it was finally passed in 2018. In both cases, conservative Republicans were blocking the policies supported by corporate interests. But that did not stop the business community from favoring the GOP with their donations. Between 2010 and 2017, the House and Senate Democratic Party caucuses received $1.6 million from their top ten business and union donors, while their GOP counterparts garnered $2.4 million. When business funders were asked why they were contributing larger amounts to those who were voting against their interests, the answer was frequently "they are in the majority, and we have other interests that we need to protect." Based on this statement, one would expect that business giving would rise as the Democrats got closer to power. In fact, that is exactly what has occurred. In the period 2018 to 2019, when Democrats were directly challenging for control of the Assembly, business interests dramatically increased campaign giving to Democrats.[50] And through the first eight months of 2020, corporate interests were investing heavily in Democratic incumbents; Dominion, for example, was spending twice the amount as they were on Republicans.[51] Many legislators do not like this system of campaign financing. "I hate this system," exclaimed G. Manoli "Manny" Loupassi, a former Republican Delegate from Richmond who lost his seat in the Democratic wave of 2017; "It makes us look like crooks and we're not."[52] As Democratic Leader in the House, I did not much like it either.

The only real prohibition involving fundraising is that legislators are not permitted to raise money during regular sessions. This creates a dynamic where fundraisers occur up until the morning of the day when a session begins. While members cannot raise money during regular session, there are no prohibitions against doing so during special sessions. In August 2020, stories emerged about prominent legislators raising money during these times. One involved a golf tournament that occurred at the same time as the session was convening by remote video conference.[53] To say that "everyone does it" does not address the public's general cynicism about this type of fund raising. And the issue is likely to become even more complicated as the General Assembly meets more frequently during the year. In 2019, for example, the legislature met in some form for 167 of 253 workdays. And it has convened special sessions in eight out of the last eleven years,[54] including 2020, when the Assembly met for the longest special session in history. If the rationale for prohibiting contributions during session is the proximity of the donation to the issues before the Body, the same rationale might be easily applied to special sessions.

PROSPECTS FOR REFORM

How many candidates for public office campaign against *a corrupt and broken* system based on the money and influence of the wealthy? Many! The overwhelming majority of the public, regardless of their political affiliation, believe that money has too much influence on elections, and that successful candidates promote policies that help their donors. A January 2019 poll, for instance, indicated that only 20 percent of Americans were satisfied with our campaign finance laws.[55] But how many citizens cast their vote based on a person's position on campaign finance reform, or their platform outlining specific changes in ethics rules? Far fewer. Unless a candidate has been directly involved in a scandal, campaign finance or ethics reform is rarely cited in polls as the main reason why a voter chooses one candidate over another.[56]

Elected officials, especially those in leadership, frequently struggle with both the public perception and the reality they face when raising money. On the one hand, they realize that while donors do not always seek influence, they frequently want access; as one donor put it, "at least I know that when I call, you will pick up the phone." Saying "no" to a prominent donor who wants you to vote in a certain way can be empowering. On the other hand, it is also difficult to win elections without communicating and extremely difficult to do this without money.

For leadership, the challenge is even more acute, because you are always raising money for your colleagues and those who you hope will join you by winning their elections. During my stint as Democratic Leader, I would frequently hear suggestions that we could win elections simply by harnessing the power of small donations and rejecting contributions from "big corporations." While a great idea, without reform applied to both parties, this approach makes it extremely difficult for the minority to fund competitive races because small donors do not tend to give freely unless gaining power seems possible or the opposing party poses a major threat to their interests. My role as Leader was to approach individuals and groups who could make large donations so I could help fund my colleagues. And until there was campaign finance reform, I was not inclined to "unilaterally disarm" when our opponents were raising large sums from major donors.

Campaign finance reform is not easy. Money always seems to *find its way* into the system, even with the most elaborate restrictions. That does not mean, however, that reform attempts should be abandoned. At the least, campaign finance and ethics rules should create incentives to reduce the likelihood that elected officials might be tempted to be influenced by donations. That means establishing reasonable limits and greater transparency in reporting. And some states are developing policies to match small donations with monies from state governments.[57] Democrats created a commission to explore reform options in 2021, and future sessions will hopefully make a serious effort to alter a system that appears to be spiraling out of control.

Enforcing campaign finance reform requires regulatory framework and personnel that may be difficult in Virginia, a state that is such an outlier in this area and has shown little interest in adopting major change. But without reform, the legitimacy of our system becomes further questioned, creating even more problems as we address major challenges in our future. Even with the best rules, a normative system must underlie them, that is, officials should *do the right thing*. This is where trust, integrity, and virtues that cannot be legislated, come into play. And the key to creating a state ethos embodying these traits will be found in those who control the levers of power, whether they be governors, legislators, or attorneys general, the so-called players in the arena.

NOTES

1. Will Rogers, "Quotes by Will Rodgers," *Will Rogers Today*, quoted in *Daily Telegram* 1538, June 28, 1931, https://www.willrogerstoday.com/quotes/will-rogers -on-politics/ (accessed June 4, 2021).

2. V. O. Key, Jr., *Southern Politics in State and Nation* (New York: Knopf, 1949).

3. Brent Tarter, quoted in Jeff Thomas, *The Virginia Way: Democracy and Power after 2016* (Charleston, SC: History Press, 2019), 27.

4. Tarter, quoted in Thomas, *Virginia Way*, 19.

5. In the late twentieth century, periodic efforts were made to disrupt this system, including the several failed statewide campaigns of Henry Howell, who ran, he said, to "Keep the Big Boys Honest." Howell was a populist who served in both the Virginia House and Senate before winning a special election in 1971 for Lieutenant Governor to serve out the term of J. Sargeant Reynolds after his death in office. One of Howell's favorite political targets was Dominion Energy, then known as Virginia Electric Power Company (VEPCO), which Howell labeled as the "Very Expensive Power Company." Howell came close to winning the governorship in 1973, when he lost to Mills Godwin by 15,000 votes.

6. See Thomas, *Virginia Way*; and Peter Galuszka, "More Stunning Public Corruption in Virginia," *Washington Post*, May 11, 2016, https://www.washingtonpost.com/ blogs/all-opinions-are-local/wp/2016/05/11/how-can-we-stem-corruption-in-virginia / (accessed June 4, 2021).

7. Rachel Weiner, "Phillip Hamilton, Ex-Virginia Delegate Jailed for Bribery, Denied New Trial," *Washington Post*, December 23, 2014, https://www.washingtonpost.com /local/virginia-politics/imprisoned-former-virginia-delegate-phillip-hamilton-denied -new-trial-by-appeals-court/2014/12/23/9530bb2e-8ad0-11e4-a085-34e9b9f09a58 _story.html.

8. Rachel Weiner, "Former Del. Ron Villanueva of Virginia Beach Pleads Guilty to Contracting Fraud," *Richmond Times-Dispatch*, March 19, 2019, https://www. richmond.com/news/virginia/government-politics/general-assembly/former-del-ron -villanueva-of-virginia-beach-pleads-guilty-to/article_5555b3f3-f518-5a77-bc12 -75497ffeb22b.html (accessed June 4, 2021).

9. R. H. Melton, "Va. Speaker Settles Sex Complaint; Wilkins Paid Woman at Least $100,000, Denies Accusations," *Washington Post*, June 7, 2002, https://www. washingtonpost.com/archive/politics/2002/06/07/va-speaker-settles-sex-complaint/ e66ad36c-2bc9-4ff3-8f28-c2d0467b81a7/ (accessed June 4, 2021); R. H. Melton, "Wilkins Resigns as Va. Speaker," *Washington Post*, June 14, 2002, https://www. washingtonpost.com/archive/politics/2002/06/14/wilkins-resigns-as-va-speaker/ b3bd41d0-4eff-4661-ae8f-be11cb955ac0/ (accessed June 4, 2021).

10. Patrick Wilson, "Del. Rick Morris, Facing Domestic Abuse Charges, Says He Won't Seek Re-election," *Richmond Times-Dispatch*, March 1, 2017, https://www. richmond.com/news/virginia/del-rick-morris-facing-domestic-abuse-charges-says -he-won/article_519629a4-11de-5eeb-b179-5309e60625eb.html (accessed June 4, 2021); Margaret Matray, "Del. Rick Morris Says He's Been Vindicated in a Child -cruelty Case. His Wife Threatens to Sue Prosecutor," *Virginian-Pilot*, August 23,

2017, https://pilotonline.com/news/local/crime/article_10711dcb-03a4-52ca-96d5 -f7ce164ca6a9.html (accessed June 4, 2021).

11. Laura Vozzella and Rachel Weiner, "Del. Joseph Morrissey Resigns in Wake of Conviction—and Promises to Run Again," *Washington Post*, December 18, 2014, https://www.washingtonpost.com/local/virginia-politics/va-del-joseph-morrissey-to -resign-in-wake-of-conviction-but-run-again-for-his-seat/2014/12/18/f50befle-86cf -11e4-b9b7-b8632ae73d25_story.html (accessed June 4, 2021).

12. Rosalind S. Helderman and Laura Vozzella, "Va. Gov. McDonnell on Two-way Street with Chief Executive of Struggling Company," *Washington Post*, March 30, 2013, https://www.washingtonpost.com/local/dc-politics/va-gov-mcdonnell-in-close -relationship-with-owner-of-struggling-company/2013/03/30/43f34fb8-97ea-11e2 -814b-063623d80a60_story.html (accessed June 4, 2021).

13. Peter Hamby, "Virginia Governor Scandal: 'That's not the guy we know,'" *CNN Politics*, August 20, 2013, https://www.cnn.com/2013/07/17/politics/mcdonnell -scandal/index.html (accessed June 4, 2021).

14. David J. Toscano, "The McDonnell Ethics Scandal: The Governor and Attorney General's Inappropriate Acceptance of Gifts," July 26, 2013, *davidtoscano. com*, https://davidtoscano.com/general-assembly-2013/the-mcdonnell-ethics-scandal (accessed June 4, 2021).

15. Rosalind S. Helderman and Matt Zapotosky, "Ex-Va. Governor Robert McDonnell Guilty of 11 Counts of Corruption," *Washington Post*, September 4, 2014, https://www.washingtonpost.com/local/virginia-politics/mcdonnell-jury-in-third-day -of-deliberations/2014/09/04/0e01ff88-3435-11e4-9e92-0899b306bbea_story.html (accessed June 4, 2021).

16. *McDonnell v. United States*, 136 S.Ct. 2355 (2016), https://supreme.justia.com /cases/federal/us/579/15-474/ (accessed June 4, 2021).

17. Jim Nolan, "Trips to Turkey, the Masters Among Gifts to Lawmakers," *Richmond Times-Dispatch*, January 30, 2013, https://www.richmond.com/news/ virginia/government-politics/trips-to-turkey-the-masters-among-gifts-to-lawmakers/ article_3a995a1f-3f73-58ff-9f41-6483f7eb0e1c.html (accessed June 4, 2021).

18. Dave Ress, "Part 6: Giving Gifts, and Gaining Influence?" *Daily Press*, November 20, 2014, https://www.dailypress.com/government/dp-nws-virginiaway -part-6-gifts-20141120-story.html (accessed June 4, 2021).

19. Anita Kumar, "Virginia Lawmakers Flying to France as Part of Lobbying Push for Uranium Mining," *Washington Post*, June 16, 2011, https://www.washingtonpost. com/local/dc-politics/virginia-lawmakers-flying-to-france-as-part-of-lobbying-push -for-uranium-mining/2011/06/15/AG0BDxXH_print.html (accessed June 4, 2021). The public became even more concerned when it was disclosed that in the following year, Virginia Uranium contributed $160,000 to state political campaigns, about 70 percent of it going to Republicans. The firm also contributed $12,500 to the Republican Party and $10,000 to Governor McDonnell's political action committee (PAC). Peter Galuszka, "The Ugly Battle Over Virginia's Uranium," *Slate*, January 10, 2013, last updated January 14, 2013, https://slate.com/technology/2013 /01/virginia-uranium-mine-the-scandals-and-dangers-of-the-first-uranium-mine-east -of-the-mississippi.html (accessed June 4, 2021).

20. Laura Vozzella, "Virginia Legislature Adopts Stricter Gift Standards for Public Officials," *Washington Post*, April 17, 2015, http://www.washingtonpost.com/local/virginia-politics/virginia-legislature-adopts-stricter-gift-standards/2015/04/17/b400b6a0-e456-11e4-905f-cc896d379a32_story.html (accessed June 4, 2021).

21. Jim Nolan and Markus Schmidt, "Legislature Approves Ethics Bill with $100 Aggregate Gift Cap," *Richmond Times-Dispatch*, April 17, 2015, http://www.richmond.com/news/virginia/government-politics/article_1d1225c8-3929-5099-8ce5-eace700186c9.html (accessed June 4, 2021).

22. Critics of Virginia's ethics frequently cite the Commonwealth's ranking in the Center for Public Integrity and Global Integrity survey of transparency and accountability.

23. Nicholas Kusnetz, "Only Three States Score Higher Than D+ in State Integrity Investigation; 11 Flunk," *Center for Public Integrity*, November 23, 2015, updated November 23, 2015, https://publicintegrity.org/state-politics/state-integrity-investigation/only-three-states-score-higher-than-d-in-state-integrity-investigation-11-flunk/ (accessed June 4, 2021).

24. As of 2019, the others were Alabama, Indiana, Iowa, Mississippi, Nebraska, North Dakota, Oregon, Pennsylvania, Texas, and Utah. See National Conference of State Legislatures (NCSL), "Campaign Contribution Limits: Overview," October 4, 2019, https://www.ncsl.org/research/elections-and-campaigns/campaign-contribution-limits-overview.aspx (accessed June 4, 2021).

25. Virginia, Legislative Information System (LIS), "Virginia General Assembly Session, HB 2732," 2019, http://lis.virginia.gov/cgi-bin/legp604.exe?191+sum+HB2732 (accessed June 4, 2021); and Virginia, Legislative Information System (LIS), "Virginia General Assembly Session, HB 1958," 2019, http://lis.virginia.gov/cgi-bin/legp604.exe?191+sum+HB1958 (accessed June 4, 2021).

26. Dave Ress,"Shad Plank: Money Talks—and It Was Loud in the Final Days of the '19 General Assembly Campaign," *Daily Press*, Dec 6, 2019, https://www.dailypress.com/government/virginia/dp-nw-shad-plank-money-talks-20191206-mqtjofdl3rgqhmekioaz54ka3i-story.html (accessed June 4, 2021).

27. Virginia Public Access Project (VPAP), "House: Historical Trends," 2019, *VPAP.org*, https://www.vpap.org/elections/house/historic/ (accessed June 4, 2021).

28. One reason for this is the fact that legislative elections in Virginia occur in the off year, that is, when no federal races are on the ballot. Louisiana, Mississippi, and New Jersey also conduct legislative elections in odd-numbered years. House campaigns in the three states raised $20 million, $8 million, and $19 million respectively in 2019. Louisiana imposes limits on individual contributions but none for political parties; Mississippi had no campaign finance limits for state legislative races; New Jersey has strict limits for individuals and organizations. A caution: each state system is different and while there may be caps on individual contributions, contributions to state races from PACs or political parties may be unlimited. Kentucky, for example, imposes a $2,000 per individual limitation, but there are no limits for parties, PACs, corporations, or unions. See National Conference of State Legislatures (NCSL), "State Limits on Contributions to Candidates 2019–2020 Election Cycle," updated

June 2019, https://www.ncsl.org/Portals/1/Documents/Elections/Contribution-Limits -to-Candidates-2019-2020.pdf?ver=2019-10-02-132802-117 (accessed June 4, 2021).

29. Peter Galuszka, "Virginia Is for Lovers of Lax Ethics and Anything-goes Politics," *Washington Post*, November 1, 2013, https://www.washingtonpost.com /opinions/virginia-is-for-lovers-of-lax-ethics-and-anything-goes-politics/2013/11/01 /757e86ce-40e6-11e3-a751-f032898f2dbc_story.html (accessed June 4, 2021).

30. VPAP reported contributions by "Dominion Energy to Virginia State Legislative Candidates in 2016–2017," as $569,962, at *VPAP.org*, https://www.vpap.org/donors /120206-dominion-energy/?start_year=2016&end_year=2017&recip_type=leg_ cands (accessed June 4, 2021); and to party legislative caucuses and legislative leadership committees in 2016–2017. VPAP, "Dominion Energy to Statewide Candidates 2016–2017," also gave $180,295 to candidates for the three statewide offices, at *VPAP.org*, https://www.vpap.org/donors/120206-dominion-energy/?start_year=2016 &end_year=2017&recip_type=statewide_cands (accessed June 4, 2021).

31. lowkell, "Final 2019 Data Show Enormous Amounts of $$$ Poured into Virginia General Assembly Races," *Blue Virginia Blog*, January 19, 2020, https: //bluevirginia.us/2020/01/final-2019-data-show-enormous-amounts-of-poured-in-to -virginia-general-assembly-races (accessed June 4, 2021). This does not include contributions made by "Clean Virginia," the PAC operated by Bills.

32. VPAP reported contributions by the "Va League of Conservation Voters to State Candidates in 2016–2017," *VPAP.org*, https://www.vpap.org/donors/148192-va -league-of-conservation-voters/?start_year=2016&end_year=2017&recip_type=all _state_cands (accessed June 4, 2021). The Virginia League of Conservation Voters (LCV) contributed most of this to the Democratic candidates for statewide offices ($2,767,236 to the Northam gubernatorial campaign, $157,308 to Mark Herring's re-election campaign for Attorney General, and $146,808 to Justin Fairfax for Lieutenant Governor), with the remaining $122,618 supporting House of Delegates candidates.

33. VPAP, "Va Uranium to All Candidates and Committees, All Years," *VPAP. org*, https://www.vpap.org/donors/148831-va-uranium/?start_year=all&end_year=all (accessed June 4, 2021).

34. VPAP, "Donations from Retail, Services to All Candidates and Committees, 2020–2021," *VPAP.org*, https://www.vpap.org/money/donors-industry-totals/3/?recip _type=all&year=2020 (accessed June 4, 2021).

35. Daniel Berti, "'Clean Virginia' Backs Candidates Ditching Dominion," *Prince William Times*, August 1, 2019, https://www.princewilliamtimes.com/news/clean -virginia-backs-candidates-ditching-dominion/article_729c6fca-b476-11e9-acd7 -93f2701380b4.html (accessed June 4, 2021). Michael Bills is not shy about his approach, stating in an interview that "If I can invest in the single millions of dollars to get (that back)—as an investor, that's really good" (quoted in Ned Oliver, "A Multi -millionaire Set Out to Counter Dominion. Now He's the State's Biggest Campaign Donor," *Virginia Mercury*, October 21, 2019, https://www.virginiamercury.com/2019 /10/21/a-multi-millionaire-set-out-to-counter-dominion-now-hes-the-states-biggest -campaign-donor/ [accessed June 4, 2021]).

36. VPAP reported contributions of $254,616, "Clean Virginia Fund to All Candidates and Committees, 2019," *VPAP.org*, https://www.vpap.org/donors/322501 -clean-virginia-fund/?start_year=2019&end_year=2019 (accessed June 4, 2021).

37. Virginia Public Access Project (VPAP), reported contributions to state-level candidates at "Clean Virginia Fund, 2020–2021," *VPAP.org*, https://www.vpap.org /donors/322501-clean-virginia-fund/?start_year=2020&end_year=2021&recip_type =all (accessed June 9, 2021). See also VAPA, "S Sonjia Smith, 2020–2021," *VAPA. org*, https://www.vpap.org/donors/3320-s-sonjia-smith/?start_year=2020&end_year =2021&recip_type=all (accessed June 9, 2021).

38. Brandon Jarvis, "Clean Virginia plans to spend $125K against Ayala after Dominion Donation," *Virginia Scope*, June 2, 2021, https://www.virginiascope. com/clean-virginia-plans-to-spend-125k-against-ayala-after-dominion-donation/ (accessed June 9, 2021).

39. Virginia Public Access Project (VPAP) reported contributions to "Taeb for Senate, All Receipts, All Years/All Filing Periods," 2019, *VPAP.org*, https://www. vpap.org/committees/325331/top_donors/ (accessed June 4, 2021).

40. In one of her more incendiary comments, Amanda Chase called upon President Donald J. Trump to declare "martial law" in order to upend Joe Biden's election to be President. "He [Biden] is not my President and never will be," she wrote, "The American people aren't fools. We know you cheated to win, and we'll never accept these results. Fair elections we can accept but cheating to win; never. It's not over yet. So thankful President Trump has a backbone and refuses to concede. President Trump should declare martial law as recommended by General Flynn." Quoted in Laura Vozzella, "Republican Contender for Va. Governor says Trump Should Declare Martial Law,'" *Washington Post*, December 15, 2020, https://www.washingtonpost. com/local/virginia-politics/chase-trump-martial-law/2020/12/15/95ca99a4-3ee5 -11eb-9453-fc36ba051781_story.html (accessed June 4, 2021).

41. Erik Ortiz, "Virginia GOP Calls Own Lawmaker's Comments on Confederate Statues 'idiotic,'" *NBC News*, June 5, 2020, https://www.nbcnews.com/news/ us-news/virginia-gop-calls-own-lawmaker-s-comments-confederate-statues-idiotic -n1225806 (accessed June 4, 2021).

42. Gregory S. Schneider, "Virginia Senator Who Called U.S. Capitol Rioters 'Patriots' Is Censured," *Washington Post*, January 27, 2021, https://www. washingtonpost.com/local/virginia-politics/amanda-chase-virginia-censure/2021/01 /27/b126bf46-60cf-11eb-9061-07abcc1f9229_story.html

43. Blue Virginia, "Time to Clean Up 'Clean Virginia?'" *Blue Virginia Blog*, July 25, 2020, https://bluevirginia.us/2020/07/time-to-clean-up-clean-virginia (accessed June 4, 2021).

44. Through March 31, 2021, Sonjia Smith had given $30,000 to Luke Torian's opponent. See Virginia Public Access Project (VPAP), "House: General Elections, November 2, 2021," *VAPA.org*, https://www.vpap.org/elections/house/candidates/ general/ (accessed June 4, 2021).

45. Virginia Public Access Project (VPAP), "Clark for Delegate—Nadarius, Since 2021" *VAPA.org*, https://www.vpap.org/committees/370874/clark-for-delegate -nadarius/ (accessed June 9, 2021).

46. Virginia Public Access Project (VPAP), "Montgomery for Delegate—Pamela, All Years / All Filing Periods," *VAPA.org*, https://www.vpap.org/committees/369935/top_donors/ (accessed June 9, 2021).

47. Virginia Public Access Project (VPAP), "Top Donors, 2020–21," *VPAP.org*, https://www.vpap.org/money/top-donors/ (accessed June 4, 2021).

48. Thomas, *Virginia Way*, 48.

49. Saslaw's opponent, while assailing large campaign contributions, nonetheless accepted $50,000 from Sonjia Smith, the spouse of Michael Bills. VPAP reported campaign contributions "Taeb for Senate, 2016–2019," *VPAP.org*, https://www.vpap.org/committees/325331/top_donors/?contrib_type=A&start_year=2016&end_year=2019 (accessed June 4, 2021). By contrast, in the twelve months prior to the 2019 primary, Dominion contributed $ 35,000 to the Senator, see VPAP, "Dick Saslaw, 2018–2019," *VPAP.org*, https://www.vpap.org/candidates/47/donor/120206/?start_year=2018&end_year=2019&contrib_type=all (accessed June 4, 2021).

50. Donation amounts are available from the VPAP at the "House Democratic Caucus," *VPAP.org*, https://www.vpap.org/committees/147803/top_donors/ (accessed June 4, 2021); and "House Republican Campaign Committee," *VPAP.org*, https://www.vpap.org/committees/148483/top_donors/ (accessed June 4, 2021), pages, using the VPAP, "top donors" filter and searching by date ranges.

51. VPAP, "Dominion Energy in 2020–2021," *VPAP.org*, https://www.vpap.org/donors/120206-dominion-energy/?start_year=2020&end_year=2021&recip_type=all (accessed June 4, 2021).

52. Dave Ress, "The Virginia Way. Part-time Legislature with Full-time Rewards," *Daily Press*, November 18, 2014, https://www.dailypress.com/news/politics/dp-nws-virginiaway-overview-20141116-story.html (accessed June 4, 2021). Ress's piece was part of a five-month investigation into the so-called Virginia Way, part of which focused on the role of money in the legislature. It concluded that legislators, though officially paid as part-timers, have access to substantial additional sources of income, coming in the form of allowances, gifts, fringe benefits, and campaign funds. Moreover, they are required to provide only the most minimal accounting for how they use that money. The piece was written prior to the ethics reforms enacted in 2015. Those reforms did not make fundamental changes in the reporting requirements.

53. Ben Paviour, "Fundraising Doesn't Stop During Virginia's Special Session," *VPM*, August 30, 2020, https://vpm.org/news/articles/16134/fundraising-doesnt-stop-during-virginias-special-session (accessed June 4, 2021).

54. Gentry Locke Attorneys, "State of Play," July 1, 2020 (presentation), https://www.gentrylocke.com/wp-content/uploads/2020/07/Q2-State-of-Play.pdf (accessed June 4, 2021).

55. Bradley Jones, "Most Americans Want to Limit Campaign Spending, Say Big Donors Have Greater Political Influence," *Pew Research Center*, May 8, 2018, https://www.pewresearch.org/fact-tank/2018/05/08/most-americans-want-to-limit-campaign-spending-say-big-donors-have-greater-political-influence/ (accessed June 4, 2021); and Frank Newport, "The Presidential Campaign, Policy Issues and the Public," *Gallop*, December 11, 2019, https://news.gallup.com/opinion/polling-matters/269717/presidential-campaign-policy-issues-public.aspx (accessed June 4, 2021).

56. Pew Research Center, "As Economic Concerns Recede, Environmental Protection Rises on the Public's Policy Agenda," February 13, 2020, https://www.people-press.org/2020/02/13/as-economic-concerns-recede-environmental -protection-rises-on-the-publics-policy-agenda/ (accessed June 4, 2021).

57. National Conference on State Legislatures (NCSL), "Public Financing of Campaigns: Overview," February 8, 2019, https://www.ncsl.org/research/ elections-and-campaigns/public-financing-of-campaigns-overview.aspx (accessed June 4, 2021).

Chapter 7

Governors Come and Go

I'm a former governor, and so I was the chief executive, and when the legislature wasn't in session, I was running the state.

—Former Indiana Governor Evan Bayh[1]

Most of us remember learning about the separation of powers in third grade civics. We were taught that there are three co-equal branches—the executive, legislative, and judiciary—and they all act to check and balance the powers of the other. Or so we thought! Personal experience suggests that legislators believe this is false, particularly in Virginia, where governors cannot serve consecutive terms and lawmakers can serve for decades. Two phrases are frequently heard around the Capitol. First, "Governors come and go; the legislature is forever." And second: "The Governor proposes; the legislature disposes."

Governors, of course, do not agree with this assertion of legislative primacy. And, in most states, the legislators are actually the people who "come and go." Only four states—California, Michigan, New York, and Pennsylvania—have legislatures that are considered "full-time" and meet almost continuously during the year.[2] In Virginia, like most other states, the legislature convenes for limited periods. Our Constitution sets a sixty-day session one year followed by a thirty-day conclave in the next.[3] This cedes the political stage to the Governor for the balance of the year.

Most governors understand their role within our system of checks and balances. In some cases, they will attempt to expand their influence for power alone, hopefully not to be slapped down by the courts or the legislature. In other instances, they seek additional control because they feel circumstances demand it. This was clearly evident during the pandemic when governors across the country not only issued numerous executive orders but took control of managing the crisis. Legislatures were only consulted when appropriations were required or statutory changes necessary.

Virginia governors have immense powers, even when the legislature is controlled by the opposing party. They propose budgets, thereby setting the financial parameters within which policy is enacted. They have the power of the "line-item veto," where they can make changes in bills, including the budget, and send the measures back to the legislature to force another vote. While the legislature is out of session, they can make interim judicial appointments to state appellate courts and to the State Corporation Commission. They can call the legislature back into what are called "special sessions" at any time for most any reason, much like Governor Ralph S. Northam did in 2019 to address gun violence. They largely control the leadership of executive branch departments, thereby influencing the implementation of policy during their terms. And, as we have seen in the responses to the pandemic, their ability to issue executive orders, especially those of an emergency nature, are extensive.

Beyond Executive Orders, one of the best examples of executive power is found in the Governor's use of the veto. Some governors have not been shy about the use of their veto pen. Though his party controlled the legislature for much of his term, Governor Jim Gilmore vetoed ninety bills over his four years. By contrast, Governors Mark Warner, Tim Kaine, and Bob McDonnell used the power more sparingly, with the three of them totaling fewer vetoes than Gilmore alone. For a variety of reasons, Governor Terry McAuliffe, who served from January 2014 to January 2018 as the 72nd Governor of Virginia, shattered the modern record for vetoes during a term, imposing his poison pen on 120 measures.

McAuliffe came to revel in his use of the veto. I distinctly remember one late evening in April 2016, as I sat with the Governor and several members of his cabinet at the Executive Mansion, celebrating the end of what is referred to in Virginia as "the reconvened" or "veto" session. This day is typically a long day when the General Assembly returns to Richmond to consider the Governors recommendations to thousands of bills passed during the previous months. We were all exhausted. McAuliffe leaned back in his chair, cigar in one hand and a scotch in the other. He was feeling good; all of his vetoes had been sustained and many of his budgetary and legislative recommendations had been accepted.[4] "I told them (the Republicans)," he explained, "I would veto any bill that compromised women's rights, reduced civil rights, or expanded gun rights; they passed them anyway and we did what we said we would do. I said I would be a brick wall against these things, and I was." Each one of McAuliffe's record-setting number of vetoes during his term was sustained by the legislature.

With the exception of the ability to present a budget and take executive actions, the annual veto session is one day where the Virginia Governor clearly dominates the legislative branch. In Virginia, the Assembly must muster votes of two-thirds of the members in each Body to override a veto.[5] In addition, the governor's use of what is sometimes called "the line-item veto" provides the ability to modify all or part of an adopted bill and resubmit it to the legislature.[6] Veto session is also the day when the minority, if the governor is from the same party, can enjoy some modicum of power.

The COVID-19 crisis illustrated the broad executive emergency powers enjoyed by governors. It is said that nothing concentrates political power in the executive branch more than a crisis, and we witnessed such a concentration during the pandemic in 2020.

The crisis altered the dynamic between the legislature and the executive, at least in the short term. In Virginia, the General Assembly was just adjourning its regular session as the pandemic hit in early March, and, with the exception of its return to Richmond that summer for a special session, played almost no role in confronting the pandemic. Governor Northam, who tends to have a collaborative governing style, did not flinch when he concluded that emergency powers were needed to combat the virus. On March 12, before the Commonwealth had reported even one death from COVID, Northam declared a "state of emergency."[7] Shortly thereafter, he closed the schools. Once executive powers were invoked, he generally continued them in place, modifying them as conditions suggested. The Governor was even able to beat back an effort to limit his executive orders to no more than thirty days without legislative approval, the measure having passed the Senate but failing in the House.[8]

Northam's approach to legislators during the crisis was not unlike his contemporaries in other states; the Governor provided information to the legislature about what he was doing rather than actively seeking their advice. His advisors were drawn from the executive agencies and not from the legislature. Republicans were especially ignored, and many did not like it. But it was the situation in which most lawmakers nationwide found themselves; the executive branch had the power to act during an emergency, and that power was being used.

Although governors in Virginia have broad executive powers, their use of them can occasionally backfire. In 2009, Kaine, both to save money and draw the public's attention to the shortfall in transportation funding, used his powers and control of the Commonwealth Transportation Board (CTB) to close nineteen of state-operated rest areas on interstates. The public rebelled; it became a campaign issue, and the next governor, McDonnell, made a point of reopening the areas immediately upon taking office. Similarly, McAuliffe issued an executive order in 2016 restoring the voting rights of all felons who had served their sentences. State Republicans sued, claiming that he did not have such broad authority to issue a blanket restoration. While the Republicans initially prevailed in the Supreme Court of Virginia, McAuliffe eventually won that battle by signing each restoration individually. Both Governors McDonnell and McAuliffe made these decisions for very good reasons; nonetheless, they serve as examples of how their powers are not unfettered.

Over the last two decades, Virginia has seen a succession of high-profile governors, two of whom eventually became U.S. Senators and several of whom have considered a run for the national office, including the presidency. In fact, one of the jokes around Richmond is that as soon as a new Virginia Governor is sworn in, he has visions of walking down Pennsylvania Avenue. Doug Wilder launched a presidential campaign during his stint as Governor. George Allen was considered a strong contender until his infamous "macaca moment" led to his defeat for re-election to the U.S. Senate in 2006.[9] Jim Gilmore became a candidate for the top spot twice, in 2008 and in 2016.[10] Current U.S. Senator Mark Warner flirted with running after having completed a very successful gubernatorial term from 2002 to 2006, during which he was able to convince the Republican-controlled legislature to support a major tax increase in 2004. Kaine was chosen as Hillary Clinton's running mate in 2016 after being one of Barack Obama's three finalists for Vice President while Kaine was still Governor in 2008. McDonnell was touted as a candidate for national office until the Jonnie Williams scandal ended his national hopes. And McAuliffe considered a presidential run in 2020. Recent Virginia Governors have clearly captured the national limelight.

I was elected to the House of Delegates in the year Tim Kaine was chosen as the Commonwealth's 70th Governor. Kaine succeeded Warner and served as Lieutenant Governor during Warner's term. Kaine and I had a lot in common. We were both Catholics, both lawyers, both former Mayors. He was arguably the most liberal person ever elected Governor in Virginia to that date, but he was not an ideologue and had a way of speaking that was both engaging and nonthreatening. He radiated compassion, perhaps a holdover from his Catholic upbringing and his stint working with missionaries in Honduras. Of all the Governors with whom I have served, he was the most adept at taking the concerns he heard from the people he met on the stump and weaving them into public comments he made to audiences minutes later.

His run for Vice President in 2016 never revealed to the Nation the Tim Kaine that we know in Virginia. He was often asked to take on the role of *attack dog*, not really his forte. He would have made a terrific Vice President (and even President). His governorship was marked by the Virginia Tech tragedy, where his compassion was on full display; a budgetary crisis of dimensions not experienced since the 1930s; and the challenge of dealing with Republican majorities in the Virginia House and Senate. He served with a Republican Lieutenant Governor and Attorney General. Despite the forces aligned against him, Kaine's term saw the permanent conservation of 400,000 acres of Virginia forests and farmland,[11] cessation of smoking in public places,[12] and increases in transportation funding not seen for the prior two decades. During his tenure, the Commonwealth was named "best-managed state," "best state for business," and "best state in which to raise a child."[13] Now a U.S. Senator, Kaine projects the voice of reason during times of chaos.

Kaine took office at a time when Republicans, still smarting from the feeling that they had fueled Warner's political success and popularity with Virginia voters, were not inclined to help a new Democratic Governor. Kaine made proposals to expand Pre-K opportunities and address transportation woes, but they fell victim to a combination of Republican intransigence and the lack of money. Kaine's tenure demonstrated how important a thriving economy is to policy success. When money is available, government can fund initiatives that residents both desire and need. The Great Recession of 2008–2009 and its accompanying shortfall in revenues forced Kaine to make major cuts in state spending to meet Virginia's constitutional requirement of a balanced budget. While he was able to limit the impact of budget cuts on education and social services, effective budget cutting was not the legacy that he desired or deserved.

One of the Governor's finest moments occurred in 2007, in the hours and days immediately following the mass shooting at Virginia Tech, which took the lives of thirty-two persons. When the shooter, Seung-Hui Cho, entered Norris Hall at the Blacksburg campus early on the morning of April 16, 2007, Kaine was halfway around the world, just having landed in Tokyo to commence a major two-week long trade mission in Asia. The trip had been planned for months and the stakes were high for the new Governor, as he was attempting to create new opportunities for the Commonwealth.

It was the middle of the night in Japan when Kaine was roused from sleep and given the news. He barely hesitated; he had to return immediately to Virginia, and dispatched his staff to locate a plane, not the easiest of tasks. In a gesture of bipartisan spirit appropriate to the moment, President George W. Bush offered to the Governor and his wife Anne Holton the opportunity to fly together to Blacksburg on Air Force One to comfort the grieving Virginia Tech community. At the memorial service held the day after the shooting, Kaine gave one of his most moving speeches, urging us "in our despair" to "not let go of that spirit of community that makes Virginia Tech such a special place."[14]

Kaine had a way of connecting with people with different points of view and incorporating their concerns into words that were nonthreatening.[15] He left the Governorship with a strong approval rating, which ultimately translated into his being elected to multiple terms in the U.S. Senate.

Kaine's popularity, however, did not transfer to the next Democratic candidate for governor. Instead, Republican Attorney General Robert F. "Bob"

McDonnell took advantage of the weak economy and backlash against President Obama and won the governorship in 2009. Coming into office with a substantial wind at his back and majorities in both the Virginia House and Senate, McDonnell was able to pursue the economic agenda on which he had campaigned. He invested in higher education, and engineered passage of the Top Jobs Act in 2011, a measure designed to increase college degrees and build more talent in the Commonwealth. He was a rising star who appeared to enjoy the national stage, giving the response to President Obama's State of the Union address in 2010 and becoming Chair of the Republican Governors Association.[16] Although any hopes he might have for national office were dashed by the ethics scandal at the end of his term, McDonnell won a major victory in 2013 when his proposal led to the first major new funding for transportation in the Commonwealth since 1986 and the administration of Governor Gerald Baliles.

Like several of the governors who preceded him, McDonnell promised the electorate that he would do something about the state's transportation challenges. But he had a problem; everyone knew that a solution required more money, and the Governor and his allies in the General Assembly were averse to raising taxes or fees. For years, the Republicans proposed taking monies from the so-called general fund of the state's budget, so named because it was that portion of the budget funded by sales, income, and other general state taxes, and was used mainly to fund education, public safety, health care, and other basic services of government. In contrast, transportation was primarily funded through the state's Transportation Trust Fund, into which revenues from the state's gas tax and federal transfers were deposited. These dollars were supposed to be used solely for transportation and remain separate from the general fund. Democrats and a key group of Republicans in the Virginia Senate resisted transferring monies from the general fund to the transportation fund on the theory that users should pay for using the transportation network, and the state should not transfer funds that traditionally covered schools, police, social services, and parks to pay to build roads. As transportation revenues languished, though, pressure increased to find a solution.

McDonnell wanted something done. He had been pushing House Speaker William J. Howell and House Republicans to "lead on this" since McDonnell's time as Attorney General, but his legislative colleagues had little appetite for any program that raised taxes. Finally, he said to Howell in 2013, "I am not leaving here until you fix this,"[17] and convinced the Speaker to carry his transportation bill. Most governors want to leave a legacy, and McDonnell was no exception.

The 2013 transportation bill breathed life into the phrase that "governors propose, but the legislature disposes." The Governor's original proposal was largely *smoke and mirrors* and provided little additional money to address the problems. But since the measure raised some revenue, an anathema to certain Republicans, everyone knew the Governor would need Democrats to pass his bill. With this came some leverage which, as leader, I hoped to exploit. In hopes of obtaining a better bill, I encouraged Democrats to threaten a "no" vote unless it was dramatically improved. If the proposal was defeated, the Governor would then be forced to send us a better one. When McDonnell learned about my efforts to scuttle his initiative, he called and forcefully told me that he did not appreciate my efforts. Some Republicans, including House Appropriations Chair Chris Jones, also opposed the initial measure, believing correctly that it would provide little money for new construction. Though his opposition was largely behind the scenes, he too was told that his concerns were not appreciated.

The Speaker wanted a bill, and he was able to recruit enough delegates (including several Democrats) to pass it out of the House. But then things began to change. Once in the Senate, McDonnell's measure was hijacked by several members of his own party, who revised it substantially to include major new transportation taxes and funding. The altered plan would increase gas taxes while allowing Northern Virginia (NoVa) and Hampton Roads to impose new regional taxes that would help regional needs. Since the altered measure now raised taxes, a majority of the House Republicans would not support it when it returned to our chamber. Delegate Tim Hugo, one of the original patrons, even withdrew support for the bill. Consequently, the only way it would pass was for Democrats to support it. While a Republican bill, the revised measure included significant new revenue. Democrats were "all in."

Once the bill got to the legislative conference committee to work out final details, the package totaled several billion dollars. At this point in the process, the Governor offered his assistance. The response of the conferees was "Thanks a lot Governor, but we've got this covered." Here was a case where the minority truly made the difference. Without the votes of Democrats, the measure would have failed; a majority of House Republicans actually voted "no." But with our support, it passed, and McDonnell was able to claim victory, again proving the adage "You can get a lot done if you do not care who gets the credit." Beyond that, this was another illustration of how a bill can end up substantially different from what it looks like at its introduction.

The transportation funding package was one of McDonnell's major accomplishments during his term. Soon, however, the credit he received collapsed under the weight of the Jonnie Williams ethics scandal. The 2013 transportation bill provides a classic example how the actions of some players in the system—in this case, the legislature—can fundamentally alter the plans of another—in this case, the Governor.

Another of the big issues during McDonnell's term involved his efforts to privatize the state-owned liquor operation known as the Virginia Alcohol Beverage Commission (ABC).[18] He proposed to sell the operation to the private sector and direct the funds to transportation infrastructure. As we are fond of saying in Richmond, his initiative quickly "caught a fever" as it mobilized a number of detractors. Members of both parties thought that privatization would lead to an increase in alcohol consumption, a loss of state revenue, and a rise in liquor prices. The privatization bill had so many problems that the Governor found it difficult to get a Republican to introduce the measure.

At the last minute, Democratic Delegate Robert Brink of Arlington thought he would have some fun by introducing the bill himself. Brink, known for a wicked sense of humor, did not support McDonnell's proposal but thought introducing it would make things uncomfortable for Republicans in the General Assembly who would be caught between loyalty to the Governor and opposition to privatization. The bill's prospects were not enhanced when budget writers reported that the ABC generates substantial monies that flow into the state's general fund, where they are used for education and other priorities. To privatize the operation would effectively transfer money from education to transportation, not a very popular political position. In addition, legislators worried that losing control of the operation could create problems in local communities, where the specter of having a liquor store on every corner was a serious concern. Finally, there has always been a strong antiliquor consumption element in Virginia politics, especially among conservatives who dominated the Republican Caucuses in the General Assembly. It did not sit well with legislators of this ilk that McDonnell's plan could make it easier to get booze.

As Brink tells the story, Speaker Howell came to him after the bill was introduced to ask if Chris Jones, the Chairman of the General Laws Committee where the bill had been sent, had called to schedule the bill for a hearing. Brink responded, "no, Mr. Speaker, no one has called to schedule a hearing." The Speaker's response was short and sweet; "Good!" he said.[19] McDonnell's bill died in the General Assembly without a vote or even a hearing.[20] In 2019, the ABC, now reorganized into the Virginia Alcohol Beverage Control Authority, had sales in excess of $1 billion and had generated almost $500 million for the state budget.[21] When it comes to state policymaking, governors can propose major initiatives, but they generally needs the support of the legislature to make the initiatives a reality.

Finally, the McDonnell years brought major efforts by Republicans to enact major new prohibitions on abortion, including one which would require women to undergo an invasive procedure before an abortion known as a "transvaginal ultrasound." McDonnell supported the legislation until it became the subject of national controversy and derision. He and his allies were forced to modify the bill, but McDonnell found ways to add administrative hurdles to access to reproductive health services. This focus tended to obscure other elements of his legacy, particularly his actions to restore voting rights to felons, his initiative to increase adoptions, and his quiet efforts at racial reconciliation.

Virginia's next governor, Terry McAuliffe, was boisterous, optimistic, and had a million ideas about how he could make Virginia better. Many also believed that his service would eventually help launch a presidential candidacy. By early 2020, he had concluded that Joe Biden was in a better position to defeat President Donald J. Trump. Instead, McAuliffe decided to seek a second, nonconsecutive term as Governor in 2021, something permitted by the Virginia constitution.

McAuliffe and I enjoyed an immediate connection. The Governor grew up one mile from me in Syracuse. Because we were both "boys from Syracuse," we had things in common from the beginning; we were both former Catholic altar boys and grew up in large families in immigrant communities. In talking one day, the Governor told me how he used to rent all of his tuxedos while in Syracuse from "Toscano's Formal Wear," my family's business. We convinced ourselves that I had actually measured the Governor for his high school prom tuxedo and began to work the story into campaign events, which usually ended with my quip about how I had "sized him up years ago."

His philosophy of governing was clear from his frequently heard assertion, "Sleep when you die." McAuliffe was energy personified, and his "tell it like it is" attitude occasionally irritated the Republicans in the House and Senate. But he believed that he only had four years to make his mark, not knowing at the time that he would again seek the office in 2021.

The Governor and his allies worked hard during those years on a wide variety of issues, the most important of which was Medicaid expansion. Although this goal was not accomplished until he left office, the Governor was adept at bringing more economic activity to the state, and he frequently produced data to show he had brought more capital investment and jobs to Virginia than any governor in history.[22] He reveled in his frequent celebration of that fact, if only to put the lie to the Republican talking point that Democrats were antibusiness. And McAuliffe was not shy about wielding his veto pen, usually on socially conservative measures such antiabortion and progun bills. During his term, none of his record number of 120 vetoes was ever overridden, not a small feat since we had to hold every single Democratic vote in the House to maintain that record.[23]

During the McAuliffe administration, I truly came to understand the importance of "being in the room at the time." Even as we were in the minority in the House, I was in the middle of countless policy and strategy discussions, from weekly breakfast meetings at the Governor's mansion to late-night sessions, occasionally with cigars and bourbon. It is during these meetings that you come to understand the role that personalities play in accomplishing things. McAuliffe was the ultimate *larger than life* personality. He was clear about what he wanted and would do all he could within the rules to accomplish his goals. He was not afraid to do things differently than they traditionally had been done in Virginia. He empowered his staff, and they worked long hours to deliver.

One major initiative of the McAuliffe term involved his efforts to restore civil rights to felons who had served their time. Virginia had one of the worst records in this area in the country; it remains one of only four states with a constitution that disenfranchises citizens with past felony convictions, and only allows restoration upon gubernatorial approval. McAuliffe boldly stated this was unfair and unjust, and, in an executive order issued in April 2016, dispensed with the case-by-case restoration approach embraced by previous Governors. Instead, the Governor's issued an Executive Order that immediately restored voting rights to all Virginians with felony convictions who, as of that date, had completed the terms of their incarceration and any period of supervised release, even if they had not applied for restoration.

State Republicans were outraged that McAuliffe would provide a blanket restoration. Although Governor McDonnell had made his own efforts to streamline the process during his term, some Republicans remained opposed to the concept of restoring civil rights to felons in the first place. They filed a lawsuit challenging McAuliffe's Order. Even some Democrats questioned the Governor's action, arguing that it was "not the way we typically do things in Virginia," and suggesting that this could turn some suburban voters against the Democrats. That was not my view. In defending his actions, McAuliffe provided Virginians with a history lesson. He discussed how felony disenfranchisement had its origins in the state's Constitution of 1902 and its racially discriminatory provisions. McAuliffe would frequently quote former State Senator Carter Glass, Jr., one of the architects of the 1902 Constitution, who said that the felon disenfranchisement provisions would "eliminate the darkey as a political factor in this State" and ensure "the complete supremacy of the white race in the affairs of government."[24]

In July 2016, the Virginia Supreme Court, in a ruling that surprised many, invalidated the blanket executive order restoring voting rights to over 200,000 citizens, holding that while the Governor had the authority to restore rights, the "tradition" was to do it "case-by-case."[25] With the court's ruling, McAuliffe could easily have said that he tried, and then moved on. But that was not his personality. Not to be denied, McAuliffe simply decided to sign individual orders to restore the rights of every single person who qualified for restoration, even if they had not yet made an application to the state. By the end of his term, he had restored voting rights to over 173,000.[26]

In this instance, personalities made the difference in effecting policy. McAuliffe felt very strongly about this change, would do all he could to effectuate it, and had the fortitude to follow it through even in the face of the numerous barriers thrown in his way. He frequently asserted that this was his proudest moment during his term as Governor. It further shows the powers of governors. McAuliffe had an idea; he wanted to make it easier for people who had served their sentences to have their rights restored. From that idea sprung a political plan to implement his proposed change. And he was in the position to make it happen.

McAuliffe's term reinforced the idea that governors need not always have the support of the legislature to make change. When it comes to job creation and economic opportunity, governors are in a unique position to market their states. McAuliffe had a national rolodex of prominent business leaders and public officials to whom he promoted the Commonwealth at every turn. He was instrumental in helping recruit Amazon's new headquarters (HQ2) to the Commonwealth and in encouraging other major companies, such as Nestle, to relocate to Virginia. As he traveled the country, he continuously spoke of how "Virginia is open for business" and brought substantial investment to the state during his tenure. In his anything but understated style, he would announce every major accomplishment as "the biggest and most significant thing that ever happened in history of the Commonwealth of Virginia." And he had the facts to back his assertions. During McAuliffe's four-year term, the state's unemployment rate fell from 5.4 percent to 3.6 percent, more than 210,000 new jobs were created, and some $20 billion in private investment was generated.[27] He took every opportunity to frame socially conservative issues embraced by Republicans, particularly those opposed to LGBTQ rights, as antibusiness. In 2017, McAuliffe was named "Public Official of the Year" by Governing magazine.

McAuliffe lived in NoVa and had a style suited to the entrepreneurial gusto of that region of the state. By contrast, his successor, Ralph Northam, a pediatric neurosurgeon and former State Senator from Hampton Roads, had a totally different approach. Northam's style was low-key, folksy, and collaborative, and had the air of a country doctor about him, perhaps a holdover from his days growing up on Virginia's Eastern Shore, a peninsula far away from the hard-driving energy of the Washington suburbs. He had Republican and Democratic friends in the legislature from his days in the State Senate and his term as Lieutenant Governor. Whether it was his style, his background, or the changing politics of the state, Northam enjoyed some early success. He was able to push Medicaid expansion through the General Assembly and provide health insurance to approximately 300,000 Virginians. His actions during the redistricting special session in 2018 created more opportunities for Democrats to win future elections. In a bold move in 2019, he engineered passage of a budget initiative that restored the ability of over 600,000 persons to have a driver's license that had previously been denied to them because they had not paid or been unable to pay their court costs and fines (in part due to the difficulty to hold down jobs without being able to drive). His help in bringing the Amazon HQ2 expansion to Virginia created thousands of jobs and brought substantial tax revenue to the Commonwealth. He was able to secure an increase in the gas tax in the Interstate 81 corridor to fund improvements to the interstate highway serving the western part of the state.

Although the publication of the blackface photo in early 2019 and the subsequent political firestorm severely crippled both his popularity and his ability to raise money, it did not affect the 2019 election, and Democrats were able to regain a majority in both the Virginia House and Senate.

Using control of both houses to his advantage, Northam became one of the most consequential governors in Virginia history. The 2020 and 2021 sessions brought key legislative victories for the Governor and the Democrats, including substantial gun safety legislation, increasing the minimum wage, and a new community college initiative to improve the workforce. Northam took particular satisfaction in signing legislation to abolish the death penalty in Virginia and legalizing the recreational use of marijuana.[28] The budgetary impacts of the COVID-19 crisis derailed, at least initially, the funding for some of these new measures. But even as some initiatives were delayed, Northam's management of the state's response to the pandemic earned him high marks.

The COVID-19 crisis also revealed Northam's backbone. Despite pressure from sectors of the business community, he kept executive orders in place designed to protect public safety and refused requests to reopen establishments that could serve to further the spread of the virus. And when President Trump requested in September 2020 that Northam send Virginia National Guard troops to Washington to intimidate and disperse citizens peacefully protesting the George Floyd murder, the Governor's answer was an unequivocal "no."[29]

It had been several decades since a Democratic governor had both Bodies of the General Assembly controlled by his Party, and the policy decisions made during those two sessions were far-reaching. At the same time, however, this period raised some thorny issues involving the balance of power between the executive and legislative branches. Northam issued more executive orders than any governor in Virginia's history, and the legislature, while occasionally complaining in private, did very little to counter this assertion of power. Unlike other states, where legislators have offered many bills to limit the uses or time periods of these orders, similar proposals in the General Assembly have gotten little traction. Whether the Virginia legislature will determine that action is necessary to address the imbalance in power will be a question for future sessions.

NOTES

1. U.S. Senator Birch Evans Bayh III, "The Exit Interviews: Sen. Evan Bayh," *NBC News*, September 13, 2010, https://www.nbcnews.com/id/wbna39082626 (accessed June 4, 2021).

2. National Conference of State Legislatures (NCSL), "Full-and Part-Time Legislatures," June 14, 2017, https://www.ncsl.org/research/about-state-legislatures/full-and-part-time-legislatures.aspx (accessed June 4, 2021).

3. In my fourteen years, the "short session" was regularly continued to forty-six days. This became so routine that many were not even aware that a resolution had to be passed to extend beyond thirty days. In 2021, Republicans objected to the extension, which required a two-thirds vote to enact. The formal session went only thirty days, whereupon the Governor called a special session so the Body could finish its work.

4. During his four years, every one of Governor Terry McAuliffe's record number of vetoes were sustained.

5. Most, but not all, state Governors count on this two-thirds rule. In Alabama, Kentucky, Indiana, and Tennessee, the legislature can override a veto on by a simple majority, thereby reducing the power of the veto.

6. In Virginia, Governor's line changes need a majority to be accepted. If they are rejected, the Governor can still veto that bill.

7. Richmond Times-Dispatch Staff, "17 Coronavirus Cases in Virginia; Northam Declares State of Emergency," *Richmond Times-Dispatch*, March 12, 2020, https://richmond.com/news/virginia/17-coronavirus-cases-in-virginia-northam-declares-state-of-emergency/article_9b6a12c4-8d79-55db-99c9-21c54147fb69.html

8. Michael Martz, "At Governor's Request, House Panel Kills Bill to Limit Public Health Emergency Orders," *Richmond Times-Dispatch*, September 18, 2020, https://richmond.com/news/state-and-regional/govt-and-politics/at-governors-request-house-panel-kills-bill-to-limit-public-health-emergency-orders/article_3cf282bc-6fb2-5e77-8ecf-5bd4bd46c030.html (accessed June 4, 2021).

9. Warren Fiske, "George Allen's 'Macaca' Moment Enshrined in a Political Manual," *Virginian-Pilot*, June 16, 2007, https://www.pilotonline.com/news/article_9e13d2bd-2bf4-5c37-ad0e-5720a7020036.html (accessed June 4, 2021); David Stout, "Senator Says He Meant No Insult by Remark," *New York Times*, August 16, 2006, https://www.nytimes.com/2006/08/16/washington/16allen.html (accessed June 4, 2021).

10. Allen Cooper, "Jim Gilmore Formally Joins GOP Presidential Race," *USA Today*, July 30, 2015, https://www.usatoday.com/story/news/politics/elections/2015/07/30/jim-gilmore-presidential-announcement/30830661/ (accessed June 4, 2021).

11. Augusta Free Press Staff, "Biscuit Run Grant Pushes State Past Kaine's 400K-acre Conservation Goal," *Augusta Free Press*, January 8, 2020, https://

augustafreepress.com/to-conserve-and-protect/ (accessed June 4, 2021). This goal was so popular that subsequent Governors Bob McDonnell and Terry McAuliffe both embraced it. McDonnell failed to reach that goal and McAuliffe decided that preserving "1000 treasures" was a better way to approach preservation than focusing on acreage.

12. Mason Adams, "Ban on Smoking Heads to Kaine," *Roanoke Times*, February 19, 2009, https://roanoke.com/archive/ban-on-smoking-heads-to-kaine/article_b2375db2 -35f5-5ab2-b2ba-51a1cdf2f88e.html (accessed June 4, 2021).

13. Jacob Geiger, "Tim Kaine Says Virginia Named Best Managed State, Best for Business While He Was Governor," *PolitiFact*, April 7, 2011, https://www.politifact. com/factchecks/2011/apr/07/tim-kaine/tim-kaine-says-virginia-named-best-managed -state-b/ (accessed June 4, 2021).

14. Tim Kaine, "Transcript of Gov. Tim Kaine's Convocation Remarks," *Virginia Tech*, April 17, 2007, https://www.remembrance.vt.edu/2007/archive/kaine.html (accessed June 4, 2021).

15. Evan Osnos, "Tim Kaine's Radical Optimism," *New Yorker*, October 17, 2016, https://www.newyorker.com/magazine/2016/10/24/tim-kaines-radical-optimism (accessed June 4, 2021).

16. James Hohmann, "McDonnell Takes to National Stage," *Politico*, August 8, 2011, updated August 15, 2011, https://www.politico.com/story/2011/08/mcdonnell -takes-to-national-stage-061368 (accessed June 4, 2021).

17. Governor Robert F. McDonnell, interview by author by telephone and email, January 30, 2020.

18. The idea originated during McDonnell's campaign for governor in 2009. On September 8, 2010, McDonnell proposed this privatization plan, arguing at the time that $400–$450 million could be generated by selling off liquor stores.

19. Former Delegate Robert Brink, interview by author by telephone, August 15, 2020, November 1, 2020, and January 12, 2021.

20. Anita Kumar, "McDonnell May Abandon His Proposal to Privatize Liquor Stores," *Washington Post*, January 13, 2012, https://www.washingtonpost.com/ blogs/virginia-politics/post/mcdonnell-may-abandon-his-proposal-to-privatize-liquor -stores/2012/01/08/gIQAWMrxvP_blog.html (accessed June 4, 2021).

21. Michael Martz, "Virginia ABC Tops $1 Billion In Sales As New Authority Updates Old Monopoly; Tito's Handmade Vodka Led Sales At $42.1M," *Richmond Times-Dispatch*, August 13, 2019, https://richmond.com/news/local/government -politics/virginia-abc-tops-1-billion-in-sales-as-new-authority-updates-old-monopoly -titos-handmade/article_fa91f440-5812-5770-9b05-f2fd722ac991.html (accessed June 4, 2021). Seventeen states either control the sale of alcohol or prohibit private enterprise from competing against a state monopoly in the wholesaling and retailing of some or all categories of alcoholic beverages. Most of these states involve state control of spirits, rather than of beer and wine. After Prohibition ended in 1933, Virginia authorized retail stores to sell beer and wine, but retained direct control over the sale of hard liquor. See National Alcohol and Beverage Control Association, "Alcohol Beverage Control Jurisdictions: A Community Choice," October 2017,

https://www.nabca.org/sites/default/files/assets/publications/statecontrol__w.pdf (accessed June 4, 2021).

22. During McAuliffe's term, both the national and Virginia economies were expanding. As a result, the unemployment rate and the number of unemployed people dropped in all ninety-five of Virginia counties and thirty-eight cities. Virginia's unemployment rate declined from 5.7 percent when McAuliffe took office in January 2014 to 3.3 percent during his last full month as governor in December 2017. During the same period, the U.S. unemployment rate dropped from 7 percent to 3.9 percent. See Warren Fiske, "Terry McAuliffe Is Mostly Right About His Jobs Record," *PolitiFact* (Virginia), December 4, 2018, https://www.politifact.com/virginia/statements/2018/dec/04/terry-mcauliffe/terry-mcauliffe-mostly-right-about-his-jobs-record/ (accessed June 4, 2021). His thirty-five domestic and international marketing missions took him to more than two dozen countries on five continents. During his term, 1,091 economic development deals were closed in the state, which brought more than $19.52 billion in capital investment to the Commonwealth. His administration was also instrumental in establishing the relationship with Amazon which permitted the Commonwealth to win the competition for the corporate giant's major "HQ2" expansion in 2018. See Gregory S. Schneider, "Va.'s McAuliffe Is Leaving Office as Master Salesman, but his Legacy Will Take Years to Play Out," *Washington Post*, January 10, 2018, https://www.washingtonpost.com/local/virginia-politics/vas-mcauliffe-leaves-office-as-master-salesman-though-his-legacy-will-take-years-to-play-out/2018/01/10/6c8f1db6-f0bf-11e7-b390-a36dc3fa2842_story.html (accessed June 4, 2021).

23. Gregory S. Schneider, "McAuliffe Breaks Record for Most Vetoes by a Virginia Governor," *Washington Post*, March 23, 2017, https://www.washingtonpost.com/local/virginia-politics/mcauliffe-poised-to-set-the-record-most-vetoes-by-a-virginia-governor/2017/03/22/6141e204-0e6b-11e7-9d5a-a83e627dc120_story.html (accessed June 4, 2021).

24. Editorial Board, "Mr. McAuliffe's Political, and Principled, Move," *Washington Post*, April 23, 2016, https://www.washingtonpost.com/opinions/mr-mcauliffes-political-and-principled-move/2016/04/23/b8191284-08ca-11e6-b283-e79d81c63c1b_story.html (accessed June 4, 2021).

25. *Howell v. McAuliffe*, 292 Va. 320, 788 S.E.2d 706 (2016), https://casetext.com/case/howell-v-mcauliffe-1 (accessed June 4, 2021).

26. At the time, this was the largest number of rights restored by a Governor in U.S. history. Sam Levine, "A Record Number of Virginians Have Gotten Their Voting Rights Back, Governor Says," *Huffington Post*, April 28, 2017, https://www.huffpost.com/entry/virginia-voting-rights-restoration_n_59038c64e4b05c39767f4b6e (accessed June 4, 2021).

27. Todd Haymore, "Haymore: McAuliffe Had a Strong Economic Record as Governor," *Roanoke Times*, April 17, 2019, https://roanoke.com/opinion/commentary/haymore-mcauliffe-had-a-strong-economic-record-as-governor/article_909f7876-6464-5d75-b0a3-205d930d6275.html (accessed June 4, 2021).

28. Governor Ralph S. Northam, interview by author in person, Richmond, Virginia, June 14, 2021.

29. Aaron Davis, "How Trump Amassed a Red-state Army in the Nation's Capital—and Could Do So Again," *Washington Post*, October 1, 2020, https://www.washingtonpost.com/investigations/how-trump-amassed-a-red-state-army-in-the-nations-capital--and-could-do-so-again/2020/10/01/2f10e17c-f9d6-11ea-a275-1a2c2d36e1f1_story.html (accessed June 4, 2021).

Chapter 8

Power in the Legislature

No man's life, liberty, or property are safe while the legislature is in session.

—Mark Twain[1]

Virginia governors cannot serve two consecutive terms, but legislators can and do serve for decades, amassing power and influence in the process. During my term in the House, Delegate Lacey Putney of Bedford broke the record for length of service, logging fifty-two consecutive years, including forty-eight on the powerful Appropriations Committee and six as its Chair. But of all the players in the legislature, there is little doubt that the Speaker of the House of Delegates is the most powerful. Speakers make all committee assignments in the Body, including choosing the chairs. They decide where bills are assigned and, in some cases, whether they are heard at all. They make parliamentary rulings from the dais that can determine the fate of legislation.

Although Delegate Kirk Cox occupied the Speaker's chair for two years prior to the Democrats taking control in 2020, my time was dominated by only one Speaker, William J. "Bill" Howell. Elected to the post as a compromise candidate in 2003, following the resignation of Vance Wilkins under a cloud of scandal, Howell spent his first years trying to restore the prestige of the position. He was determined not to repeat what he perceived to be the autocratic and partisan approach of Speakers of both parties who preceded him. He embraced, for example, the principle that the minority party should be accorded proportional representation on committees. Imbued with a quick wit frequently on display at the dais, he had a way of disarming members who, in the heat of debate, came close to crossing the line of decorum and civility. Members generally liked him whether they agreed with him or not—and accorded him respect that went beyond the formal power of his position.

Howell practiced law in a refurbished log cabin just outside of Fredericksburg. Part of the initiation for new legislators involved each of them driving to the Speaker's office to introduce themselves and exchange pleasantries about their hopes and priorities. It usually involved making an ask for a committee assignment. The custom was viewed by some as quaint and by others are merely a reinforcement of the power relations between the Speaker and the new member. In fact, it was both. And it was a key introduction to the informal norms of the Body. He was establishing that there would be personal connections that transcended political party. Although much important legislation passed or failed along party lines, there would also be a personal element upon which the Speaker and members of each party could rely as circumstances required. Howell served as Speaker until his retirement in 2018, after thirty years of service in the Body.

Although Speakers shape the House in ways that can last for decades, Bill Howell rarely put his name on individual bills, preferring instead to work behind the scenes. He was instrumental in helping Governor Tim Kaine pass a smoking restriction that had few Republicans adherents until Howell weighed in. He was instrumental in promoting land preservation and conservation through expensive tax credits that would prompt wealthy landowners to place their properties under conservation easement.[2]

In my fourteen years, I remember few times where Howell sponsored bills. He once proposed to waive liability for certain corporations who had purchased asbestos companies but did not seem to be terribly upset when the measure died on the House floor. He advocated for a new state song; his proposal passed, but at the cost of the Senate's imposing its own tune, so Virginia now has two. But of all the measures where he made his policy mark, it was the 2013 transportation bill. He not only sponsored the bill but also moved forcefully for its passage.

For Howell, generally an opponent of tax increases, this bill was a huge departure from his usual approaches. But he had come to see that new revenues were necessary to address the Commonwealth's critical needs. Politically, he was concerned that a failure to address transportation would hurt Republicans in suburban districts if the General Assembly did not act to ease concerns about traffic congestion. And while the majority of his caucus ultimately opposed the measure, he corralled enough support on his side that when House Democrats delivered their thirty-four votes, the bill became law.

State legislatures are composed of people from varied backgrounds with different skills and distinctly individual personalities. Some might be referred to as "show horses," "instigators," "troublemakers," or even "bomb throwers," while others are described as "work horses," "policy wonks," "quietly effective," "persuasive advocates," or "influencers." All state legislatures have certain people who stand out and receive headlines, even if they may never pass substantial bills or have much impact on policy. They often view their role as "stirring the pot." They are frequently, though not always, extremely bright and can have oratory skills superior to others in the

Chamber. Over the years, the Virginia General Assembly has either enjoyed or endured (depending on one's perspective) the presence of a number of these. Two of the most celebrated were Delegate, and now Virginia Senator, Joe Morrissey and Delegate Bob Marshall.

Morrissey, whose nickname was "Fighting Joe," began his political career as Richmond's Commonwealth's Attorney from 1989 through 1993. He gained fame for fighting, not just for the "little guy," but for actual fisticuffs with a legal opponent. Morrissey won election to the Virginia House in November 2007, and immediately distinguished himself with his oratorical flourishes. He gained national attention in 2013 by carrying an AK-47 onto the House floor and, during a speech advocating gun restrictions, raising it over his head in dramatic fashion. It was not loaded, but "Fightin' Joe" did not volunteer that fact when he displayed it to the Body. Morrissey was smart and one of the best orators in the House. He was flamboyant, charismatic, and his constituents loved him. But he never passed a single bill of any importance while in the House, partly because he was a Democrat and partly because many of his colleagues would not work with him to achieve his goals.[3]

Morrissey resigned the House after a scandal erupted involving an under-age intern at his law office. He then unsuccessfully ran for both the Virginia Senate and for Mayor of Richmond. Several years following Morrissey's guilty plea to a charge involving the intern, they married, and now have three children. In 2019, he defeated incumbent Democratic Senator Rosalyn Dance in a primary and won the general election for the seat. It appears that he learned from his House experience, as he has had greater success as a legislator in the Senate. In 2020, for example, he passed a bill that changed a Virginia practice in existence since 1796 whereby prosecutors could force criminal defendants to be tried by a jury. This practice frequently resulted in either longer sentences upon conviction or increased pressure on defendants to accept plea agreements even if they maintained their innocence.[4]

In securing passage, Morrissey continued to revel in his pugilistic approaches, threatening to recruit a candidate to run against House Democratic Criminal Justice committee chair Mike Mullen simply because the Delegate raised questions about a bill. "You have badly underestimated me," said the Senator in a text message to the Delegate. "Good luck in your primary."[5] During debate of the issue on the Senate floor, Republican Leader Tommy Norment referred to Morrissey's tactics as "putrid," but the measure passed and was signed into law by Governor Ralph S. Northam. Mullen, like most Democrats, voted for it.

Morrissey garnered headlights preaching a liberal agenda; Bob Marshall was a perfect conservative foil, and they would frequently engage in long debates on the House floor. Marshall billed himself as the "Chief Homophobe" in the House, and there was a certain irony that he was defeated by Danica Roem, who openly acknowledged her transgender status, in the 2017 Blue Wave election.

Marshall was fond of telling the story about how he entered politics supporting the liberal Hubert H. Humphrey, then a Democratic Senator from Minnesota. But he frequently took positions to the Right of even the most conservative Republicans in the House, thereby providing some level of consternation within his own caucus. He constantly introduced legislation that made the Republican leadership squirm and was not shy about questioning the wisdom of the Speaker Howell, especially when the Delegate's parliamentary motions were ruled "out of order." Yet through sheer persistence, Marshall helped to engineer the successful legal challenge that undermined some of the transportation funding initiatives passed during Governor Kaine's administration[6] and was the force behind the so-called Marshall-Newman Amendment, a constitutional initiative that upon its passage by Virginia voters in 2006, prohibited same-sex marriage in the Commonwealth.[7] The federal court decision in *Bostic v. Schaefer*,[8] and the U.S. Supreme Court decision in *Obergefell v. Hodges*,[9] voided the Virginia action, but this did not stop Marshall from consistently railing against "gay marriage" on the House floor.

Marshall never passed many bills, but he was a frequent irritant, both to the Republican majority and to the House Democrats, especially with his ideologically motivated bills, floor amendments, and speeches outlining a far-right agenda infused with a healthy dose of conspiracy theory.[10] He did not hesitate to publicly criticize Republican Delegates for not being conservative enough. Partly because of that, members of the Republican Caucus would frequently tell the Democratic leadership how great it would be if we would defeat him. They never gave him much financial support during elections until 2017, when they intervened at the last minute in a halfhearted (and ultimately unsuccessful) effort to save him. Both Morrissey and Marshall could be personally engaging, which made it more difficult to ignore their outlier status as legislators.

The Chamber has also enjoyed a number of wonderful speakers, some of whom could determine the outcome of bills based on their oratory. One who could swing votes on the House floor, based solely on his words and the force of rational argument, was Delegate Ken Melvin from Portsmouth, who retired from the General Assembly in 2009 and then became a Circuit Court judge. Members called him "the terminator" because of his ability to defeat bills on the house floor. But he was also known as a careful legislator who could parse the criminal code like few others. Democratic House Leader Ward Armstrong was also known for his speechmaking, but being in the minority, he was rarely able to affect the outcome of a measure. And veteran legislator Delegate Ken Plum of Reston could make the liberal case as well as anyone.

Republicans had their own persuasive advocates, who could both articulate "the values thing" from their side and delve into the nuances of policy. Former Speaker M. Kirkland Cox of Chesterfield was one; he would occasionally give impassioned speeches on the floor, usually around the issue of abortion, but was also capable of dissecting the state budget and crafting policy in the area of higher education. Another was Delegate Lee Ware. Ware was a conservative in the Edmund Burkean tradition. He was erudite, thoughtful, and rarely, if ever, embraced a tax increase. He was profoundly conservative, both fiscally and socially. When Ware would rise on the House floor, Delegates on both sides of the partisan divide would listen. He believed in the positive elements of "the Virginia Way," which to him meant the ability to "disagree without being disagreeable."

Though Ware and I differed mightily on many social policies, we were both deeply skeptical of Dominion Energy and its influence on Virginia politics. Ware identified with ratepayers and believed that Dominion was constantly pushing legislation to limit the oversight of the Virginia State Corporation Commission (SCC) and therefore place more costs on consumers. Both of us were also skeptical of special tax credits given to certain industries. Ware, a strong believer in the private marketplace, felt that these credits often had the effect of picking winners and losers.[11] Moreover, once the credits were passed, their yearly costs were "baked into the budget" without any yearly review. This created financial demands on the budget each year and took away the control of the legislature to make appropriations on an annual basis.[12] Ware loved to debate ideas and would annually host dinners where conservative speakers would come to Richmond to discuss people like G. K. Chesterton and conservative Catholic thought.

Each State house also has its workhorses, who had subject matter expertise and to whom others looked for guidance. Delegate David Bulova was a solid environmentalist who understood nuance in ways most others did not. Delegate Mark Sickles became an expert on health policy as related to the budget, and members always looked to then Delegate, now Senator Jenn McClellan when education was being debated. And some committees had a much greater workload than others. The Virginia House Courts of Justice Committee was one such group, putting in long hours and frequently struggling with every comma, apostrophe, and period in a piece of legislation. House Courts has historically handled more legislation than any committee in the General Assembly, and I was appointed to the group during my first session in 2006. Most of the members were lawyers, the major exception being Vivian Watts, who herself was a force on the Committee and came to know more criminal law while serving than some defense attorneys. Committee members are proud to be successors of famous Virginians who served on this Committee, including James Madison, Patrick Henry, and the influential Chief Justice of the United States, John Marshall.

Committee members would frequently work late into the night refining legislation because they understood that the statutes passed could have an impact on whether a person would lose their liberty. In the days prior to Republican control, the Courts Committee became known for what many in the Assembly called "the night of the long knives," a special evening late in the General Assembly session when former Democratic Leader C. Richard Cranwell and members of both parties worked, often late into the night, and engaged in an equal opportunity killing spree of large numbers of bills—both Republican and Democratic—that they did not consider ready for prime time.

Of all the committees I witnessed, Virginia House Courts was perhaps the least partisan. While it was stocked with conservative *law-and-order* legislators, many of whom were former prosecutors, most were also attorneys and could appreciate the give-and-take of good legal arguments. The Committee certainly passed a wide variety of conservative measures over the years that I opposed, but it most always gave the public and opposing viewpoints a hearing. Bob McDonnell was the Chair of the Committee until he became Attorney General in 2006, after which the major forces on this Committee were his successor as Chair, Dave Albo, and Republican Delegate Rob Bell.

Albo was from Fairfax and was more moderate than Bell, whose district abutted mine in Albemarle. In his twenty-four years in the House, Albo had become known for his analytical skills, his commitment to work long hours, and his sense of humor. He was viewed as a moderate who helped engineer the defeat of some of the most conservative bills proposed by his colleagues. When Albo did not like a bill, including several antiabortion measures, he would often assign it to an ad hoc "Constitutional Law subcommittee" that he would stack with progressive Democrats and Republicans he could trust in order to kill the measure. While Chair of the House Courts of Justice Committee, he would occasionally alert Democrats to "pay attention" to bills that he supported such as extensions of the death penalty, but that he knew we would want to oppose. These small courtesies are lacking in today's political environment and testimony to Albo's collegiality. And he was not afraid to raise taxes. He strongly supported a string of transportation bills, including the 2013 measure that raised money by increasing the gas tax, an anathema to some of his Republican colleagues.

The exchanges between Albo and Bell, who became Chair after the former's retirement, were often priceless, especially when they involved the constitutional nuances of various conservative proposals. But when it came to the criminal law, their impact was immeasurable. The joke around both caucuses was that Bell wanted to put more and more people in jail for longer and longer periods, and the only thing stopping him were constraints in the budget. This was perhaps a bit harsh, but he would nonetheless push several major initiatives each year for a mandatory minimum sentence or an enhanced penalty for some offense.

The other place where Bell made his mark was in the area of mental health. In the session following the Virginia Tech shootings in 2007, Bell and I served on a committee that made major changes in how the state could provide emergency assistance to persons with mental health challenges who were risks to themselves or to others. He was on the front lines of this effort, and the committee spent countless hours reviewing bills word-by-word and reforming the mechanisms by which people could be detained if they were a danger. The work was especially difficult. The words of the new statutes needed to provide society with protections without unjustifiably restricting the rights of others. This was legislative practice at its best, detached from the partisan disputes of the day.

After a tragic attack on Senator Creigh Deeds by his son, who suffered from mental illness and was unable to secure treatment at a critical time, Bell joined with the Senator on a multiyear effort to reform mental health policy and funding in the Commonwealth. Called the "Deeds Commission on Mental Health," this initiative was created in 2014 and continued into 2021. Their work does not always receive the publicity it deserves, but it remains one of the most critical undertakings authorized by the General Assembly.

Many people see the House and Senate of each state as very similar Bodies. They are not. Each Body has its own personality and can struggle mightily with the other, even if controlled by the same party. Such was the case in Virginia during my time in office, when Republicans often controlled both Bodies. For much of this time, the Senate was viewed as more moderate and took pleasure killing some of the more outrageous measures passed by their House colleagues. In fact, a strange dynamic existed where House Republicans would pass measures that some did not think were good public policy, recognizing that they would be killed in the Senate. They could vote for bills that appealed to their base, knowing that they would never become law. After Democrats took control of both Bodies in 2020, similar dynamics occurred as Delegates and Senators would frequently differ, even if they were from the same party.

The House has always been viewed as more boisterous and colorful than the Senate, which some commentators used to describe as a group of grandparents looking for a nap. This was, of course, unfair to the Senate, whose median age has declined dramatically in the last decade, and whose character has changed as it became more partisan. In the House, however, elements of humor could find their way into the most contentious debate, in part because Speaker Howell had a quick wit and was not shy about using it. Contributing to the House atmosphere was the occasional use of colorful props. During one debate on predatory lending, Republican Delegate Glenn Oder from Newport News pulled a large stuffed-animal of a shark from his desk, named it "Sharkie," and proceeded to regale the Body about how high interest loans exploited the military and the poor. Delegate Scott Surovell, a Democrat representing Fairfax, did not like tax credits given to film companies and took the occasion to put on dark sunglasses a la the "Blues Brothers" and summons a large replica of ET to illustrate his point. Both of these delegates were known for the substantive legislation they pushed; they also enjoyed a joke.

The Senate, of course, included many persons of legislative consequence. Janet Howell ran the Senate Finance Committee with acumen and humor. Dr. Mamie Locke's calm persona concealed a commitment to Civil Rights that was unmatched in the Body. Yvonne Miller and L. Louise Lucas were powerful advocates for many issues. Scott Surovell introduced so many bills of major consequence that many wondered if he ever slept. But the most consequential senator was the Democratic Leader during much of the last two decades, Richard "Dick" Saslaw of Fairfax. Saslaw was first elected to the House in 1976, and then to the Senate four years later. He was criticized by the progressive wing of the Democratic Party later in his career as the "Senator from Dominion Energy" and for some of his views of predatory lending. But he knew much more about energy policy than many of his critics. And while not afraid to embrace reform, he was skeptical about moving too quickly and concerned that poorly crafted legislation might actually increase the utility bills of his constituents.

Saslaw could be brusque and occasionally dismissive. And he was certainly direct in explaining his views, often commencing his explanation with the words "let me tell you this . . . " One conservative talk show host took to calling him "the Godfather" because of his demeanor and his impact on the Senate. But this occasionally gruff exterior masked a love for the Commonwealth and a desire to increase the opportunities for those who lived within it. He was also a stitch, and he would tell countless stories that would prompt a smile or generate outright laughter.

One of the best stories involved gun control. Saslaw was among the strongest advocates for reasonable gun safety measures in the Assembly, often drawing criticism from gun advocates from around the state. Saslaw reports that on one day in 2007, he found himself jammed into an elevator at the General Assembly building with a group of gun lobbyists wearing camouflage and sporting large orange stickers on their chests that read "GUNS SAVE LIVES." This prompted the Senator from Fairfax to quip, in a reference to the 1972 movie about a group of friends who confront some unsavory characters during a canoe trip in rural Georgia, "I see we're debating a gun bill. Half of the cast of *Deliverance* is in town." The activists, of course, took offense, and were able to get the *Washington Post* to write about the incident.

When interviewed, Saslaw did not miss a beat, and rather than deny the remark, chose to embellish it. "How do they know I was referring to them," he said, "and not the other side? I never said anything other than we must be debating the gun bill. I never said which side" looked like they came from the movie. He maintained that all criticism stopped at that point. Saslaw has been in the middle of most every significant change in Virginia in the last three decades—from the 2013 transportation bill to Medicaid expansion in 2018 to major gun safety legislation in 2020.

The Republican side of the Senate had godfathers of their own, and one of the most prominent was Tommy Norment. Hailing from the Williamsburg / James City County area of the Commonwealth and an attorney with the prestigious law firm of Kaufmann & Canoles, Norment could deal with the best of them, and his quips alternated between insight and snark. Originally elected as a Democrat to the James City County Board of Supervisors, Norment changed parties and successfully ran for the State Senate in 1992. [13] Viewed for years as a member of the moderately conservative Republican element in the Senate, embodied in people like John Watkins and Walter Stosch, Norment's politics moved to the right as his party and his caucus colleagues became more conservative. Nonetheless, some Republicans do not consider him conservative enough; *Bearing Drift*, the self-styled "conservative voice" of Virginia Republicanism website, accused him of "massive, ego-driven hypocrisy" for his votes supporting everything from Mark Warner's tax package in 2004 to raising the minimum wage in 2020,[14] and for his friendship with Saslaw.

Norment has also been criticized for allegedly intervening in the *House* Republican primary fights in 2019 that deposed incumbents Delegates Chris Peace and Bob Thomas. These disputes were frequently not even over ideology; in Peace's case, Norment objected to the Delegate's legislation about Airbnb as well as his concerns about the Colonial Downs racetrack in the Senator's district. Over the last several years, Norment successfully beat back challenges to his own leadership, the first from former state Senator Tom Garrett in 2016 and another in 2019, after the Minority Leader proposed a minor gun safety measure. Norment's proposal enraged conservatives, prompting Bill Stanley from Franklin County to resign his position as Republican whip and causing gubernatorial hopeful Amanda Chase to bolt from the caucus altogether. Few Republican Senators shed tears about Chase's departure. As detailed in chapter 6, she managed to antagonize legislators of both parties. Two years later, Norment actively pushed Chase's censure by the Senate.

PICKING JUDGES

Virginia legislatures make their marks not just in the laws that they pass. They also leave their stamp on the judiciary. The Commonwealth is unique among the states in how it selects judges.[15] Many states choose judges by popular election. In Virginia, judges from the juvenile courts to appellate and Supreme Court are chosen exclusively by the legislature. The Governor has no role, unless a vacancy arises while the legislature is in recess. In those cases, the chief executive appoints, and the legislature considers ratifying the choice when it reconvenes. In most cases, the legislature adopts the Governor's choice. But recent events show that this is not a certainty. Legislatures love their prerogatives, and, in Virginia, judicial selection is one of them.

One reason for holding the majority in the House or Senate involves the ability to pick judges. In Virginia, judicial selection has largely been a one-party debate, replete with personal vendettas to be settled and ideological cards to be played. Until the Democrats gained control in 2020, the Republican legislative leadership generally dictated the judicial choices. They did not hide their desire to stock the judiciary with conservative, law-and-order types. Occasionally, a quiet liberal would slide into an appointment as a juvenile or general district court judge in an urban jurisdiction or Northern Virginia (NoVa), but that has been the exception rather than the rule. The reason for this is clear. At every step in the process, a person designated as a judge becomes someone who is more easily considered for the next higher position. Circuit Court judges are often chosen from juvenile and general district court judges. Court of Appeals judges are often chosen from Circuit Court judges. Supreme Court Justices are often chosen from Court of Appeals judges.

Hence, appointing judges with certain ideological predispositions creates a talent pipeline for positions where case law is established for the next generation. This is not to say these appointees are unqualified; there are many good attorneys in Virginia who are more than capable of taking the bench, and most of the appointments are taken from this group. But the focus has tended to be narrow and has been done for a purpose.

Many of these appointments do not attract much public scrutiny. For a judge to be confirmed in Virginia, they need only to receive the votes of a majority of those elected in each Chamber. While there is much infighting within and between House and Senate about prospective nominees, there is almost no debate when the recommendation reaches the floor of each Body, and rarely do opponents of a nominee vote "no." This is considered "bad form," a violation of the norms of the General Assembly. Members who oppose a nominee will instead withhold a "yes"; they will simply sit in their seat and not vote at all. Occasionally, though, the culture wars show their ugly sides in judicial selection. Two cases in point are those of Tracy Thorne-Begland and Jane Marum Roush.

Tracy Thorne-Begland joined the U.S. Navy after completing college. He distinguished himself by finishing first in his flight training class and flew A-6 Intruders out of U.S. Naval Air Station (NAS) Oceana in Virginia Beach. It was during this time that he told his Navy colleagues about his sexual orientation. Prior to his discharge in 1995, he was awarded the U.S. Navy Achievement Medal for "superb leadership, exceptional professionalism and total devotion to duty." He then entered law school, graduated in 1997, and became a prosecutor. After serving twelve years in that role, Thorne-Begland was nominated for an open seat on the General District Court of Richmond in 2012. He seemed eminently qualified and had gained the support of Delegate G. Manoli Loupassi, then an influential Richmond Republican on the judicial selection committee of House Courts of Justice. Thorne-Begland would have been the first openly gay person appointed to a judicial position in the Commonwealth. At his hearing before the committee, only three questions were asked, none of which involved his sexual orientation, and he was deemed "qualified" in a unanimous vote.

But behind the scenes, action had commenced to kill the appointment. Then Delegate Ben Cline, a member of the Courts committee and now a U.S. Congressman, had, following the hearing, notified Victoria Cobb and the Family Foundation, the most prominent social conservative advocacy group in the state, about the nomination. Arguing that Thorne-Begland would bring an "aggressive activist homosexual agenda" to the bench,[16] the Family Foundation marshaled its forces, and Thorne-Begland became the target of a vicious campaign to discredit him. Four House Delegates, who were military veterans, Rich Anderson, Scott Lingamfelter, Mark Dudenhefer, and Chris Stolle, were recruited to publicly criticize Thorne-Begland's military service. His appointment was now in jeopardy.

On the day before the House vote, Governor McDonnell, hoping to avoid more embarrassment after the "transvaginal ultrasound" debate earlier that spring, suggested that the decisions about judges should be made on the basis of qualifications, not sexual orientation. But his suggestion made no difference. When the vote was taken on May 12, 2012, Thorne-Begland received only thirty-three votes of the fifty-one he needed in the House for appointment. Particularly jarring, however, was the number of explicit "no" votes, against the typical norms in the House.[17] Despite the protestations of Senators Adam Ebbin of Alexandria and Donald McEachin of Richmond, Thorne-Begland did not even receive a vote in the Senate. Virginia once again received headlines and condemnation from across the Nation; in this case, it was for a vote to deny a qualified applicant simply because he was gay.[18]

Thorne-Begland was ultimately vindicated. Since the General Assembly had rejected the nominee and adjourned without filling the vacancy, Richmond Circuit Court judges exercised their power under the Virginia State Constitution, and, in June 2012, appointed Thorne-Begland as a temporary judge to fill the slot for which he was rejected. He served six months without controversy, and on January 15, 2013, the House of Delegates elected him to a full six-year term by a vote of sixty-six to twenty-eight. As before, many Republicans broke House tradition to cast "no" votes, but not enough to derail his appointment. The Senate followed with a vote of twenty-eight to zero, with twelve Republican senators not voting, and Thorne-Begland was appointed. As an indication of the rapid changes occurring in the Nation, when the judge came before the Body for reappointment in 2019, little controversy remained, and he was approved unanimously in the House and with only two negative votes in the Senate.

Another instance where politics triumphed over competency involved the effort to elevate the Honorable Judge Jane Marum Roush to the Virginia Supreme Court. Roush was just finishing her twenty-second year as a Circuit Court Judge in Fairfax County in April 2015 when Virginia Supreme Court Justice LeRoy F. Millette Jr. announced his retirement. Since the legislature was "in recess," Governor Terry McAuliffe was authorized under the Constitution to fill the position.[19] This would allow the Justice to begin serving immediately, even though the appointment would require approval by the General Assembly when it next reconvened.

McAuliffe and his staff conducted a several month search for a replacement for Millette. A dozen applicants were considered, and Judge Roush rose to the top of the list. She seemed like a great pick; she had presided over the DC sniper case of John Malvo and was viewed as smart and fair. As members from both parties put it in a letter to McAuliffe, Roush "is one of the premier judges in all of Virginia . . . . Judge Roush is nonpolitical, and most importantly, she knows that a judge applies, not writes, the law."[20] Among her strongest supporters was Albo, Republican Chairman of the House Courts of Justice Committee, who co-authored the letter. Believing that she would enjoy bipartisan support, McAuliffe appointed Roush, who assumed the bench at the end of July.

The judicial honeymoon was short-lived. Two days later, Speaker Howell and the Senate Majority Leader Norment announced that both Republican Caucuses would support a different nominee, an African American Court of Appeals judge named Rossie D. Alston, Jr., when the General Assembly session reconvened. McAuliffe was not pleased. And neither was Albo, who had gone out on a limb for a candidate he believed to be highly qualified. While conceding that Roush was well qualified,[21] Norment and Howell grumbled about not being sufficiently consulted prior to the appointment and sought to assert the legislative prerogative to make their own choice. This would prove to be the first time that the General Assembly had refused to approve a recess judicial appointment of a governor since 1900.[22]

To heighten the insult to McAuliffe and Roush, the Republicans stated that they would not afford the new Justice the courtesy of an interview. Saslaw and I cried foul, asserting that the Virginia Constitution "makes very plain" that the General Assembly, not the Republican Caucuses, has the duty to select jurists.[23] Using some artful parliamentary maneuvers and the defection of one Republican Senator, the Democrats in the Senate were able to deny Alston the position during an August session of the General Assembly.[24] Yet when the Body reconvened in January 2016, Republicans delivered on their promise. Roush was denied the position in favor of conservative jurist Stephen R. McCullough.[25] The public, which never much follows these judicial selection processes, read numerous stories about this assertion of partisan political power directed against a highly qualified woman. Independent of the clear right of the legislature to determine this appointment, the process appeared arbitrary and unfair, and the GOP was blamed for it.

Virginia is one of only two states where legislators choose judges; most other states involve elections of some kind. And Virginia's choices are not subject to gubernatorial veto.

The Virginia legislature likes its prerogatives, and judicial selection is among its most important. These judges often serve longer periods than many lawmakers, and their impact can be felt for decades. Hence, it is unlikely that the judicial selection process in Virginia will be altered any time soon. Legislators have occasionally considered the creation of a standing commission to recommend judges to the Assembly, but with the exception of a minor effort made by Republicans when they gained the majority in the early 2000s, these proposals have gained little traction.

NOTES

1. Mark Twain [Samuel Clemens], *Mark Twain, Selected Writings of an American Skeptic,* ed. Victor Donyo (Buffalo, NY: Prometheus Books, 1983), 253.

2. Albemarle County, a portion of which I represented, was among the counties where citizens took aggressive advantage of the credits and placed substantial acreage under easement using them.

3. An illustration of how some of his House colleagues reacted to Joe Morrissey speeches can be found in the following exchange from March 12, 2010. Morrissey could occasionally poke fun at himself and rose that day to declare the following: "Mr. Speaker . . . Would the Journal reflect that today, March 12, 2010, *I did not* make a motion of personal privilege" (emphasis in the original). Almost immediately,

Republican Bill Janis from Henrico, jumped to his feet to respond: "Mr. Speaker, I move that a thousand copies of the gentleman's speech be printed," to which Speaker Howell quipped, "I would remind the gentleman the morning hour is not over yet." Humor sometimes has a way of making a point. See Joe Morrissey and Bill Janis, quoted in Family Foundation, "Quote of the Day," March 11, 2010, https://www.familyfoundation.org/blog-posts/tag/Morrissey+Moments (accessed June 4, 2021).

4. Ned Oliver, "'A Revolutionary Change': Va. Lawmakers Vote to Reform 224-year-old Jury Sentencing Law," *Virginia Mercury*, October 17, 2020, https://www.virginiamercury.com/2020/10/17/a-revolutionary-change-va-lawmakers-vote-to-reform-224-year-old-jury-sentencing-law/ (accessed June 4, 2021).

5. Rachel Weiner and Laura Vozzella, "'Revolutionary' Criminal Sentencing Change Passes in Virginia," *Washington Post*, October 23, 2020, https://www.washingtonpost.com/local/legal-issues/sentencing-reform-virginia/2020/10/23/59ad16dc-149b-11eb-ba42-ec6a580836ed_story.html (accessed June 4, 2021).

6. Michael Laris, "Legal Challenge Launched Against New Northern Virginia Transportation Spending," *Washington Post*, August 16, 2013, https://www.washingtonpost.com/local/trafficandcommuting/legal-challenge-launched-against-new-northern-virginia-transportation-spending/2013/08/16/b17b1a48-068a-11e3-88d6-d5795fab4637_story.html (accessed June 4, 2021).

7. The amendment was approved by the voters by a 57 to 43 percent margin. See Virginia, SB 526 Constitutional Amendment [Marshall-Newman Amendment], April 17, 2006, https://leg1.state.va.us/cgi-bin/legp504.exe?061+sum+SB526 (accessed June 4, 2021).

8. *Bostic v. Schaefer,* 760 F.3d 352 (4th Cir. 2014), https://casetext.com/case/bostic-v-schaefer (accessed June 4, 2021).

9. *Obergefell v. Hodges*, 135 S. Ct. 2584 (2015), https://www.lexisnexis.com/community/casebrief/p/casebrief-obergefell-v-hodges (accessed June 4, 2021).

10. In several sessions, Marshall proposed legislation that would have a "person" to exist at conception and given "unborn children at every stage of development . . . all the rights, privileges, and immunities available to other persons, citizens, and residents of the Commonwealth." (His 2012 version was filed at Virginia, Legislative Information System (LIS), "HB 1 Unborn Children," November 21, 2011, http://leg1.state.va.us/cgi-bin/legp504.exe?121+sum+HB1 [accessed June 4, 2021]). Some Republicans were rightly worried the measure went farther than an attack on *Roe v. Wade*, with some wondering in private whether the bill might prevent contraception. HB 1 passed the House and got out of a Senate committee, but never received a floor vote. see Jim Nolan and Wesley P. Hester, "In Stunning Turnaround, Senate Scraps 'Personhood' Bill," *Richmond Times-Dispatch*, February 24, 2012, https://www.richmond.com/news/in-stunning-turnaround-senate-scraps-personhood-bill/article_9e005130-2c00-5256-9ed4-ff2d6da65c19.html (accessed June 4, 2021). A similar attempt by Marshall in 2009 (Virginia, Legislative Information System [LIS], "HB 1639 Human Beings, Preborn," Session 2009, http://lis.virginia.gov/cgi-bin/legp604.exe?ses=091&typ=bil&val=hb1639 [accessed June 4, 2021]) was frustrated by procedural maneuvering by the Republican Chairman of the House Courts of Justice committee, Dave Albo, who wanted to kill the measure without outraging the GOP's

conservative base. His solution was to convene a special subcommitteecalled the "Constitutional Law subcommittee" and stock it with progressive Democrats like me and Republicans who represented more moderate districts. We then held a four-hour hearing, allowed all perspectives to be heard, and then tabled the measure. The bill had technically received a hearing, but the outcome was never seriously in doubt.

11. David J. Toscano and R. Lee Ware Jr., "Shining Some Sunlight on $200 Million in Virginia Tax Breaks," *Washington Post*, March 25, 2011, https://www. washingtonpost.com/opinions/shining-some-sunlight-on-200-million-in-virginia-tax -breaks/2011/03/22/AFsCI8XB_story.html (accessed June 4, 2021).

12. While generally skeptical of the tax credits, Ware was nonetheless a major proponent of the Land Preservation Tax Credit, one of the costliest credits in the Virginia Code. Over the years, the credit has been modified somewhat, with the result that the yearly cost has declined, but the annual transfers from the budget, usually to large landowners who place their property under conservation easement, can be as high as $75 million.

13. Tommy Norment defeated incumbent William Fears after the Democrat made the impolitic statement on the Senate floor against increasing penalties for drunk driving, saying, "We're going to take all the sport out of drinking and driving."

14. Publius, "How Tommy Norment Led Republicans Over the Cliff," *Bearing Drift*, November 18, 2019, https://bearingdrift.com/2019/11/18/how-tommy-norment -led-republicans-over-the-cliff/ (accessed June 4, 2021).

15. David J. Toscano, *Fighting Gridlock: How States Shape the Nation and Our Lives* (Charlottesville: University of Virginia Press, 2021).

16. Laura Vozzella, "Virginia Delegate Vows to Block Gay Judge," *Washington Post*, May 14, 2012, https://www.washingtonpost.com/blogs/virginia-politics/post /virginia-delegate-vows-to-block-gay-judge/2012/05/14/gIQA75SuOU_blog.html (accessed June 4, 2021).

17. When members feel they cannot support a judge, the tradition is simply not to vote. Consequently, a "no" vote is very unusual. Dahlia Lithwick, "Another Virginia Disgrace," *Slate*, May 15, 2012, https://slate.com/news-and-politics/2012/05/tracy -thorne-begland-and-the-virginia-house-of-delegates-the-state-legislature-rejects-the -judicial-nomination-of-a-prosecutor-just-because-hes-gay.html (accessed June 4, 2021). A judge must receive fifty-one votes in the House and twenty-one votes in the Senate to be approved and not merely a majority of the votes cast. Therefore, an abstention has the same practical effect as a negative vote but does not carry the same political weight or have an adverse effect on the reputation of a newly-approved judge.

18. Sabrina Tavernise, "Gay Prosecutor Is Denied Virginia Judgeship Despite Bipartisan Support," *New York Times*, May 15, 2012, https://www.nytimes.com/2012 /05/16/us/politics/gay-prosecutor-is-denied-judgeship-in-virginia.html (accessed June 4, 2021).

19. John J. Dinan, *The Virginia State Constitution* (Westport, CT: Praeger, 2006), 32.

20. Tom Jackman, "Fairfax Judge Jane Marum Roush Named to Virginia Supreme Court," *Washington Post*, July 27, 2015, https://www.washingtonpost.com/

local/fairfax-judge-jane-marum-roush-named-to-virginia-supreme-court/2015/07/26/ e9c18238-324e-11e5-8353-1215475949f4_story.html (accessed June 4, 2021).

21. Laura Vozzella, "McAuliffe Suggests He Was Victim of Republican 'Set-Up' in Judicial Battle," *Washington Post*, December 9, 2015, https://www.washingtonpost. com/local/virginiapolitics/mcauliffe-suggests-he-was-victim-of-republican-set-up -in-judicial-battle/2015/12/09/b050b1f6-9e99-11e5-a3c5-c77f2cc5a43c_story.html (accessed June 4, 2021).

22. Carl Tobias, "Electing Justice Roush to the Supreme Court of Virginia," *Washington & Lee University Law Review Online* 72, no. 2 (2015): article 8, 360, https://scholarlycommons.law.wlu.edu/wlulr-online/vol72/iss2/8.

23. Tobias, "Electing Justice Roush," 368.

24. Jenna Portnoy, "Va. Democrats Revive Roush Judgeship," *Washington Post*, August 17, 2015, https://www.washingtonpost.com/local/virginia-politics /va-democrats-revive-roush-judgeship/2015/08/17/0555b808-4518-11e5-8e7d -9c033e6745d8_story.html (accessed June 4, 2021).

25. In 2019, only 25 percent of Virginia state court judges were female, fewer than most other states, and less than the national average of 34 percent, noted in National Association of Women Judges (NAWJ), "2019 US State Court Women Judges," *NAWJ*, 2019, https://www.nawj.org/statistics/2019-us-state-court-women-judges (accessed June 4, 2021). Only seven states have fewer female judges than Virginia. The state with the most female judges is Minnesota has the highest at 48 percent. The good news is that the last decade saw improvement. In 2008, 19 percent of Virginia's state court judges were female; the national number was 25 percent.

Chapter 9

Advocates

Never doubt that a small group of thoughtful, committed citizens can change the world; indeed, it's the only thing that ever has.

—Margaret Mead[1]

Lisa Smith never fancied herself as an activist—and still does not. Her primary concern was always for her daughter Haley, who, at five months of age, started experiencing scary seizures, the cause of which remained unknown for years. Haley was ultimately diagnosed at six years old with Dravet Syndrome, a catastrophic form of epilepsy for which there was neither a cure nor medication that could allow the condition to be controlled. For Haley, every seizure was perceived as possibly her last. She was in and out of hospitals. At thirteen years of age, she was experiencing about 1,000 Grand Mal seizures per year. Her family had tried countless pharmaceuticals and numerous combinations of them, most of which did little but to render her listless and sleepy almost constantly. Lisa was looking for an answer and concluded that one could be found in changing Virginia law to make cannabidiol (CDB) oil, a derivative of cannabis, available to her daughter. Their story illustrates the uniqueness of a citizen legislature, and how individual advocates can affect change.

In 2012, Lisa became aware of CBD oil while searching the internet in hopes of finding some relief.[2] Initially, she was leery of using a cannabis-based product for her daughter. But she had seen the practical results of use of the oil, and the family was out of options. Lisa knew she was onto something that could help not only her daughter but also thousands of others who are subject to these types of seizures. She also knew that possession of the substance was illegal in Virginia and transporting it across state lines was a federal offense. If Haley was to gain regular access to this treatment, laws had to change.

Lisa joined a group called "Virginia Parents for Medical Marijuana," which had been lobbying to legalize marijuana for medical use in the

143

Commonwealth. Her goals were initially more limited than those of the group; she wanted CBD oil to become available to assist in the treatment of epilepsy. She was not advocating to legalize marijuana in the state but wanted permission to possess certain oils made from cannabis plants with a doctor's certification. Having lived in Virginia for years, and knowing its general conservatism, she knew this change would be a tough sell. But she was pleasantly relentless, providing anyone that would listen with the facts to counter the tendencies to view this measure as the "camel's nose under the tent" toward eventual marijuana legalization.

Smith had an important ally—Ralph S. Northam—who, as a pediatric neurologist, had treated Haley for a limited period early in her life. When running for Lieutenant Governor, Northam publicly signaled a willingness to fight to make CBD oil available to "patients like Haley." Northam suggested that Smith and the advocates recruit a Republican in the House to introduce legislation. Delegate Dave Albo of Fairfax was approached, and he told the advocates that before he introduced any bill, he wanted them to prepare informational packets for each member of the House Courts of Justice Committee, and then speak to each one of them far in advance of when the bill would be introduced. Smith had now entered the realm of citizen advocacy.

Throughout the summer and fall, Smith and others met with key legislators around the state, learning the lesson that one cannot simply introduce a good bill and lobby for it during the session. Instead, the work often needs to be done in advance, so that objections can be addressed and fixed out of the limelight and pressure cooker of a legislative session. In 2015, the bill was introduced by two Fairfax representatives, Republican Dave Albo in the House and Democrat Dave Marsden in the Senate. And it was then that I first met Lisa and Haley Smith. Haley was fourteen years old at the time. It was difficult for her to talk, and she was so tired that she was largely confined to a wheelchair. But armed with just a smile and her Teddy Bear, she was able to connect with legislators in a way few other advocates could. The proposed bill was innovative; federal law still made transportation of these substances' illegal, so straight legalization of the oil for medicinal purposes would not work. Instead, the 2015 legislation created what lawyers call "an affirmative defense" to possession, meaning that people could not be prosecuted for possession if a doctor had certified the CBD was being used for treatment of glaucoma, cancer, or epilepsy.[3] These included parents and caregivers like Lisa, who might possess marijuana oils based on a doctor's recommendation.[4] The bill passed with almost no opposition, largely because it was pitched as different from medical marijuana. Along the way, even the most conservative legislators embraced Smith's efforts. And Haley won friends that hopefully will last a lifetime. Senator Charles William "Bill" Carrico, a former state trooper and among the most conservative members of the Body, for example, initially was extremely skeptical of the proposal. But when hearings were held, Carrico was deeply moved. Listening to both Lisa and Haley, he became an advocate. And Haley now refers to Carrico as "scarecrow, daddy-oh." Such is the charm of legislating in the states.

When Haley was able to finally access the CBD oil in late March 2015, her life changed. She was immediately able to stay awake all day and much better able to communicate. She was livelier than ever before. One state law had made a difference. What was the key to the success of Lisa and Haley Smith? "When you find like-minded, passionate people," Smith explained, "you can move mountains." "Our group was effective because we all came from different backgrounds, had different political views, and we left our egos at home."[5]

IT TAKES TIME

Early on the morning of April 14, 2007, Lori Haas answered the phone call from her daughter Emily and heard words she will never forget: "Hi, mommy, I've been shot."[6] A sophomore at Virginia Tech and the oldest of Lori's three children, Emily had been shot twice in the head, and thirty-two of her friends and colleagues had been murdered, by a solo gunman in the largest mass shooting on a college campus in the United States to that date. Amazingly, she recovered, and Lori, who described herself at that time as a stay-at-home mom with no political involvement other than attending an occasional school board meeting, tried to make sense of it. "Different people react to tragedy in different ways," she said. "For me, I constantly asked myself 'how could this happen, how did he get the gun?'" Not knowing much about issues surrounding gun violence, she plunged into the research. "I had to learn everything from scratch," she explained. She met Andrew Goddard, another parent whose son had been seriously wounded, and they began meeting with legislators and traveling to Richmond to argue for change. Soon thereafter, she became the Virginia Director of the Coalition to Stop Gun Violence, perhaps the oldest gun safety group in the Nation.

At first, Lori was met in Richmond with skepticism and outright hostility. At the time, the General Assembly was dominated by legislators who were either conservative and did not support gun rights or by moderates who were scared to death of the National Rifle Association (NRA). Bill after bill would be introduced, only to be defeated. For Haas and other advocates, this was disheartening. Eventually, the state's politics began to change. In 2013, Terry McAuliffe was elected Governor, even after receiving a "F" rating from the NRA. The new Governor, as well as Lieutenant Governor Northam and Attorney General Mark Herring were committed to gun safety initiatives. But electing statewide candidates would not be enough. While McAuliffe's veto had successfully torpedoed bills that expanded access to guns, Haas remained frustrated by the lack of positive legislation. "After several years of work," said Haas, "I realized that if you could not change the minds of legislators to support our views, you had to change the persons who sat in their seats."[7] Lori then began mobilizing resources to elect a new group of legislators more favorable to these measures. In cooperation with Everytown for Gun Safety and other gun safety advocacy groups, heavy investments were made in a series of elections that eventually helped lead to the Democratic take-over in 2020.

Although she is now a registered lobbyist, Lori epitomizes the citizen advocate, who is passionate about an issue, and believes that an individual or a small number of people can make a difference. Within several years of the Tech shooting, she had transformed herself into a force with whom to reckon. U.S. Senator Mark Warner described her as "relentless, respectful, tough."[8] "She is passionate and has no fear," explained Brian Moran, former Delegate and Secretary of Public Safety under Governors McAuliffe and Northam; "She will as quickly engage her strongest supporter as she will her most ardent opponent."[9] Haas always emphasized the importance of understanding the environment in which advocates work. "You just can't parachute into the legislative arena and change everything," she explained. "It takes time to understand the players, the culture of the place, the politics."[10] In the 2020 session, the Virginia General Assembly passed major gun safety measures upon which Lori Haas had worked for years. On April 10, 2020, Governor Northam signed the bills, which included a "Red flag law" designed to keep guns out of the hands of people whose behavior evidences a risk of harm to themselves or others, the restoration of the one-gun-a-month purchase restriction, and universal background checks, among others. At his side were the legislative patrons of the measures, some executive branch cabinet officers, and one citizen advocate who clearly made a difference—Lori Haas.

TRAGEDY BRINGS CHANGE

Much like Haas, the families of Gil and Dan Harrington, and John and Susan Graham became involved as citizen advocates because of tragedy. Both were linked by the murders of their daughters, Morgan and Hannah. Morgan Dana Harrington, a student at Virginia Tech, went missing during a concert in Charlottesville in October 2009. After an exhaustive search, her body was discovered in a remote rural area in adjacent Albemarle County. No perpetrator was initially identified. The Harrington's launched a national nonprofit called "Save the Next Girl" to promote awareness of abductions and attacks on young women. At their instigation, the General Assembly passed a resolution drawing attention to the challenges of locating missing persons. Gil Harrington was a frequent attendee of committee meetings to testify for various criminal justice initiatives.

Hannah Elizabeth Graham, an eighteen-year-old second-year University of Virginia (UVA) student, was murdered five years later, also in Charlottesville. Initially, there appeared to be no link between the two murders. But the events surrounding them seemed eerily similar. Both victims were young, clearly abducted against their will, and their bodies were discovered in the same remote area in the surrounding county. Unlike the Harrington case, however, there was surveillance video showing Graham with a possible perpetrator named Jesse Matthew, a Charlottesville cab driver with a history of assaultive behavior.[11] Police searched Matthew's residence and discovered evidence linking him to Graham's abduction. By then, Matthew had fled the area, and was arrested shortly thereafter in Texas near the Mexican border. Shortly thereafter, forensic evidence assembled in the Harrington investigation appeared to link Matthew to that crime as well. He eventually confessed to both, entering a plea to both murders on March 2, 2016. He was given multiple life sentences.

Given his criminal history, many wondered about how Matthew could have remained free to commit these heinous offenses. Could he have been charged and convicted of the Harrington murder earlier, and therefore would never have met Hannah Graham? Albemarle County Sheriff John "Chip" Harding thought he had an answer.

I had known Chip for years, having first met him while I was Charlottesville Mayor and he was a Captain in the City's police department. He was sincere, and always looking for new ways of improving law enforcement. Chip had become interested in the power of deoxyribonucleic acid (DNA) identification to convict the guilty and exonerate the innocent. He was especially intrigued about how this evidence might have been used to capture Matthew before he had killed Graham. Harding argued that if a DNA sample had been taken upon Matthew's conviction for trespassing in 2010, he would have been linked to a brutal 2005 assault in Fairfax, arrested and jailed, and would have never met Graham.

In 2010, Virginia only collected DNA samples from convicted felons and from a small number of misdemeanants, and Harding thought the law should change. He had assembled the experience of many other states and had concluded that laws that required the taking DNA samples from those who had been convicted of any misdemeanor helped law enforcement in their attempts to solve other crimes. He had been working first with the Harringtons and eventually with the Grahams on this idea. Because Delegate Rob Bell and I represented Albemarle County and Harding knew us both, he suggested that we try to change the law.

I was never perceived as a "law and order" Delegate, and rarely introduced criminal justice bills. But this proposal hooked me from the beginning. Not only would it help arrest and convict wrongdoers, but it also could exonerate the innocent. I introduced my first bill in this area in 2015. Mark Obenshain had a similar bill on the Senate side, and the Republicans concluded that his would be the vehicle for any change in the statute. The measure had widespread support but the costs of taking DNA samples for so many misdemeanors were high, and the bill's scope was reduced substantially. This left some crimes exempt from the requirement, particularly assault and trespassing. The measure passed, and I planned to make an effort in the next year to add more offenses.

In 2017, I introduced a bill to further expand the list of misdemeanors. Again, there were concerns about costs; expanding the list could add almost $500,000 per year to the state budget, and legislators were skeptical. Instead of the measure being rejected outright, it was instead referred to the Virginia State Crime Commission for study. Commission referral is sometimes used as a good way to kill a bill, but that would not happen in this case. Commission staff was very interested in exploring the relationship between misdemeanor offenses and future felonies. They conducted an elaborate study of the subject,[12] and recommended that a number of offenses be added to those for which DNA was collected. With this, I had the imprimatur of a body perceived as a defender of law and order. Both Obenshain and I reintroduced our bills in 2018.

Prior to 2018, I had little contact with Gil Harrington and had never spoken with the Grahams. But introduction of this new bill changed that. And without their advocacy, the 2018 measure would never have passed. Many in the legislature had met Harrington, but few had encountered the Grahams, who had remained largely out of public view since their daughter's death. During that legislative session, the Grahams appeared before numerous committees to describe their daughter and how this bill might have saved her life. Any objection to adding more misdemeanors collapsed under the weight of the emotional testimony of the Grahams. They were quiet and reserved, but each time they testified, you could feel their ongoing pain. They knew nothing would return their daughter to them, but like the Harringtons, felt they should act to prevent similar tragedies in the future.

As is the case with many criminal justice bills, it is not just a question of whether the measure is a good idea but whether it can be funded. The bill almost died at the last minute when the House Appropriations Committee attempted to remove one of important misdemeanor to save on costs. After the Grahams spoke, the committee restored the misdemeanor, and indicated that they would find money to support the bill. Again, the power of a personal story and the influence of effective citizen advocates was able to make major change at the state level. The bill was passed, and Governor Northam signed it in a special ceremony on June 21, 2018. Both the Grahams and Gil Harrington were present. A photo of the signing is prominently displayed on my bookcase next to Gil Harrington's autographed book[13] as a testament to what citizen advocates can accomplish, even in the aftermath of tragedy.

THE PROFESSIONALS

As previously mentioned, it surprises many people to discover that while Members of the U.S. Congress have as many as eighteen staff members to assist them with the running of their offices and policy development, Virginia Delegates and Senators usually have only one or two. And unlike a full-time legislature, Virginia is only Constitutionally mandated to meet for sixty days in even-numbered years and thirty days in odd-numbered years. Under these conditions, Virginia lawmakers come to depend on the analysis of others outside of their immediate offices for assistance. They include staff members from the executive branch, and the nonpartisan state employees who staff the various committees of the General Assembly. Legislators benefit from members of the public, many of whom come of Richmond during session to advocate for bills or argue against them. But another key element in making a citizen legislature work involves the role of paid lobbyists.

The public perception of lobbyists owes much to those who work in Washington and inhabit the swanky offices of K Street while enjoying extensive expense accounts. Virginia lobbyists are typically quite different. Many have worked for years in the Virginia system, and have grown accustomed to its tradition of civility and aspirations of fair dealing. Many have more institutional knowledge than the legislature, and the larger firms have deep connections to those who control the levels of power. Nonetheless, most lobbyists view their success as dependent upon the building of trust with policymakers over long periods of time. Their approach is generally transactional—not ideological—and the adage that "your worse enemy today can be your best friend tomorrow" is largely embraced by this group as they ply their trade in the halls of the Capitol.

Consequently, the quickest road to lobbyist failure is by providing legislators inaccurate or inadequate information. There is nothing that a legislator hates more than to be coaxed into a position based on inaccurate information, only to be undercut in a public way at the last minute. The good lobbyists will provide a legislator with both the pros and cons of the bill as well as who is likely to support and oppose the bill both on Capitol Square and in the public at large. This will help the legislator make an educated judgment about how to vote and how to explain a bill as needed. If the legislator comes to feel that the lobbyist is misleading in their presentation, any trust that existed previously may never be restored.

The lobbying corps in Virginia has changed dramatically over the years. When I first took office in 2006, there were 834 registered lobbyists in the entire Commonwealth. By 2020, that number had risen to 2,865.[14] And lobbying today is much more sophisticated, with firms employing different persons who can approach specific legislators depending on their party, personalities, and politics. There are Democratic and Republican lobbyists working the same bill in the same firm. And on major issues, it is not uncommon for many different firms to be involved, each working different angles of the legislation.

Virginia witnessed this dynamic during the casino gambling debate in 2019 and 2020. Until that time, gaming interests found it difficult to make much progress, primarily because Speaker William J. Howell was adamantly opposed. But with the retirement of the Speaker and the changing character of the legislature, proponents of casino gambling saw an opportunity. In 2020, companies that already had an active lobbying presence in Virginia such as the Colonial Downs racetrack and 7-Eleven were engaged. But so too were new groups such as Caesars, MGM Grand, and even the National Basketball Association. These groups hired so many of the major lobbying firms in Richmond that when a local company approached me about the possibility of hiring a lobbyist of their own, every major Richmond firm had already been engaged and was therefore unable to undertake the representation. And the money spent was substantial. According to the Virginia Public Access Project (VPAP), almost $1 million was spent by gaming interests on lobbying activity between May 2019 and April 2020. Racetrack owner Colonial Downs reported the fourth highest spending of *all* lobbyists during that period, an amount in excess of $330,000.[15]

The expectation that gambling would be a major focus in 2020 also led to a dramatic increase in political contributions from these companies. The developers of the proposed Bristol Resort and Casino in southwest Virginia, for example, formed their own political action committee (PAC), and proceeded to donate $311,500 to fifty state Senate and House campaigns during August and September of 2019.[16] The same individuals behind this PAC, who made their money largely in the coal industry, had previously given $200,000 to then-Speaker Kirk Cox's PAC in 2018.[17] Clearly, much money was at stake and proponents of gaming sought not only to be well represented by lobbyists, but to curry favor with those who were making the decisions.

The public has a jaundiced view of lobbyists, but it is difficult for a part-time, citizen legislature to function without them. They have access to substantial amounts of information that they can offer to assist with policy decisions. The key to making the arrangement work for the public is character—of both the legislator and the lobbyist. The legislator needs to view the lobbyist as the source of information, not the director of decision-making. At the same time, the lobbyist must respect the independent judgment of the lawmaker and understand that they represent a constituency that may or may not be supportive of the bill that is being pushed.

In some cases, lobbyists can also be instrumental in reconciling seemingly contradictory positions on a bill. It is also not uncommon for legislators to instruct lobbyists from different perspectives to forge a compromise that each can live with. When this happens, legislators refer to the solution as creating "peace in the valley," and the compromise is often sold to other legislators in that fashion. I have seen numerous instances where several groups with differing perspectives on a bill are asked to meet to develop a compromise which then can be presented to the relevant committee. Are the legislators ceding control of the process at that point? To some extent, that is true. But many of these issues are so complex that it requires the careful review of the language of the legislation, and sometimes the lawyers for the advocacy groups can provide effective assistance to ensure a bill operates in the proper, and the intended, fashion.

Two experienced lobbyists who understand these dynamics are Whitt Clement and Don Hall. Clement was elected to the House of Delegates in 1998 from Danville, an area that tended to vote Democratic at that time. With his lawyerly skills and his Southern style, he eventually gained a position on the Appropriations Committee. As the Danville area became more conservative, the GOP targeted his seat in the 2001 redistricting, thereby making his re-election more problematic and prompting him to leave the House. Clement then joined the Warner administration and became the Commonwealth's 10th Secretary of Transportation. In 2005, he left that position to join the firm of Hunton & Williams (now Hunton Andrews Kurth LLP), and built its governmental relations section into a lobbying powerhouse. In 2021, Clement became the Rector of UVA's Board of Visitors.

Don Hall never sought public office. His experience was shaped instead by his service in the U.S. Marine Corps. Brash, direct, and engaging, Hall assumed leadership of the Virginia Auto Dealers Association (VADA) in 1988 and has remained in charge ever since. A tall, solidly built man, he is a forceful advocate for the 450 dealers he represents and their 35,000 employees. "Don is definitely someone you want on your side," said H. Carter Myers III, retired president and CEO of Charlottesville-based Carter Myers Automotive, a member of the VADA for decades.[18] Franchise dealers exist in every county, city, and town in the Commonwealth, and Hall was adept at mobilizing them every time it was necessary to deliver a certain message to Delegates and

Senators. It was not uncommon for them to pack a committee room to support or oppose a measure, usually winning the day. As a result, Virginia has some of the most favorable franchise dealership laws in the country.

Hall is not shy about discussing his craft. "Lesson 101 in lobbying is that to be effective, you need to be honest and maintain your credibility," he said; "this business is all about trust and relationships. If you lose these, you are done."[19] Clement agrees: "I once had a lobbyist directly lie to me about a bill. I told her never to come back. Within two years, she had left the lobbying corps."[20]

Both Clement and Hall remember their work on the 2013 transportation bill and were witnesses to how the measure, proposed by Governor Bob McDonnell, was transformed during the legislative process. Clement was working with the road builders and had recognized, from his days as Secretary of Transportation, that monies were being sucked from the state's roadbuilding fund simply to maintain the transportation network. He recognized, as did many others, that without additional monies, Virginia would soon become a state where no new roads could be built. Once the bill was introduced, Clement and his allies went to work on legislators to argue for more revenue. He described how the McDonnell initiative was transformed from one where little new monies were proposed to one where substantial new investments would be made. Lobbyists for the road builders and other transportation interests prevailed in changing the legislature's basic approach to the legislation as well as many of its details. "I think the bill got away from the Governor," explained Clement, "and key players in the House and Senate decided to raise more money, especially for Hampton Roads and Northern Virginia."[21]

But not every lobbyist got what they wanted in the transportation deal; Don Hall was one of them. Some of those new monies came at the expense of Hall's auto dealers, who had been concerned about raising the 3 percent sales tax on automobiles as part of the bill. Like Clement, Hall also realized that the state needed new money for roads and felt proud that he had been able to convince his dealers to support adding an additional 1 percent onto the cost of a car. But when the final bill emerged from the conference, the sales tax increase was higher than he expected. Hall felt betrayed, believing that he had a deal for the tax to remain at 4 percent in return for the dealers' support of the legislation. But given that the final details had been hammered out behind closed doors by a conference committee of House and Senate Leaders, there was little he could do. Similarly, Governor McDonnell could do little but to support the measure. The legislature had taken control of a bill that initially appeared to do very little and turned it into something that had major impact. The Governor could not risk undercutting one of his major initiatives, and eventually took credit for the final plan.

Clement and Hall admit that the General Assembly has changed a lot during their time in Richmond. "It used to be that delegates and senators came to the assembly after being community leaders," Clement explained. "Some were active in local government, others were bankers, lawyers, or people who had substantial roots independent of being involved with a party. It did not cost very much money to run, and you were not beholden to parties or large donors for the resources necessary to win." Clement says that he did not even have a fundraiser in Richmond until the twelfth year he had been in office; today, there are fundraisers every day of the week when the Assembly is not in session. "The urgency to raise money, and the constant need to draw political contrasts between the parties" he argued, "is making it more difficult for Delegates and Senators to work together. Clearly, some members approach their work today more like Washington politicians than at any time in memory." Hall spoke about the change in this way: "fewer members recognize that there are 'shades of gray' in many bills. For the state legislature to work," he argued, "members should attempt to understand and incorporate the reasonable arguments from those with whom you disagree. Unfortunately, there is an increasing tendency to work just with those in your camp, and policy can suffer as a result."

ATTORNEYS GENERAL

A discussion of advocates would not be complete without examining the role of another professional--the Commonwealth's chief lawyer—its Attorney General (AG). States' Attorneys General are not typically recognized by the American public. While some have gone on to higher positions after the tenures as their state's top attorney, including most recently Vice President Kamala Harris from California, many citizens do not understand precisely what they do.[22] In fact, when people campaign for the job they have to spend much of their time explaining that they will not be the state's "top cop" and have many powers and responsibilities outside of criminal law. Virginia is among the forty-three states and Washington, DC, where attorneys general are directly elected by the people.[23]

The office traces its roots to England, where it was created as a vehicle to protect the Crown. In this country, its role was much the same—until the American Revolution. At that time, the job of the attorney general was transformed. The position became viewed as the protector of the public, the "people's lawyer." In Virginia, the AG has been directly elected since 1851, and unlike the governor, can serve successive terms. The position is considered part of the executive branch.

In the last several decades, state Attorneys General offices have become increasingly sophisticated operations where the priorities are more reflective of national issues than ever before. Beginning with tobacco litigation in the early 1990s[24] and continuing with drug and environmental actions of recent years, state Attorneys General have become advocates for changes in social policy through their litigation. They have done this without the passage of any legislation or even with the involvement of the institutions typically viewed as those who initiate change in the country—the executive and the legislature. It is one of the untold stories of why states matter.

In Virginia, recent experience has shown how national politics can shape the efforts of Attorneys General. When Bob McDonnell was elected AG in 2005, he viewed the job primarily as being the chief lawyer for the executive and state agencies, from universities to the Department of Transportation. He nonetheless held strong views that differed from those of the Governor. As one of his first actions of his new administration, Governor Tim Kaine signed an executive order adding sexual orientation to the state's antidiscrimination policy, something that Mark Warner had done at the end of his term. At the request of Delegate Bob Marshall, Attorney General McDonnell issued and publicized an opinion suggesting that the new Governor had exceeded his authority. Around Capitol Square, those who took issue with the AG's view were frequently heard to say, "it is his opinion, and worth nothing more,"[25] but McDonnell had entered the fray of politics and clearly aligned himself with those who opposed Kaine's Order.

McDonnell's term as AG began at a time when the role of state Attorneys General was being reinvented and taking on a decidedly more political character. Republicans and Democrats had frequently worked together on major cases such as the tobacco litigation. That began to change in 1999, when the Republican Attorneys General Association (RAGA) was established to push a partisan agenda apart from the traditional National Association of State Attorneys General (NAAG).[26] Not to be outdone, the Democrats created their own group several years later, the Democratic Attorneys General Association (DAGA). Both RAGA and DAGA began raising substantial campaign dollars for state Attorneys General races across the country but the groups nonetheless operated under an informal "incumbent rule" by which they would not target sitting Attorneys General of the other party in elections. Ironically, it was a Virginia campaign in 2017 that brought a change in the informal rule. In that year, RAGA unsuccessfully targeted Democrat Mark Herring in his re-election bid. Democrats subsequently began targeting incumbent Republican AGs in other states.[27]

During McDonnell's stint as AG, state offices became even more political, as conservative AGs joined together to attack President Barack Obama's efforts to combat climate change and pass the *Affordable Care Act* (ACA).[28]

When Ken Cuccinelli succeeded McDonnell, he immediately increased the partisan focus of the position. He became the first state AG to file a lawsuit challenging the constitutionality of the ACA, doing so several months into his term and on the day the bill was signed into law, March 23, 2010.[29] He was also a climate change skeptic, and initiated a state-sponsored attack of one of its chief proponents, environmental scientist Michael Mann. In 2010, Cuccinelli claimed that Mann, who had worked at the UVA from 1999 to 2005, may have violated the *Virginia Fraud Against Taxpayers Act* (FATA) in securing of major research grants and used a relatively unknown statutory provision called a "civil investigative demand" to request a wide variety of records held by the UVA.[30] The University fought the effort, claiming that it posed a threat to academic freedom and would have a chilling effect on research in the state. Ultimately, Virginia's Supreme Court dismissed Cuccinelli's efforts,[31] but not before thousands of dollars in private and tax-payer monies were used in prosecuting and defending the suit.[32] Much of the scientific community across the country was outraged by Cuccinelli's actions, and even some of Mann's own scientific detractors were critical of the AG's efforts to question the scientific process.

AG Cuccinelli also became a point person for conservative legal advocates concerned about gay rights and immigration. Part of the Virginia AGs portfolio involves providing legal representation for the state's colleges and universities, and Cuccinelli felt compelled to write these clients in early 2010 to advise them to rescind their policies banning discrimination based on sexual orientation.[33] In July 2010, Cuccinelli filed an *amicus* brief in support of eight other states defending an Arizona immigration enforcement statute against legal attacks from the Obama administration. He then angered immigrant groups and civil libertarians with an August 2010 legal opinion stating that state and local law enforcement officials were permitted to investigate the immigration status of anyone that they had stopped.[34]

Cuccinelli also gained notoriety when he gave new lapel pins to his staff showing a modification of the historic state seal of Virginia to cover up the left breast of Virtus, the Roman goddess of bravery and military strength, which had been exposed on the seal and on the state flag since it had been adopted in 1776.[35]

Cuccinelli was also not hesitant about injecting himself into policy debates. Like Governor McDonnell, he was Roman Catholic, and felt very strongly about abortion; this issue was for him not about politics, but about basic values that he believed were under attack. But Cuccinelli did not always see eye-to-eye with Governor McDonnell, especially after the AG called for a special session on ethics reform following the revelations that McDonnell had taken gifts from Jonnie Williams.[36] After his stint as AG, Cuccinelli ran against Democrat Terry McAuliffe for governor in 2013, losing by 2.5

percent. Since then, he has remained active as a conservative commentator on the Fox News talk show circuit, arguing against undocumented immigrants attending universities and for the repeal of birth right citizenship. He was also a major supporter of Donald Trump, eventually being appointed Acting Deputy Secretary of Homeland Security in 2019.

When Mark Herring succeeded Cuccinelli in 2014, the priorities of the office changed dramatically. His 2013 AG election victory was anything but a mandate. The beneficiary of substantial last-minute funding support from groups like Everytown, the Michael Bloomberg-funded gun safety organization, Herring bested his opponent, Senator Mark Obenshain, by only 165 votes. But his small margin did not prevent Herring from showing Virginians his decisiveness. In the first two weeks of his term, the new AG garnered national headlines when he announced that he would not defend Virginia's Marshall-Newman Amendment, the Commonwealth's constitutional prohibition against marriage equality, in court.[37] The decision raised many issues, not the least of which involved an AGs responsibility to defend the laws of the state, even those which he or she believes are unconstitutional. In this instance, Herring argued that he had no duty to defend an unconstitutional law, but his action left some wondering how he might pick and choose which state laws to defend. And while the U.S. Supreme Court's 2015 decision in *Obergefell v. Hodges* confirmed the new AGs view of the Marshall-Newman, Herring's decision sparked considerable debate about the role AGs in defending laws enacted by the state. It is a thorny issue affecting not only Democratic and Republican attorneys general, but also governors who propose laws and legislatures that enact them. And this issue is further complicated by differences in state constitutional and statutory requirements of AGs. Many states do not include explicit language imposing a "duty to defend" all laws and, in a hyperpartisan environment, states attorneys general are increasingly being influenced by politics as they consider their proper roles in protecting the public interest.[38]

Herring, like Cuccinelli, was viewed as an activist AG. He joined with other Attorneys General across the country to push consumer rights litigation that brought millions of dollars to the Commonwealth. He engaged in the legal debates about gun safety, criticizing the emerging Second Amendment sanctuary movement by issuing an opinion stating that such resolutions passed by many local governments had "no legal force."[39] And when President Trump imposed a travel ban in 2017 to curtail immigration, Herring joined Attorneys General to combat it.[40]

With the exception of their mutual skepticism of the utilities, AG Herring's approach on climate was quite different from his predecessor.[41] After winning re-election easily in 2017, Herring joined a coalition of Attorneys General and local governments in the November 15, 2019 filing of a lawsuit opposing

U.S. Environmental Protection Agency (EPA) efforts during the Trump presidency to block actions by states designed to reduce air pollution.[42]

The Republican legislature did what they could to stop AG Herring's activism, largely without effect. Similar to North Carolina Republicans, who cut Democrat Joel Stein's budget by $10 million in 2017,[43] Virginia's GOP-controlled legislature trimmed Herring's budget in protest and included language restricting the Attorney General from employing independent counsel to prosecute the most complex consumer litigation targeted at corporations.[44] They also authorized a review of his office in 2017 by the state's independent watchdog agency, Joint Legislative Audit and Review Commission (JLARC). The request backfired as the Commission's report concluded that Herring's office "provides first-rate legal services."[45]

AG Herring continued to press his advantage as he considered whether to seek the governorship in 2021 (ultimately he lost his bid to win a third term). Shortly after Virginia became the thirty-eight state to ratify the Equal Rights Amendment (ERA), the national archivist, who certifies the ratification of amendments, indicated that, upon the guidance of the United States Justice Department in the Trump administration, the measure would not be added to the U.S. Constitution as its Twenty-Eighth Amendment.[46] Herring and two other state Attorneys General immediately filed a federal lawsuit to compel the measure's inclusion.[47] Throughout his administration, AG Herring continued to join other state Attorneys General in numerous fights against initiatives of President Trump. He also made progress on gun safety initiatives, pressing for universal background checks, and was able to eliminate the state's huge backlog of untested rape kits.[48] He was the classic Advocate, and his tenure provides yet another example of how AGs in the state are influencing policy across the Nation.

NOTES

1. While the original source of this widely used quote by Margaret Mead is unknown, reference to it is found in Frank G. Sommers and Tana Dineen, *Curing Nuclear Madness: A New-Age Prescription for Personal Action* (Toronto: Methuen, 1984), 158.

2. Cannabidiol (CBD) is a chemical compound extracted from cannabis that does not create a psychoactive response or marijuana "high."

3. Rachel Weiner, "Marijuana Oil Now Allowed in Virginia for Victims of Severe Epilepsy," *Washington Post,* February 26, 2015, https://www.washingtonpost.com/local/virginia-politics/marijuana-oil-now-allowed-in-virginia-for-victims-of-severe-epilepsy/2015/02/26/b3e1a3a8-bdd4-11e4-8668-4e7ba8439ca6_story.html (accessed June 5, 2021).

4. Laura Vozzella, "Bill Meant to Pave Way for Marijuana-Oil Production Advances in Virginia," *Washington Post*, February 15, 2016, https://www.washingtonpost.com/local/virginia-politics/bill-meant-to-pave-way-for-marijuana--oil-production-advances-in-virginia/2016/02/15/c9f9b63c-d429-11e5-be55-2cc3c1e4b76b_story.html (accessed June 5, 2021).

5. Lisa Smith, interview by author by telephone, November 2, 2020.

6. Lori Haas, "Virginia's New Gun Restrictions Have Been 13 Years in the Making," *Virginia Mercury*, April 16, 2020, https://www.virginiamercury.com/2020/04/16/virginias-new-gun-restrictions-have-been-13-years-in-the-making/ (accessed June 5, 2021).

7. Lori Haas, interview by author by telephone, November 20, 2020.

8. Alan Suderman, "For Virginia Tech Parents, New Gun Laws a Long Struggle," *ABC News*, February 23, 2020, https://abcnews.go.com/US/wireStory/virginia-tech-parents-gun-laws-long-struggle-69159946 (accessed June 5, 2021).

9. Former Virginia Delegate and Secretary of Public Safety Brian Moran, interview by author by telephone, March 5, 2020.

10. Lori Haas, interview.

11. Lisa Provence, "99 Problems That Could Lead to DNA Collection," *Cville*, January 20, 2015, https://www.c-ville.com/99-problems-lead-dna-collection/ (accessed June 5, 2021).

12. This is consistent with other research suggesting that DNA databases are linked to lower rates of recidivism. See Jennifer L. Doleac, "The Effects of DNA Databases on Crime," *American Economic Journal: Applied Economics* 9, no. 1 (2017): 165–201, https://doi.org/10.1257/app.20150043

13. Gil Harrington and Jane Lillian Vance, *Murdered Dead and for Good* (Nepal: Vajra Books, 2017).

14. Virginia Public Access Project (VPAP), "Lobbying in Virginia," 2020, https://www.vpap.org/lobbying/ (accessed June 5, 2021).

15. VPAP, "Lobbying: Spending," 2019–2020, https://www.vpap.org/lobbying/spending/all/?disclosure_period=15 (accessed June 5, 2021). Queen of Va Skill & Entertainment and MGM Resorts, two other gambling companies, spent over $212,000 and $161,000, respectively, during the same period. Five other similar companies spent over $100,000 each.

16. Ed Silverstein, " Bristol, Virginia Casino Developers Donate $310,000 to State Political Campaigns," *Casino.org*, October 21, 2019, https://www.casino.org/news/bristol-virginia-casino-developers-donate-310000-to-state-political-campaigns/ (accessed June 5, 2021).

17. Ned Oliver, "Bristol Bigwigs Pump $200,000 into Kirk Cox's PAC Amid Casino Push," *Virginia Mercury*, October 25, 2018, https://www.virginiamercury.com/2018/10/25/bristol-bigwigs-pump-200000-into-kirk-coxs-pac-amid-casino-push/ (accessed June 5, 2021).

18. Louis Llovio, " Marine Imprint Drives VADA Exec," *Richmond Times-Dispatch*, March 8, 2010, updated Sep 18, 2019, https://richmond.com/business/marine-imprint-drives-vada-exec/article_b146f5ed-c91c-50ad-87dd-686c63876859.html (accessed June 5, 2021).

19. Don Hall, interview by author by telephone, November 19, 2020.

20. Former Delegate Whitt Clement, interview by author by telephone, November 10, 2020.

21. Whitt Clement interview.

22. In recent Virginia history, both Jim Gilmore and Bob McDonnell served terms as Attorney General before becoming Governor.

23. In Maine, the attorney general is selected by the state legislature, and the attorney general is appointed by the governor in the states of Alaska, Hawaii, New Hampshire, New Jersey, and Wyoming. The Tennessee attorney general is appointed by the state Supreme Court.

24. Individual attorneys and states had been suing the tobacco companies for years, but not until the early 1990s did a group of creative lawyers hit on a strategy that worked. The new state lawsuits were brought not on behalf of individual plaintiffs, who the companies would often blame for smoking, but instead sought recovery for Medicaid and other public health expenses incurred in the treatment of smoking -induced illnesses. As Mike Moore, the Mississippi Attorney General who brought one of the earliest suits said, "the lawsuit is premised on a simple notion: you caused the health crisis; you pay for it" (Michael Janofsky, "Mississippi Seeks Damages from Tobacco Companies," *New York Times,* May 24, 1994, https://www.nytimes.com /1994/05/24/us/mississippi-seeks-damages-from-tobacco-companies.html, [accessed June 5, 2021]). This tobacco litigation eventually involved forty-six states and their respective Attorneys General, and, in 1998, extracted a $246 billion settlement from Philip Morris, Reynolds Tobacco, Brown & Williamson, and Lorillard Tobacco Company, the largest monetary settlement in the history of litigation. States benefited mightily from this action; Virginia received an estimated $4.1 billion and used part of the money to establish the Tobacco Indemnification and Community Revitalization Commission, which has made grants in tobacco-producing areas of the Commonwealth for years. See Virginia, Joint Legislative Audit and Review Commission (JLARC), *Review of the Tobacco Indemnification and Community Revitalization Commission,* Report to the Governor and the General Assembly of Virginia, June 2011, http://jlarc. virginia.gov/pdfs/reports/Rpt412.pdf (accessed June 5, 2021). Beyond the tangible benefits of the settlement, however, it emboldened states Attorneys Generals around the country to cooperate with each other on a variety of similar lawsuits. For more on this history, see Allan M. Brandt, *The Cigarette Century: The Rise, Fall, and Deadly Persistence of the Product That Defined America* (New York: Basic Books, 2007).

25. While Attorney General, McDonnell occasionally became embroiled in other social issues, such as when he criticized the Sex Workers Art Show at the College of William & Mary and issued an opinion that forbade the sale of the group's books on school grounds. Lindsay Barnes, "Lust Bust: Porn Case Prompts Statewide Crackdown?" *Hook,* February 7, 2008, http://www.readthehook.com/81766/news -lust-bust-porn-case-prompts-statewide-crackdown (accessed June 5, 2021).

26. One area where there is still some level of bipartisan cooperation involves opioid drugs. In February 2020, a bipartisan coalition of forty state attorneys general, including Virginia's Mark Herring, announced a $1.6 billion global settlement with the largest generic opioid manufacturer, designed to cover the costs of opioid

addiction treatment. The company also agreed to more stringent regulatory and marketing prohibitions. Sheila Kaplan and Jan Hoffman, "Mallinckrodt Reaches $1.6 Billion Deal to Settle Opioid Lawsuits," *New York Times*, February 25, 2020, https://www.nytimes.com/2020/02/25/health/mallinckrodt-opioid-settlement.html (accessed June 5, 2021).

27. Dan Levine, "Exclusive: As Democratic Attorneys General Target Trump, Republican AGs Target Them," *Reuters*, March 28, 2017, https://www.reuters.com /article/us-usa-politics-republican-ags-exclusive/exclusive-as-democratic-attorneys -general-target-trump-republican-ags-target-them-idUSKBN16Z1A5 (accessed June 5, 2021).

28. U.S. Congress, *Patient Protection and Affordable Care Act* (ACA) *of 2010*, 124 Stat. 119, Pub. L. 111–148, 111 Cong., 2nd sess., March 23, 2010, https://www.govinfo.gov/app/details/PLAW-111publ148/PLAW-111publ148 (accessed June 9, 2021).

29. Joshua Hersh, "Cuccinelli's War," *New Republic*, March 17, 2011, https://newrepublic.com/article/85327/cuccinelli-virginia-health-care-tea-party (accessed June 5, 2021). The case was subsequently dismissed in 2011. See Anita Kumar and N. C. Aizenman, "Appeals Court Dismisses Virginia's Health Law Challenge," *Washington Post*, September 8, 2011, https://www.washingtonpost.com/national /health-science/appeals-court-dismisses-virginias-health-law-challenge/2011/09/08/ gIQAB81xCK_story.html (accessed June 5, 2021).

30. Rosalind S Helderman, "State Attorney General Demands Ex-professor's Files from University of Virginia." *Washington Post*, May 4, 2010, https://www.washingtonpost.com/wp-dyn/content/article/2010/05/03/AR2010050304139.html (accessed June 5, 2021). See also Virginia, General Assembly, *Virginia Fraud Against Taxpayers Act* (FATA), § 8.01–216.1, c. 842 (2002), https://law.lis.virginia.gov/ vacode/8.01-216.1/ (accessed June 23, 2021).

31. *Kenneth P. Cuccinelli, II, in his capacity as Attorney General of Virginia v. Rector and Visitors of the University of Virginia*, 283 Va. 420, 722 S.E.2d 626 (2012), http://www.courts.state.va.us/opinions/opnscvwp/1102359.pdf (accessed June 5, 2021).

32. Kumar, Anita, "Va. Supreme Court Tosses Cuccinelli's Case Against Former U-Va. Climate Change Researcher," *Washington Post*, March 2, 2012, https://www.washingtonpost.com/blogs/virginia-politics/post/va-supreme-court-tosses-cuccinellis -case-against-u-va/2012/03/02/gIQAeOqjmR_blog.html (accessed June 5, 2021).

33. Brittany Daniels, "Cuccinelli Says Colleges Can't Protect Gays," *Loudoun Times Mirror*, March 8, 2010, https://www.loudountimes.com/news/cuccinelli-says -colleges-can-t-protect-gays/article_30543555-931c-532c-88a8-0a39c0c010e1.html (accessed June 5, 2021).

34. Previously, the ability to check status was limited to those who were arrested. While the opinion did not carry the force of law, it received considerable publicity. Critics noted that the General Assembly had rejected a number of measures that Cuccinelli was now asserting was the law. See Anita Kumar and Rosalind S. Helderman, "Virginia Permits Wider Police Immigration Status Check," *Washington*

Post, August 3, 2010, https://www.washingtonpost.com/wp-dyn/content/article/2010 /08/02/AR2010080205229.html (accessed June 5, 2021).

35. Rosalind S. Helderman, "Cuccinelli Says He Chose New Lapel Pins to Cover History, Not Breasts," *Washington Post*, May 3, 2010, http://voices.washingtonpost. com/virginiapolitics/2010/05/cuccinelli_says_he_chose_new_la.html (accessed June 5, 2021).

36. Chris Gentilviso, "Bob McDonnell Declines Ken Cuccinelli Request for Special Session on Virginia Ethics Reform," *Huffington Post*, August 6, 2013, https://www.huffpost.com/entry/bob-mcdonnell-ken-cuccinellli_n_3710198 (accessed June 5, 2021). Cuccinelli himself was reported to have received gifts from Jonnie Williams and had purchased stock in the company run by the entrepreneur but was never charged with any wrongdoing. See Jim Nolan, "Cuccinelli Discloses More Gifts from Star Scientific CEO," *Richmond Times-Dispatch*, April 27, 2013, https://www. richmond.com/news/local/government-politics/cuccinelli-discloses-more-gifts-from -star-scientific-ceo/article_9b2bcfc8-ed4c-574c-9746-3fdd387e7ec3.html (accessed June 5, 2021); and Jessica Taylor, "Cuccinelli Cleared of Wrongdoing in Star Scientific Disclosures," *MSNBC*, September 13, 2013, http://www.msnbc.com/the -daily-rundown/cuccinelli-cleared-wrongdoing-star-scie (accessed June 5, 2021).

37. Timothy Williams and Trip Gabriel, "Virginia's New Attorney General Opposes Ban on Gay Marriage," *New York Times*, January 23, 2014, https://www. nytimes.com/2014/01/24/us/new-virginia-attorney-general-drops-defense-of-gay -marriage-ban.html (accessed June 5, 2021); Daniel Rothberg, Daniel, "Virginia Official Refuses to Defend Gay Marriage Ban," *Los Angeles Times*, January 23, 2014, https://www.latimes.com/nation/la-na-gay-marriage-virginia-20140124-story. html (accessed June 5, 2021). This action caught many Virginia politicos by surprise; even Governor McAuliffe had little if any advance notice of the Attorney General's dramatic announcement.

38. Neal Devins and Saikrishna Bangalore Prakash, "Fifty States, Fifty Attorneys General, and Fifty Approaches to the Duty To Defend," *The Yale Law Journal*, 124, No. 6 (2015): 2100–2187, https://www.yalelawjournal.org/feature/state-attorneys -general-and-the-duty-to-defend (accessed Sept. 19, 2021).

39. Gregory S. Schneider, "Virginia AG Herring: 'Second Amendment Sanctuary' Proclamations Have No Force," *Washington Post*, December 20, 2019, https://www. washingtonpost.com/local/virginia-politics/virginia-ag-herring-second-amendment -sanctuary-proclamations-have-no-force/2019/12/20/5f7adcb2-234b-11ea-a153 -dce4b94e4249_story.html (accessed June 5, 2021); and Patrick Wilson, "AG Herring Issues Opinion Saying Gun Sanctuary Resolutions Have No Legal Effect," *Richmond Times-Dispatch*, December 20, 2019, https://www.richmond.com/news/virginia/ag -herring-issues-opinion-saying-gun-sanctuary-resolutions-have-no/article_1fd8a88e -f904-5ebd-bcb7-6e86e4234c20.html (accessed June 5, 2021). Many of the local government attorneys representing their clients shared this view.

40. Caroline Cournoyer, "More State AGs Join Lawsuits Against Trump's Immigration Ban," *Governing*, February 1, 2017, https://www.governing.com/ topics/public-justice-safety/tns-state-ags-lawsuits-trump-immigration.html (accessed June 5, 2021).

41. Both Cuccinelli and Herring were very critical of Dominion Power. In 2019, Cuccinelli even joined with the progressive group, Clean Virginia, to argue for the deregulation of the utilities. See Gregory S. Schneider, " Coalition of Unlikely Allies Calls on State to Break Up Utilities, Deregulate Energy," *Washington Post*, May 7, 2019, https://www.washingtonpost.com/local/virginia-politics/coalition-of-unlikely -allies-calls-on-state-to-break-up-utilities-deregulate-energy/2019/05/07/72916a2e -70e9-11e9-8be0-ca575670e91c_story.html (accessed June 5, 2021). Herring has consistently argued that the Virginia State Corporation Commission should retain broad authority of regulate utility rates for the benefit of the consumer, even if the legislature disagreed.

42. Virginia, Office of Virginia Attorney General, News Release, "Attorney General Herring Sues EPA Over Attacks on Clean Air and Climate Change Efforts," November 15, 2019, https://www.oag.state.va.us/media-center/news-releases/1577 -november-15-2019-herring-sues-epa-over-attacks-on-clean-air-and-climate-change -efforts (accessed June 5, 2021). During the first two years of Trump's presidency, Attorneys General filed sixty-one lawsuits against the administration, challenging rules such as the EPA rollback of the Clean Air Act and child separations at the border. See Jared Bennett, "Why State Attorneys General Races Are The Next Frontier For Out-Of-State Influence," *Center for Public Integrity*, November 3, 2018, https: //publicintegrity.org/politics/state-politics/why-state-attorneys-general-races-are-the -next-frontier-for-out-of-state-influence/ (accessed June 5, 2021).

43. Republican legislators became upset when Joel Stein announced a decision not to defend the state's voter ID law before the U.S. Supreme Court in 2017. See Anne Blythe, "GOP Lawmakers Target Democrat Josh Stein with Surprise Budget Cuts," *News & Observer*, June 21, 2017, https://www.newsobserver.com/news/politics -government/state-politics/article157510939.html (accessed June 16, 2021).

44. When the GOP controlled the legislature in 2019, they attempted to prevent Mike Bloomberg from assisting the Attorney General in hiring outside counsel to pursue climate change litigation by including language in the state budget requiring those working for the Attorney General to be state or federal government employees paid solely with public funds. See Valerie Richardson, "Virginia Blocks Mike Bloomberg's Climate Lawyers," *Washington Times*, April 18, 2019, https://apnews.com/38938e39 f23c6b8f3a900b221797143e (accessed June 5, 2021).

45. Patrick Wilson, "JLARC Gives Good Review to Virginia Attorney General's Office," *Richmond Times-Dispatch*, November 25, 2019, https://www.richmond.com /news/virginia/jlarc-gives-good-review-to-virginia-attorney-general-s-office/article _a408652e-6288-58fa-a018-2512af36bf70.html (accessed June 5, 2021).

46. U.S. National Archives and Records Administration (NARA), Press Release, "NARA Press Statement on the Equal Rights Amendment," January 8, 2020, https:// www.archives.gov/press/press-releases-4 (accessed June 5, 2021).

47. Patricia Sullivan, "Herring, Other State AGs File Lawsuit Demanding Addition of ERA to Constitution," *Washington Post*, January 30, 2020, https: //www.washingtonpost.com/local/virginia-politics/era-lawsuit-herring/2020/01/30 /027eb956-42dc-11ea-aa6a-083d01b3ed18_story.html (accessed June 5, 2021).

48. Tom Jackman, "Virginia Eliminates Backlog of 2,665 Untested Rape Kits," *Washington Post*, July 8, 2020, https://www.washingtonpost.com/crime-law/2020/07/08/virginia-eliminates-backlog-2665-untested-rape-kits/ (accessed June 5, 2021).

Chapter 10

Hot Buttons

With liberty and justice for all . . . the born and unborn.

—Unidentified Virginia Republican members in the
House chamber at the end of the pledge of allegiance that
opens each daily formal session of the body, 2008

The daily floor sessions of most state legislative Bodies open with the Pledge of Allegiance, and Virginia is no exception. But early in my first term, I noticed a strange occurrence during this morning ritual. Emanating from the Republican side of the aisle as we finished the Pledge each day was a soft murmur with words not easily identifiable and difficult to assign to any specific individual. This went on for several weeks, and I incorrectly believed that the phrase being uttered was some kind of joke, akin to the "play ball" recitation you would hear at the conclusion of the Pledge at a sports event. But this was no joke. Upon inquiring of my seatmate what was being said to conclude the phrase "with liberty and justice for all," the answer came: "for the born and unborn." The culture wars were alive and well in the Virginia House of Delegates, the longest serving democratic Body in the Western world.

ABORTION AS LITMUS TEST

This experience was disturbing in so many ways. First, it was a corruption of the Pledge itself, ironic considering the criticism that many had leveled at Colin Kaepernick and NFL players who "took a knee" during the national anthem in the mid-2010s to protest social injustice. Second, it was cowardly; it was almost impossible to know which delegates were reciting the phrase and therefore who to hold accountable. And finally, the words ensured that we would begin our day emphasizing division on an issue that was deeply personal for many members. After several weeks, the murmur went away, and I always assumed that the Speaker had instructed his colleagues that such a display was beneath the Body.

While few people have ever heard about the corruption of the Pledge, they became acutely aware of abortion disputes in the Commonwealth in 2012, when a Senator Jill Holtzman Vogel introduced Senate Bill 484, a measure to require doctors to perform an invasive ultrasound procedure on a woman at least twenty-four hours prior to her undergoing an abortion. When initially filed, the bill was merely viewed as another way that conservatives could create additional roadblocks for women who sought abortions. In reading the actual language of the bill, however, it created greater alarm. As proposed, Vogel's bill would require a woman who wanted an abortion during the first twelve weeks of pregnancy to have a probe inserted into her vagina and then moved around until the ultrasound image was produced. If passed, the state would be forcing an invasive medical procedure upon women whether they or their doctors wanted it.

Ralph Northam, a medical doctor and a state Senator at the time, was the first Virginia lawmaker to publicly use the word "transvaginal" to describe the procedure. Blasting the measure on the Senate floor, he argued that a woman seeking an abortion in Virginia would be forcibly penetrated for no medical reason. While Republicans denied the assertion, amendments proposed that would have required the consent of patients prior to the procedure, or to permit physicians to opt-out altogether, failed on party-line votes.

In the House, Democratic Caucus Chair Charniele Herring characterized the legislation as "state-sponsored rape," and nighttime talk shows went wild.[1] Jon Stewart had a field day on the *Daily Show*, and Seth Meyers and Amy Poehler took aim at the state's proposed law on *Saturday Night Live*. To add fuel to the fire, Delegate Todd Gilbert, who eventually became the Republican Floor Leader and later Speaker of the House, stated during public debate that "in the vast majority of these cases, these [abortions] are matters of lifestyle convenience."[2] He apologized the next day.

Governor Bob McDonnell became increasingly concerned as he watched the controversy unfold on national television. Virginia was being made to be a national laughingstock. The Governor was looking for a way out of the political firestorm. At the same time, he was staunchly antiabortion, and had to be careful about alienating his conservative base. After initially stating that he would sign the bill, he announced that he would not accept it in the form passed by the Senate.[3] The controversy continued to build as the bill worked its way through the House. Something needed to be done. One early evening from my sixth-floor offices immediately across from those of the Speaker of the House, I watched as the Governor and his team arrived to huddle with Republican leadership. They initially had not accepted the word of Dr. Ralph

Northam about the intrusiveness of the procedure but now had now obtained "second opinions" from several their members, including Republican Delegate Chris Stolle of Virginia Beach, himself a physician, who confirmed Northam's impression of the bill.

For McDonnell, abortion was the taking of a life, and he wanted to make the practice more difficult. He was proud of his record in this area and argued that tougher state regulations adopted in the early 2010s had led the abortion rate to plummet in Virginia between 2011 and 2017.[4] He distrusted what he described as the "abortion industry" for allegedly misrepresenting the truth. But after studying the measure, he concluded that even this procedure was too intrusive. He told House Republicans to "fix it."[5] After several late-night meetings, McDonnell and his advisors prevailed, and the Republicans backed away from the initial version, and proposed a substitute to eliminate the requirement for the insertion of the probe.

Because of his reputation as a moderate, Delegate Dave Albo was assigned to argue the bill on the floor. During debate, Albo acknowledged the controversy with a personal story. He proceeded to describe his unsuccessful attempts to seduce his wife, who had become angry after learning that he supported the initial bill. Viewing this on the floor struck many as weirdly funny, tragic, and outrageous, all at the same time; the Delegate was suggesting, tongue-in-cheek, that we vote "yes" to help his marriage.[6] The measure passed, with most Democrats voting "no."

Virginia legislators from both parties hold very strong views on this issue. For many conservatives, it is what drew them to politics, and is central to their core values. And for many Democrats, particularly women, reproductive rights are one of their key issues. Among the most vocal of the "pro-life" legislators was Delegate Kirk Cox, former Speaker of the House, who would give a speech every year discussing this issue. He felt so strongly about it that in 2019, in a move totally unprecedented for a Speaker of the House, he came down from his elevated dais to stand on the House floor to give an impassioned speech opposed to abortion. Before an April 2019 "antiabortion" rally in Richmond, he asserted that "[t]here's not a more important issue that I've dealt with in my career in the legislature than life."[7]

When Republicans controlled the House, most every year would see another bill or resolution designed to restrict or condemn abortion. In 2017, at the urging of Delegate (now U.S. Congressman) Ben Cline, the House passed the so-called "Day of Tears" resolution encouraging Virginians to fly their flags at half-staff on the anniversary of *Roe v. Wade*.[8] And during the budget debates, the House would always pass language to deny funding for Planned Parenthood. These actions became so predictable that they took on the character of a scripted play, where both sides played their appointed roles with passion and conviction. But there are few reasons to doubt the sincerity of legislators on both sides of this issue, and they would probably take these positions even if their constituents did not support them.

Nationally, various legislatures have recently passed antiabortion bills in hopes of getting a court case before the U.S. Supreme Court that would overturn *Roe v. Wade*, and some Virginia legislators have not been shy in supporting them. When Alabama, for example, passed a measure that would punish a doctor who performs an abortion with a Class A felony—punishable by life, or ten to ninety-nine years in prison, more time than convicted rapists face in the state,[9] one Virginia Delegate, Bob Thomas of Fredericksburg, said in a radio interview that the near-total abortion ban did not go far enough.[10] As of May, 2021, seventeen states had passed laws to prohibit abortion at or before twenty weeks of pregnancy and ten would prevent nearly all abortions if *Roe v. Wade* was overturned.[11] In May 2021, the U.S. Supreme Court accepted a case from Mississippi that has the potential to overturn or modify *Roe v. Wade*.[12]

Most Republicans would find it difficult to obtain the nomination for any office without proclaiming support for "the unborn," and some reproductive rights advocates have imposed the same type of litmus test for Democrats. For years, many Democrat defenders of reproductive choice employed the phraseology used by President Bill Clinton that abortion should be "safe, legal and rare." More recently, however, the phrase has come under attack, with some arguing that it imposes a stigma upon women who have need for the procedure. In fact, some groups would deny an endorsement to a candidate who incorporated the word "rare." I bristled at this requirement, feeling that it only fed the narrative of conservative activists that advocates only want to increase the practice.

GUNS

If you were to choose one issue that embodies the shift in the politics of the Commonwealth over the last decade, it would be the issue of guns. Republicans, especially in rural areas, never had much difficulty in touting their strong support for "the right to keep and bear arms," and actively sought the endorsement of the National Rifle Association (NRA); it would often be the defining issue that would get their voters to the polls. Democrats used to walk a finer line. Gun safety advocates tended not to be single issue voters, and guns ranked lower in their hierarchy of concerns. Consequently, even if candidates strongly supported gun safety initiatives, they usually discussed them in the context of their respect for the Second Amendment and how they would never "take your guns away." This nuanced position began to change in the 2010s! Democrats, especially in the suburbs, began to campaign vigorously on gun safety issues. With Northern Virginia (NoVa) and suburbia in the political ascendency, the hold of the NRA was loosening. And some voters had now made gun safety a priority issue that determined their vote.[13]

Like many other states, Virginia has many legislators who are outspoken in their support of guns rights. House Speaker Gilbert has not been shy about embracing the NRA and has publicly stated that "I don't mind supporting and being supported by America's No. 1 longest civil rights organization."[14] Several Virginia elected officials have also made it a practice to carry concealed weapons during session. Senator Amanda Chase famously proclaimed that her .38 pistol, which she prominently displayed on many occasions while presenting her bills, was her "personal ERA,"[15] Senator John A. Cosgrove Jr. drew headlines when he left his pistol (presumably unloaded) in a committee room after leaving a hearing, and former Delegate David Ramadan carried two and perhaps three pistols on his person as he roamed the halls of the Capitol.

Of all the stories involving guns, the most interesting involved Jack Reid, a Henrico Delegate who served seventeen years in the House until his retirement in 2007. Reid made it a daily practice to carry his loaded semiautomatic .380 handgun to his office located on the seventh floor of the General Assembly building (immediately below mine on the eighth floor). Upon arrival, he would typically remove the clip and store the weapon in his desk drawer. On January 26, 2006, however, his plans went awry. As he was releasing the clip, the weapon discharged, and the bullet was only stopped by lodging in Reid's Kevlar bulletproof vest hanging on the door. Although there were many rumors suggesting that Reid had actually fired at the vest, none of them were substantiated, and the extremely embarrassed Delegate personally apologized for the incident on the floor of the House.[16]

Until very recently, the guns rights lobby generally had its way with the Virginia General Assembly. I learned that lesson early in my career. In 2008, I introduced a bill to conform Virginia's protective order prohibitions against firearms possession to federal law. The idea originated from a Commonwealth's Attorney in a jurisdiction adjacent to mine, who had identified a loophole in the Virginia law. She was prosecuting a man who had previously been convicted of domestic abuse and was subject to a protective order designed to protect his victim. Law enforcement had arrested the man after being called to the home of the victim; she said she was being threatened, and that the man had a gun. The sheriff arrived to find the man sitting in the living room with a gun between his legs. Though arrested and charged with violating the protective order, he was acquitted. In Virginia, individuals subject to a protective order could neither purchase nor transport a firearm. But they could *possess* one—and that, technically, was what he was doing.

My bill would have barred purchasing, transportation, or *possession* of a gun. Groups like the Commonwealth's Attorneys Association, the Sheriffs Association, and the police organizations all supported the bill, as well as domestic violence advocates. I was hopeful about the bill's passage as I presented it to committee and heard all the testimony for it. But it all came undone as Morgan Griffith, then the House Majority Leader and a future U.S. Congressperson, emerged from the back door leading to the committee room. He arrived with Philip Van Cleave, the head of the Virginia Citizens Defense League (VCDL), a group even more conservative than the NRA. Griffith and Van Cleave savaged the bill, and it was quickly defeated by the Republican majority in the committee. [17]

It would be years before I proposed another gun safety measure. I fully supported reasonable measures like universal background checks but chose instead to sign on to the proposals of others. After the August 2017 "United the Right" demonstration in Charlottesville, where hundreds of people marched in the streets with firearms and semiautomatic rifles, I felt I should try again. Gun regulation is an area where many states, including Virginia, have actively prohibited localities from passing certain gun ordinances.[18] I sponsored a bill that would give places like Charlottesville the ability to control firearms being carried during demonstrations, something they did not have in 2017. It was killed by a Republican-controlled subcommittee after the guns' rights lobby argued against it. During my fourteen years, I cannot recall a significant gun safety measure passing the General Assembly.

Virginia has the fifth highest gun ownership of any of the states.[19] Until recently, the state's gun policy has largely been dictated by the NRA, whose headquarters is located in NoVa, and by more conservative gun rights groups such as the VCDL. When Republicans controlled both Houses of the General Assembly and the governorship, they passed several measures expanding gun rights, including a law that allowed citizens to carry a concealed weapon into places where alcohol is served. Virginia is still one of some thirty-one states which permit the "open carry" of handguns, and these advocates would take full advantage of it.[20]

Governor Terry McAuliffe ended the expansion of gun rights after he took office in 2013. Proposals to allow citizens to carry concealed guns into churches or even airports fell victim to the Governor's veto pen. More elected officials and candidates began proposing gun safety measures than ever before, and money was mobilized for campaigns to push gun safety, with the result that the NRA has been massively outspent in recent state elections.[21] The 2019 election in Virginia brought the state a Democratic majority clearly committed to gun safety measures, and they moved quickly in 2020 to enact new policies reflecting that view.[22]

Nonetheless, there remains strong support for gun rights in many places in Virginia. As it became clear that the ascendency of the Democrats would mean passage of gun safety measures, some localities proclaimed themselves "2nd amendment sanctuaries," mimicking the pronouncements of sheriffs and local officials in other states who asserted they would refuse to enforce gun safety measures that they considered unconstitutional.[23] Within a month of the November 2019 election in Virginia, fifty-nine localities (counties, cities, and towns) passed sanctuary resolutions.[24] By the time the General Assembly reconvened in January 2020, over one hundred localities had adopted resolutions of this type, including the City of Virginia Beach. Major protests occurred at the Capitol.

The rhetoric surrounding the "2nd amendment sanctuary" movement proved disturbing.[25] Words like "nullification" and "interposition," common at the time of massive resistance to desegregation, and even harkening back to the secessionist arguments prior to the Civil War, were heard once again in the Commonwealth and in the Nation. "Our first line of defense is to stop these [gun safety] laws from getting passed," said Bedford County Supervisor John Sharp. "We need to show them [the legislature] a crowd like they have never seen. They need to be afraid, and they should be afraid."[26] In Tazewell County, Virginia, the county administrator stated that "we are 'ordering' a militia by making sure everyone can own a weapon."[27] False allegations circulated on the Internet that the Governor was ready to confiscate guns of law-abiding citizens and even "kill" them if they failed to comply with what the protesters deemed to be unconstitutional policies.[28] While the sanctuary resolutions provided solace to opponents of gun safety legislation, most were legally problematic.[29]

Neither large protests nor the emergence of sanctuary jurisdictions, however, would deter the Democrats, who felt that public opinion and the 2019 election gave them a mandate to act.[30] The 2020 session passed initiatives that they had advocated for years. In a series of generally party-line votes, the legislature reinstituted the "one-gun-a-month" regulation, adopted measures for universal background checks, and created Emergency Risk Protection Orders (ERPOs) designed to keep guns away from individuals with acute mental health problems. They also made good on their pledge to prohibit the carrying of firearms into the House gallery and onto the House floor.[31]

Conflicts over gun rights and safety are yet another manifestation of the cultural divergence occurring in the country. The sanctuary movement highlights a sense of alienation present in the more traditional, rural areas of the country, where some citizens feel that they are "losing their way of life" due to national and state action.[32] This sentiment is also evident when immigration issues are discussed. Increasing diversity is viewed by some as a threat to their culture and way of life; in some polls, nearly one half of respondents say that "things have changed so much" and that they feel "like strangers" in their own country.[33]

IMMIGRATION

About 13 percent of Virginia residents are immigrants, and one in nine is a native-born U.S. citizen with at least one immigrant parent.[34] Recent estimates placed the undocumented population at 275,000, and nearly 10,000 Deferred Action for Childhood Arrivals (DACA) recipients reside in the Commonwealth.[35] In the last decade, one of Virginia's major issues involved whether the state would force localities to report the presence of undocumented immigrants held in local jails to the U.S. Immigration and Customs Enforcement (ICE).

Following the 9/11 attacks, the U.S. Congress made changes in the *Federal Immigration Act*. A provision of the *Act*, Section 287(g), allows local law enforcement to perform certain functions under the supervision of ICE. Localities had mixed views of this approach, fearing the local costs involved in the effort. Called the Section 287(g) program, there was no requirement that localities or states participate at all, and some chose either limited cooperation or opted out altogether.[36] In the 2010s, conservatives in the General Assembly proposed bills targeted at localities who rejected the federal initiative, calling them "sanctuary jurisdictions." Technically, there are few sanctuary jurisdictions in the United States and presently none in Virginia. But that did not prevent legislators from offering bills that would force localities to enter into cooperative agreements with ICE. When these bills have passed, Democratic governors typically vetoed them.[37]

Another debate in the immigration arena involved whether to permit individuals who were brought to this country as children by undocumented persons (the "Dreamers") to attend college at in-state tuition rates. While states are required to provide all students, including undocumented ones, with a K-12 public education,[38] there are differences among the states about whether in-state college tuition should be extended to the undocumented residents. As of January 2020, there were seventeen states that have extended in-state tuition rates to undocumented students who met specific requirements.[39] Virginia had frequently considered such legislation, but it failed in every legislative session—until Democrats took control. Carrying the banner for this initiative since he arrived in 2011 has been Democratic Delegate Alfonso Lopez from Arlington, the first Latino ever elected to the Virginia House. As the son of a Venezuelan immigrant who arrived in this country without documentation, Lopez worked tirelessly to promote the rights of New Americans and argue for those who had little power or wealth. After nine years of hard work and frustration, Lopez was finally successful in 2020, and Dreamers in Virginia now have access in-state tuition.[40]

Finally, immigration issues are frequently intertwined with public safety. The issuance of driver's licenses, a state responsibility, is an example. Over the years, the House of Delegates has heard, usually in the form of emotional floor speeches, numerous examples where an undocumented person driving without a license has caused a terrible accident with massive loss of life. These are wrenching stories, and they make it difficult for legislators to move beyond the emotion to assess whether the issuance of licenses or privilege cards might increase the safety of the driving public or make it easier for injured persons to be compensated. As of February 2020, fifteen states and the District of Columbia had enacted laws to allow unauthorized immigrants to obtain driver's licenses.[41] Effective January 1, 2021, Virginia was added to the states which permit the issuance of driver's permits to certain categories of undocumented persons.[42]

CONCLUSION

Of the issues that I faced during my time as a Delegate, abortion, guns, and immigration were those that generated the most heat and the least light in policy debates. The views associated with guns, abortion, and immigration seem to be at the core of two widely divergent perspectives on the nature of the country and its future. LGBTQ issues could have been included as well, but attitudes in this area changed rapidly in my fourteen years of service, especially after the U.S. Supreme Court's decision on marriage equality. In 2021, Critical Race Theory[43] and "defund the police" became taking points for debate and division. It is difficult to predict the next issue in the culture wars, but there is little doubt that it will provide fodder for warriors in various camps for passionate arguments in the years ahead.

NOTES

1. Richmond Times-Dispatch Staff, "McDonnell Denounces Ultrasound Bill: House Passes Weaker Version," *Richmond Times-Dispatch*, February 22, 2012, https://www.richmond.com/archive/mcdonnell-denounces-ultrasound-bill-house-passes-weaker-version/article_d44a0394-a781-567a-a11a-4f5d74b75816.html (accessed June 5, 2021).

2. John Celock, "Virginia Ultrasound Bill: Republican Lawmaker Calls Abortion 'Lifestyle Convenience,'" *Huffington Post*, February 16, 2012, https://www.huffpost.com/entry/virginia-ultrasound-bill-republican-abortion-lifestyle-convenience_n

_1276799 (accessed June 5, 2021); Dahlia Lithwick, "Virginia's Proposed Ultrasound Law Is an Abomination," *Slate*, February 16, 2012, https://slate.com/human-interest /2012/02/virginia-ultrasound-law-women-who-want-an-abortion-will-be-forcibly -penetrated-for-no-medical-reason.html (accessed June 5, 2021).

3. Richmond Times-Dispatch Staff, "McDonnell Denounces Ultrasound Bill."

4. Former Governor Robert F. McDonnell, interview by author by telephone and email, January 30, 2020 and January 5, 2021. This period saw the closure of five clinics in Virginia, including two of the state's largest providers of abortion services. The Guttmacher Institute, a Washington, DC-based research group that supports reproductive choice, confirmed the governor's statistics, finding that pregnancy terminations dropped during this time by 41.5 percent, one the largest declines in the Nation. While the study confirmed McDonnell's view that fewer clinics meant fewer reported abortions, Guttmacher also suggested that one reason for the drop was better access to contraception. See Elizabeth Nash and Joerg Dreweke, "The U.S. Abortion Rate Continues to Drop: Once Again, State Abortion Restrictions Are Not the Main Driver," *Guttmacher Institute*, September 18, 2019, https://www.guttmacher.org/gpr /2019/09/us-abortion-rate-continues-drop-once-again-state-abortion-restrictions-are -not-main (accessed June 5, 2021).

5. Governor Robert F. McDonnell, interview by author by telephone and email, January 30, 2020 and January 5, 2021. When a Governor tells legislators to "fix it," it becomes clear very quickly that a bill needs to be changed. After all, Governors have a veto pen. The problem, of course, is that the Governor had to placate his conservative base, so the "fix" could not appear to be an accommodation to the critics.

6. John Hudson, "Ultrasound Bill Ruins Night of Sex for Virginia Lawmaker," *Atlantic*, February 24, 2012, https://www.theatlantic.com/politics/archive/2012/02/ ultrasound-bill-ruins-night-sex-virginia-lawmaker/331288/ (accessed June 5, 2021).

7. Mel Leonor, "Estimated 6,500 Rally Against Abortion at Virginia State Capitol," *Richmond Times-Dispatch*, April 3, 2019, https://www.richmond.com/news/virginia/ government-politics/estimated-rally-against-abortion-at-virginia-state-capitol/article _4faf0023-fd81-5632-9cc2-b7ce1dcc82eb.html (accessed June 5, 2021).

8. Graham Moomaw, "Virginia House Approves 'Day of Tears' Resolution to Encourage Half-staff Flags Over Abortion," *Richmond Times-Dispatch,* January 18, 2017, https://www.richmond.com/news/virginia/virginia-house-approves -day-of-tears-resolution-to-encourage-half/article_8fbfe938-86d9-5d33-9816 -616c601c7e75.html (accessed June 5, 2021). See also *Roe v. Wade*, 410 U.S. 113 (1973), https://supreme.justia.com/cases/federal/us/410/113/ (accessed June 6, 2021).

9. Emily Wax-Thibodeaux, "Restrictive Abortion Bill Weighs on Alabama Republicans, Who Struggle With Lack of Exceptions for Rape, Incest," *Washington Post*, May 13, 2019, https://www.washingtonpost.com/national/restrictive-abortion -law-weighs-on-alabama-republicans-who-struggle-with-lack-of-exceptions-for-rape -incest/2019/05/13/bec7b736-759e-11e9-b3f5-5673edf2d127_story.html (accessed June 5, 2021).

10. Josh Israel, "Republican Vows to Bring Near-total Abortion Ban to Virginia," *Thinkprogress*, May 15, 2019, https://thinkprogress.org/virginia-lawmaker-vows -georgia-style-abortion-ban-if-the-gop-controls-wins-the-upcoming-elections

-94cfc51628f2/ (accessed June 5, 2021). Virginia Delegate Bob Thomas was perhaps attempting to recapture a portion of his conservative base, some of whom he offended when he voted to expand Medicaid in 2018; he lost a primary bid in 2019 to a more conservative candidate.

11. Guttmacher Institute, "Abortion Policy in the Absence of *Roe*," May 18, 2021, https://www.guttmacher.org/state-policy/explore/abortion-policy-absence-roe (accessed June 5, 2021).

12. Robert Barnes, "Supreme Court to Review Mississippi Abortion Law That Advocates See as a Path to Diminish *Roe v. Wade*," *Washington Post*, May 17, 2021, https://www.washingtonpost.com/politics/courts_law/supreme-court-abortion-roe-v -wade/2021/05/17/cdaf1dd6-b708-11eb-a6b1-81296da0339b_story.html (accessed June 5, 2021).

13. A study by Schoen Consulting commissioned by Everytown for Gun Safety found that in Northern Virginia (NoVa), 82 percent of voters felt a candidate's stance on gun issues was important in receiving their vote. In the Richmond suburbs, 87 per-cent of voters found it important, while in the Hampton Roads area, 83 percent of vot-ers said that a candidate's stance on gun safety made a difference on how they voted. See Schoen Consulting, Memo to Everytown for Gun Safety, "Re: 2019 Virginia General Assembly Polling by Region Summary," *Everytown*, August 21, 2019, https: //everytown.org/documents/2019/08/2019-va-general-assembly-polling.pdf.

14. Max Thornberry, "House Delegate Race Pulls No Punches," *Northern Virginia Daily*, October 10, 2019, updated October 25, 2019, https://www.nvdaily.com /nvdaily/house-delegate-race-pulls-no-punches/article_554b370e-de59-562a-827e -0998a16afeb3.html (accessed June 5, 2021).

15. Amanda Chase is among the most controversial of the Senators in the Virginia Senate. See Patrick Wilson, "After Denying Foul Language, Chase Admits She Did 'Drop the F Bomb' During an Altercation with Officers," *Richmond Times-Dispatch*, April 29, 2019, https://www.richmond.com/news/virginia/government-politics/after -denying-foul-language-chase-admits-she-did-drop-the/article_845e22e3-65bd-579d -8051-4e922ecc9e6e.html (accessed June 5, 2021). In 2021, Chase was censured by the Senate for a wide variety of behaviors.

16. Chris L. Jenkins and Rosalind S. Helderman, "Gun-Toting Delegate Misfires at Va. Capitol," *Washington Post*, January 27, 2006 , https://www.washingtonpost. com/archive/politics/2006/01/27/gun-toting-delegate-misfires-at-va-capitol/1174f47f -21f3-45b4-b4c4-8f54a2d1dc3f/ (accessed June 5, 2021). While I never heard the shot, my office was on the eighth floor, directly above John S. Reid's, and the ceilings in the old building were not especially thick.

17. In 2020, the statute was finally changed to include possession as one of the prohibitions.

18. Joseph Tartakovsky, "Firearm Preemption Laws and What They Mean for Cities," *Municipal Lawyer* 54, no. 5 (2013): 6–9, 30–31, https://www.gibsondunn. com/wp-content/uploads/documents/publications/Tartakovsky-Firearm-Preemption -Laws-ML-09.2013.pdf (accessed June 5, 2021).

19. Jeff Edwards, "Gun Ownership Mapped: How Many Guns Each State Had in 2017?" *Hunting Mark*, February 18, 2018, https://huntingmark.com/gun-ownership-stats.

20. Giffords Law Center to Prevent Gun Violence, "Open Carry: Guns in Public," 2018, https://lawcenter.giffords.org/gun-laws/policy-areas/guns-in-public/open-carry/ (accessed June 5, 2021).

21. The National Rifle Association (NRA) has not helped itself with a number of scandals in which it has become embroiled over the last few years. See Claire Hansen, "What's Going on with the NRA?" *US News and World Report*, August 15, 2019, https://www.usnews.com/news/national-news/articles/whats-going-on-with-the-nra (accessed June 5, 2021). In the 2019 Virginia elections, the NRA was massively outspent by gun safety groups like Giffords PAC, so named for Congresswoman Gabby Giffords, and Everytown for Gun Safety, which was projected to invest $2.5 million in state races. See Laura Vozzella, "Giffords Gun-control Group Spends $300,000 on Ads Targeting Va. Republicans," *Washington Post*, October 9, 2019, https://www.washingtonpost.com/local/virginia-politics/giffords-gun-control-group-spends-300000-on-ads-targeting-va-republicans/2019/10/08/f63f5e52-e9f3-11e9-9306-47cb0324fd44_story.html (accessed June 5, 2021).

22. A postelection poll conducted in December 2019 by the Wason Center at Christopher Newport University showed strong support among Virginia voters for gun safety measures; 86 percent of respondents supported requiring background checks on all gun sales, and 73 percent favored the passage of a "red flag" law to allow guns to be temporarily removed from someone deemed a threat. Laura Vozzella, "Virginians Mostly Welcome Democratic Takeover, CNU Survey Finds," *Washington Post*, December 16, 2019, https://www.washingtonpost.com/local/virginia-politics/virginians-mostly-welcome-democratic-takeover-cnu-survey-finds/2019/12/15/a9e909e0-1f90-11ea-a153-dce4b94e4249_story.html (accessed June 5, 2021).

23. Organizers of the pro-gun sanctuaries readily admit that they borrowed this idea from local activists across the Nation who have created immigration sanctuaries designed to defy the Trump administration's efforts to enforce tougher immigration laws. See Daniel Trotta, "Defiant U.S. Sheriffs Push Gun Sanctuaries, Imitating Liberals on Immigration," *Reuters*, March 4, 2019, https://www.reuters.com/article/us-usa-guns-sanctuary/defiant-us-sheriffs-push-gun-sanctuaries-imitating-liberals-on-immigration-idUSKCN1QL0ZC (accessed June 5, 2021).

24. Gregory S. Schneider, "In Virginia, and Elsewhere, Gun Supporters Prepare to Defy New Laws," *Washington Post*, November 23, 2019, https://www.washingtonpost.com/local/virginia-politics/in-virginia-and-elsewhere-gun-supporters-prepare-to-defy-new-laws/2019/11/23/4a95fcc2-0c86-11ea-bd9d-c628fd48b3a0_story.html (accessed June 5, 2021), and David J. Toscano, "The Gun Sanctuary Movement is Exploding," *Slate,* Dec 11, 2019, (accessed June 5, 2021).

25. Michael Paul Williams, "Williams: The 'Second Amendment Sanctuary' Movement is a Sham. But More Local Control is a Good Idea." *Richmond Times-Dispatch*, November 27, 2019, https://www.richmond.com/news/plus/williams-the-second-amendment-sanctuary-movement-is-a-sham-but/article_919f752a-05b2-5be3-9a7e-8049ca7f62a8.html (accessed June 5, 2021).

26. David "Adam" McKelvey, "McKelvey: A Framework for True 2nd Amendment Sanctuary," *Roanoke Times*, November 27, 2019, https://www.roanoke.com/opinion /commentary/mckelvey-a-framework-for-true-nd-amendment-sanctuary/article _700ee127-81a2-50b9-8c7a-234647a3c92e.html (accessed June 5, 2021). Following passage of an Extreme Risk Protection Order (ERPO) law in New Mexico, a representative of the state Sheriffs' Association said a large majority of sheriffs would refuse to confiscate a person's firearms if given a court order to do so."We don't work for the governor. We don't work for the Legislature," Cibola County Sheriff Tony Mace told the Santa Fe New Mexican. "We have discretion to use whichever laws we want." Jens Gould, "Governor Signs Controversial 'Red-flag' Bill into Law," *Santa Fe New Mexican*, February 25, 2020, https://www.santafenewmexican.com/news /legislature/governor-signs-controversial-red-flag-bill-into-law/article_e36b14d2 -57e5-11ea-aa8a-3ff1fb8231bc.html?utm_campaign=2020-02-26+SD&utm_medium =email&utm_source=Pew (accessed June 5, 2021).

27. Jim Talbert, "Tazewell County Becomes Second Amendment Sanctuary, Adds Militia Ordinance during Widely Attended Meeting," *Bristol Herald Courier*, December 3, 2019, updated December 11, 2019, https://www.heraldcourier.com /news/tazewell-county-becomes-second-amendment-sanctuary-adds-militia -ordinance-during/article_6a3d4e37-64f2-5365-9b71-7e4a694602e3.html (accessed June 5, 2021).

28. Beginning on December 25, 2019, Facebook posts began to appear and be replayed with the following statement attributed to Governor Northam: "You will give up your guns, if you don't, I'll have the National Guard cut your power, your phone lines, and your internet. Then, if you still refuse to comply, I'll have you killed." *Politifact* ruled these statements as "pants on fire" lies. Bill McCarthy, "No, Northam Will Not Cut Off Power, Kill Virginians Who Refuse to Give Up Guns," *PolitiFact*, January 2, 2020, https://www.politifact.com/facebook-fact -checks/statements/2020/jan/02/facebook-posts/no-northam-will-not-cut-power-kill -virginians-who-/ (accessed June 5, 2021). And the Governor was so concerned about this rhetoric that he specifically denied it during the annual State of the Commonwealth address on January 8, 2020.

29. Amy Friedenberger, "Attorney General Mark Herring, in Advisory Opinion, says Second Amendment Resolutions Have 'No Legal Effect,'" *Roanoke Times*, December 20, 2019, https://www.roanoke.com/news/local/attorney-general-mark -herring-in-advisory-opinion-says-second-amendment/article_c01780bd-535d-5c1e -a322-0f6e6d3adbdb.html (accessed June 5, 2021).

30. A March 2019 study by Quinnipiac reported that 93 percent of American voters support a bill that would require "background checks for all gun buyers" (including those conducted at gun shows and by online vendors), including 89 percent of Republicans and 87 percent of gun owners. Quinnipiac University Poll, "U.S. Voters Oppose Trump Emergency Powers on Wall 2–1 Quinnipiac University National Poll Finds; 86percent Back Democrats' Bill on Gun Background Checks," *Quinnipiac*, March 6, 2019, https://poll.qu.edu/Poll-Release-Legacy?releaseid=2604 (accessed June 5, 2021). And an April 2018 poll found that 85 percent of registered voters support laws that would "allow the police to take guns away from people who have

been found by a judge to be a danger to themselves or others" (71 percent "strongly supported"). Emily Guskin and Scott Clement, "Has Parkland Changed Americans' Views on Guns?" *Washington Post*, April 20, 2018, https://www.washingtonpost.com/news/the-fix/wp/2018/04/20/has-parkland-changed-americans-views-on-guns/ (accessed June 5, 2021).

31. One of the interesting dilemmas faced by Democrats when they considered banning guns from the House chambers was enforcement. Democrats knew that as many as ten members carried a concealed weapon every day and were concerned that they might try to precipitate an arrest not only to test the rule but become a hero to their base. Democratic leadership decided that they would pass the ban, but not force Republican members to be searched before entering the Chamber. And Republican members discreetly avoided confrontation by keeping their firearms hidden.

32. Alienation in rural life has been most recently detailed in J. D. Vance, *Hillbilly Elegy: A Memoir of a Family and Culture in Crisis* (New York: Harper Press, 2016); Timothy P. Carney, *Alienated America: While Some Places Thrive While Others Collapse* (New York: Harper Collins, 2019); and Arlie Russell Hochschild, *Strangers in Their Own Land: Anger and Mourning on the American Right* (New York: New Press, 2016).

33. Peter Wehner, *The Death of Politics: How to Heal Our Frayed Republic After Trump* (New York: Harper One, 2019), 16

34. American Immigration Council, "Fact Sheet: Immigrants in Virginia," *American Immigration Council*, August 6, 2020, https://www.americanimmigrationcouncil.org/research/immigrants-in-virginia (accessed June 5, 2021).

35. American Immigration Council, "Fact Sheet."

36. See U.S. Immigration and Customs Enforcement (ICE), "Delegation of Immigration Authority Section 287(g)," in *Illegal Immigration Reform and Immigrant Responsibility Act of 1996, Immigration and Nationality Act*, https://www.ice.gov/identify-and-arrest/287g (accessed June 2, 2021).

37. Mel Leonor, "Northam Vetoes 'Sanctuary Cities' Bill," *Richmond Times-Dispatch*, March 19, 2019, https://www.richmond.com/news/local/government-politics/northam-vetoes-sanctuary-cities-bill/article_a0594c7e-b87f-5e4e-9eb8-feb32abdbfc7.html (accessed June 5, 2021).

38. *Plyler v. Doe*, 457 U.S. 202 (1982), https://supreme.justia.com/cases/federal/us/457/202/ (accessed June 5, 2021).

39. National Conference of State Legislatures (NCSL), "Undocumented Student Tuition: Overview," March 14, 2019, updated September 19, 2019, http://www.ncsl.org/research/education/undocumented-student-tuition-overview.aspx (accessed June 5, 2021).

40. Kate Masters and Ned Oliver, "House, Senate Pass Long-anticipated Immigrants' Rights Bills," *Virginia Mercury*, February 12, 2020, https://www.virginiamercury.com/2020/02/12/house-senate-pass-long-anticipated-immigrants-rights-bills/ (accessed June 5, 2021).

41. NCSL, "States Offering Driver's Licenses to Immigrants," February 6, 2020, https://www.ncsl.org/research/immigration/states-offering-driver-s-licenses-to-immigrants.aspx (accessed June 5, 2021). For more information, see National

Immigration Law Center (NILC), "State Laws Providing Access to Driver's Licenses or Cards, Regardless of Immigration Status," *NILC.org*, updated August 2019, https://www.nilc.org/wp-content/uploads/2015/11/drivers-license-access-table.pdf (accessed June 5, 2021).

42. Masters and Oliver, "House, Senate."

43. Critical race theory is an academic concept that was developed primarily by legal scholars more than 40 years ago. Its core premise is that racism is not simply a product of individual prejudice but is rooted in our legal system and other institutions. See Lauren Camera, "What Is Critical Race Theory and Why Are People So Upset About It?" *US News*, June 1, 2021, https://www.usnews.com/news/national-news/articles/what-is-critical-race-theory-and-why-are-people-so-upset-about-it (accessed June 23, 2021).

Chapter 11

Because We Can

Though the will of the majority is in all cases to prevail, that will, to be rightful, must be reasonable.

—Thomas Jefferson, First Inaugural Address, March 4, 1801[1]

Being in the minority is frustrating and discouraging. Serving as the Leader of the Minority can magnify those feelings tenfold. You can win small skirmishes, occasionally embarrass the opposition, and receive compliments from supporters on fighting *the good fight*. But most every day, after making the most reasonable arguments in support of your position, you commonly cast your vote on critical issues only to find that you have lost . . . again. And, on certain occasions, the majority will pass a bill, or defeat one, simply because they can. Even little bills without consequence can fall victim to this fate to enact retribution for something that was said or done by the patron or a member of his or her party. During my years as Minority Leader, this happened periodically, and these actions frequently had nothing to do with policy. But it was not just Republicans who did it. In 2020, Republican Delegate Glenn Davis made the unfortunate mistake of criticizing Democratic leadership for a parliamentary ruling made one day before four of his bills were up for a vote. Only one of the measures was the least bit controversial, but the Democrats killed them all—just because they could.[2]

I do not regret for a minute my experiences as Democratic Leader. There is a significant role for active and engaged minorities in our system of checks and balances; such groups are essential to ensure governmental accountability and so all voices are heard. And members of the minority party can make a big difference. The unified House Democratic minority provided the key votes in passing major legislation such as the 2013 transportation bill and Medicaid expansion in 2018. Democrats were able to sustain numerous gubernatorial vetoes that prevented detrimental laws from taking effect. But it is not the same as having control over the making of major policy. Just ask my colleagues who seized control of the House in 2020. Since I was never in the majority, I had to live with decisions made by the majority simply because they had the votes. The most significant of these involved redistricting and voting rights.

VOTING RIGHTS AND REDISTRICTING

The Privileges and Elections Committee is the oldest standing committee in the Virginia House of Delegates, tracing its origins back to the House of Burgesses in the 1600s when it had the title of "Committee for the Examination of Elections and Returns." Its members have included George Washington, Thomas Jefferson, and Patrick Henry. It was historically viewed as among the most important committees in the House, as it dealt with elections and rules of parliamentary procedure. Today, it is the committee where bills relating to redistricting, election rules, and voting rights are considered. While never serving on this committee, I attended many of its sessions

Until 2020, most efforts made by Democrats over the last two decades to make voting easier were rejected. Instead, Republicans imposed major restrictions on voting rights, such as the requirement that Virginians carry a picture ID into the polls to vote. Virginia was one of a number of state legislatures controlled by Republicans that made such changes during this period. The arguments for these measures were largely the same as those heard in other statehouses. Without more regulations, the GOP argued, fraud would increase. Democrats countered with evidence that election fraud was miniscule and suggested that the Republican measures were designed to suppress the vote, especially in minority communities. Through their control of this committee and the House, the GOP was able to dictate Virginia electoral rules for the greater part of two decades.

Redistricting is perhaps the best example of how the majority party maintains its power—simply because it can. When California Democrats redrew their state legislative districts in 1980, it was so blatantly partisan that it drove the state's Republicans into an electoral hole from which they have never recovered. When the GOP protested, the response they received from the architect of the plan, former U.S. Representative Philip Burton, was indicative of how parties in control drew maps simply because they had the power to do so. "What's the matter?" Burton was reported to say. "Can't they take a joke?"[3]

But redistricting is no joke. Like other states, Virginia redistricts every ten years and 2011 was my first experience with the process. Prior to the 2011 redistricting, Democrats held thirty-nine seats out of one hundred, and Republicans preferred that they win no more. In an approach that can only be labeled "masterful," Republican leadership in the House, led by Delegate S. Chris Jones, a pharmacist from Suffolk who eventually became the Chair of the House Appropriations Committee, developed a plan that they thought would solidify their power for a decade. It concentrated Democratic voters into certain districts, while diluting the party's strength in surrounding areas. In some of the Democratic districts represented by African American delegates, voter history predicted that as much as 70 percent of the electorate would support a Democrat. Looking at a color-coded map of the districts, blue dots represented by Democrats were surrounded by a sea of red. The more that Democratic votes were concentrated into these districts, the more options were created for Republicans in the surrounding ones.

The Republican 2011 redistricting strategy was simple. First, Republicans in the House made an implicit deal with the Senate, then controlled by Democrats, that the House would not object to the lines drawn by the Senate so long as the Senate supported the House map. The GOP map drawers then went to African Americans in the House to seek their input on the districts they would like to see. Some African Americans effectively participated in drawing their own districts. One member of the Virginia Legislative Black Caucus (VLBC) even asked Jones to draw her lines so that one potential competitor would no longer be in her district. Jones complied. Jones was frank in describing the effort. "At the time, we were concerned about the *Voting Rights Act*," he said, "and we wanted to draw lines that would meet the preclearance standard of the Obama justice department."[4] At the time, redistricting plans in the South needed the approval from the U.S. Department of Justice (DOJ) before taking affect, a practice designed to protect the voting rights of African Americans. Republicans would be submitting their plan to a department with President Barack Obama appointees. Obtaining support from African Americans was viewed as key to gaining preclearance. After Jones received input from African American delegates, he and his allies went to work. The GOP established lines so that districts presently represented by African Americans would include more than a certain percentage of black voters. In those targeted districts, at least 55 percent of the voting population would be African American.

Ironically, it was this racially-centric approach that provided the basis for the federal court decision overturning the plan years later. In 2013, the U.S. Supreme Court in the *Shelby County v. Holder* case[5] gutted the *Voting Rights Act* and released a number of Southern states from the preclearance requirement. Ironically, this case was used to find the Virginia redistricting map was an unconstitutional gerrymander based on race. In 2011, Republicans protected African Americans because they thought it would buttress their legal position. They were wrong.

Finally, the Republicans made other deals with some House Democrats in Northern Virginia (NoVa) to shore up their districts and gain an additional level of support for their plan. Former Delegate Bob Brink of Arlington describes his exchange with Chris Jones to illustrate the point. "Chris," he said, "do you really care about the map in northern Virginia?" Jones responded in the negative, saying that "when you move lines in NOVA [NoVa], you either get more Democrats in a district or you bump up against the Potomac. Besides, I get lost every time I drive up there."[6] Eventually, the redistricting plan in the House passed by a wide majority; I was one of only twelve House Democrats who voted "no."

As Democrats had done years earlier, the Republican plan also placed incumbents from the opposition party into districts designed to force retirements. It eviscerated the district of Democrat Delegate Paula Miller from Norfolk, forcing her to retire. It moved substantial numbers of Republican voters into the district of ten-term veteran Delegate William Barlow, who was then swamped in his re-election bid.[7] And it ended the career of Delegate Ward Armstrong, the feisty populist from Henry County. Armstrong had not endeared himself to Republicans during his three-year stint as Democratic Leader, and when population changes required that one district in the southern part of the state be eliminated so a new one could be created in NoVa, the Republicans decided that Armstrong's district would be the one. While Armstrong ran the next year in an adjacent district, spent over $1 million, and performed several points better than previous Democrats, he lost. Partisan redistricting had ended his legislative career.[8]

When I first arrived in the General Assembly in 2006, I understoodredistricting only in the most academic way. I never realized the importance of the process in controllingf the state legislatures, the political composition of the U.S. Congress (the states also draw lines for Congress), and the direction of the country. But as I watched what was happening across the Nation, it became clear that the Republicans were engaged in a coordinated campaign to control the U.S. Congress, and thereby the country, through redistricting in the states.

In state after state, control over redistricting allowed one party to win a much higher percentage of seats than the overall percentage of voters that supported their party. In 2011, Virginia was considered a *purple* state, with the electorate evenly divided. Yet the House had only thirty-nine Democrats out of one hundred. I became a strong proponent of nonpartisan redistricting approaches that could draw fairer lines than either party would create when in the majority. The Republican redistricting of 2011 made the Democratic prospects for gaining the majority in the House exceedingly difficult. When I became Democratic Leader in late 2011, one of my goals was to change these lines, hopefully sooner rather than later. That opportunity finally came in 2018.

COURTS UPEND THE GOP PLAN

In 2014, plaintiffs from twelve separate Virginia House districts filed a federal lawsuit allegedly that the 2011 redistricting plan was an unconstitutional, racial gerrymandering prohibited by the U.S. Constitution. These arguments were based on those that had been successful in a 2015 case that overturned the Virginia Congressional maps drawn by the legislature in the same year. As a result, Democrats gained another U.S. Congressional seat in the next election.

The case involving the House of Delegates districts took years before the court finally issued its ruling. At trial, Delegate Jones admitted that the goal was to create districts in which at least 55 percent of the voters were African Americans so that the plan could meet the requirements of the *Voting Rights Act of 1965* and gain the approval of the U.S. DOJ.[9] Jones asserted that he had sought Democratic cooperation in building the plan. Though some delegates denied this, it was clear that some communication had occurred and that the Democrats who had voted for the plan either had their districts improved or not adversely affected.

Clearly, there was a racial element to the plan; African American Democratic Delegate Lionel Spruill, Sr., in speaking on the House floor in support of the Republican map, even exclaimed "I was black before I was a Democrat." With the notable exceptions of Delegates Rosalyn Tyler and Jeion Ward, all African Americans in the House voted for the map, giving the Republicans a talking point to argue that this was not a "racial gerrymander," and that it had significant Democratic and African American support.

By the time the redistricting trial ended, I was confident, based on recent case law and Jones's statement about establishing racial criteria in the contested districts, that the federal court would overturn the plan. The U.S. Supreme Court had already concluded that similar approaches were constitutionally impermissible. The question was how long it would take, and when House elections in new districts would occur. Finally, in June 2018, the U.S. District Court for the Eastern District of Virginia issued its opinion. Not surprisingly, it held that eleven of the twelve challenged districts were racially gerrymandered and therefore unconstitutional.[10] The Court's order gave the legislature "the opportunity" to redraw the districts to address the constitutional infirmities by October 30, 2018.[11] Most Democrats were shocked at how long it took the court to reach a decision; the 2017 election was the fourth House election conducted using what the Court ultimately determined to be an unconstitutional map.

In 2018, the legislature was still in Republican hands and there was some concern that some Democratic members would repeat history by striking individual deals with the GOP, leading to a new map that would make it more difficult to win the majority. I was determined not to let this happen.

We were also worried that Republicans would delay the process until it was not possible to run in new districts in the fall 2019 election. But 2018 was very different than 2011. First, the Democratic Governor Ralph S. Northam could exercise his veto if an unfair map was to pass the Assembly. [12] Whether he would do it in the face of a strongly bipartisan map supported by prominent African Americans, however, was not a surety. Second, Democrats now had forty-nine members in the House, fifteen of whom had emerged from their recent elections and first legislative session with a very strong allegiance to their party. An agreement with Republicans would therefore be less likely in 2018 than it was in 2011. Third, the composition of the VLBC was very different. Only three members remained from the group serving in the House in 2011, and the VLBC was now younger, more partisan, and less inclined to make a deal with Republicans.

Republicans found themselves between the proverbial "rock and a hard place." While still in the majority, albeit barely, any new maps that they might draw almost inevitably would create more districts where Democrats would have an advantage over Republican incumbents. Any chance in having the case overturned by the U.S. Supreme Court was made less likely because the Justices, in a supermajority decision, had already instructed the lower court that it should apply the standard that had already been used to overturn the Congressional districts. Both parties knew that producing a new map before the 2019 election was key to Democrats winning the majority before the next redistricting scheduled after the 2020 U.S. Census. For the Republicans, this meant a strategy of delay. Democrats, however, felt the need to move quickly.

Democrats best hope of getting a good map rested in having the federal courts draw it. To do this, we would need to show that the legislature was unable to do so. Our biggest worry was that Republicans would make deals with enough members of our caucus to gain a majority support for a new map. We could not let that happen. We needed a unified caucus, especially among our African American members. Hence, we engaged House members of the VLBC to develop and present a plan that we knew would be rejected by the Republicans. This would demonstrate to the Court that we had reached an impasse. And we needed to do this as soon as possible.

Throughout the summer, House Democrats publicly demanded that the Speaker call us back into session to produce a plan. As expected, he ignored the requests and did not even respond to our letters. At the same time, we convened the democratic delegates in the eleven affected districts, most of whom were members of the VLBC, to draw our own map. Gaining their unanimous support for a plan would not only show we could produce a map, but make it less likely that any of our members would desert us.

This effort took weeks of careful and deliberate negotiations, of modifying precinct lines again and again, always considering the implications not only for the eleven districts that required change, but also for adjacent districts. The discussions were difficult at times. Some of our longest-serving members had grown comfortable in their districts and were concerned about possible reductions in the percentage of African American voters that might be moved from their present districts. And some members in adjacent districts wanted more Democratic voters than the veterans were willing to give. Delegate Lamont Bagby (Chair of the VLBC), Delegate Charniele Herring (House Democratic Caucus Chair), Brad Komar (the Governor's PAC Director), and technical advisors from the National Democratic Redistricting Committee (NDRC) exercised great patience in getting the map drawn. There were several occasions when it appeared that the deal would fall apart, and one delegate from Newport News delayed her approval for much longer than any of us wanted. But a plan was finally adopted, and we unveiled it several days before the special session commenced.

During this process, the federal court threw the Republicans a curve ball. In early August 2018, the Court asked the majority party if they even intended to produce a revised map and gave them until August 24 to respond. As the Republicans equivocated, Governor Northam accelerated the process by calling the special session on the issue for August 30.

The House of Delegates convened on that date, and our introduced map was referred to the Privileges and Elections Committee. As expected, Republicans criticized it as overly partisan. We were also scolded for putting several sitting Republican lawmakers into the same districts, something we neither intended and nor knew until the map was scrutinized in committee. In fact, I had specifically instructed our line drawers not to look at where Republican delegates resided as our map was drawn. During the session on August 30, Republicans spent hours criticizing our plan, but took no action, offered no plan, failed to set a timetable to return to Richmond, and simply adjourned. The federal court must have been watching; within thirty minutes of adjournment, the Court denied the request by Republicans to "stay" the Court's order requiring the House to draw new districts.

After weeks of hoping they could run out the clock, the Republicans were now forced to act. But they had few cards left to play. It would be difficult to secure support from the VLBC for any plan proposed by the GOP; the caucus had already embraced a map and changing it would be viewed as capitulation. The Republicans chose instead to state publicly their intention to offer their own map by late September in hopes that they would get the Court to back down from drawing a map of their own. But the federal court had other plans. On September 13, it ordered each side to designate a "special master" to draw a map within two weeks. The Republicans decided to reconvene the Privileges and Elections Committee for September 27, 2018 and issued a general statement of their intent to call the entire Body into session sometime in mid-October. Their plan was still delay, delay, delay.

Only two days prior to the September 27 meeting, Republicans offered a map which did little to unpack the districts, and overtly stated that their purpose was to "maintain the present partisan composition" of the House. In a straight party line vote, the committee approved the GOP map twelve to ten. The Republicans had hoped to show the court that they had some bipartisan support and were moving to produce a map that could pass the legislature, but Democratic unity frustrated their plans. Shortly thereafter, Governor Northam indicated that he would veto the Republican plan.

The Republicans continued to delay. First, they attempted to convey the impression that they were on the verge of generating a bipartisan map. They spoke to several younger Democratic members and got them to make statements suggesting a bipartisan compromise. Second, they worked behind the scenes in an effort to split off members of the VLBC. Jones even enlisted the help of now Virginia Senator Spruill in hopes of influencing his colleagues. But even that failed; House members were reluctant to be influenced by someone outside our Body, even if he was African American. Finally, they wrongfully hoped that Brent Kavanaugh's appointment to the U.S. Supreme Court would ensure a reversal of the lower court's ruling. All of these efforts failed. Governor Northam declared that the legislature had reached an impasse, and the Court proceeded to draw its own map.

At the end of February, the federal court issued the new map that, as expected, gave Democrats a fighting chance at the majority. Speaker Cox and Chris Jones were now in districts where Democratic performance was projected to be 52 percent or more; the Speaker's district swung some twenty points in the blue direction. House Republicans kept hoping that an appeal to the U.S. Supreme Court would save them, but month after month passed with no decision. Primaries were held in June 2019 with the new districts. Then, on June 17, 2019, the word came; in a five-to-four decision which crossed ideological lines, the Court dismissed the appeal, and the Republicans were left to compete in districts that were no longer drawn for their advantage.[13] The goal of changing the 2011 redistricting map had been accomplished. Democrats were now poised to capture the majority.

EXCEPTIONS PROVE THE RULE

Although majorities are fond of exercising their power, there are occasions, independent of court disputes, when participants act differently than what their power might allow. When that occurs, it can represent a powerful statement of the importance of upholding the rules and traditions of democracy. One of the most dramatic such incidents occurred in 2013 and involved Speaker of the Virginia House of Delegates William J. Howell. Like many other states, Virginia employs a legislative concept known as "germaneness" when considering amendments attached to bills. Under the rule, an amendment to a bill may not expand a measure's original purpose or transform its general scope. This rule is designed to prevent amendments that have little relevance to an original bill from being added to it. One could not amend a bill on animal control, for example, by adding language to fund a new road. Nonetheless, even such rules require interpretation and enforcement. In the House, when there is an objection to an amendment for germaneness, it is the Speaker of the House who determines whether the proposal can be considered. Speakers may choose, for convenience or politics, to ignore precedent and adopt a certain position simply to support the majority—because they can.

The most significant parliamentary ruling I ever witnessed occurred in February 2013. Early in the session, the Virginia House had passed, and sent to the Senate, an innocuous bill that made minor technical adjustments in several electoral districts for the upcoming elections. At the time, the Senate consisted of an equal number of Democrats and Republicans—until one day, when one of the Senate's longest-serving Democratic members, an African American veteran of the Civil Rights movement, took leave to attend President Obama's second inaugural. Republican Senators, recognizing that they had temporarily gained the majority, seized the moment to push through thirty-six-page amendment to the bill that made massive changes in districts across the state. Democrats cried foul, but the amended legislation, which was designed to ensure a Republican Senate legislative majority for a decade, passed twenty to nineteen.

Since the Senate had made changes to a House measure, the bill had to return to our Chamber for approval. As typical, it was sent directly to the House floor without any committee deliberations. Senate Republicans were betting that GOP members of the House would support the brazen power grab. Under the rules, the amendment was clearly not germane. It dramatically altered the original measure's original purpose and scope and therefore should be ruled out-of-order. And most everyone knew it.

Howell now faced a serious dilemma. If he ruled the amendments out-of-order, he would anger Senate Republicans. If he allowed the amendments to remain, he would violate the formal rules, the informal norms, and prior precedents of the House. Such an action would only increase partisanship in the Body. A lot was at stake.

After delaying for almost two weeks, the Speaker finally placed the bill on the floor for debate and a vote. When it was called, I attempted to be recognized to move to strike the amendment. Instead, the Speaker called on Delegate Robert "Bobby" Orrock, the Republican parliamentarian. The Speaker would call on Orrock whenever a parliamentary motion would be made. As soon as Orrock was recognized, it was clear that Howell had decided to rule the amendments out-of-order; he would not allow the Democrats to gain credit for defeating the measure.[14] "I have the responsibility and obligation," he explained from the dais, "to uphold the honor, dignity and integrity of both this office and the institution as a whole." He then ruled the amendments out-of-order.[15]

After the vote, the House Republican Caucus briefly considered removing the Speaker, going so far as requiring him to leave the room while they decided his fate. He retained his position, and while Senate Republicans were not pleased, Howell had reinforced the traditions and norms of the Body so critical for transactional decision-making.[16] It was not easy, but it was right. And it reinforced the notion that a democratic Body that had operated for 400 years had much to celebrate.

When the Democrats took control of the House and Senate in 2020, one of the first things watched by observers was whether they would operate much like the Republicans had done previously. At the close of the 2019 session, the General Assembly, with the votes of Democrats in both Houses, had passed a proposal to amend the Virginia Constitution to create a commission to presumably draw new districts in the 2021 redistricting process. The proposal arrived at the last minute of the legislative session and was not the best of all redistricting reform plans. Many felt that it gave too much power to legislators and were troubled because any impasse would be decided by the Virginia Supreme Court.

Under Virginia law, the measure was required to be passed a second time by the 2020 session and then approved in a general election by the voters in order to take effect. Opposition to the amendment began to emerge in the fall of 2019. Delegates like Democrat Mark Levine of Alexandria argued that under the amendment, any redistricting plan proposed could be shelved by only two legislators on the commission, with the result that the map-drawing power would devolve quickly to the Virginia Supreme Court, a body he claimed would be biased because most of its justices had been appointed by the Republican majority.[17] Susan Swecker, Chair of the Democratic Party of Virginia, voiced her opposition as well. But most importantly, the amendment drew fire from African Americans in the House, many of whom were concerned about the lack of protections for people of color in commission deliberations. They now numbered seventeen in the House, and could make their power felt if they acted together. African Americans in the House had always been concerned about a system which would take control over drawing legislative lines away from them, especially when Democrats now had the majority. They worried that smaller numbers of African Americans would be elected if nonpartisan redistricting occurred. In an effort to stick together, Democrats had long meetings, frequently punctuated by charges that one person or another was acting in bad faith or, worse yet, with racial insensitivity.

As the session approached adjournment, it appeared that new Speaker Filler-Corn was blocking efforts to consider the amendment. With a majority of House Democratic Caucus members concurring, she supported the decision of Privileges and Election Chair, Democratic Delegate Joseph Lindsey, of Virginia Beach, to delay docketing the legislation for a hearing and vote before his committee.[18] Pressure for a vote began to build from redistricting reformers and media outlets; to do nothing, they argued, would reinforce voter cynicism and be hypocritical.[19] But why? There is a reason why the Virginia Constitution requires a proposed amendment to be passed twice by the legislature; it is to allow time for reflection and for the possibility that lawmakers might change their minds before submitting a measure to the voters. Nonetheless, the Democrats were feeling the heat. Republicans kept agitating for the measure to be considered, and even filed for a "discharge" of the bill from the committee so it could go directly to the House floor.[20]

The discharge motion created problems for the Democrats. Under usual circumstances with Democrats controlling fifty-five votes and the discharge action considered as a "procedural" rather than a "substantive motion," one would expect the Republican effort to fail. The strong feelings some Democrats had for redistricting reform, however, injected risk into such a vote. A vote to discharge the bill from the committee would prove a terrible blow to Democratic control of the House agenda, the new Speaker's control of the Body, and hand a major victory to the GOP. That vote had to be avoided at all costs. Nonetheless, House Democrats knew that between five and ten of their colleagues would support the amendment if it came to a floor vote. With the GOP's forty-five members expected to vote yes, the measure would likely pass.

Differences emerged not only within the House Democratic Caucus, but also between the Senate and the House. African American leaders in the Senate, notably Louise Lucas, Mamie Locke, and Jennifer McClellan, supported the amendment and did not share the views of their VLBC colleagues in the House. They pushed for the resolution to be docketed for a vote and suggested that the Senate might otherwise refuse to take up some key measures considered important by House Democrats. In the last days of the session, the Speaker authorized the Privileges and Elections Committee to take up the measure. It passed easily, primarily because Republicans voted in a block for it. Opponents of the resolution mounted one last effort on the House floor, introducing a substitute measure which would have delayed placing the amendment in the constitution for several years. It failed in a close vote with Republicans making the difference. When the final votes on the amendment were tallied, only nine Democrats voted for the resolution, but, with forty-five votes from Republicans, it passed easily.[21] It was the only major defeat for Democratic House leadership in the 2020 session. And despite the assertion by House leadership that the voters would reject the amendment, it was approved by a wide 66 percent to 34 percent margin, and is now part of the Virginia Constitution.

Democrats could have easily stopped the amendment before it got onto the ballot and would then have been able to control the entire redistricting process in 2021. The fact that they did not do so may be an indication that this majority party will operate differently than others have in the past. We will see whether the adage "just because they can" will apply as the Democrats continue their total control of the levers of state government.

NOTES

1. Thomas Jefferson, "Thomas Jefferson's First Inaugural Address," March 4, 1801, *First Amendment Watch, New York University*, ed. Stephen D. Solomon, November 27, 2017, https://firstamendmentwatch.org/thomas-jeffersons-first-inaugural-address/ (accessed June 5, 2021).

2. Graham Moomaw, "A Va. Republican Criticized Democrats in a Tweet. Then They Killed 4 of His Bills," *Virginia Mercury*, February 10, 2020, https://www.virginiamercury.com/blog-va/a-va-republican-criticized-democrats-in-a-tweet-then-they-killed-3-of-his-bills/ (accessed June 5, 2021).

3. Alan Ehrenhalt, "Will We Ever Slay the Evil Gerrymander? One State Took a Small Step This Week, but We're a Long Way From Eliminating Noncompetitive Districts and Partisan Malfeasance," *Governing*, November 4, 2020, https://www.governing.com/assessments/will-we-ever-slay-the-evil-gerrymander.html (accessed June 5, 2021).

4. Former Delegate S. Chris Jones, interview by author by telephone, October 12, 2020. See also U.S. Congress, *Voting Rights Act of 1965*, Pub. L. 89–110, 89th Cong., 1st sess., August 6, 1965, https://www.ourdocuments.gov/doc.php?flash=false&doc=100 (accessed June 5, 2021).

5. *Shelby County v. Holder*, 570 U.S. 529 (2013), https://supreme.justia.com/cases/federal/us/570/529/ (accessed June 5, 2021).

6. Former Delegate Robert Brink, interview by author by telephone, August 15, 2020, November 1, 2020, and January 12, 2021.

7. Julian Walker, "Redistricting plans are approved [by] General Assembly," *Virginian-Pilot*, April 8, 2011, https://pilotonline.com/news/government/politics/virginia/article_0887636d-2fd7-5232-b804-166ec05bb4bb.html (accessed June 5, 2021).

8. Anita Kumar, "Va. House of Delegates Race Between Armstrong, Poindexter Turns Heated and Costly," *Washington Post*, October 22, 2011, https://www.washingtonpost.com/local/dc-politics/va-house-of-delegates-race-between-armstrong-poindexter-turns-heated-and-costly/2011/10/19/gIQAsDdm7L_story.html (accessed June 5, 2021).

9. The redistricting map was drawn prior to the five-to-four U.S. Supreme Court decision in *Shelby County v. Holder*, 570 U.S. 529 (2013), that effectively nullified the heart of the *Voting Rights Act of 1965* by allowing nine states, including Virginia, to avoid previous requirements that any fundamental changes in their election laws (including redistricting) receive preclearance from the U.S. Department of Justice (DOJ) prior to implementation. See Adam Liptak, "Supreme Court Invalidates Key Part of Voting Rights Act," *New York Times*, June 25, 2013, https://www.nytimes.com/2013/06/26/us/supreme-court-ruling.html (accessed June 5, 2021); and U.S. Congress, *Voting Rights Act of 1965*, Pub. L. 89–110, 89th Cong., 1st sess., August 6, 1965, https://www.ourdocuments.gov/doc.php?flash=false&doc=100 (accessed June 5, 2021).

10. *Bethune-Hill v. Virginia State Bd. of Elections*, 326 F. Supp. 3d 128 (E.D. Va. 2018), https://casetext.com/case/bethune-hill-v-va-state-bd-of-elections-6 (accessed June 5, 2021).

11. Gregory S. Schneider, "Federal Court Releases Plans for Possible Redistricting in Virginia, Refuses to Delay Process," *Washington Post*, December 7, 2018, https://www.washingtonpost.com/local/virginia-politics/federal-court-releases-plans-for-possible-redistricting-in-virginia-refuses-to-delay-process/2018/12/07/a1a58be6-f728-11e8-8d64-4e79db33382f_story.html (accessed June 5, 2021).

12. States matter even in these instances. In some states, governors do not have the ability to veto state legislative maps. In Florida, Maryland, and Mississippi, governors cannot veto state legislative plans approved by the legislature. In North Carolina, neither congressional nor state legislative plans are subject to gubernatorial veto. Brennan Center for Justice, "Who Draws the Maps? Legislative and Congressional Redistricting," *Brennan Center*, January 30, 2019, https://www.brennancenter.org/analysis/who-draws-maps-states-redrawing-congressional-and-state-district-lines (accessed June 5, 2021).

13. *Virginia House of Delegates v. Bethune-Hill*, 587 U. S. ___ (2019), https://www.justice.gov/crt/case-document/virginia-house-delegates-v-bethune-hill-supreme-court-decision (accessed June 5, 2021). The Justices never actually reached the merits of the case, that is, whether this was an unconstitutional racial gerrymandering. Instead, they held that the House Republicans did not have "standing" to bring the appeal. The majority held that since the case was brought against the Commonwealth, the only proper appellant would be the State of Virginia, and its Attorney General, Mark Herring, had chosen not to file an appeal.

14. Laura Vozzella, "Va. House Speaker Kills GOP Senate Redistricting Plan," *Washington Post*, February 6, 2013, https://www.washingtonpost.com/local/va-politics/va-house-speaker-kills-controversial-gop-redistricting-plan/2013/02/06/14863cda-7081-11e2-8b8d-e0b59a1b8e2a_story.html (accessed June 5, 2021).

15. William J. Howell, "Howell: For the Honor of the Institution, Amendments Ruled 'Out of Order.'" *Richmond Times-Dispatch*, February 7, 2013, https://www.richmond.com/opinion/columnists/howell-for-the-honor-of-the-institution-amendments-ruled-out/article_0fc62f9e-2bdc-5893-817e-b0723887b318.html (accessed June 5, 2021).

16. Contrast Virginia House of Delegates William J. Howell's actions with the tactics Republicans in North Carolina used to override Democratic Governor Roy Cooper's veto of the state budget in 2019. Press reports suggest that Republican leadership misled Democrats into thinking that no vote would be taken on whether to sustain the Governor's veto of the budget; based on this assurance, several Democrats were absent when the measure was brought up on the House floor. With a number of Democrats out of the room, the Republicans had enough votes to override the veto. Chaos ensued, as the small number of Democrats vocally protested, so much so that the police had to be called. For some observers, those actions further destroyed the guardrails of trust in the state, already weakened as the result of the political hardball that had been played for years in Raleigh. What elected officials frequently forget in these battles is that they may win significant victories, but the hard feelings will remain for years, and the other party may act the same way if given the opportunity. See Dawn Baumgartner Vaughan, Lauren Horsch, and Paul A. Specht, "NC House Overrides Budget Veto in Surprise Vote with Almost Half of Lawmakers Absent," *Raleigh News & Observer*, September 11, 2019, https://www.newsobserver.com/news/politics-government/article234962017.html (accessed June 5, 2021).

17. Mark Levine, "Why I Oppose a Partisan Judicial Virginia Gerrymander," *Washington Post* (Opinion), December 11, 2019, https://www.washingtonpost.com/opinions/local-opinions/why-i-oppose-a-partisan-judicial-virginia-gerrymander/2019/12/11/000777c8-1b9d-11ea-87f7-f2e91143c60d_story.html (accessed June 5, 2021). During floor debate, Levine suggested, in citing a text from a friend, that raw politics might be at work: "Why do we bother to elect Democrats if they just willingly hand their power back to Republicans anyway?" "Your colleagues are bringing a bouquet of flowers to a gunfight."

18. Joseph Lindsey had never hidden his views on the amendment, claiming it was "piss poor."

19. Editorial Board, "On Redistricting, Will Virginia Democrats Choose Hypocrisy or Principle?" *Washington Post*, February 7, 2020, https://www.washingtonpost.com/opinions/on-redistricting-will-virginia-democrats-choose-hypocrisy-or-principle/2020/02/07/5560377e-4914-11ea-9164-d3154ad8a5cd_story.html (accessed June 5, 2021).

20. A discharge motion is an action to force a bill, which is held up in a committee, directly to the floor for a vote. It requires majority approval, but it is rarely used because it is a direct challenge to the Speaker's authority.

21. As an indication of the level of distrust between the two bodies, the House did not immediately transmit its decision to the Senate, leading some to wonder

whether there would be a Motion to Reconsider the vote in order to kill the amendment. Senators threatened to kill several House initiatives, including minimum wage increases, unless the House sent the resolution over to the other Body. This was eventually done, but not before a very public display of contention. Mel Leonor and Justin Mattingly, "After Wrangling on Redistricting, Legislature Extends Session to Finish Work on Key Bills Before Finalizing Budget," *Richmond Times-Dispatch*, March 8, 2020, https://richmond.com/news/plus/after-wrangling-on-redistricting-legislature -extends-session-to-finish-work-on-key-bills-before-finalizing/article_eebfb445 -b4c3-59c9-8b1e-943b9503ab23.html (accessed June 5, 2021).

Chapter 12

The Power of Forty-Nine

I would expect Democrats to pick up four to six seats . . . . If it went to 10, I'd say it sends a loud message across the country about the energy within the grassroots Democratic base and lack of energy in the Trump base.

—Quentin Kidd, Christopher Newport University professor and Virginia political pundit, November 2, 2017, just prior to Virginia Democrats flipping fifteen seats in the House of Delegates[1]

The polls on November 7, 2017 closed at 7:00 pm, and my wife and I had just made the long drive from Charlottesville to Fairfax in the pouring rain. We proceeded to the Democratic war room located in a Tysons Corner hotel complex with anticipation *and* trepidation. We were confident that Lieutenant Governor Ralph S. Northam would win his gubernatorial race and hopeful that Democrats would gain several seats in the House. But previous experience dictated caution. My first election cycle as Democratic Leader in 2013 showed us ahead in the polls in eight races with two weeks to go. Our hopes then were dashed on election night, due largely to the public backlash against Democrats generated by the collapse of President Barack Obama's *healthcare.gov* website that had been unveiled two weeks earlier. Democrats lost six of those House races by a cumulative total of 800 votes, and while our numbers increased that year, we still held only thirty-four of one hundred seats. Terry McAuliffe won the Governorship by three points, but even he will admit that if the election had been held two weeks later, he might have lost.

This night would be different. Instead of frustration and disappointment, we were greeted by cheers, jubilation, and occasional chants of "Mr. Speaker." In race after race, a Blue Wave was washing over Virginia. Democrats were sweeping Prince William County seats, had won three in the Richmond area, and knocked out two incumbents in Loudoun County. By 9:00 p.m., Democrats had flipped five seats from red to blue. It then increased—to eight, then thirteen, and for a moment, we appeared to have won the majority. The euphoria lasted for thirty minutes, when we were informed that Donte Tanner, an U.S. Air Force veteran who appeared to be defeating Republican Caucus Chair, Delegate Tim Hugo, had lost his lead because of an error in transposing some numbers. And Shelly Simonds, a school board member and late entry in the race in the Newport News area against Republican incumbent, Delegate David Yancey, was now behind by thirteen votes. The majority, which at 10:00 p.m. appeared to be in sight, had slipped from our grasp. At the end of the night, Democrats held forty-nine seats, and we needed strategy and some luck to get us the majority.

THREADING THE NEEDLE

By early the next morning, our strategy was clear. First, we had to win one of the several recounts, and our best chance involved the Simonds / Yancey race. Second, we would need to invalidate, or at least delay, the results in House District 28 (HD 28), a seat located in the Fredericksburg area and previously represented by the Speaker. In that race, we discovered that voters had been given ballots to vote in the wrong district. If we could show that this irregularity could have made a difference in the result, we might prevent anyone from being certified to be seated until after the opening of session. Winning the Newport News seat and preventing certification in HD 28 would leave Democrats with a fifty to forty-nine majority when session convened. We would then control the reorganization of the House, and could elect the Speaker, appoint committees, and write the rules for the session. Democrats would be in charge.

I was confident that we would win the recount in Newport News, and was right—for about twelve hours. Simonds initially won the recount by one vote! Republican incumbent David Yancey had conceded. Her victory meant that the worst we could do would be a fifty-to-fifty partisan composition in the House, *even* if we lost the contest in HD 28. Our excitement, however, was short-lived. In a move that appeared highly irregular, Republicans announced the next morning that they had found a ballot that should be counted for Yancey. We argued that this was too late to be counted, but, after hours of consideration, the three-judge panel overseeing the recount gave it to the Republican. The race was now tied, and it would be decided by lot, a little-known statutory requirement that determines the winner in case of a tie. We appealed the judges' decision, but the higher court ruled against us, and the winner would now come down to the luck of the draw. We waited weeks for this to occur, but when the lot was drawn just after Christmas, we were on the losing end.[2] We later lost our legal case in HD 28. The election cycle left us at forty-nine, a great triumph in most circles, but so disappointing for how it all ended.

"SOMETHING'S HAPPENING HERE"

One year earlier, few would have predicted the 2017 wave. Donald J. Trump had just won the presidency and the negative tone of his administration began immediately. So too did the resistance to his policies. Large numbers of Americans, particularly the progressive wing of the Democratic Party, were not going to take the Trump victory lying down. They had been activated, and many of them decided to seek public office. Since Virginia was the first state to have elections following the Trump win, we saw this energy in many of our candidates. Most had never previously held public office and were running insurgent campaigns, especially in their primaries.

This progressive energy that was sweeping the Commonwealth spilled over into Charlottesville. Notwithstanding my position as House Democratic Leader, I drew a primary challenge from a leftist graduate student at the University of Virginia (UVA). A self-proclaimed Democratic socialist, he cared little about my positions or my history as an advocate for progressive programs, but wanted to foment a change in the system, and recruited a committed group of followers to engage the fight.

He attempted to make the Atlantic Coast Pipeline (ACP), a proposed major fossil fuel infrastructure project that would run through several states with a path through Virginia to the west and south of Charlottesville, the major issue in the campaign. It made little difference that delegates had no vote on the project. Anything less than outright denunciation was viewed as support of greedy corporate interests. He also alleged that I had received hefty campaign contributions from Dominion Power, the major partner in building the pipeline, in hopes of linking those contributions to my failure to stop ACP.

I took the challenge lightly and focused instead on helping many other candidates across the state. My environmental bona fides were clear, having consistently supported renewable energy and opposed coal. I had won yearly accolades as a "Legislative Hero" from the Virginia League of Conservation Voters (LCV), the leading environmental advocacy group in the state. But my district was changing; it was becoming younger and more progressive. I had not had a challenger for years and, in that environment, one can get a little complacent. In the last month of the primary, I turned some of my attention away from helping others across the state to focus more on my own race. With years of goodwill built up in the district, I prevailed, winning almost 68 percent of the vote.

A similar dynamic occurred in the gubernatorial primary, as Albemarle County resident Tom Perriello mounted a challenge to Lieutenant Governor Northam's efforts to gain the nomination. I had known Tom and his family for years. He served as our U.S. Congressman for two years, and his dad was my son's pediatrician. Tom was gutsy, voting for the *Affordable Care Act (ACA)* while representing a district where many voters strongly opposed it.[3] He likely lost his reelection bid as a result. Perriello then went to work for the Obama Administration's State Department and had recently returned from diplomatic service in the Congo and Central Africa when he announced his run. His energy and progressivism provided Northam and the Democratic establishment a real challenge. When the primary votes were counted that June, he won about 80 percent of the vote in Charlottesville, and garnered 44 percent statewide.

I had announced my support for Northam months before Perriello had entered the race and felt that I needed to honor my commitment. This was difficult, as I had always been a big fan of Tom and was an early supporter of his U.S. Congressional bid in 2008. I remember the excitement of his election night, celebrating with Tom on the phone while reporting his upset victory to him as he drove through Nelson County on his way back to Charlottesville. He flirted with running for Governor in the Democratic primary against Terry McAuliffe in 2013, but his deliberations came late, and he ultimately abandoned the effort before it seriously began. Tom called for advice while my friend and then-assistant David Brown and I were in a car driving to a fundraising event in Northern Virginia in early 2013. Five minutes previously, I had received a call from McAuliffe asking if I had heard anything about a Perriello bid and asking me to intervene to argue against it. I conveyed my view to Tom that not only would he not win, but he would also seriously divide the party in the effort. Tom never entered the 2013 race, and McAuliffe became a terrific Governor.

When Tom declared for Governor four years later, he spoke to very few Democrats before announcing, and I was not among his confidants. He made the same case to Virginia voters that he had made to me four years earlier—that the presumptive nominee (in this case, Ralph Northam) could not win in November because he could not galvanize the base. Like many of us, Tom underestimated the antipathy toward Trump in the state. Northam ultimately bested the Republican nominee, Ed Gillespie, by nine percentage points, the largest margin in a statewide election by a Democrat in more than three decades. To his credit, Perriello worked very hard to help Northam win.

THE FIRST BLUE WAVE

The 2017 Blue Wave devastated the Republicans, particularly in Prince William County, where so much demographic change had been occurring. In House District 31 (HD 31), social worker Elizabeth Guzman trounced her opponent, sixteen-year veteran Republican Delegate Scott Lingamfelter. In the adjacent district, Virginia Military Institute (VMI) graduate and public defender Jennifer Carroll Foy won handily in a campaign during which she gave birth prematurely to twins, who then remained in intensive care for weeks during the fall. Single mom Hala Ayala, a cybersecurity expert who Democrats had recruited for years, dispatched three-term legislator Delegate Rich Anderson. And, in the biggest surprise of the night, Danica Roem became the first openly transgender candidate to win a state delegate seat anywhere in the country, defeating self-described homophobe and twenty-six-year veteran of the House, Delegate Bob Marshall, by more than six points. By the end of that November election evening, Democrats had swept all but one of the Prince William County seats.

The election produced other upsets. Democratic socialist Lee Carter defeated former police officer Delegate Jackson Miller. Anthropologist Debra Rodman bested veteran physician and budget conferee Delegate John O'Bannon in the Richmond suburbs. Teacher Schuyler VanValkenburg won an open seat to succeed retiring Delegate Jimmie Massie, and nurse practitioner Dawn Adams scored an upset over Delegate Manoli Loupassi.

Our polling indicated that voters disliked Trump, but we would need to also emphasize specific local issues to show how electing a Democrat would make a difference. In Virginia Beach, Kelly Convirs-Fowler beat incumbent Delegate Ron Villanueva, largely because of a scandal involving his company. Roem emphasized long-needed transportation fixes in her race against Bob Marshall. The Blacksburg area, a formerly blue district that had swung Republican in the early 2010s, was won by Chris Hurst, a former local television news anchorman who lost his girlfriend to gun violence when she was murdered with her cameraman on live television while conducting an interview. Hurst spent almost a million dollars on his race against Delegate Joseph R. Yost, focusing on college campuses and younger millennials.[4]

In most districts, Democrats hammered healthcare and used Medicaid expansion as an issue to drive turnout in their districts. As we gathered new data into the fall, and Trump kept sliding in the polls, it was clear that a wave was possible and that we had to get on top of it so we could ride it to victory in November.

Turnout was key. Our caucus consultant, Craig Varoga, had put together a chart based on Democratic performance in the various districts where a

Republican House member represented a district won by Hillary Clinton in 2016. There were seventeen of these districts, which is how we developed the slogan "17 in 17." This chart, which affectionately became known as the "wave chart," numerically showed how election results could change based on increases in Democratic turnout. Democrats were immediately competitive in five to six seats if turnout was typical for a Governor's year race. But if turnout jumped by 5 percent, Democrats could beat seventeen incumbents. The 2017 actual increase in turnout was 4.7 percent, and Democrats flipped fifteen seats.[5] It certainly helped that Northam's margin (+9) was larger than any major Democrat in a statewide race since Tim Kaine's five-point margin in 2005, and was larger than either McAuliffe in 2013 (+3) or even Obama in 2008 (+6).[6] In only three of the fifteen House pickups—Tran, Hurst, and Carroll Foy—did the Delegate candidate's winning percentage exceed Northam's in that district.

THE BEST LAID PLANS

My plan had always been to retire as House Democratic Leader following the 2017 election. Thinking that we would win seven or eight races that day, I would simply declare victory and then leave the leadership, which had been taking an increasing toll on my personal life, my legal career, and even my health. After seven years in the job, I was becoming someone I did not want to be—not so patient, frequently frustrated, and rarely enjoying the position. I had tried to leave leadership after the 2015 election, but as Michael Corleone in *The Godfather III* once lamented, "just when I thought I was out, they pulled me back in." My 2015 resignation lasted less than twenty-four hours, as my caucus mates prevailed upon me to remain; future Speaker Eileen Filler-Corn even drove to Charlottesville to convince me to stay. As the 2017 fall election season continued, I became more convinced that it was time for me to go and thought a postelection announcement would be the best way to exit gracefully.

But the 2017 election did not end on election night, and that delayed my plans. Weeks would go by before several contested races would be settled. We also had many new members in the caucus and some continuity made sense. Beyond that, we now had new opportunities to pass Medicaid expansion and handle redistricting in a way that could create a new Democratic majority. To step down at that moment just did not make sense; there was critical work to do. I would remain Leader for one more session, during which Virginia would witness the "power of 49."

The 2017 election decimated Republican leadership, already affected by retirements. Republican Whip Jackson Miller lost, and caucus chair Tim Hugo narrowly escaped defeat; he would lose in 2019. Democrats defeated four members of the House Appropriations Committee (another retired), including two budget conferees. The Chair of the House Transportation Committee lost. The Chair of House Courts of Justice retired. Of the large Fairfax County delegation, only had one Republican (Hugo) remained. Except for several precincts, Prince William County had become totally blue. Three districts surrounding Richmond moved into the Democratic column. The Republican Caucus became, on average, older and more rural. Democrats entered the 2018 General Assembly Session with momentum and a caucus that looked much more like Virginia—47 percent women, 43 percent people of color, and one-third under the age of 40 years old—than the other side of the aisle. The entire dynamic of the Virginia House of Delegates had changed.

DOMINION DISRUPTED

Democrats were now positioned to influence outcomes in ways only dreamed about a decade earlier. One such area involved energy policy. For years, this arena had been dominated by Dominion Energy.[7] A company with operations in eighteen states, it was slow to embrace the push for renewable energy, adopting pilot projects but preferring to assert control over as many of these new initiatives as possible.[8] Whenever a renewables bill would be proposed, Dominion would argue that they should recover the costs inherent in its implementation. The company maintained an army of effective and personable lobbyists in Richmond who influenced lawmakers on legislation and provided their supporters with contributions at campaign time.

Virginia's electric industry consists of three investor-owned utilities (IOUs), the two largest of which are Dominion Energy and Appalachian Power (APCO). The system also includes thirteen member-owned electric cooperatives, located mostly in rural areas. The state's electric IOUs are regulated, but municipal systems,[9] electric co-ops, and gas utilities are not. In 2017, the state relied heavily for its power generation on natural gas (48.5 percent of generation) and nuclear (33.3 percent). Coal has now been relegated to a distant third place at only 11.7 percent, down from 36.5 percent in 2009, and solar provides a mere 0.3 percent.[10]

The other major player in the energy arena is the Virginia State Corporation Commission (SCC). Created by Virginia's Constitution of 1902 to combat the monopoly power of railroads, and telephone and telegraph companies, the SCC has the authority to set electric utility rates based on the utility's costs of service, and establish a utility's rate of return, or authorized profit level, after considering factors such as the riskiness of the utility company and general economic conditions. The SCC is led by three commissioners, each of whom is appointed by a joint vote of both houses of the Virginia General Assembly.[11]

Historically, the SCC has appeared resistant to the expansion of renewable energy, concerned that it would simply increase costs to consumers. Some of these concerns were justifiable, especially when considering the costs of building wind farms off the Virginia coast. But others were questionable, most notably those associated with the expansion of solar installations in residential neighborhoods. This dynamic frequently creates dilemmas for Virginia legislators. While some favor more oversight by the Commission, they also realize that this can lead the regulators to reject proposals by the utilities that are judged too costly to consumers. As a result, the legislature has had the tendency to dictate to the Commission the kinds of projects that should be approved as deemed to be "in the public interest." This designation almost forces the Commission to approve certain projects, independent of their impact on electric bills. In many cases, the utilities are willing to go along, knowing that the risk of investing in costly projects such as offshore wind will be limited due to their ability to recapture their costs through higher rates.

Nearly every major piece of legislation affecting the energy sector in Virginia in the last two decades has enjoyed the support of the utilities. Even reregulation in 2007 had industry support, in part because that law placed some restraints on the SCC's ability to cut rates by extending the rate review period from every year to every other. But that was not enough; the utilities, risk averse as they are, would yearly push the legislature to enact even more changes. In 2015, for example, they secured passage of a bill that purported to "freeze" rates for several years. Sold as a consumer protection measure designed to limit price hikes derived from the federal Clean Power Plan, the legislation prevented base rate increases, but also suspended the SCC's ability to conduct biennial reviews for both APCO (until 2020) and Dominion (until 2022). This effectively prohibited the SCC from reducing electricity rates, even if the Commission determined that rates were too high. To placate the Governor and skeptical legislators, the utilities included sweeteners in the form of weatherization assistance for low-income households, and enlisted help from lobbyists and public relations firms to convince lawmakers and the public of the merits of the "rate freeze." It worked; most legislators were persuaded that the plan would be a good deal for their constituents, and few opposed the bill.[12]

The projected pressure on costs used as justification for the rate freeze never materialized; instead, wholesale costs declined—and utility profits soared. A report released by the SCC in September 2017 found that the IOUs earned excess profits in 2016 above what they would have earned under the law prior to 2015. APCO earned an excess of approximately $28 million, while Dominion's totaled approximately $252 million.[13]

Legislators were upset; the 2015 bill was supposed to help consumers, not to enrich the utilities. The utilities, especially Dominion, were concerned about the potential political fallout from these revelations. Pressure was mounting to become more active in the renewables field. At the same time, Dominion was taking a public relations beating in certain parts of the state because of its investment in the ACP and the Mountain Valley pipelines, two huge and expensive natural gas infrastructure projects. Activists were increasingly restive, and legislators progressively uncomfortable, with the level of the company's political contributions.[14] Dominion needed to change the narrative and hoped that new legislation would help. What developed was the *Grid Transformation and Security Act of 2018.*[15]

THE *GRID TRANSFORMATION AND SECURITY ACT* OF 2018

Prior to the 2018 session, Dominion Energy convened meetings with Leaders of both parties to propose a plan by which the company could use their excess profits to invest in more renewables. The company also suggested more undergrounding of power lines and modernizing the grid, two ideas that were attractive to legislators, but which had prompted skepticism from SCC staff due to their high costs. Dominion also approached environmental groups to explain their new commitment to solar and wind energy. Finally, the utility sought the aid of the Virginia Poverty Law Center (VPLC) to buttress its argument that low-income Virginians would benefit from a new approach.[16]

A powerful array of legislators was enlisted to support the new bill. In the House, Republican Delegate Terry Kilgore, the Chair of the House Commerce and Labor Committee, and Democrat Delegate Lamont Bagby, Chair of the Virginia Legislative Black Caucus (VLBC), were chief copatrons. In the Senate, Democratic Leader Dick Saslaw, Republican Leader Tommy Norment, and Virginia Beach Senator Frank Wagner introduced the measure. All but Bagby were known as Dominion advocates; his name on the bill, however, would provide additional help in securing the support of African Americans in both bodies, who might otherwise be influenced by consumer groups such as the VPLC. Major solar and wind power interests lined up behind the bill because of its significant commitment to increasing use of renewables. The measure also included substantial rebates to consumers derived from previous years' "overearnings." Governor Northam's office got actively involved in pushing the goals, if not the specifics, of the legislation.

Nonetheless, there were skeptics. The Southern Environmental Law Center (SELC) objected to new constraints on the SCC's regulatory authority. The Attorney General Mark Herring's office and SCC staff raised questions about how the new provisions would affect ratepayers and whether the proposed rebates of excess profits were enough. Both were also concerned that the bill would further limit the power of the SCC to deny costly requests for certain kinds of investment because the legislature had redefined them as being "in the public interest."

One of the most significant criticisms involved language in the bill to allow utilities to charge ratepayers twice for the same infrastructure investment; this came to be known as the "double dip." Dominion professed that the bill neither was written nor intended to include such a provision. But as concerns about a hidden "double dip" grew and more criticisms came to light, even some of the bill's proponents began to get nervous. With floor votes on both the Senate and House bills approaching, additional benefits in the form of weatherization assistance for low-income customers were added to mollify consumer groups and the VPLC. The amount of overearnings to be returned to consumers was increased. The SCC staff remained skeptical and said so in committee hearings. Nonetheless, the Senate version of the bill passed handily in that Body, and the matching House measure was approved by the Commerce and Labor Committee on a seventeen to four vote.

But then the unthinkable happened. For the first time in recent memory, a measure developed and supported by the major utilities would be altered on the House floor in a way they did not support. When I arrived in the Capitol that on February 11, 2018, I planned to attack the "double dip" by attempting to remove it from the bill on the House floor. These efforts almost always fail. A similar amendment had been squashed in the Senate, so I was not terribly optimistic. Yet, Democrats now numbered forty-nine, and I thought that several Republicans, most notably Delegate Lee Ware, an outspoken opponent of the entire bill, might vote to strip the provision.

The effort would only work if few people were given advance notice. Otherwise, Dominion would mobilize its lobbying team to split away enough Democrats to kill the amendment. When the bill was called, the amendment was offered. "If there is a double dip in this bill," I said, "passing the amendment will fix the problem. If there is no double dip, the language will do no harm and simply clarify that fact." Patron Delegate Kilgore made his rejoinder, and then it was time to vote. I sat back in my seat, feeling I had given it my best shot but thinking that the amendment would be defeated. I then looked at the voting board; six Republicans joined all forty-nine Democrats, and the amendment passed fifty-five to forty-one. Murmurs filled the Chamber as the implications sank in. Dominion Power had lost a key vote on the House floor, the first time in recent history where such a public defeat had occurred.[17] We had witnessed the "power of 49." With the amendment in place, the bill passed handily.

For advocates of renewables, passage of SB 966 was celebrated as a victory. The commitment to deploy 3,000 megawatts of new solar and wind—enough to power 750,000 homes—by 2022 was significant, as were the new investments in grid modernization, and the pledge to spend $870 million on energy efficiency programs over the next decade. The law required Dominion to issue $200 million in refunds to customers who were overcharged during the rate freeze, while APCO would have to issue $10 million, a big win for consumers. And, in the year following, the company appeared to deliver on portions of its promise, announcing plans to build a major offshore wind facility which was projected to provide electricity to as many as 650,000 homes at peak wind.[18] In the next sessions, even more changes were made in the energy arena. By 2020, Dominion even pledged that it would seek to reduce its carbon emissions to "net zero" by 2050.[19] And it was the "power of 49" and events of the 2018 session that really set the stage for future change.

MEDICAID EXPANSION

June 7, 2018, dawned crisply on the Virginia piedmont. The rain and floods of the past week had subsided. The sky was clear and blue. Virginia Governor Ralph Northam emerged from the gleaming white state Capitol to sign a budget that would add Virginia to the list of thirty-two other states that had embraced Medicaid expansion at the time. Northam was joined on the Capitol steps by thirty of my colleagues and stood before hundreds of excited onlookers. As we gazed into the distance at the Richmond skyline and at the puffy white clouds gently floating across the horizon, the significance of the moment took hold. After five years of arguing, cajoling, pleading, and strategizing, we had won the greatest victory during my time in the General Assembly. With one vote and the stroke of a Governor's pen, insurance options emerged for almost 400,000 Virginians. It was a great day for Virginia and again clear evidence of the "power of 49."

The debate over Medicaid expansion had its roots in the 2010 passage of the *Affordable Care Act* (ACA). One hallmarks of the ACA was the requirement that Medicaid, the state-federal partnership to provide insurance and care to low-income elderly, disabled, and children, be expanded in each of the states to include larger numbers of the poor. As an inducement, the federal government would initially pay for 100 percent of the expansion, to gradually decrease to 90 percent. This would provide a great benefit to states like Virginia, where the federal government funded only one-half of Medicaid costs and the state paid for the balance.

Given its controversy, it was expected that many lawsuits would be filed contesting the constitutionality of the ACA. What was not expected, however, was the U.S. Supreme Court's decision in *NFIB v. Sebelius*, the 2012 case which held that the individual mandate that undergirded the legislation was constitutional but the requirement that all states would be required to expand Medicaid was not.[20] This put the states in the middle of the growing maelstrom involving "Obamacare," as the ACA was called, and served as the lightning rod for countless political disputes in the following years.

Our first legislative session following the Supreme Court decision began in January 2013, and Democrats naturally tried to pass expansion. But with only thirty-three members in the House, there was little we could do except make speeches about how expansion would be good for Virginia. As early as 2013, Virginia was an outlier. States were expanding Medicaid throughout the Nation, including those with Republican Governors such as Arizona (Janice K. Brewer), Florida (Rick Scott), and Ohio (John Kasich). By January 2015, twenty-eight states had accepted the Medicaid expansion, including ten with Republican Governors.[21] Republicans in Virginia, however, continued to say no.

There were several reasons why even Republican states were expanding. First, large numbers of their residents would benefit from expansion. Under the ACA, Medicaid would be available for anyone with an income less than 138 percent of the federal poverty line—more generous coverage than any state had previously offered. Subsidies were then targeted to citizens who earned over that amount. Without expansion, significant numbers of individuals remained either too wealthy to enroll in Medicaid or too poor to gain coverage on the new health care exchanges. They fell into what was called "the coverage gap." Only if a state expanded Medicaid would those in the gap gain access to coverage. Second, most hospitals, particularly smaller ones in rural areas, would be direct beneficiaries of expansion. Rather than losing money on treating persons who would never be able to pay for the cost of care, Medicaid expansion would provide the hospitals additional reimbursement to help their finances. In many rural communities, hospitals were not only key places for health care, but the major employer. And many now faced threats of closure. Expansion would assist communities by maintaining and creating jobs and by increasing economic activity.

Finally, expansion was projected to help state budgets and ensure that taxpayer monies flowing to Washington, DC would be returned to them as part of Medicaid reimbursements. When expansion was first debated, it was projected that Virginians would send $10 billion in tax dollars to Washington for support of the *ACA* between 2013 and 2018; proponents argued that the money should come back to the Commonwealth to help people and create jobs.

In the House, these arguments fell on deaf ears. The Republicans could not stand the prospect of supporting anything linked to President Obama. In the Senate, however, a critical mass of Senators wanted expansion and initially held up the 2013 transportation bill in hopes of striking a "grand bargain" that would give Governor Bob McDonnell his transportation victory in exchange for Medicaid expansion. This compromise fell apart at the last minute, and legislators decided instead to create the Medicaid Innovation and Reform Commission (MIRC). This could serve as a vehicle for cutting Medicaid costs (at the time, the percentage of the state budget dedicated to Medicaid was rising faster than almost any other program and had reached 20 percent of the discretionary budget) and as an avenue by which Medicaid might be expanded without a vote of the entire General Assembly. Some Republicans, particularly in the Senate, believed that this was only way to pass expansion in the face of massive GOP opposition in the House.[22] Expansion would automatically occur once the state's Department of Medicaid Assistance Services (DMAS) met the reform criteria developed by the MIRC.

Though some thought that MIRC would be a waystation on the road to expansion, they were soon disappointed. The state made many reforms designed to cut costs proposed by the MIRC, but the Republicans simply added new requirements to prevent expansion.

When Governor Terry McAuliffe was elected, he immediately asserted the need for expansion, and stated he would not sign a budget that did not include the change. McAuliffe's comment merely stiffened the spine of conservative Republicans in the House to block expansion at any cost. McAuliffe did everything he could short of vetoing the entire budget to achieve expansion. He rehired Dr. Bill Hazel, McDonnell's former Secretary of Health and Human Services, a man with strong ties to the Republicans and well respected on both sides of the aisle. McAuliffe engaged legislators personally, inviting them to the Executive Mansion for his well-stocked bar and his infamous kegerator, the newly installed dispenser of craft brews from across the Commonwealth. His staff provided detailed analyses of the positive elements of expansion, including how it would affect voters in rural and red districts where objections to Obamacare were so strong. He even tried to "line-item veto" a provision in the budget so he could authorize expansion administratively. None of it worked.

Perhaps McAuliffe's best chance at getting expansion occurred in 2014, his first year in office. Though the House remained firmly in Republican hands, the Senate was evenly divided between Democrats and Republicans, and many Senators were willing to accept expansion by inserting it in the budget under the guise of what was labeled "Marketplace Virginia." But the House was firmly opposed, with the result that the General Assembly deadlocked over the budget. The session adjourned without passing a budget, and a special session was immediately called to see if the dispute could be resolved. Budget discussions extended into June. Some thought that McAuliffe and some Senate Republicans would cut a deal, outlast the House, and secure a victory for expansion.

House Republicans, however, had plans of their own. They approached Phillip Puckett, a longtime Democratic Senator from the southwest, to encourage him to resign his senate seat and take a job with the Virginia Tobacco Commission. Created in 1999 from a huge federal tobacco settlement, the Tobacco Commission was largely viewed as a vehicle for dispensing favors to southern and southwest Virginia. The Commission had been controlled by Republicans for years, and its operations periodically drew criticism. John W. Forbes II, former Secretary of Finance in Governor Jim Gilmore's administration and member of the Commission, was convicted for embezzling $4 million in the early 2000s from the fund.[23] A 2011 study by the Joint Legislative Audit and Review Commission (JLARC), Virginia's independent watchdog group, concluded that while some of the $756 million spent to date had helped economic growth, much of the spending had only a "marginal impact."[24]

It now appeared that the Commission was being used as a political tool to frustrate the public desire to expand Medicaid. When Democrats discovered the scheme, they screamed "foul" and argued that this was the worst kind of politics. But it was too late; despite the best efforts of McAuliffe and others, not only did Puckett resign, but he did do so immediately, giving the Republicans a twenty to nineteen margin in the Senate.[25]

With majorities in both bodies, Republicans immediately convened in Richmond to pass a budget that excluded expansion. McAuliffe was incensed, calling Puckett immediately after the vote and reportedly telling him "We just lost the vote, 20 to 19, in the Senate. Medicaid is done. I hope you sleep easy tonight, buddy."[26] Yet, McAuliffe and his team persisted. They developed a theory under which they could expand by executive action. Republicans not only rejected the approach but took actions to stop it. First, they hired attorneys to produce a memo showing the legal problems with the plan. Second, they inserted an amendment into budget bills stating that no monies could be expended on expansion "unless included in the appropriations act." This came to be known as the "Stanley Amendment," so named for Bill Stanley, a Senator from the southwest and an ardent opponent of expansion.

Each successive session brought other attempts at expansion, but the changing character of the Senate was making it more difficult. Republican Ben Chafin was elected to replace Puckett, and while he ultimately voted for expansion in 2018, he was consistently a "no" in the earlier sessions. In 2015, two of the more centrist Senate Republicans, Walter Stosch and John Watkins, retired, and were replaced by more conservative legislators

(Siobhan Dunnavant and Glen Sturtevant). The 2015 election brought House Democrats numbers to thirty-four, but the Senate Democrats failed to pick up any seats. Expansion seemed out of reach.

Throughout much of this period, most major business groups in the Commonwealth, including the Chamber of Commerce and the Virginia Hospital & Healthcare Association (VHHA), argued that expansion was a job creator and an economic development tool. VHHA hired Sean Connaughton, the former Secretary of Transportation under Governor McDonnell and a major Republican, as their CEO, and began a major campaign to mobilize support. Studies showed that expansion would create at least 30,000 jobs and inject federal dollars into many local economies. Since the enactment of the *ACA*, Virginians had been sending about $5 million per day of their tax dollars to Washington. If the state expanded, the federal government would return much of these revenues. For Virginia, waiting so long to expand had already meant the loss of $10 billion—monies that would never be recovered.

FIRST BLUE WAVE BRINGS CHANGE

The November 2017 election changed the political dynamics surrounding expansion. Ralph Northam, who campaigned openly for the initiative, was elected Governor by a wide margin. Victories by Democrats in the House left them one coin toss from parity. By the time that the 2018 legislative session convened in January, House Republican leadership began to signal that a deal might be struck on expansion. Newly designated Speaker Kirk Cox suggested that Republicans might support Medicaid expansion if a work requirement for recipients were included.[27] Long-time opponent Delegate Kilgore published an op-ed in the *Roanoke Times* in which he appeared open to expansion.[28] Although House Republican leadership never explicitly explained why their position had changed, they were to claim some credit for what was likely to pass because of the Democratic electoral victories. The opposition to expansion was still strong in the Republican ranks, but there were enough caucus members now in favor that the measure would ultimately pass the House.

Though McAuliffe's term was ending, he still had one more opportunity to push expansion.[29] He did this in his last formal budget unveiled in December 2017. The proposed budget included Medicaid expansion—and the federal revenues that would come with it. The Governor then used the additional revenue to fund popular initiatives. For Republicans to reject expansion, then, would require them to make cuts to very popular programs in order to balance the budget, a requirement of state law.

The other key element in McAuliffe's last budget was called a "hospital provider assessment." Under this arrangement, Virginia hospitals would be assessed fees based on revenues they would receive from expansion. These fees would then be sent to the state and would be used to fund the state's share of expansion. This amounted to about $200 million per year and allowed McAuliffe to crow that no state tax dollars would be used to fund expansion, since 90 percent would be paid from the return of federal dollars and the other 10 percent would come from the assessment. Because he left office before his proposed budget was considered, he never actually signed the bill creating expansion. But it was his budget that set the table.

Even with most House Republicans opposed to expansion, the House passed a budget on February 22, 2018 that included the provision. The Republicans included language requiring Governor Northam's administration to seek a waiver from the federal government to permit the state to impose a work or a community service requirement as a condition for new enrollees to receive benefits. But this requirement included so many exemptions that it was doubtful that it could be used to deny anyone who really needed benefits. And the budget did not condition expansion on Washington's approval of the waiver.

Over many years, you learn that the things that you do not say can be just as important as those that you do. Consequently, after making countless speeches in support of expansion in years previous, there was no need to say anything on the floor during the expansion debate (indeed, it might have proven counterproductive). Instead, Democrats simply listened as Republican House Appropriations Committee Chair Chris Jones recited the arguments for expansion that we had made for years. While most House Republicans voted against the budget (thirty-two in fact), Democrats delivered our forty-nine, and the measure passed. Elections truly make a difference.

Passage of the House budget placed Senate Republicans in a dilemma; to reject expansion and the provider assessment meant they would have to cut $600 million from spending initiatives, not a pleasant challenge. In addition, their own arguments opposing the expansion of Medicaid were losing force. For years, the Republicans had been adding people to the Medicaid rolls, but in the least efficient and most costly way possible. Instead of embracing expansion, where the federal government would assume over 90 percent of the costs, Republicans had been adding beneficiaries for whom Washington only paid 50 percent. This was done primarily by authorizing "Medicaid waiver" slots to provide state assistance to disabled Virginians. Each time the Commonwealth provided another "waiver," it was agreeing to pay 50 percent of the costs for this very expensive but undoubtedly necessary assistance. Similarly, when more Virginia veterans were added to the Medicaid Addiction and Recovery Treatment Services (ARTS) program in 2017, the reimbursement rates received from Washington were lower than what would have arrive under the proposed Medicaid expansion program.

The key advocate for expansion in the Senate remained Emmet W. Hanger, Jr., the Chair of Senate Finance, and a person who had studied this issue for years. Hanger was under tremendous pressure from both sides. Advocates of expansion had counted on Hanger to support their efforts, but in years past, he had equivocated. Years earlier, he had supported the MIRC initiative to gain expansion without an up-or-down vote in the General Assembly. But by 2018, the MIRC had been abolished, and the only way expansion would occur was through the budget. The House had included expansion in their budget; now, it was up to the Senate.

Senator Norment, ever the strategist, attempted all forms of parliamentary maneuvers to prevent Medicaid expansion from being included. But he misjudged Hanger, his understanding of the rules, and his willingness to use the power of his Chairmanship. Hanger knew his vote for expansion would draw him a primary opponent but felt empowered by how he weathered a similar challenge in 2015. He saw through the Norment subterfuge and, rather than indulging his fellow Senator, short-circuited the debate once he had won the critical vote, and abruptly adjourned the meeting.[30] Norment protested, but he and the conservatives were left with nowhere to go, except to the Senate floor, where they did not have the votes. Hanger was awarded the "Hero in Health Care Extraordinaire" from the Virginia Health Care Foundation for his work in passing the Medicaid expansion.[31]

With the passage of Medicaid expansion, one of the major goals of my service had been met. By January 2020, more than 375,000 people had gained coverage under the expanded Medicaid eligibility guidelines. And while the pandemic undoubtedly boosted the numbers, enrollment in Virginia's expanded Medicaid reached over 452,000 people by late 2020.[32] Ironically, many of the beneficiaries of expansion were the constituents in rural areas who had voted for Republicans who opposed the initiative. They might never support a Democrat. But to those of us who supported expansion, this mattered little. It was all about the idea of a Commonwealth, and the belief that all state residents should have access to insurance, no matter their income, where they lived, or for whom they voted.

On my office wall hangs a poster signed by Ralph and Pam Northam, which says "Victory in Virginia: Medicaid Expansion is Here." It will forever serve as a reminder of the positive role of government and how perseverance in pursuit of a good cause will eventually win the day. With the expansion of Medicaid, a huge goal of the Democrats had been met. Next would be the push to the majority.

NOTES

1. Trip Gabriel, "In Obscure Virginia Races, a Test of Anger at the President," *New York Times*, November 2, 2017, https://www.nytimes.com/2017/11/02/us/virginia -legislature-election-trump-.html (accessed June 5, 2021).

2. In 2019, in her third run for the seat, Shelly Simonds won.

3. U.S. Congress. *Patient Protection and Affordable Care Act* (ACA) *of 2010*. 124 Stat. 119, Pub. L. 111–148. 111 Cong., 2nd sess. March 23, 2010. https://www.govinfo. gov/app/details/PLAW-111publ148/PLAW-111publ148 (accessed June 9, 2021).

4. Young voter turnout was strong in Blacksburg and Radford, the homes to Virginia Tech and Radford University. Chris Hurst won 54.4 percent of the vote, one of the few districts where our Delegate candidate won with a higher percentage than Governor Ralph Northam. And young voter involvement was higher than in most gubernatorial years. About 34 percent of this age group (ages 18–29 years) voted in 2017, eight points higher than in 2013 and double the percentage of those who voted in 2009. Estimates placed Northam's support among this electorate at 69 percent. Center for Information & Research on Civic Learning and Engagement (CIRCLE), "Virginia Youth Voter Turnout Doubled between 2009 and 2017, Estimates Suggest," *Circle*, November 8, 2017, https://civicyouth.org/virginia-youth-voter-turnout-doubled -between-2009-and-2017-estimates-suggest/ (accessed June 5, 2021).

5. Only in Virginia Beach's House District 85 (HD 85), where teacher Cheryl Turpin put together a terrific campaign and won by a whisker (50.85 percent), did we pick up a seat that was not one of the so-called Hillary 17. During the months prior to November, I showed the wave chart to countless donors and supporters; the usual response was "David, we love you, and will support your efforts, but this is quite a reach."

6. Former Vice President Joe Biden's victory over President Donald J. Trump in 2020 was ten points.

7. Created in 1901 as the Virginia Passenger and Power Company to operate elec- tric railways and power plants, it became the Virginia Railway and Power Company in 1909 and began operating Norfolk streetcars shortly thereafter. It morphed into the Virginia Electric Power Company (VEPCO) in the 1920s and operated Richmond streetcars. Its transit operations were sold in 1944, making it exclusively a monopoly power company. In 1947, the company, with more than 11,000 stockholders and about 450,000 gas and electric customers, became an independent, investor-owned utility (IOU). Dominion Resources was created as a holding company in 1983, and VEPCO operates within it. In 2017, Dominion Resources rebranded itself as Dominion Energy, and was ranked number 238 on the Fortune 500 in 2019.

8. Jeff St. John, "How 4 Top US Utilities Are Grappling with Climate Change and the Energy Transition (or Not)," *Grid Edge*, January 22, 2020, https://www. greentechmedia.com/articles/read/how-4-top-u-s-utilities-are-grappling-with-the -energy-transition (accessed June 5, 2021).

9. There are sixteen localities in Virginia which own their electric utility and sell electricity on a retail basis, the largest of which is Danville. Municipal Electric Power

Association of Virginia (MEPAV), "Member Utilities," *MEPAV*, 2021, http://www.mepav.org/members-localities/ (accessed June 5, 2021).

10. Net Generation by State by Type of Producer by Energy Source (EIA-906, EIA-920, and EIA-923); quoted in State Policy Opportunity Tracker (SPOT), "State Brief: Virginia," 2019, https://spotforcleanenergy.org/state/virginia/ (accessed June 5, 2021).

11. A good history of the Commission can be found in Preston C. Shannon, "The Evolution of Virginia's State Corporation Commission," *William & Mary Law Review* 14, no. 3 (1973): article 3, https://scholarship.law.wm.edu/wmlr/vol14/iss3/3 (accessed June 5, 2021).

12. In the years following its passage, there was considerable criticism of the "rate freeze" legislation, much of which was justified. Nonetheless, it is important to remember that this was occurring at a time when many officials and elected leaders were concerned about the financial impacts that the Clean Power Plan would have on ratepayers. The market was collapsing for coal generation and the Virginia State Corporation Commission (SCC) was projecting that ratepayers might be on the hook for billions that would be required for new investments. Governor Terry McAuliffe was so worried at the time that he personally lobbied U.S. Environmental Protection Agency (EPA) Chief Gina McCarthy to modify Virginia's $CO2$ emission targets. McAuliffe was also insistent that Dominion include new monies for home weatherization, especially in low-income neighborhoods; he got his wish, and the utility committed to spend an estimated $25 million over five years on weatherization programs for the poor.

13. Virginia, State Corporation Commission, "Status Report: Implementation of the Virginia Electric Utility Regulation Act," September 1, 2017, https://www.scc.virginia.gov/comm/reports/2017_veurcomb.pdf (accessed June 6, 2021).

14. Patrick Wilson and Graham Moomaw, "Dominion Executives Bundle Donations to Virginia Lawmakers' Campaign Accounts," *Richmond Times-Dispatch*, October 13, 2017, https://www.richmond.com/news/special-report/dominion/dominion-executives-bundle-donations-to-virginia-lawmakers-campaign-accounts/article_2dc5e500-ae9e-11e7-825f-cf7d0872e492.html (accessed June 6, 2021).

15. Virginia, General Assembly, *Grid Transformation and Security Act of 2018,* Chap. 296, S 966, March 9, 2018, https://lis.virginia.gov/cgi-bin/legp604.exe?181+ful+CHAP0296+pdf (accessed June 11, 2021).

16. For years, Dominion had been criticized as a laggard in its commitment to solar and wind, and the utility was determined to change this perception. By comparison to utilities in neighboring states, particularly North Carolina, its investment in solar was negligible, and according to the American Council for an Energy Efficient Economy (ACEEE), it was also ranked fiftieth out of fifty-one large utilities in its commitment to energy efficiency, narrowly avoiding last place.

17. Daniel Marans, "Virginia Democrats Score a Surprising Win Against Powerful Utility Monopoly," *Huffington Post*, February 13, 2018, https://www.huffpost.com/entry/virginia-democrats-score-surprising-win-against-utility-monopoly_n_5a8266eae4b0892a0352426d (accessed June 6, 2021). Republican leadership immediately began to scurry around their side of the floor, as they began to realize that most

of them had just voted to oppose a major consumer protection measure. Greg Habeeb, a savvy Republican from Roanoke, jumped to his feet, moved to reconsider the vote, and the Republican majority, most of whom earlier had voted against the amendment, passed it *en masse* in a voice vote, thereby avoiding being on the record for allowing a power company to charge customers twice for the same thing.

18. Mel Leonor, "Dominion Plans to Build Nation's Largest Offshore Wind Farm Off Coast of Virginia," *Richmond Times-Dispatch*, September 19, 2019, https://www.richmond.com/news/virginia/dominion-announces--turbine-offshore-wind-project-in-virginia-beach/article_1f4fbead-03dc-59f5-a770-4a29f1fe8dd1.html (accessed June 6, 2021).

19. Dominion has considerable investments in nuclear power generation, which makes that goal more feasible than many utilities. Mel Leonor, "Dominion Pledges 'Net Zero' on Carbon Emissions by 2050," *Richmond Times-Dispatch*, February 11, 2020, https://www.richmond.com/news/virginia/dominion-pledges-net-zero-on-carbon-emissions-by/article_7da942eb-71d8-5e40-a328-0f0e6559f92e.html (accessed June 6, 2021).

20. *National Federation of Independent Business (NFIB) v. Sebelius*, 567 U.S. 519 (2012), https://supreme.justia.com/cases/federal/us/567/519/ (accessed June 11, 2021).

21. Andrew Prokop, "The Battle Over Medicaid Expansion in 2013 and 2014, Explained," *Vox*, May 12, 2015, https://www.vox.com/2015/1/27/18088994/medicaid-expansion-explained (accessed June 6, 2021).

22. At the time, Attorney General Ken Cuccinelli, in two separate legal opinions, took the position that this was an unconstitutional delegation of authority to an unelected body. Norman Leahy and Paul Goldman, "Medicaid: Will McAuliffe Play the Cuccinelli Card?" *Washington Post*, May 7, 2014, https://www.washingtonpost.com/blogs/all-opinions-are-local/wp/2014/05/07/medicaid-will-mcauliffe-play-the-cuccinelli-card/ (accessed June 6, 2021).

23. Michael Martz, "Tip Spurred Forbes Case," *Richmond Times-Dispatch*, December 19, 2010, updated September 19, 2019, https://richmond.com/news/tip-spurred-forbes-case/article_372a0766-cf79-5c3a-8e5e-4ae2b7563ad9.html (accessed June 6, 2021).

24. Virginia, Joint Legislative Audit and Review Commission (JLARC), "Review of the Tobacco Indemnification and Community Revitalization Commission," Report to the Governor and the General Assembly of Virginia, June 2011, http://jlarc.virginia.gov/pdfs/reports/Rpt412.pdf (accessed June 5, 2021).

25. Washington Post, "Puckett's Departure Deconstructed: Senator Resigning Killed McAuliffe's Secret Medicaid Plan," *Washington Post*, November 23, 2014, https://www.dailypress.com/government/dp-pucketts-departure-deconstructed-senator-resigning-killed-mcauliffes-secret-medicaid-plan-20141123-story.html (accessed June 6, 2021).

26. Washington Post, "Puckett's Departure Deconstructed."

27. Laura Vozzella, "Speaker of Va. House Signals Willingness to Consider Medicaid Expansion, But With Strings Attached," *Washington Post*, January 29, 2018, https://www.washingtonpost.com/local/virginia-politics/speaker-of-va-house

-signals-willingness-to-consider-medicaid-expansion-but-with-strings-attached/2018 /01/29/57585ca4-0538-11e8-b48c-b07fea957bd5_story.html (accessed June 6, 2021).

28. Terry Kilgore, "Kilgore: The Next Step for Rebuilding Southwest Virginia's Economy," *Roanoke Times*, February 15, 2018, https://www.roanoke.com/opinion /commentary/kilgore-the-next-step-for-rebuilding-southwest-virginia-s-economy/ article_5661305e-9900-5e2e-bcf8-eef11959e0fb.html (accessed June 6, 2021).

29. In Virginia, the outgoing Governor submits a new two-year budget just prior to the expiration of his or her term. The incoming Governor and the legislature can then amend it, but the template is largely that of the outgoing Governor.

30. Laura Vozzella, "Sen. Emmett Hanger's Gavel Thwarts GOP Leader's Effort to Block Expansion of Medicaid," *Washington Post*, reprint news *leader.com*, May 30, 2018, https://www.newsleader.com/story/news/local/2018/05/30/gop-leader -tries-fails-last-ditch-effort-head-off-medicaid-expansion-emmett-hanger-virginia /654596002/ (accessed June 6, 2021).

31. Michael Martz, "Northam, Hanger to be Honored for Medicaid Expansion Push," *Richmond Times-Dispatch*, September 22, 2018, https://www.richmond. com/news/local/government-politics/northam-hanger-to-be-honored-for-medicaid -expansion-push/article_26f26a69-ef9a-5e9d-8659-0e67247ae028.html (accessed June 6, 2021).

32. Louise Norris, "Virginia and the ACA's Medicaid Expansion," *Healthinsurance. org*, December 2, 2020, https://www.healthinsurance.org/virginia-medicaid/ (accessed June 6, 2021).

Chapter 13

Trifecta

This changes everything.

—Virginia Speaker of the House Eileen Filler-Corn,
upon Democrats gaining control in 2020[1]

On opposite sides of the Virginia House Chambers, Democratic Majority Leader Charniele Herring and her Republican counterpart Todd Gilbert both slumped in their seats following yet another grueling floor session. It was "crossover," the day on the legislative calendar by which all bills originating in one Body must pass that Body for them to crossover to the other for consideration; otherwise, the measures are dead for the year. The days leading up to and including crossover are exhausting. Hundreds of bills are considered, and the sessions typically are a whirlwind of parliamentary maneuvers, motions, and debate. In the Virginia Senate, the 2020 version of crossover finished at 12:48 a.m., technically a violation of General Assembly rules. But, with Democrats in control of both Bodies, they simply redefined a "legislative day" in order to "extend" the session for the extra forty-eight minutes. The House session was not as long, but Gilbert, Herring, and their lieutenants had been engaged in fights all day, and both were glad the session was over.

Minority Leader Gilbert, born in Texas and educated at the University of Virginia (UVA) and Southern Methodist University Law School, had been elected in the same year as I—2005.[2] Representing ruby red and rural Shenandoah County, he rose quickly within the Republican ranks, becoming Deputy Majority Leader in 2010. An imposing figure at 6 feet 4 inches tall, 240 pounds, and head totally shaven, Delegate Gilbert became Majority Leader in 2018 when Delegate Kirk Cox became Speaker. Even Gilbert would acknowledge his conservatism, especially on guns and abortion.[3] He was masterful at maintaining party discipline on key votes, frequently lumbering down the House aisles cajoling, collaring, and coercing Republicans to support a caucus position. Watching him hover over a Delegate who needed to change their vote was a thing to behold.When Republicans retook the House in 2022, Gilbert became Speaker.

Until 2020, being in the majority gave Gilbert many parliamentary maneuvers at his disposal. He could re-refer a bill from the floor back to committee, either to kill it or to change it to the liking of caucus leadership. And when all else failed, he could always move for a recess, an action that would invariably pass because the majority controlled the votes. When Republicans became the minority, Gilbert's role totally changed. He could raise points of order, pose pointed questions, and argue the caucus position, but he no longer had control. His power had been reduced to theatrics and press releases, and, as I watched him during the 2020 session, I sympathized. Having served in that position, I understood the limited tools available to the minority. Even if you feel you have a winning procedural argument, it takes only the gavel of the Speaker or the votes of the majority to hand you a defeat. Being in the minority is not an enviable position, no matter how talented you may be.

When Democrats gained the majority in 2020, Delegate Herring won the position of Majority Leader, the first African American ever to serve in that role. Herring and Gilbert had gotten to know each other well over the years, serving together on the Criminal subcommittee of the House Courts of Justice Committee, the Body that considers more bills than any other, and which is not averse to frequently meeting late into the evening to refine criminal justice bills where semicolons and commas can determine whether a citizen's liberty can be denied and for how long. But the two could not be more different. While both lawyers, Herring represents one of the most Democratic areas in the Commonwealth—Alexandria—and her views reflect that. An advocate for affordable housing, gun safety, and women's rights, she became one of the national faces of Virginia Democrats' fight against the transvaginal ultrasound bill in 2012, appearing on countless national talk shows to discuss this controversial action.

Growing up as a U.S. Army brat, Delegate Herring experienced personal misfortune that led her to be homeless for a time. She eventually graduated from George Mason University and Catholic University Law School. She never forgot the efforts by Republicans to prevent her installation as a Delegate in the House after she won a special election to replace former Delegate Brian Moran in early January 2009. Herring had clearly won, if only by sixteen votes. Yet Republicans prevented her from being seated for almost three weeks, arguing that she should be prohibited from joining the Body until a recount confirmed her win. She sat in the House gallery every day, patiently waiting for her chance to take her seat on the floor below. On January 26, 2009, the recount was completed, and she finally was sworn in as Delegate.[4] Herring eventually became state Democratic Party Chair, ran unsuccessfully for U.S. Congress, and was elected House Democratic Caucus Chair before becoming Majority Leader in 2020.

Not only were Herring and Gilbert different from each other, but so too were their caucuses. While in the majority, House Republicans were extremely disciplined and would not typically allow legislation to be considered if it did not enjoy majority support within its membership. They rarely played their cards until necessary and kept their internal debates largely hidden from the public. In contrast, the Democratic Caucus seemed to leak information constantly. Some members gained benefits by providing our strategy to the Republicans in advance of its unveiling. And apart from moral suasion, there were few ways of enforcing discipline. Unlike the Republican leadership, who could remove members from committees and table their bills if their members got out of line, the minority leadership in the House did not have the luxury of appointing its members to committees. There were few negative consequences for disregarding the will of the caucus. Over the years, the caucus became more cohesive as we both lost several members who revealed our secrets and gained others who understood better the importance of sticking together. This cohesion would be tested when Democrats gained the majority in 2020.

PUSH TO THE MAJORITY

House Democrats felt that 2019 would be the year to regain the majority. With new legislative district lines drawn by the court, and President Donald J. Trump still in the White House, conditions were favorable. The party had substantial momentum after 2017, and gained more in 2018, when Tim Kaine easily won reelection to the U.S. Senate and three new women were added to the party's Congressional delegation.

The federal court's drawing of the new House district lines in 2019 provided new Democratic opportunities in at least six districts. But it would not be easy. Some Republican Delegates most affected by the new districts were popular among the voters, and not all the Democratic challengers were the strongest candidates. In addition, 2019 was an off-off year election with no statewide race driving turnout. In 2017, turnout had hit 47.6 percent of registered voters. By contrast, the 2015 off-off year turnout in Virginia was only 29.1 percent. If 2019 turnout numbers remained similar to those in 2015, Democrats would likely remain in the minority. In addition, the 2019 scandals affecting Ralph S. Northam, Justin E. Fairfax, and Mark Herring could both dampen turnout and impact the ability to raise the money necessary for the fall.[5]

To further complicate matters, several Democratic bills in the 2019 session became very controversial and threatened to make the push for the majority more challenging. The first involved reproductive rights and a bill brought by Delegate Kathy Tran from Fairfax. Tran, whose personal story as a Vietnamese immigrant and whose intellect and personality suggests a bright future for her in Virginia politics, created a firestorm as she was presenting a bill designed to protect a woman's right to terminate a third-trimester pregnancies. Although the same bill had been proposed in previous sessions, Tran's responses in a subcommittee hearing were used by Republicans to suggest she advocated "infanticide." The main portions of the bill would have removed unnecessary and costly requirements that did little to ensure the health of women seeking these rare abortions. Nonetheless, other provisions reduced the role of physicians in decisions involving the procedures. To further complicate matters, Governor Northam, when asked about the bill on a radio program, responded in a way that simply fueled the "infanticide" narrative.

Another example of going off message involved the introduction of a bill by Delegate Lee Carter of Manassas to repeal the "right-to-work" provisions in state law. Carter sought to repeal a law that had been on the books for more than fifty years. It was unclear clear whether he had approached organized labor before he introduced the bill, but he had not discussed the issue with Democratic House leadership. Because Democrats were in the minority, Carter knew that the bill had no chance of passage. But leadership understood the problems it created for Democrats. They would either vote for a measure that could not pass and alienate the business community and independents in the process. Or they would vote against the measure and incur the wrath of organized labor.

Sly smiles ran across the faces of House Republican leadership when they discovered that Carter had filed his bill. They knew that the measure could not pass but thought they could use it to their advantage. It would allow them to paint Democrats as antibusiness and use the proposal as an example of what could happen to "one of the best states for business" if the Democrats took control of the legislature. They also knew that forcing a floor vote on this issue would also divide Democrats, some of whom would be very uncomfortable voting for it. Speaker Cox initially referred the bill to the Rules Committee, from which, under House Rules, it could be sent directly to the House floor without taking an up-or-down vote in the committee. This was a strategy that allowed Republicans to avoid taking a formal position on the bill in committee but force all Delegates to register a vote on the House floor. It had been used in the past to compel Democrats to take politically unpopular votes on measures that no one believed would ever pass.

As expected, once the right-to-work repeal was introduced, labor not only embraced it but made it a litmus test by which they would judge whether to support a candidate (or even the caucus) in the fall 2019 campaign. With Republicans in the majority, I knew the bill would never become law. But I also knew that bringing it to a floor vote would divide our caucus and potentially put some members in political peril. In short, this bill could never reach the House floor.

There was only a small chance to prevent the entire Body from considering the measure. This strategy involved getting organized labor to lobby Republican Delegates from districts that had larger numbers of union households to support the bill. These Republicans would quickly understand that voting on this measure would put them in an untenable position. If the bill got to the floor, they would have to support their leadership and vote "no," since to do otherwise would ensure the bill's passage. A "no" vote, however, could mobilize labor in their districts, something they could ill afford in the fall election. Ironically, then, working the bill in this way actually undermined its chances of getting to the House floor. This was a subtle play, but the only chance of preventing a floor vote and putting our members in a difficult position on a bill that would not pass. In the end, Delegate Carter's bill never got to the floor, and was never even considered in committee.

It was clear that the House of Delegates would change dramatically after the 2019 election, even if the Democrats did not gain a majority. Five Republicans joined me in announcing their retirement that spring, and two more—Delegates Bob Thomas of Stafford and Chris Peace of Hanover—were defeated in party primaries. Four of those retiring served on the Appropriations Committee, including its Vice-Chair, Delegate Steve Landes. No matter what happened in the fall election, the Body would have at least ten new members, and the possibility existed that Republicans could lose eight of their twelve members on Appropriations.

As the election cycle commenced, Republicans attempted to exploit the allegations against Lieutenant Gov. Fairfax to create divisions within Democratic constituencies, particularly between African Americans and women. They pushed for a House-initiated investigation into the allegations. Advanced primarily by Delegate Rob Bell of Albemarle, these calls for an inquiry appeared to be designed more to create political theater and embarrassment for the Democrats than to discover the truth. The offenses for Fairfax were accused occurred decades ago, long before he had been elected Lieutenant Governor. A strong argument could be made that they were more appropriately considered in a court of law. The House had no more authority to investigate Fairfax's behavior than it did the actions of any other elected official who had allegedly committed an offense years before his or her election. Moreover, during recent Virginia history, neither the House nor the

Senate had convened hearings to investigate alleged criminal behavior of elected officials, even when it had occurred while they were serving in office. And there had been plenty of chances. Neither former Delegates Phillip Hamilton (convicted of felony bribery and extortion), Ron Villanueva (pled guilty to conspiracy to defraud the U.S. government), Rick Morris (charged but not convicted of felony child abuse), Joe Morrissey (charged with felonies; convicted of misdemeanor of taking indecent liberties with a child), nor former Governor Bob McDonnell (convicted of eleven conspiracy and public corruption charges that were ultimately reversed on appeal) were subjected to House or Senate inquiries.

When the two women accusers appeared on national television in early April, Fairfax responded, first by releasing the results of two polygraph tests which he argued cleared him, and second, by asking the prosecutors in the jurisdictions where the alleged events occurred to conduct their own investigation, something that neither of his accusers said they desired. Republicans hoped to build their case to remain in power by attempting to link the scandals to Democratic candidates through a series of ads throughout the fall. Bell continued the drumbeat to have a legislative hearing, but Democrats were not taking the bait. And the public never really embraced Republican demands for a hearing. There was little evidence that the Fairfax scandal affected the fall campaigns at all.

The problems of Northam and Fairfax had little impact on the fall election. But gun violence did. When a disgruntled city employee murdered twelve people in a mass shooting in Virginia Beach in May, Northam called the General Assembly into special session to consider gun safety legislation.[6] This elevated the issue, and Democrats immediately presented eight separate measures for consideration, including mandatory background checks and a "red flag" law, both of which enjoyed broad public support. When the Assembly reconvened on July 9, Republicans did nothing, instead adjourning after ninety minutes, with no plan to reassemble until after the election.[7]

For those in the electorate already incensed by the lack of action on guns, this move further intensified their motivation to push for change in November.[8] And for Northam, it was a key element in his slow rehabilitation. By late summer, polling data indicated that Northam was putting the blackface scandal behind him, and that it was having little impact on House contests.[9] Perhaps more importantly, President Trump's approval rating was in the midthirties in many competitive districts.[10] Another wave now appeared possible.

Many of the Republicans were running campaigns as if they were Democrats.[11] Chris Jones, in an almost hopeless situation because his new district drawn by the court was predominately Democratic, never used his party label on his literature, preferring the word "independent" to describe his partisan status. He campaigned as the person who helped pass Medicaid expansion. Delegates David Yancey in Newport News, Tim Hugo in Fairfax, and Chris Stolle and Glenn Davis in Virginia Beach all stated they were now willing to consider "some reasonable" gun measures. Davis even sent mail comparing so-called *lies* of his Democratic opponent to those of Donald Trump. Cox de-emphasized his conservative ideas in favor of a campaign that focused on his being a retired Little League coach.

When the dust settled on November 5, 2019, turnout statewide exceeded 42 percent, thirteen points higher than the comparable election in 2015. Democrats had won six more seats, giving them a fifty-five to forty-five majority. For the first time in twenty-six years, Virginia Democrats would control the House, Senate, and governorship. I could retire at the end of 2019 knowing that several important goals we had sought for a decade had either been achieved or were within reach. First, Medicaid expansion had passed. Second, the unconstitutional redistricting of 2011 had been overturned. And now, Democrats had regained the majority.

A BOLD AGENDA

The 2020 Virginia legislative session was historic.[12] It started dramatically, when Delegate Eileen Filler-Corn was elected the new Speaker, the first woman to be chosen for this position in the Body's 401-year history. A veteran legislator who enjoyed good relationships with most caucus members, Filler-Corn was from vote-rich Northern Virginia (NoVa). She had cultivated many of the grassroots activist groups and was a terrific fundraiser. As a leading proponent of gun safety measures, she was perfectly positioned to lead on this critical issue. She was deliberate, and understood both what she knew, and importantly, what she did not. And she had largely avoided the various controversies involving Dominion Energy.

Speaker Filler-Corn's election had historical significance, but the real change came through legislation. House Democrats decided early that they would *go bold* and embrace a progressive agenda. And the results were amazing to observers who had watched the Assembly for decades. Despite the challenging learning curve for a new Speaker, new committee chairs, and twenty-five Democratic members with two years or less experience,[13] 48 percent, or 824, of the 1,734 bills that were introduced in the House were passed by midsession,[14] including eighty-eight that were previously defeated in Republican-controlled committees in 2019.[15] And the change agenda continued into 2021. The bills represented positions Virginia Democrats had advocated for years,[16] including:

1. Ratifying the ERA, the 38th state to do so.[17]
2. Eliminating the requirement of producing a photo ID to vote.[18]
3. Removing restrictions on abortion that had previously been enacted by Republicans.[19]
4. Passing a LGBTQ nondiscrimination bill.[20]
5. Enacting major energy and climate change measures to reduce carbon emissions.[21]
6. Increasing the minimum wage.[22]
7. Adopting gun safety legislation.[23]
8. Granting collective bargaining rights to some public employees.[24]
9. Legalizing small amounts of marijuana for recreational use.[25]
10. Abolishing capital punishment, the twenty-third U.S. state and the first in the South to do so.[26]

When the 2020 session began, Virginia was unaware of the future economic impact of the pandemic, and Democrats passed a budget built upon projected new revenues because of a booming economy. It included major new investments in education, including pre-K, transportation, and housing. All were initiatives that were deemed impossible to fund only a few years earlier.[27] Governor Northam explained the changes in this way: "The stars were aligned. We had just elected Democratic majorities in the House and Senate and had a public clamoring for progressive change in the aftermath of Donald Trump's presidency and the killing of George Floyd."[28] Celebrating the changes, Speaker Filler-Corn exclaimed that voters "wanted change; they wanted action. And we are doing just that."

Republicans did not agree.[29] "What we're really seeing is like a jewelry store smash and grab," said Senator Bill Stanley, then a possible Republican candidate for Governor in 2021; "They're going to grab everything they possibly can while they can get it before the lights go on and the siren goes off."[30] Similarly, Minority Leader Gilbert decried Democrat measures, asserting that they would "have the cumulative effect of making living here and working here a lot more expensive."[31] Leaders of both parties agreed on one thing; it was a new day in Richmond.

Not since 1994 had Virginia Democrats occupied the governorship and controlled both the House and the Senate. The Republicans had their own trifecta during the last two years of the Gilmore administration and again in 2012 and 2013, when Bob McDonnell was Governor. But the Virginia Senate was much more moderate at the time and provided some balance to the House's conservative instincts. By 2020, conditions had changed. Many progressives had been elected in 2017 and 2019. Progressive elements across the state felt that the electoral results were largely due to their efforts and believed there was a clear mandate to push their agenda. Newly elected members, primarily within the House, were willing to oblige, and introduced so many progressive measures they almost overwhelmed the legislative drafters. One member explained the rationale: "why should we wait?" he inquired; "the voters elected us knowing that we were progressives and they wanted us to lead. That is precisely what we are doing."

Over the last decade, most trifectas have occurred in red states and benefitted Republicans. The GOP has not been shy in using total control to push its conservative agenda, and recent events further document this fact.[32] Trifectas for Democrats, however, have been rarer. After the 2020 election, Democrats had trifectas in fifteen states and Republicans enjoyed them in twenty-one, up three from 2018.[33]

When trifectas initially come to states, several trends emerge. First, unless the trifecta occurs as the result of a shift of the party of the Governor, the major impetus for change emanates from the legislature. When trifectas came to Virginia, New York, and Colorado, the energy for change came from newly elected House and Senate members. Second, accountability can no longer be avoided; the majority is in total control and what passes and what fails is up to them. "All I'll say is, hey, voters will hold elected officials accountable for their votes," said Doris Crouse-Mays, who directs the Virginia American Federation of Labor and Congress of Industrial Organizations (AFL-CIO).[34] Virginia Democrats were no longer in the minority. No longer could they simply propose wonderful ideas without thoroughly exploring all the implications of the measures, including their costs. And mistakes in legislation, including those that can occur when deliberation time is short, becomes a risk. It was now time to govern.

Finally, trifectas interject a different dynamic into our system of checks and balances. When both houses are controlled by the same party, "the other Body" often serves as a break on the pace of change. When Republicans were in control, the state Senate and the House appeared at times to be at each other's throats. A similar relationship emerged in the years of the Democratic trifecta. The state Senate modified or even defeated certain progressive initiatives of the House, specifically rejecting paid family leave and the elimination of "right-to-work."[35] And both Bodies insisted that were not being accorded enough respect from the other. Governors, who would typically use their veto power as a check on the power of the legislature, are less likely to use this tool when faced with a legislature controlled by the same party. As an example, Governor Northam vetoed four bills in 2020, all measures introduced by Republicans. By contrast, he vetoed fourteen in 2019, when Republicans were in control of the legislature.

FISSURES TO REMEMBER

Despite their successes, Democrats in 2020 and 2021 had their share of disagreements. Two of the most significant involved redistricting reform and climate change legislation. Chapter 11 explained how the 2011 redistricting plan was undone by the courts, and how the newly-drawn districts contributed to the Democrats resuming control of the House. But redistricting reform was still on the table, and the 2020 session would illustrate how it proved an especially vexing problem for House Democrats. For years, Democrats had argued that Virginia's system of redistricting was severely broken and embraced the argument that the only solution rested in a constitutional amendment that would require the state to use a nonpartisan commission to draw district lines. Consequently, when such a measure was proposed in 2019, many Delegates and Senators voted for it. All amendments to the Virginia Constitution require passage of the exact language of the measure by the General Assembly in two successive sessions separated by an election. They must then be approved by the voters in a general election. Hence, the measure had to be reapproved, this time by the 2020 Assembly session, before it went before the voters. And House Democrats were having second thoughts. The amendment drew increasing criticism from their political base. Race was a central issue, as African Americans in the House suggested that a failure to vote "no" on the amendment would be taken as a sign of racial insensitivity. Senate Democrats, including prominent African Americans like Jennifer McClellan, Mamie Locke, and Louise Lucas, generally supported the amendment, thereby setting up further division between the party caucuses in each Body. The Senate could not understand why House members would seem to backtrack on commitments earlier made to a commission.

Despite the opposition of House Democratic leadership when the measure was finally considered in the last week of session, it passed easily. Only nine Democrats voted for it, the margin of victory provided by forty-five Republicans. As an indication of the level of distrust between the two Bodies, the House did not immediately transmit its decision to the Senate, leading some to wonder whether there would be a Motion to Reconsider the vote to kill the amendment. Senators threatened to shelve several House initiatives, including minimum wage increases, unless the House sent the resolution over to the other Body. The amendment finally passed, but not before a very public display of contention.[36] It was the only major defeat for Democratic House leadership in the 2020 session. And despite the assertion by House leadership that the voters would reject the amendment, it was approved that fall by a 66 percent to a 34 percent margin and is now part of the Virginia Constitution.

Similar divisions were present in the policy debates over energy and climate change. The 2020 session began with Dominion Energy on the defensive, and observers were predicting major change in this arena. Much of the discussion focused on the *Virginia Clean Energy Act* (VCEA), a major initiative designed to significantly increase the state's commitment to renewables. VCEA had prominent sponsors and was pushed by major environmental groups.[37] But its passage remained problematic until the final days before adjournment. Democrats knew that Republicans would oppose the bill and criticize it as another example of unrealistic antibusiness attitudes of Democrats that would increase the cost of electricity. What surprised them was the reluctance of some of their colleagues to embrace the measure.[38]

Dominion Energy began the session by calling the bill "too complex"; of course, every single major piece of energy legislation supported by the utility giant over the last twenty years had been every bit as complicated. Disputes also arose about the bill's costs and benefits. Proponents asserted it would save consumers money and create 1,000 "clean energy" jobs per year by 2050.[39] Experts from the Virginia State Corporation Commission (SCC), who have historically argued that more renewables meant higher costs, asserted that passage of VCEA would increase rates.[40] With the exception of Senator Dick Saslaw, Democrats largely disputed the SCC analysis. "You can't do this stuff for free," Saslaw exclaimed, clearly irritated by the debate. "Everybody says that we've got a climate problem, and you know, you can't fix the climate problem for free. You all need to understand that."[41]

Democratic opposition was led by Delegate Sam Rasoul of Roanoke city, who first proposed a Virginia version of the "Green New Deal" in 2018 and reintroduced it in 2020. During his time in the House, Rasoul had tried to position himself as the darling of progressives and had ambitions for higher office. He frequently differed with Caucus leadership about campaign strategy and policy initiatives. His bill, while expressing great aspirations, was a policy mess. If passed, it would likely have shut down power plants without energy replacements, and seriously compromise the ability to create any energy infrastructure except solar and wind. Rasoul was critical, as were many of his colleagues, of the massive new natural gas pipelines being advocated by Dominion Energy, but his measure seemed to impose a moratorium on *all* pipeline investments and might prevent even the maintenance and improvement of the many smaller gas pipelines that had crisscrossed the Commonwealth for years and were the vehicles by which thousands of Virginians gained access to natural gas for heating.

The 2020 session saw a plethora of energy reform proposals, including those that would provide customers with retail choice to purchase energy from electricity generators other than Dominion, give the SCC more power to regulate rates, and establish more rigorous targets for renewables and energy efficiency in the state.[42] Governor Northam continued to champion efforts to join the Regional Greenhouse Gas Initiative (RGGI), which was now an easy sell with Democrats in control. Of these, VCEA would make the greatest change in energy policy.[43] As opposition emerged, it fell upon two Assembly workhorses and the sponsors of the bill, Richmond Senator Jennifer McClellan and Arlington Delegate Rip Sullivan, to carry it across the finish line. McClellan had established herself during her ten years in the House and four in the Senate as a person who did her homework and was effective in building coalitions to pass bills. VCEA passed the Senate easily, but the House would prove more difficult. With forty-five Republican votes against and progressives like Rasoul, Delegate Sally Hudson of Charlottesville, Delegate Carter, and others expressing reluctance, there was little margin for error. Sullivan needed an insurance policy, and he found it in Republican Terry Kilgore, the longtime Delegate from Scott County and former Chair of the Commerce and Labor Committee.[44] Kilgore exchanged his vote for a pledge not to immediately shutter Dominion's major natural gas generation plant in Wise County.[45] When the measure, including its landmark provisions for the state's electricity to be carbon-free by 2045, substantial expansion of wind power, dramatic new targets for energy efficiency and storage, and major support for distributed generation like rooftop solar, reached the House floor, it passed fifty-one to forty-five.[46] Sullivan, who already had won a major victory in the 2020 session with the passage of the gun safety measure called the Extreme Risk Protective Order (ERPO), had helped engineer another triumph for the Democrats. Virginia was now poised to become one of the leaders in the new energy economy, and Democratic leadership had won yet another major success.[47]

IF YOU CAN SEE THE CHANCE, TAKE IT

When the legislature and the Governor are from the same party, opportunities are available that may never come again. The urgency is especially acute when a party has been out of power for years, as was the case for Democrats before they took control in 2020. That legislative session, and the special session that followed, will be forever viewed as historic, even as the budgetary impacts of COVID-19 would temporarily defer some of the initiatives that required additional monies to fund.

Once in control, Democrats kept pushing their advantage. In a 2020 special session, they passed several measures to rein in police brutality, prompting Republicans to allege Democrats were trying to "defund the police." In 2021, Virginia became the first Southern state to abolish the death penalty. The Commonwealth became the first in the South to legalize small amounts of marijuana for recreational use. For many of us who had served in the legislature even as recently as 2015, these changes were breathtaking. As late as 2015, Republicans were adding to the list of criminal offenses for which conviction made the perpetrator eligible for the death penalty. There was a small group of us in the House—about ten to thirteen—who would always vote against the expansion of the ultimate sanction. Now, the entire penalty had been removed.

Legalization of cannabis was more complex and driven by a complex array of forces. Advocates of racial equity stressed the fairness of the change and how its implementation would eliminate some of the arbitrary police stops and incarceration of African Americans. Others saw the revenue potential; full legalization and taxation of sales was projected to bring an additional $300 million per year to the state's coffers. Nonetheless, the Commonwealth was not ready to change the drug's availability overnight. At the instigation of the Senate and Democrats like Scott Surovell, an attorney from Fairfax who had become a force for moderation after he left the House and now relished tamping down some of the progressive initiatives of the other Body, full legalization should be phased in over time. The measure that passed did not permit smoking marijuana in public. Said Surovell, "this is not going to generate some ganja fest at Jiffy Lube pavilion out in the parking lot, because that is smoking in public." But Democrats believed that legalization's time had simply come. The change prompted Senate Finance Chair Janet Howell to quip, "One of the reasons I support making it come into effect soon is if we don't, and we have to wait another three years, I'll be in my 80s before I can do legally what I was doing illegally in my 20s."[48]

Time will tell how Virginians will react to these changes; when a political landscape shifts very quickly, there is always the risk that the majority will *overreach*. In the attempt to move quickly, the consideration of possible unintended consequences may take a back seat to the exhilaration of changing laws which have been in place for years, if not decades. In the case of marijuana legalization, Virginia not only embraced change, but one commentator's analysis of state laws produced by the National Organization for the Reform of Marijuana Laws (NORML) argued that the Commonwealth now has "most lenient law in the nation for possession of a pound of pot."[49] Voters will ultimately determine whether this is an example of *too much, too fast*.

Lawmakers hoping that their changes are viewed as legitimate should always be mindful of the norms and rules of the decision-making process itself, both in terms of its fairness to the minority and in how it involves those most affected by change—the public. This Nation's experience with this challenge over the last several decades has been problematic at best. Fortunately, the public's view of the Commonwealth's processes is generally favorable. Whether they refer to it as "the Virginia Way" or simply see it as deliberate and careful, Virginians seem most comfortable with a legislative process that does not embrace innovation for its own sake, but instead brings change incrementally. The ultimate verdict on the Democratic initiatives passed in the last several years will be provided at the ballot box, but whatever occurs in the next elections, the 2020 and 2021 will be among the most consequential in decades.

NOTES

1. Eileen Filler-Corn, interview by author in person, January 20, 2020.

2. As an indication of fast turnover in the Virginia House, only three members remain from the fifteen elected with me in 2005—Rosalyn Tyler of Sussex, David Bulova of Fairfax, and Todd Gilbert. Tyler was defeated in 2021.

3. Ned Oliver, "A Kinder, Gentler Todd Gilbert? 'It Depends on the Day and the Issue,'" *Virginia Mercury*, November 19, 2019, https://www.virginiamercury.com/blog-va/a-kinder-gentler-todd-gilbert-it-depends-on-the-day-and-the-issue (accessed June 6, 2021).

4. Olympia Meola, "Va. House Swears in Delegate after Recount," *Richmond Times-Dispatch*, January 26, 2009, updated September 19, 2019, https://richmond.com/article_ee04e3e9-51bf-5df7-aa64-3fc48b0f42ad.html (accessed June 6, 2021). The racial makeup of the 46th district is approximately 52 percent white, 29 percent African American, and 9 percent Asian, making Herring one of the few African Americans in the House whose district's African-American composition is less than 30 percent.

5. "If all three statewide Democratic officials are under a cloud of scandal like this," said Quentin Kidd, Director of the Judy Ford Wason Center for Public Policy at Christopher Newport University, in February 2019, "I don't see how it doesn't have a demoralizing effect on Democratic voters and an energizing effect on Republicans." Alan Greenblatt, "Virginia Scandals Threaten Democrats' High Election Hopes," *Governing*, February 6, 2019, https://www.governing.com/topics/politics/gov-virginia -governor-northam-fairfax-herring-blackface-assault.html (accessed June 6, 2021).

6. Gregory S. Schneider, "Gov. Ralph Northam Will Convene Special Session of Virginia Legislature to Take Up Gun Control," *Washington Post*, June 4, 2019, https://www.washingtonpost.com/local/virginia-politics/virginia-gov-northam-calls -for-special-session-of-legislature-to-take-up-gun-control/2019/06/04/40efb24c-86d2 -11e9-a870-b9c411dc4312_story.html (accessed June 6, 2021).

7. Patrick Wilson, "Republicans Reject Northam's Call for Quick Action on Guns, Say They'll Study Proposals Until After Nov. Elections," *Richmond Times-Dispatch*, July 9, 2019, https://www.richmond.com/news/plus/republicans-reject-northam-s -call-for-quick-action-on-guns/article_55830dcb-20c8-58c8-bb41-dc0b44a05be0. html (accessed June 6, 2021). Somewhat lost in the headlines about inaction was the fact that the Republicans had referred all of the bills to the Virginia State Crime Commission, which was established primarily to address criminal justice issues.

At the time, Senator Mark Obenshain, the Chair of the Commission, remarked that "We're going to look at that from a data-driven standpoint," the Harrisonburg Republican told the *Roanoke Times*. "I am confident that we will emerge with real policy proposals that are going to make Virginia a safer place." Virginian-Pilot and Daily Press Editorial Board, "Editorial: Crime Commission Disappoints Virginia," *Virginian-Pilot*, November 15, 2019, https://www.dailypress.com/opinion/vp-ed -editorial-crime-commission-guns-1115-20191115-hhg3ufejurf4nmuafsolgcx7ym -story.html (accessed June 6, 2021). The Crime Commission met in the fall and heard substantial testimony, some of which included empirical studies that purported to show how certain legislation actually reduced gun violence. This included a major study from researchers at Boston University, by Michael Siegel and Claire Boine, *What Are the Most Effective Policies in Reducing Gun Homicides?* Regional Gun Violence Research Consortium Policy Brief (Albany, NY: SUNY Rockefeller Institute of Government, 2019), https://rockinst.org/wp-content/uploads/2019/08 /8-13-19-Firearm-Laws-Homicide-Brief.pdf (accessed June 6, 2021). Yet after the Republicans were trounced in the November election, the Commission issued a three-page report which said nothing, and GOP leadership cancelled the special session scheduled for later in November. See Ned Oliver, "Virginia GOP's Promised Gun-law Study Yields Three-page Report that Makes No Recommendations," *Virginia Mercury*, November 12, 2019, https://www.virginiamercury.com/2019/11 /12/virginia-gops-promised-gun-law-study-yields-three-page-report-that-makes-no -recommendations/ (accessed June 6, 2021).

8. Polling data supports a dramatic shift in the saliency of the issue. A 2018 poll reported that only 9 percent of Virginia voters said "gun policy" was the most important issue facing the country. By contrast, a *Washington Post*-Schar School poll, conducted just one month before the 2019 elections, reported that gun policy was the top issue for Virginia voters, with 75 percent saying it was "very important." Gregory S. Schneider, Laura Vozzella, and Scott Clement, "Poll Finds Virginia Voters Focused on Gun Policy Ahead of Pivotal Election," *Washington Post*, October 4, 2019, https: //www.washingtonpost.com/local/virginia-politics/new-poll-finds-virginia-voters -focused-on-gun-policy-ahead-of-pivotal-election/2019/10/03/db034922-e472y11e9 -a331-2df12d56a80b_story.html (accessed June 6, 2021).

9. A poll conducted in December 2019 by the Wason Center at Christopher Newport University showed that Northam's approval rating was largely restored from what it was before the scandal, with 52 percent approving, and 36 percent disapproving of his performance. Laura Vozzella, "Virginians Mostly Welcome Democratic Takeover, CNU Survey Finds," *Washington Post*, December 16, 2019, https://www. washingtonpost.com/local/virginia-politics/virginians-mostly-welcome-democratic -takeover-cnu-survey-finds/2019/12/15/a9e909e0-1f90-11ea-a153-dce4b94e4249 _story.html (accessed June 6, 2021).

10. An October 2019 poll by the Wason Center at Christopher Newport University reported that 54 percent of Virginia voters were more likely to vote for a state legislative candidate who supported impeaching President Donald J. Trump (and 40 percent felt strongly about it). Christopher Newport University, Judy Ford Wason Center for

Public Policy, "Virginia State Senate Survey," October 28, 2019, https://cnu.edu/wasoncenter/surveys/2019-10-28-va-senate-survey/ (accessed June 6, 2021).

11. Reid J. Epstein, "In Virginia Election, Suburban Republicans Sound a Lot Like Democrats," *New York Times*, October 31, 2019, updated November 5, 2019, https://www.nytimes.com/2019/10/31/us/politics/virginia-elections-republicans.html (accessed June 6, 2021).

12. In 2020 and in even-numbered years, the Virginia General Assembly meets for sixty days. This is called the "long Session" and includes consideration of the biennial budget. In odd-numbered years, the Assembly is authorized to meet for thirty days, though recent practice has involved them extending this to forty-six days; this is called the "short session." The origins of Virginia's "long" and "short" sessions is found in 1970 amendments to the Constitution, which provide for annual sessions.

13. In the 2017 and 2019 electoral cycles, the House added thirty-eight new Delegates who were not serving in January 2017.

14. Virginia Public Access Project (VPAP), "Crossover 2020: A Little Over Half of Bills in the General Assembly Are Still Alive," *VPAP.org*, February 13, 2020, https://www.vpap.org/visuals/visual/crossover-2020/ (accessed June 6, 2021). In 2020, the 1,734 bills introduced in the House of Delegates were an increase of about 8 percent over 2018, when Democrats were one seat short of parity. The number of bills introduced in the House has increased about 25 percent since 2016. See Michael Martz, "Glut of General Assembly Legislation 'Just Overwhelming the System,'" *Richmond Times-Dispatch*, February 12, 2020, https://www.richmond.com/news/plus/glut-of-general-assembly-legislation-just-overwhelming-the-system/article_90c9039c-7488-53ef-aca3-d95b26c4f5ae.html (accessed June 6, 2021). Senate bills doubled during this period. The number of bills introduced by Democrats in the House between 2017 and 2020 tripled in number from about 400 to over 1,200 in 2020. Virginia Public Access Project (VPAP), "Spike in Democrat-Sponsored Bills," *VPAP.org*, January 20, 2020, https://www.vpap.org/visuals/visual/spike-democrat-sponsored-bills/ (accessed June 6, 2021).

15. Virginia Public Access Project (VPAP), "Similar Bills, Different Fates," *VPAP.org*, February 12, 2020, https://www.vpap.org/visuals/visual/similar-bills-different-fates/ (accessed June 6, 2021).

16. Mel Leonor, "Democratic Majority Delivers on Liberal Agenda in Virginia, a Remade Southern State," *Richmond Times-Dispatch*, March 8, 2020, https://www.richmond.com/news/plus/democratic-majority-delivers-on-liberal-agenda-in-virginia-a-remade/article_d215569e-6f58-52ea-9fd9-b556096e8280.html (accessed June 6, 2021).

17. Gregory S. Schneider, Laura Vozzella, and Patricia Sullivan, "'A Long Time to Wait': Virginia Passes Equal Rights Amendment in Historic Vote," *Washington Post*, January 15, 2020, https://www.washingtonpost.com/local/virginia-politics/2020/01/15/0475d51a-36f1-11ea-9541-9107303481a4_story.html (accessed June 6, 2021).

18. Justin Mattingly, "Along Party Lines, Senate Backs Removing Photo ID Requirement for Voting," *Richmond Times-Dispatch*, February 4, 2020, https://richmond.com/news/plus/along-party-lines-senate-backs-removing-photo-id

-requirement-for-voting/article_fab96d92-9f49-5120-8ccf-9e500fb7dbfe.html (accessed June 6, 2021).

19. Ned Oliver, "Virginia Lawmakers Vote to Repeal Mandatory Ultrasound, Waiting Period for Abortion," *Virginia Mercury*, January 29, 2020, https://www.virginiamercury.com/2020/01/29/virginia-lawmakers-vote-to-repeal-mandatory -ultrasound-waiting-period-for-abortion/ (accessed June 6, 2021).

20. Graham Moomaw and Ned Oliver, "Virginia Becomes First Southern State to Pass Sweeping LGBTQ Nondiscrimination Bill," *Virginia Mercury*, February 6, 2020, https://www.virginiamercury.com/blog-va/virginia-becomes-first-southern -state-to-pass-sweeping-lgbtq-nondiscrimination-bill/ (accessed June 6, 2021).

21. Associated Press, "Virginia Lawmakers Pass Major Renewable Energy Legislation," *New York Times*, February 11, 2020, https://www.nytimes.com/aponline /2020/02/11/us/ap-us-virginia-renewable-energy.html.

22. Ned Oliver, "Senate Democrats Vote to Increase Minimum Wage to $15, But Only in Northern Virginia," *Virginia Mercury*, February 11, 2020, https://www.virginiamercury.com/blog-va/senate-democrats-vote-to-increase-minimum-wage-to -15-but-only-in-northern-virginia/ (accessed June 6, 2021).

23. Universal background checks, a red flag law, reimposing prohibitions against buying more than one gun per month were among the highlights. The Virginia Senate, however, rejected enactment of an assault weapons ban. Graham Moomaw and Ned Oliver, "Va. Democrats Have Passed Most of Their Gun-control Bills. A Big One is Still Missing," *Virginia Mercury*, January 30, 2020, https://www.virginiamercury.com /2020/01/30/va-democrats-have-passed-most-of-their-gun-control-bills-a-big-one-is -still-missing/ (accessed June 6, 2021).

24. Southern states have been the most resistant to granting employees bargaining rights. Three of them specifically ban all government employees from unionizing: North Carolina, South Carolina, and Virginia. In Texas and Georgia, only police and firefighters can negotiate contracts together.

25. Ned Oliver, "Marijuana Will Be Legal in Virginia on July 1. Here's What Is and Isn't Permitted Under the New Law," *Virginia Mercury*, April 7, 2021, https://www.virginiamercury.com/2021/04/07/marijuana-will-be-legal-in-virginia-on-july-1-heres -what-is-and-isnt-permitted-under-the-new-law/ (accessed June 6, 2021).

26. Gregory S. Schneider, "Virginia Abolishes the Death Penalty, Becoming the First Southern State to Ban Its Use," *Washington Post*, March 24, 2021, https://www.washingtonpost.com/local/virginia-politics/virginia-abolish-death-penalty/2021/03 /24/8d6eda46-8bf6-11eb-9423-04079921c915_story.html (accessed June 6, 2021).

27. Newly appointed House Appropriations Chair Luke Torian, the first African American selected for this position, crowed, upon the passage of the Body's 2020–2021 budget, that it was the "most progressive" in the state's history. Gregory S. Schneider, "Flush With Cash, Virginia Lawmakers Push Bigger Raises for Teachers," *Washington Post*, February 16, 2020, https://www.washingtonpost.com /local/virginia-politics/flush-with-cash-virginia-lawmakers-push-bigger-raises-for -teachers--though-not-as-much-as-educators-seek/2020/02/16/91bd6f92-4e9c-11ea -9b5c-eac5b16dafaa_story.html (accessed March 1, 2021).

28. Governor Ralph S. Northam, interview by author in person, Richmond, Virginia, June 14, 2021.

29. For further criticism, see Steve Haner, "Sweet 16 (Tax Bills) Will Cost Virginians Billions," *Bacon's Rebellion* (blog), March 11, 2020. https://www. baconsrebellion.com/wp/sweet-16-tax-bills-will-cost-virginians-billions/ (accessed June 6, 2021).

30. Alan Suderman and Sarah Rankin, "Virginia Emerges as South's Progressive Leader Under Dems," *AP News*, February 15, 2020, https://apnews.com/55cdfed8d8 f1bf661bc94f860a522fd7 (accessed June 6, 2021).

31. Graham Moomaw, "In Five Weeks, Virginia Democrats Reshape Decades of State Policy," *Virginia Mercury*, February 12, 2020, https://www.virginiamercury. com/2020/02/12/in-five-weeks-virginia-democrats-reshape-decades-of-state-policy/ (accessed June 6, 2021). "I think they are moving very far, very fast," said Todd Gilbert. "What you're seeing is a huge shift in the way Virginia operates going forward." Gregory S. Schneider, Laura Vozzella, and Patricia Sullivan, "Virginia Democrats Push Liberal Agenda—With a Dose of Caution," *Washington Post*, February 2, 2020, https://www.washingtonpost.com/local/virginia-politics/virginia -democrats-push-progressive-agenda--with-a-dose-of-caution/2020/02/11/3c4e7388 -4c37-11ea-b721-9f4cdc90bc1c_story.html (accessed June 6, 2021).

32. The GOP "trifecta" states have tried to eliminate restrictions on gun rights, stop cities from becoming "sanctuaries" for undocumented immigrants, include work requirements for Medicaid recipients and passed numerous abortion prohibitions designed to create a Supreme Court review of *Roe v. Wade*. Perry Bacon Jr., "What Republicans and Democrats Are Doing in the States Where They Have Total Power," *FiveThirtyEight*, ABC News, May 28, 2019, https://fivethirtyeight.com/features/what -republicans-and-democrats-are-doing-in-the-states-where-they-have-total-power/ (accessed June 6, 2021). See also *Roe v. Wade*, 410 U.S. 113 (1973), https://supreme. justia.com/cases/federal/us/410/113/ (accessed June 6, 2021).

33. Multistate, "2020 Election: State Government Trifectas," December 1, 2020, (Presentation), https://s3.amazonaws.com/multistate.us/production/landingpages /lpmf1up6XCQeO4Ltg/attachment/Deck_%202020%20State%20Elections%20_ %20MultiState%20(6).pdf (accessed June 6, 2021).

34. Ned Oliver, "$15 Minimum Wage, Paid Sick Days Hang in Balance as Democrats Debate Labor Priorities," *Virginia Mercury*, February 18, 2020, https: //www.virginiamercury.com/2020/02/18/15-minimum-wage-paid-sick-days-hang-in -balance-as-democrats-debate-labor-priorities/ (accessed June 6, 2021).

35. Oliver, "$15 Minimum Wage."

36. Mel Leonor and Justin Mattingly, "After Wrangling on Redistricting, Legislature Extends Session to Finish Work on Key Bills Before Finalizing Budget," *Richmond Times-Dispatch*, March 8, 2020, https://richmond.com/news/plus/after -wrangling-on-redistricting-legislature-extends-session-to-finish-work-on-key-bills -before-finalizing/article_eebfb445-b4c3-59c9-8b1e-943b9503ab23.html (accessed June 6, 2021).

37. Gloria Li, "Virginia Clean Economy Act Offers Growth, Jobs, and Savings," *Advanced Energy Perspectives* (blog), January 8, 2020, https://blog.aee.net/virginia

-clean-economy-act-offers-growth-jobs-and-savings (accessed June 6, 2021). See Virginia, General Assembly, *Virginia Clean Energy Act* (VCEA), HB 1526, April 12. 2020, https://lis.virginia.gov/cgi-bin/legp604.exe?201+sum+HB1526 (accessed June 11, 2021).

38. Sarah Vogelsong, "On Eve of Clean Economy Act Vote, a Split Emerges Among Democrats," *Virginia Mercury*, February 10, 2020, https://www.virginiamercury.com /2020/02/10/on-eve-of-clean-economy-act-vote-a-split-emerges-among-democrats/ (accessed June 6, 2021).

39. Mike Tidwell and Ruth McElroy Amundsen, "Opinion: With Energy Policy, There's No Free Lunch," *Washington Post*, January 17, 2020, https://www. washingtonpost.com/opinions/local-opinions/with-energy-policy-theres-no-free -lunch/2020/01/17/b13fd97c-3650-11ea-9541-9107303481a4_story.html (accessed June 6, 2021). Attempting to project these types of numbers over three decades is, of course, an extremely difficult undertaking.

40. Simply joining Regional Greenhouse Gas Initiative (RGGI) was projected to cost consumers $2.00 to $2.50 extra per month. Sarah Vogelsong, "At Senate Panel, a Clash Over the Costs of Shifting Away from Carbon," *Virginia Mercury*, February 9, 2020, https://www.virginiamercury.com/2020/02/09/at-senate-panel-a-clash-over-the -costs-of-shifting-away-from-carbon/ (accessed June 6, 2021).

41. Vogelsong, "At Senate Panel."

42. Sarah Vogelsong, "With New Democratic Leadership, General Assembly Faces Flood of Energy Proposals," *Virginia Mercury*, January 6, 2020, https://www. virginiamercury.com/2020/01/06/with-new-democratic-leadership-general-assembly -faces-flood-of-energy-proposals/ (accessed June 6, 2021).

43. Tidwell and McElroy, "Opinion: With Energy Policy."

44. After Democrats took over in 2020, they changed the name of the committee from "Commerce and Labor" to "Labor and Commerce."

45. The original bill would have forced the closure by 2030 of Dominion Energy's hybrid energy center in Wise County, which opened in 2012. The plant has been touted as the cleanest burning facility of its kind in North America, providing power for 150,000 homes and serving as the source of about 500 jobs both at the facility and for related businesses. Significant revenues from the facility also flow to Wise County and the town of St. Paul.

46. Sarah Vogelsong, "Virginia Clean Economy Act Clears General Assembly, Aided by Beefed-up Ratepayer Protections," *Virginia Mercury*, March 6, 2020, https: //www.virginiamercury.com/2020/03/06/virginia-clean-economy-act-clears-general -assembly-aided-by-beefed-up-ratepayer-protections/ (accessed June 6, 2021). The bill required Dominion Virginia and the smaller Appalachian Power Company (APCO) to supply 30 percent of their power from renewables by 2030, and to close all carbon-emitting power plants by 2045 for Dominion and by 2050 for Appalachian.

47. Despite this victory for advocates of renewables, skepticism lingers as to whether Dominion can meet the goals established, both within the bill and in their public statements. A report released less than a week after the bill's approval by Synapse Energy Economics suggested that Dominion would need to acceler-ate its investments in renewables to reach its goals. Catherine Morehouse, "Duke,

Dominion, Southern won't hit clean energy targets at current pace: Report," *Utility Drive*, March 10, 2020, https://www.utilitydive.com/news/duke-dominion-southern -wont-hit-clean-energy-targets-at-current-pace-re/573769/ (accessed June 6, 2021). In addition, questions remain about the costs to ratepayers generated by the bill. See Lee Ware, "Dominion Energy Will Get a 'Blank Check' From the Virginia Clean Economy Act," *Richmond Times-Dispatch*, March 11, 2020, https://www.richmond. com/opinion/columnists/lee-ware-column-dominion-energy-will-get-a-blank-check/ article_aea195ab-2e41-54b7-b02d-bcd67b1528c8.html (accessed June 6, 2021).

48. Oliver, "Marijuana Will Be Legal." The criticism seemed a bit broad, particularly since many of the provisions of the bill would not take effect for several years.

49. Warren Fiske, "PolitiFact VA: Cox Questions Strength of New Marijuana Law," *VPM*, April 26, 2021, https://vpm.org/news/articles/21921/politifactva-cox -questions-strength-of-new-marijuana-law (accessed June 6, 2021). The law arguably made the Commonwealth the only state where possession of a pound of marijuana is not a crime, and its $25 civil fine will be among the Nation's lowest.

Conclusion

Reimagining the Virginia Way

Change is inevitable, and the disruption it causes often brings both inconvenience and opportunity.

—Robert Scoble[1]

The year 2020 will be remembered as one of the most critical years in our Nation's history. The President was impeached but not convicted (the spectacle was repeated in 2021). The COVID-19 pandemic wreaked havoc on our lives and economy. We endured unprecedented wildfires in the West that brought the challenge of climate change into clearer view. As we entered the fall, the Nation wondered whether our democracy could survive another four years of a Donald J. Trump administration beset with corruption, deceit, and ineptitude. And even after Joe Biden won the prevailed by over 7 million votes, and won the Electoral College by a substantial margin, the Nation questioned when and whether Trump would voluntarily vacate the White House.

Then, on January 6, 2021, this country entered a new phase in the fight for American democracy. With exception of the British attack on Washington in 1814, there has never been an assault and occupation of the U.S. capitol. And certainly, never one that involved American citizens and that was incited by the President of the United States. It reinforced for many that we are in the fight of our lives. Trump has now gone from office, but his presence remains, and significant portions of the Republican Party are either fearful of him or fully embrace his politics. Significant numbers of Americans, including many Virginians, do not believe Joe Biden legitimately won the presidency, a fact that prompted one Virginia pundit to remark, "This is the new Lost Cause in Virginia politics."[2]

Virginians have typically been uncomfortable with disruptive change. But the arrival and persistence of the pandemic gave them little choice, as adjustment after adjustment was dictated by the invisible virus. From the education of our children to where we worked, from how we shopped to our manner of socializing, citizens were buffeted by forces that few would have imagined when 2020 began. COVID-19 numbers began to spike that fall, and while the Commonwealth did better than most, over 510,000 of our relatives, friends, and neighbors (including almost 8,000 Virginians) were dead by the end of February 2021.

Disruption also came as a reaction to the murder of George Floyd, which prompted a much-needed racial reckoning. For the most part, protests were nonviolent, but there was looting and rioting in several of our cities, including Richmond, and many Virginians greeted the rallying cry of "defund the police" with different responses, depending on where they lived and their view of race relations. President Trump and his supporters did little to calm the storm. The rhetoric contributed to a further fracturing of racial divisions, though polls indicated that Americans were ready to adopt reasonable measures to rein in police abuses.

Protests over racial injustice, whether they involved Major League baseball's opening day scene of the Yankees and Nationals holding a "Black Lives Matter" banner while kneeling together in a dramatic sign of solidarity, the NBA boycott, or street demonstrations in numerous cities, helped generate change. Within two weeks of Floyd's killing, Richmond witnessed the removal of three major Confederate statues from Monument Avenue, all of which had dominated the landscape for over a century. And states across the Nation enacted a variety of police and criminal justice reforms. Our whole world was changing and the whole world was watching, usually with hope and occasionally with apprehension.

Helping drive the change in the Old Dominion was Democratic control of the legislature, which brought passage of many new laws. But as the 2020 legislative session ended, Virginians quickly became focused on a state of emergency and a series of executive orders; COVID-19 brought a concentration of power in the Governor's office and forced the legislature to hold a session outside of Capitol building for the first time in over one hundred years. Governor Ralph S. Northam called a special session on the budgetary impacts of COVID-19 and criminal justice reform, and it became one of the longest special sessions in history, starting on August 18 and continuing until November 9, 2020.

The Nation emerged from the 2020 election more politically divided than ever. The character of state legislatures changed very little, though Republicans gained a few seats and were able to beat back major pushes by Democrats in Texas, Michigan, North Carolina, and Maine. After the November 2020 election, there were twenty-four Republican trifectas (an increase of three), fifteen Democrats trifectas, and twelve divided governments. Republicans emerged with twenty-seven governorships, a net gain of one. The results in Virginia were never really in doubt. Biden won by ten points and U.S. Senator

Mark Warner prevailed by a larger margin. Democratic control in Richmond was not affected since elections for the House of Delegates would not occur until 2021.

Virginians hoped that 2021 would bring less chaos and more regularity. But they would have to wait out the last chaotic weeks of the Trump administration. A vaccination campaign that began slowly at the end of 2020 picked up steam after Biden's inauguration, and COVID-19 cases eventually began to drop. Problems from the economic dislocation of 2020 remained, and the state's budget was initially challenged. Eventually, many residents of the Commonwealth began to return to some semblance of their former lives.[3] But for all the discussion of *normalcy*, our recent experience with economic disruption, politics, health, and race suggested that *normal* would not be enough. Our failure to live up to the promise of this Nation was taking its toll, especially on those with little wealth or power. Merely returning to normal would not be an option.

BEYOND NORMALCY?

Throughout this book, there has been frequent reference to the embodiment of so-called Virginia exceptionalism—"the Virginia Way." Constructed during the days of Jim Crow and massive resistance, when the state was run by oligarchs who believed that the Virginia Way meant civility for civility's sake, and "to get along" meant to "go along," the concept needs a massive overhaul, if not a total discard. It is time for a newer—and bolder—Virginia Way, still respectful in how we deal with disagreement, but more progressive in its policies and inclusive in its politics.

This new approach will first acknowledge our history, and how policies have frequently operated to disadvantage racial minorities and others without power. As historian John Hope Franklin once wrote, "If the house is to be set in order, one cannot begin with the present; he [*sic*] must begin with the past."[4] That compels creation of a new Virginia Way that not only celebrates diversity but is also inclusionary in how decisions are made and benefits distributed. In contrast to the past, a bold Virginia Way would neither be an inflexible defender of the status quo, nor a means for keeping people *in their place*. Instead, it should serve as a vehicle for getting more citizens of different experiences and backgrounds "into the room" where decisions are made. This may take more effort, but the results will mean a more equitable Commonwealth.

Additionally, this new approach would include even more concerted efforts to build economic opportunity throughout the Commonwealth. This phrase is heard all the time, but its meaning would take on a different character. Our future will likely be shaped by the development of new sources of talent that will generate higher levels of productivity and greater wealth for Virginians. That will undoubtedly mean more education after high school and greater involvement from those who either have been unwilling or unable to secure advanced education or training. Those who have been left out need to be brought in. A recent analysis by the Conference Board of the Committee for Economic Development (CED) supports what has been known for years—that the greater the educational attainment, the higher a person's economic success.[5] Virginia has a strong system of colleges and universities, but our workforce development efforts have occasionally been viewed as fragmented.[6]

Developing more talent means increasing efforts to assist rural and urban areas beset with poverty,[7] and ensuring that those concerns are reflected in budgetary priorities and legislation.[8] But economic opportunity needs to be more than just about inclusivity, if only because economic growth generates the revenues necessary to fund the core services of government, especially those that help most in need. A bolder approach may not always cast government as an exclusive provider of opportunity but instead as a facilitator of creative problem-solving. In some cases, training is more appropriately conducted by an employer-community college partnership; in other instances, a union or a private company would make the most sense. Choices should not be made based on ideological predisposition, but instead on what will prove most effective.

Some of this work is presently being done by the State Council of Higher Education for Virginia (SCHEV), which has set an audacious goal of making the state "the most educated by 2030"[9] and the Virginia Business Higher Education Council, whose Growth4VA initiative purports to make the Commonwealth "the Top State for Talent."[10]

Such an emphasis on talent development also means permitting more innovation in local communities, and a relaxation of unreasonable restraints upon localities who want to try new things to combat seemingly intractable problems. In these instances, it will always be a question of balance, and tipping the scales too much one way or the other may lead the state in directions either uncomfortable to its residents or frustrate efforts to build a talent pool for the future.

A bold approach does not mean that past success is simply jettisoned. Civil discourse remains a norm to be cultivated. And Virginia's economic advantages should be strengthened, not disparaged. Compared to many states, the Old Dominion is better situated both economically and fiscally. We retain a Triple-A (AAA) bond rating and a history of strong managerial capacity and sound budgeting. Our educational system, while ripe with challenges, ranks consistently among the best in the Nation. The expansion of Medicaid has strengthened our safety net. Our unemployment rate is lower than most states, and we have benefitted from economic expansion in ways that many states have not. But emphasizing those things we do well should not be an excuse to operate the state on autopilot. Just the opposite! History teaches us that great places do not just happen; they are products of decisions and choices—good, bad, and indifferent—made by people over periods of time. And by leaders who focus on future challenges and address them before they become crises.

So, what is to be done? The following policy and process initiatives are worthy of consideration.

ATTACKING DISPARITIES IN EDUCATION

Virginians understand that the state has many school divisions that outperform the national average and a number that lag substantially behind. The systems that underperform are typically found in our urban centers and in our poorer rural areas. But for all the discussion, the Commonwealth has only nibbled around the edges of the major sources of disparity. Some of these can be traced to the standards of quality (SOQs) and the school funding formula. Others have their origins in racial and class inequality.

Article VIII, Section 1 of Virginia Constitution is explicit in its support of education: "The General Assembly shall provide for a system of free public elementary and secondary schools for all children of school age throughout the Commonwealth, and shall seek to ensure that an educational program of high quality is established and continually maintained."[11] The state's Supreme Court, however, has largely ducked the issue of what precisely this means, leaving it instead to the legislature and the executive branch to determine the proper funding scheme. Under the same constitution, the Board of Education is required to formulate SOQs for public schools. It is not the only basis upon which educational funding is appropriated, but it is the most significant. Every two years, the state conducts an exercise called "rebenchmarking for the standards of quality." The Commonwealth looks at the programmatic and staffing needs in the K-12 system, and then determines the costs of funding them. This serves as the basis for school funding in the state budget, with the approved funds going to local divisions. But we all know that this does not solve funding disparities. Poorer jurisdictions have greater challenges than richer ones, even as they benefit disproportionately from the composite index and school funding formula.

One reason for this, and a criticism of the SOQ approach, is that it fails to account for the higher cost that divisions have in educating students in poverty. The state has attempted to accommodate for this, mostly by providing supplemental funding through what is called the "At-Risk Add-On" program.

In existence since 1992, its funding has never been included in the SOQs, and therefore has always been subject to the ups and downs of tax revenues coming into state coffers. In late 2019, the state Board of Education recommended a change in the At-Risk Add-On program to include more funding for prevention, intervention, and remediation as part of SOQ.[12] But the price tag was high, the pandemic intervened, and the proposal was placed on hold. Building these factors into the SOQ would mean that at-risk funding would not be an annual political football. Localities might still need to provide their own monies to match the state funding, but more state resources would be built into the budget.

Adjustments might also be needed in the school funding formula and the composite index to further adjust for a locality's ability to pay. This may be the most difficult task of all, because it would mean that the wealthier counties, primarily in the northern part of the state, would potentially lose at the expense of the poorer cities and counties to the south. Every year that Northern Virginia (NoVa) increases its influence and power in the General Assembly makes it less likely for this to occur. Perhaps the only way to do this would be in a year when revenues were projected to be high enough that no school division would actually lose money.

Other investments in both personnel and facilities are needed to enhance school performance. Virginia continues to lag other states in its teacher salaries. In 2019, Virginia had the eight highest average salary for full-time employees but ranked thirty-fourth in average teacher pay. In his 2021 run for governor, Terry McAuliffe seized on this statistic, arguing that the Commonwealth's average teacher salary was 29 percent lower than the $73,890 average salary for all full-time workers—the largest gap in the Nation.[13] For years, the Commonwealth provided extra monies for teachers who work in NoVa, called the "cost to compete." This has been justified by the relatively higher costs of living in the region. But why not provide special incentives for teachers to teach in poverty areas? The issue of teacher salaries is a perennial one, and the state's funding formula only creates more complexities for local governments. When the state authorizes a teacher pay hike, the locality must match the state's contribution in some percentage for it to take effect in their division; some jurisdictions find that impossible to do. What emerges, then, are salaries that differ widely across the state. In 2019, the highest average yearly teacher salaries were found in the counties of Prince William ($65,902), Fairfax ($68,883), Alexandria ($74,738), Falls Church ($77,157), and Arlington ($78,617). These salaries are much higher than the national average, mainly because localities are willing and able to provide greater supplements to boost the monies provided by the Commonwealth.[14] By contrast, teachers in counties such as Grayson and Russell, both located in southwestern Virginia, average less than $40,000 per year.

And what about investments in better school buildings? A Virginia Department of Education analysis requested by Governor Bob McDonnell in 2013 found that more than 60 percent of Virginia's 2,030 school buildings were more than forty years old, and that it would take an estimated $18 billion renovate all schools built before 1983.[15] Bill Stanley, a state Senator from rural Franklin County, has tried several times recently to replenish the school construction fund, without success. "It is hard to learn if your school building is crumbling around you,"[16] said Stanley, citing studies linking facilities and educational performance.[17] Despite bemoaning "our crumbling schools" in his inaugural, Governor Northam was unable to find the monies for substantial new investments to help urban and rural jurisdictions alike. Federal stimulus money may provide a vehicle for a down payment,[18] but this will continue to be an ongoing issue, especially in poorer jurisdictions.

ADDRESSING LOCAL FISCAL STRESS

Beyond schools, there are tremendous differences in the financial ability of localities to meet the needs of their residents. In 2017, largely in response to a fiscal crisis in Petersburg, the General Assembly created a fiscal stress index that measures a locality's ability to generate additional local revenues from its tax base.[19] The index was designed to provide an early warning system to allow the state to provide technical assistance to localities in need. Of the twenty-four localities labeled as having "high" fiscal stress, twenty-two were cities.[20] Considering both cities and counties, the most fiscally stressed tend to be smaller jurisdictions. A recent analysis of the ninety-seven cities and counties with populations less than 50,000, showed that fifty-six (57.7 percent) have "above average" or" high" fiscal stress.[21]

There is a racial component to this. The wealthiest Virginia jurisdictions are all located in NoVa and are predominately white. These include Loudoun (57.1 percent white), Fairfax (51.5 percent white), and Arlington (62.5 percent white). Many of the least wealthy localities are located, not surprisingly, in the southern part of the state, and are overwhelmingly African American. These include Petersburg (76.7 percent black), Emporia (62.5 percent black), and Martinsville (45.5 percent black).[22]

While the stress index illustrates the problem, the real challenge for state lawmakers is how to use it. To date, the state has largely been content to help through the Auditor of Public Accounts by reorganizing the stressed locality's budgeting and accounting approaches.[23] This has been useful for cities such as Petersburg, but what about others? Many "stressed" localities simply do not have the capacity to raise revenue to meet the needs of their residents. And when one considers that most all the fiscally stressed cities, either large and small, operate their own school divisions populated by children that require more intervention and generate more costs, the dynamic becomes even more difficult to overcome.

Some states have statutes permitting takeover of localities or departments within them in cases of extreme fiscal crisis.[24] Michigan, for example, has authority to designate an "emergency manager" to oversee and reorganize localities in extreme distress. This process was used somewhat successfully in Detroit but failed miserably when applied to Flint and its water crisis several years later. In Virginia, we tend to believe that "it can't happen here." Nonetheless, in the aftermath of COVID-19, greater attention should be paid to community resiliency, and tools that may needed to address communities in need. The success of any such measures would certainly depend on involving stakeholders in any of these efforts.

No one should underestimate the political difficulty inherent in greater state intervention.[25] But observers of local government have always been concerned that underlying economic conditions as well as inefficient economies of scale (for example, managing a small school division with many students in need) will further impoverish areas of the state. This has been part of the rationale for statutes encouraging the consolidation of independent cities and towns with surrounding or adjacent counties.

DIVERSIFYING THE ECONOMY AND REFORMING TAXATION

In recent years, the Virginia economy has remained dependent on federal spending, especially in the defense sector. The Commonwealth has consistently ranked among the top three states in both defense and federal spending per capita. This has meant jobs for Virginians and tax revenues for the state. As recently as FY 2015, Virginia was one of three states with annual total federal salaries and wages above $20 billion, the other two being Texas and California.[26] Virginia also has one of the highest concentrations of veterans of any state and is second to California in total U.S. Department of Defense employees. The Hampton Roads area has one of the largest concentrations of military personnel and assets anywhere in the world, including a U.S. Naval base that is second to none.

This reliance can be both a blessing and a curse. For example, even as the pandemic decimated some segments of the Virginia economy, federal spending provided a cushion against some of the budget challenges faced in other states. But when the federal government adopted sequestration in 2011 and embraced automatic budget cuts, Virginia, which was still finding its way out of the 2007–2008 Great Recession, was hammered. Growth stagnated, lagging many states,[27] and the state's budget was challenged. As we emerge from the pandemic, Washington may eventually have to address an increasing deficit, which may portend future reductions in federal spending. That is why Virginia governors have spoken so often about diversifying our economy to be less dependent on federal spending.

There are many great options available. Given our port, expanding international trade is a great opportunity.[28] The Commonwealth is placing a large bet not only on offshore wind power but also upon building a supply chain of manufacturers that can provide materials to other states up and down the East Coast.[29] After years of ignoring the expansion of broadband into underserved areas, the Commonwealth took some tentative steps to make this technology available in hopes of addressing the digital deserts found in many areas of the state.[30] The Amazon HQ2 deal showed that the Commonwealth could outcompete other states on the basis of its strengths in education and in workforce availability, two investments that cannot be overlooked if the state wants to recruit and to retain high tech business.

Other industries may help the budget picture. Legislation passed in 2020 will expand the gaming industry, which is projected to generate $367 million in new tax revenue annually.[31] In 2021, the Commonwealth joined fifteen other states that had legalized the use of recreational marijuana. Although the state left undecided the rules for the drug's sale or taxing, it had commenced a process by which a projected $300 million in annual revenues could be added to state coffers.[32] These actions are not panaceas but are indicative of the type of approaches necessary for diversification. And it will take advocates and innovative thinkers to make them happen.

One of the larger issues involving expanding economic opportunities and addressing disparities involves tax policy. Since countless books with contradictory conclusions have been written on the subject, I will not wade into this political minefield in a substantive way. Nonetheless, there is broad consensus in the state that our tax system was created during an economic period that no longer exists and could use modification in light of present realities. We do not tax services, though they are one of the fastest growth areas of our economy. While the Business, Professional, and Occupational License (BPOL) tax is a local fee that greatly helps some stressed cities, it remains a holdover from the War of 1812 and is viewed as a damper on local startups.[33] The Commonwealth provides too many tax subsidies to private interests, some of which no longer serve their original intended purpose or whose goals might be accomplished in other ways.[34] And while we have been eliminating lower income Virginians from paying income taxes, our brackets have not changed in decades, and our system is not progressive.

It is almost impossible to tackle this challenge one bill at a time during the pressure of a legislative session. In 2021, the General Assembly authorized a major study to determine what tax reforms might be enacted to spur our economy and provide services to our people. But change will require champions at the legislative and executive levels to really have an impact.

EMBRACING GOVERNMENTAL REFORM

The Commonwealth's governmental structure could use some updating considering recent economic, social, and cultural change. Three are especially worthy of consideration. The first would require amending the Virginia Constitution to permit governors to succeed themselves. The single-term limit has been Virginia law since the Commonwealth's 1851 Constitution. As recently as fifty years ago, fifteen states prohibited their governors from serving two consecutive terms, including Pennsylvania, Indiana, and most of the South, but Virginia is now the *only* state with this arrangement. Most Virginia governors are only hitting their stride when their time in office is over. Economic development initiatives and long-term structural changes are difficult to accomplish in four years. Moreover, voters never get the chance to cast a ballot expressing their view of whether the governor has done a good job, and should continue in office.

Our budget cycle is also complicated by this practice. Since Virginia works on a two-year budget that is approved in the even-numbered year, incoming governors immediately face a budget that has been crafted and introduced by their predecessor. Just before leaving office, the governor must present a new two-year budget. In most cases, by the time the legislature considers the proposal, few representatives from the previous administration remain to argue for it. That budget then is reworked to reflect the priorities of the incoming governor. Consequently, a Virginia governor effectively has only one budget that is theirs alone, and that occurs halfway through the four-year term. Constitutional amendments to change the present arrangement have passed recently in the Virginia Senate but have consistently been rejected in the House.

Another area worth reform involves the relationship between state and local governments. Some suggest that one solution could be found in the relaxation of the Dillon Rule and granting greater control to localities. But it is not clear that enactment of "home rule" is a panacea. Some communities could thrive, but others will remain challenged by underlying economic realities. At the same time, relaxation of the Dillon Rule may permit localities to construct unique and innovative approaches to problem-solving. As an example, some jurisdictions have major affordable housing problems, and wish to address them through what is called "inclusionary zoning," an approach that would require a developer of new housing to set aside units deemed affordable by the locality. Since such an approach is prevented by Virginia law, the only way for a locality to get such a power is by convincing the Assembly to pass legislation that enables that specific locality to do so.

Modifying or eliminating the Dillon Rule is easier to discuss in principle than it is to accomplish in practice. When Virginia was rewriting its Constitution in the early 1970s, it flirted briefly with transforming itself into a "home rule" state. The Commission on Constitutional Revision, the group empowered by the General Assembly to develop recommendations for the new Constitution, initially proposed home rule for all localities with a population greater than 25,000.[35] Changing the doctrine could have been as simple as including language in the proposed Constitution, the entirety of which would then have been submitted to the voters for approval. By the time the recommendation was considered by the General Assembly, however, resistance had emerged from two unexpected sources, the Virginia Municipal League (VML) and the Virginia Association of Counties (VACo), usually the strongest advocates for empowering localities. Concerned that passage of home rule provisions would simply mean that the General Assembly would pass a series of general laws preempting the ability of localities from exercising real power, they lobbied against the change, and it was not included in the proposed new Constitution.[36]

Revising the Dillon Rule is neither easy nor a panacea. Since the Dillon Rule is not a statute, changing one Code provision will not transform it. There is also considerable opposition from business interests, who fear that relaxation would create inconsistent policies across jurisdictions and that differential regulations, labor policies, and tax provisions could create havoc for economic development. Finally, even if Virginia were to move to a structure more consistent with home rule, the state would still be in a position where it could "preempt," by explicit action, those actions of a locality that it found unreasonable.

Lawmakers serious about the relaxation of the Dillon Rule should consider suggestions of the National League of Cities (NLC) to add a constitutional amendment to permit localities of a certain size to adopt policies unless they are specifically preempted by the state. At present, state preemption is largely implicit, that is, there is a presumption against localities. Localities who currently seek to innovate often have the burden to show their actions are not prevented by state law. If a constitutional amendment was adopted to force preemption to be explicit, the burden would then shift to the state to specifically assert policies that a locality could not adopt.[37]

Finally, there is little doubt that economic competitiveness is enhanced when localities cooperate across jurisdictional lines. Virginia's unique system of independent cities, an arrangement different from those found in any of the other forty-nine states, may actually discourage this. In most states, residents of cities are also residents of a county; towns and cities are part of the larger entity, and services are shared among them. But not Virginia! The Commonwealth has an "either/or" designation for people living in a specific location. We live in cities or counties, but not both. The Commonwealth has debated the effectiveness of this arrangement for decades. In 1967, the Hahn Commission issued a prescient report asserting that "demands of urban life impose an increasingly heavy burden on the fiscal resources of local government in the metropolitan areas. Problems generated outside local boundaries become problems which local governments must solve."[38] Subsequent studies drew the same conclusion.

In response to these analyses, the state passed new laws, and created a vehicle by which independent cities could be absorbed into counties. Called "reversion," this process has been successful in consolidating several localities. But as suburban counties gained more power in the General Assembly, a major tool by which cities could expand their revenue base—annexation—was placed on hold. The moratorium now remains in place through 2024, and a recent study suggested that it should be extended permanently.[39]

Across the Commonwealth, there continues to be strong interest in regional approaches, especially in economic development. The successful recruitment of Amazon's HQ2 was a product of many factors, not the least of which was the joint pitch by four NoVa jurisdictions to woo the giant.[40] GO Virginia,[41] an initiative pushed by the private sector and funded by a combination of state, local, and private monies, is fostering regional economic development across jurisdictional lines and using state law that allows localities to share in revenue generated from projects that are being developed outside of their jurisdictions. This creates opportunities for cities that have few sites for major industry to jointly participate with counties that have land to generate revenue for both. Challenges will remain for smaller localities who suffer from a lack of economies of scale, but regionalism holds promise for those who embrace it.

REINFORCING OUR POLITICAL GUARDRAILS

The last four years have accelerated a trend that has been building for decades—the erosion of trust that Americans have for each other and their government. President Trump did not create this problem, but he exploited it and, in the process, made it substantially worse. For many, our public sphere has ceased being a place where we can reconcile our differences, but instead as a battleground for partisan and cultural warfare. We used to experience this as a problem reserved to U.S. Congress and the executive. No longer! It has spread into statehouses around the Nation, including Virginia. And it threatens our ability not only to solve critical problems but also the nature of democracy itself.

When I first arrived in Richmond in 2006, most of my colleagues believed that whatever your partisan differences, leaders would find ways to cobble together good policy. One good summary of this aspirational sentiment was provided by former Republican State Senator John Chichester, who served from 1984 to 2007:

> In large part, [he said] the Virginia Way is rooted in the deep sense of responsibility that goes with occupying the space of our founding fathers—those who shaped this great nation with a bold vision that continues to inspire the world . . . . We can take comfort from the lessons of Virginia history. At those crucial points in our journey, Virginia's political leaders will reach deep and find fortitude and courage. They will coalesce and make that unpopular choice, if it truly is necessary to preserve the treasure that is our Commonwealth.[42]

Chichester was appealing to a governing philosophy that rewarded compromise and civility, two qualities which many believe remain essential to the preservation of democracy, and key to any reimagination of the Virginia Way.

Resolving the fault lines of our divergence will require much effort, and Virginia is in a unique position to lead this endeavor, if only because it is what people expect of us. Polarization has many sources and addressing them will require a multifaceted approach.

First, hyperpartisan redistricting is clearly one culprit. When lines are drawn to create safe districts for one party or the other, a tendency emerges where key decisions about candidates are made in primaries that are overly influenced by the extremes of each party. This creates more of an ideological divide when it comes to governance. With Virginia's 2020 passage of a constitutional amendment requiring a bipartisan commission to draw district lines, the state is charting a new course. Lawmakers will still pass play roles in passing criteria that will help guide the commission in their work, and the public will then judge whether this new structure will reduce the role of redistricting in our polarization.

Second, our system of campaign financing continues to fuel our political divisions. Each year, spending in states sets new records. The National Institute on Money in Politics projected total spending in the 2020 cycle at $1.9 billion, up from nearly $1.6 billion in the 2016 contest.[43] Virginia state legislative campaign spending dwarfs those of many other states. In 2019, candidates for the House of Delegates spent a total of $68 million on seats that pay $17,600 per year; their Senate colleagues spent $56 million for seats that pay $400 more. By contrast, the total spent on 110 Michigan state house races in 2018 was $27.6 million. In neighboring Wisconsin, senate and house races that year cost $36 million.[44] Rarely do the costs of individual state legislative races in most states exceed $1 million. That is a lot of money to spend—and it is only increasing.[45]

Although campaign finance reform does not typically rise to the top of concerns of Virginia voters, many elected officials are increasingly troubled by the amounts of money flowing into races in the Commonwealth and what it means for the character of our democracy. Not only are there concerns about contributions currying political favor but worry that the increasing expense of running for office discourages some qualified persons from considering public service. Beyond that, more money allows candidates and their surrogates to spend greater amounts on negative advertising, which has the effect of demonizing opponents and poisoning relationships that lawmakers may need as they construct policy.

Campaign finance reform is more complicated than merely complaining about *Citizens United* and creating clever slogans that generate much heat but shed little light on what can be accomplished. Recognizing that the structure of our financing may be contributing to polarization is an important first step.[46] And in Virginia, we will have to walk before we can run. That would involve placing a cap on individual contributions, out-of-state contributions, and if possible, ideologically based political action committees (PACs).[47]

Ultimately, preserving the guardrails of democracy is a function not only of institutions, but also of the people who run them, the citizens who elect them to do so, and the traditions by which they operate. The inability to agree upon facts and information is difficult. But the peddling of deceptive narratives and the trading in false hopes threatens the basis of democratic legitimacy. Leadership in both parties can play critical roles in tamping down excesses emanating from their respective bases. Democrats certainly can admit that not all Republican ideas to improve our electoral system are evil and Republicans need to acknowledge that our most recent election was perhaps the fairest in recent history. Any time a new majority considers steamrolling the minority (you did it to us, why shouldn't we do it to you?), it should take a deep breath and ask whether the change being advanced is important enough to damage the relationships within the Body.

When given the chance, then, elected officials should do what they can to reinforce the rules, norms, and traditions of key institutions. When Georgia Secretary of State Brad Raffensperger defended his state's counting of votes during the 2020 election, he was protecting the essence of democracy. When Speaker Bill Howell ruled against the attempt by Republicans in the state Senate in 2013 to push through a draconian redistricting plan by attempting to circumvent the rules, he asserted the importance of defending the traditions and norms of the institution. These are stories worth repeating to each generation of lawmakers. Virginia has a history of bipartisan cooperation when it comes to budgetary matters. Republican Appropriations Chair Chris Jones would specifically ask the minority about their priorities as the budget was being developed, and often incorporated these initiatives. In that way, the budget that emerged would have some level of bipartisan support even if it was largely controlled by the majority. The institution will benefit if both parties continue the practice.

It can be difficult for lawmakers to ask themselves, "how am I contributing to this political dysfunction?" But it is a question that has been posed for centuries and is at the heart of the responsibilities of a leader. Conservative thinker Edmund Burke argued this in his address to the Bristol, England electors in 1774, asserting that a "representative owes you not his industry only, but his judgment; and he betrays, instead of serving you, if he sacrifices it to your opinion."[48] Burke would likely cringe if he could witness the contortions of politicians who substitute the feelings of their political base for their exercise of independent judgment.

Words and actions will always matter, and the words and actions of elected officials influence more than most. The best lawmakers recognize this and understand the importance of supporting democratic norms in a humble and empathetic way. If we are ever to reimagine the Virginia Way, this principle would be central to it. Good leaders understand that in our system of *representative* government, elected officials do not *have* power. They *hold* power—in sacred trust for the people they represent. For all the trappings inherent in elected office, most representatives in Virginia remain regular people trying to do the best they can for those they represent. Their constituents come in all stripes, some rich, some poor, a mixture of races and of ethnic groups, young and old, liberal and conservative, friendly and obnoxious, the wide diversity that makes this state a great place to live. They all have needs, hopes, and perspectives, but at base, their most important desire is to be heard. In the Commonwealth of Virginia, one of our greatest challenges is to create the space to do this, to listen and to learn, and even to change our minds as we do. The good news for Virginia is that for all the partisan rancor, we still have a government that works. And while we reject its oppressive past, we aspire to elements of a bold and reimagined Virginia Way that includes civil discourse, respect for each other, thoughtful debate and discussion, support of the rule of law, and even redemption. It is upon these principles that the Commonwealth can survive—and thrive—in the decades ahead.

NOTES

1. Scoble, quoted in Robert Scoble and Shel Israel, *Age of Context: Mobile, Sensors, Data and the Future of Privacy* (Scotts Valley, CA: CreateSpace, 2006).

2. Statement of Quentin Kidd, quoted in Ally Schweitzer, "Poll: Majority of Virginia Republican Voters Say Biden Did Not Win the Election Legitimately," *dcist.com*, February 23, 2021, https://dcist.com/story/21/02/23/majority-of-virginia-republican-voters-say-biden-did-not-win-election-legitimately/ (accessed June 6, 2021).

3. In 2021, parts of the Virginia economy, and the tax collections in the state, came roaring back, with the result that the state projected a surplus at the end of the fiscal year, even without the federal stimulus transfers. Graham Moomaw, "Defying Early Expectations, Virginia Is Coming Out of the Pandemic Flush with Cash," *Virginia Mercury*, June 17, 2021, https://www.virginiamercury.com/2021/06/17/defying-early-expectations-virginia-is-coming-out-of-the-pandemic-flush-with-cash/ (accessed June 19, 2021).

4. John Hope Franklin, "Rediscovering Black America: A Historical Roundup," *New Times on the Web*, September 8, 1968, http://movies2.nytimes.com/books/99/08/15/specials/franklin-roundup.html (accessed June 6, 2021).

5. Committee for Economic Development (CED), Conference Board, "The Future of Work: How America Can Meet the Upskilling Challenge," *Ced.org*, February 2020, https://www.ced.org/solutions-briefs/the-future-of-work-how-america-can-meet-the-upskilling-challenge (accessed June 6, 2021). The Conference Board of the CED, in 2020 found, using data assembled just before the pandemic, that men between the ages of twenty-five and fifty-four years old with at least a bachelor's degree were eight percentage points, on average, more likely to be working or looking for work than the same age cohort without a four-year degree. This was an increase of five points over data compiled in 1980.

6. Virginia. Joint Legislative Audit and Review Commission (JLARC), "Virginia's Workforce Development Programs," Report to the Governor and the General Assembly of Virginia, House Document 8 (2015) Commonwealth of Virginia, December 2014, http://jlarc.virginia.gov/pdfs/reports/Rpt463.pdf (accessed June 6, 2021).

7. James A. Bacon, "Virginia's Rural Development Strategy—and Suggestions for Improvement," *Bacon's Rebellion* (blog), November 11, 2019, https://www.baconsrebellion.com/wp/virginias-rural-development-strategy-and-suggestions-for-improvement/ (accessed June 6, 2021).

8. This also involves providing more protections to those who can be exploited because of their economic vulnerability. See Ned Oliver, "Pew: Virginia's Payday and Title Loan Laws Among Laxest in the Nation," *Virginia Mercury*, October 10, 2019, https://www.virginiamercury.com/blog-va/pew-virginias-payday-and-title-loan-laws-among-laxest-in-the-nation/ (accessed June 6, 2021).

9. State Council of Higher Education for Virginia (SCHEV), "The Virginia Plan for Higher Education: Annual Report 2019 Summary," January 2021, https://www.schev.edu/index/statewide-strategic-plan/annual-report (accessed June 6, 2021).

10. Growth4VA, "Virginia Business Higher Education Council Launches Growth4VA Campaign," n.d., https://growth4va.com/2017/09/23/virginia-business-higher-education-council-launches-growth4va-campaign/ (accessed June 6, 2021).

11. Virginia. *Constitution of Virginia*, Article VIII. Section 1, Education, https://law.lis.virginia.gov/constitutionexpand/article8/ (accessed June 6, 2021)

12. Virginia, Department of Education, "Standards of Quality (SOQ) Proposals for Board of Education Consideration," Presented to the Board of Education, October 16, 2019 (Presentation), https://www.doe.virginia.gov/boe/meetings/2019/10-oct/item-f-attachment-a.docx (accessed June 6, 2021).

13. Warren Fiske, "Va. Teachers Pay Ranks Last in U.S. Compared to Full-time, Year-round Workers," *PolitiFact*, March 22, 2021, https://www.politifact.com/factchecks/2021/mar/22/terry-mcauliffe/va-teachers-pay-last-compared-full-time-year-round/ (accessed June 6, 2021).

14. Mechelle Hankerson, "What's the Average Teacher Salary in Virginia? Depends Who Does the Math, Lawmakers Find." *Virginia Mercury*, November 20, 2019, https://www.virginiamercury.com/blog-va/whats-the-average-teacher-salary-in-virginia-depends-who-does-the-math-lawmakers-find/ (accessed June 6, 2021).

15. Kate Masters, "In the Final Days of Session, Funding School Construction Remains a Budget Debate," *Virginia Mercury*, March 6, 2020, https://www.virginiamercury.com/2020/03/06/in-the-final-days-of-session-funding-school-construction-is-still-a-budget-debate/ (accessed June 6, 2021).

16. Virginia Senator William Stanley Jr., interview with author by telephone, November 15, 2020.

17. Daarel Burnette II, "Does Moving to a Brand New School Building Improve Student Learning?" *Education Week*, April 17, 2019, https://www.edweek.org/education/does-moving-to-a-brand-new-school-building-improve-student-learning/2019/04 (accessed June 6, 2021).

18. Roanoke Times, "Editorial: Virginia Should Use Its Federal Stimulus Money for School Construction," *Roanoke Times*, March 23, 2021, https://roanoke.com/opinion/editorial/editorial-virginia-should-use-its-federal-stimulus-money-for-school-construction/article_33e3f45c-88ea-11eb-8424-670b65cfd62f.html (accessed June 6, 2021).

19. Some twenty states across the Nation have such laws. Pew Charitable Trusts, "3 Steps States Can Take to Strengthen Localities' Fiscal Health: Early Action Can Prevent More Costly Interventions," Pew Fact Sheet, *pewtrusts.org*, June 30, 2020, https://www.pewtrusts.org/en/research-and-analysis/fact-sheets/2020/06/3-steps-states-can-take-to-strengthen-localities-fiscal-health (accessed June 6, 2021).

20. Virginia, Department of Housing and Community Development (DHCD), "Report on Local Vulnerability Analysis," Presented to Commission on Local Government (CLG), Commonwealth of Virginia, July 2020, https://www.dhcd.virginia.gov/sites/default/files/Docx/clg/fiscal-stress/local-vulnerability-report.pdf (accessed June 6, 2021).

21. Virginia, Commission on Local Government (CLG), "Report on Annexation Alternatives to the General Assembly of Virginia," Commonwealth of Virginia, House Document No. 11, November 2018, 17, https://www.dhcd.virginia.gov/sites/default/files/Docx/clg/gena-assem-studies/report-on-annexation-alternatives-housedocument-11.pdf (accessed June 6, 2021).

22. University of Wisconsin Population Health Institute, "Virginia: 2020 County Health Rankings State Report," March 9, 2020, https://www.countyhealthrankings.org/sites/default/files/media/document/CHR2020_VA_0.pdf (accessed June 6, 2021).

For full disclosure, Albemarle County, a portion of which I represented, is Virginia's sixth healthiest county and is also overwhelmingly white (77.3 percent).

23. Martha S. Mavredes, "Local Government Fiscal Distress Monitoring," Auditor of Public Accounts, Commonwealth of Virginia, June 2019, http://www.apa.virginia. gov/reports/LocalFiscalDistressMonitoring2018.pdf (accessed June 6, 2021), see 4–5 for details some of the state assistance provided.

24. Pew Charitable Trust, "The State Role in Local Government Financial Distress," *pewtrusts.org*, July 2013, https://www.pewtrusts.org/~/media/assets/2016 /04/pew_state_role_in_local_government_financial_distress.pdf (accessed June 6, 2021). See also Stephen Eide, " DE-MUNICIPALIZATION: How Counties and States Can Administer Public Services in Distressed Cities," Report for the Manhattan Institute, July 2019, https://media4.manhattan-institute.org/sites/default/files/R-0719 -SE.pdf (accessed June 6, 2021).

25. In the Flint, Michigan example, the emergency managers made decisions with little input from residents, and those residents are still paying the price for state over-reach and poorly made decisions. Derek Robertson, "Flint Has Clean Water Now. Why Won't People Drink It?" *Politico*, December 23, 2020, https://www.politico. com/news/magazine/2020/12/23/flint-water-crisis-2020-post-coronavirus-america -445459 (accessed June 6, 2021).

26. Old Dominion University, "2017 State of the Commonwealth Report, Center for Economic Analysis and Policy," November 2017, https://www.ceapodu.com/wp -content/uploads/2017/11/SOC-2017-FINAL.pdf (accessed June 6, 2021).

27. Old Dominion University, "2017 State of the Commonwealth Report."

28. Elizabeth Cooper, "Casting a Wider Net: An Expanding Port of Virginia Considers New Revenue Opportunities," *Virginia Business*, September 3, 2019, https: //www.virginiabusiness.com/article/casting-a-wider-net/ (accessed June 6, 2021).

29. Sydney Lake, "Va. Offshore Wind Industry Could Create 5.2K Jobs, Study Finds," *Virginia Business*, September 29, 2020, https://www.virginiabusiness.com /article/va-offshore-wind-industry-could-create-5-2k-jobs-study-finds/ (accessed June 6, 2021).

30. Evan Feinman and Kyle Rosner, "Bridging the Digital Divide: A Report from the Office of the Governor," *Virginia Town & City* 56, no. 1 (Jan/Feb 2021): 18–19, https://www.vml.org/wp-content/uploads/pdf/VTCJanFeb21_web.pdf (accessed June 6, 2021).

31. Ned Oliver and Graham Moomaw, "Report: Casinos Could Bring State Millions, But Wouldn't Be Economic Driver Developers Have Pitched," *Virginia Mercury*, November 25, 2019, https://www.virginiamercury.com/2019/11/25/report -legalizing-casino-gambling-sports-betting-could-bring-virginia-367m-in-new-tax -revenue/ (accessed June 6, 2021).

32. Virginia, Joint Legislative Audit and Review Commission (JLARC), "Key Considerations for Marijuana Legalization," JLARC Report 542, November 16, 2020, http://jlarc.virginia.gov/landing-2020-marijuana-legalization.asp (accessed June 6, 2021). Most states have legalized, not by legislative action but by citizen initiative, a process not authorized in the Commonwealth. See also Sophie Quinton, "Voters Approve Marijuana Measures in Five States," *Pew Stateline*, November 4,

2020, https://www.pewtrusts.org/en/research-and-analysis/blogs/stateline/2020/11/04/voters-approve-marijuana-measures-in-five-states?utm_campaign=2020-11-04+SD&utm_medium=email&utm_source=Pew (accessed June 6, 2021).

33. Virginia. Joint Legislative Audit and Review Commission (JLARC), "Technical Report: Impact of Changing the Basis of the BPOL Tax From Gross Receipts to Income," Commission Draft, October 15, 2013, https://www.alexandriava.gov/uploadedFiles/finance/info/JLARC%20BPOL%20report.pdf (accessed June 6, 2021).

34. Virginia. Joint Legislative Audit and Review Commission (JLARC), "Infrastructure and Regional Incentives," Commission Draft, Report 536, September 14, 2020, http://jlarc.virginia.gov/pdfs/reports/Rpt536.pdfVirginia (accessed June 6, 2021).

35. Virginia, *The Constitution of Virginia: Report of the Commission on Constitutional Revision to His Excellency, Mills E. Godwin, Jr., Governor of Virginia, the General Assembly of Virginia, and the People of Virginia, January 1, 1969* (*Commission on Constitutional Revision*) (Charlottesville, VA: Michie Company, 1969), 228–230. The precise recommendation would provide that "a charter county or a city may exercise any power or perform any function which is not denied to it by this Constitution, by its charter, or by laws enacted by the General Assembly . . . " A history of the debate over including a home rule in the 1971 Virginia *Constitution* is found in Richard Schragger and C. Alex Retzloff, "The Failure of Home Rule Reform in Virginia: Race, Localism, and the Constitution of 1971," April 13, 2020, Essays on the Constitution of Virginia (University of Virginia Press, 2021), Virginia Public Law and Legal Theory Research Paper No. 2020–35, https://ssrn.com/abstract=3574765 (accessed June 6, 2021).

36. A. E. Dick Howard, *Commentaries on the Constitution of Virginia* (Charlottesville: University Press of Virginia, 1974), vol. 2, 811–812. See also Jack Spain Jr., "The General Assembly and Local Government: Legislating a Constitution 1969–1970," *University of Richmond Law Review*, 8, no. 3 (1974): article 2, 387–432, http://scholarship.richmond.edu/lawreview/vol8/iss3/2 (accessed June 6, 2021).

37. National League of Cities (NLC), "Principles of Home Rule for the 21st Century," 2020, https://www.nlc.org/wp-content/uploads/2020/02/Home20Rule20Principles20ReportWEB-2-1.pdf (accessed June 6, 2021).

38. Virginia, Senate, "Report of the Virginia Metropolitan Areas Study Commission," to the Governor of Virginia and the Members of the General Assembly of Virginia, Hahn Commission, Senate Document No. 16, 1967, published 1968, https://rga.lis.virginia.gov/?OpenForm (accessed June 6, 2021).

39. Virginia, Commission on Local Government (CLG), "Report on Annexation Alternatives."

40. Victor Hoskins and Stephanie Landrum, "Opinion: Regionalism Is Working for Northern Virginia," *Washington Post*, September 18, 2020, https://www.washingtonpost.com/opinions/local-opinions/regionalism-is-working-for-northern-virginia/2020/09/17/ae5814f2-f781-11ea-89e3-4b9efa36dc64_story.html (accessed June 6, 2021).

41. Trevor Metcalfe, "Hampton Roads Plan to Bring Offshore Wind Supply Chain to Region Gets GO Virginia Funding," *Virginian-Pilot*, September 14,

2020, https://www.pilotonline.com/inside-business/vp-ib-wind-grant-0914-20200914 -id6gmqhmmbahjb22xr5vvc4rw4-story.html (accessed June 6, 2021).

42. John Chichester, "Epilogue: The Virginia Way," in *Governing Virginia*, ed. Anne Marie Morgan and A. R. Pete Giesen Jr. (Boston, MA: Pearson Learning Solutions, 2012), 229, 233.

43. Stacy Montemayor, Pete Quist, Karl Evers-Hillstrom, and Douglas Weber, "Joint Report Reveals Record Donations in 2020 State and Federal Races," National Institute on Money in Politics, *FollowTheMoney.org*, November 19, 2020, updated December 22, 2020, https://www.followthemoney.org/research/institute-reports /joint-report-reveals-record-donations-in-2020-state-and-federal-races (accessed June 6, 2021).

44. Craig Mauger, "The Cost of Campaigns for the Michigan House Rises . . . Once Again," *Michigan Campaign Finance Network*, March 28, 2019, https://mcfn.org/ node/7197/the-cost-of-campaigns-for-the-michigan-house-rises-once-again (accessed June 6, 2021); Riley Vetterkind, "Record $36 Million Spent on Wisconsin Legislative Races in 2018," *Wisconsin State Journal*, March 6, 2019, https://madison.com/ wsj/news/local/govt-and-politics/record-36-million-spent-on-wisconsin-legislative -races-in-2018/article_48a207c1-a13d-5d97-87b0-6b1dddd029dd.html (accessed June 6, 2021).

45. In 2017, for example, four House members spent over $1 million on their individual races. Two years later, that number rose to nineteen, with two of them (Tim Hugo in Fairfax and Kirk Cox in Chesterfield) each spending over $2 million. Of the nineteen spending $1 million or more, seven lost their races, including Hugo. See Virginia Public Access Project (VPAP), "House: General Elections, 2017 and 2019," House of Delegates Campaign Spending, *VAPA.org*, https://www.vpap.org /elections/house/candidates/general/?year=2017&competition=all&party_in_power =all (accessed June 6, 2021).

46. Ezra Klein, *Why We're Polarized*, Kindle ed. (New York: Avid Reader Press/ Simon & Schuster, 2020). Klein cites Raymond J. La Raja, and Brian F. Schaffner, *Campaign Finance and Political Polarization: When Purists Prevail* (Ann Arbor: University of Michigan Press, 2015), 119, who analyzed data from fifty states, and concluded that the more powerful the political party in a state, the lesser the polarization in the state legislature. Similarly, Klein cites a study by Michael J. Barber, "Ideological Donors, Contribution Limits, and the Polarization of American Legislatures," *Journal of Politics* 78, no. 1 (2015): 296–310, https://www.journals. uchicago.edu/doi/pdf/10.1086/683453 (accessed June 6, 2021), that argues that candidates in states with greater emphasis on individual donations tend to be more polarized than in states where there is greater spending by Political Action Committees (PACs) or parties.

47. This may increase the role of political parties, which has been changing in recent years. Parties historically have served a role in identifying and cultivating candidates with a demonstrated track record of effective community work rather than an ideological focus or driving ambition. Much of that function is going away as primaries have become the method of choice for candidates, but is that always the best way? In 2021, the Democratic contest for Lieutenant Governor had twelve

different candidates, a recipe for the most ideologically pure contestant to win the nomination with perhaps as little as 10 percent of the vote. Experiments are also occurring across the country with "ranked choice voting," or "instant runoff," a system by which people vote for multiple candidates, in order of preference. If no one initially gains a majority of the vote, the second-place votes are then allocated among candidates, until someone crosses the 50 percent threshold. In theory, this will reduce ideological polarization by forcing candidates to appeal to a larger segment of the electorate. Virginia's Republican Party used this technique to choose their statewide candidates in 2021. See Andrew Yang and Bill Weld, "Andrew Yang, Bill Weld: Why Ranked Choice Voting Will Improve America's Elections," *USA Today*, October 2, 2020, https://www.usatoday.com/story/opinion/2020/10/02/why-ranked-choice-voting-improve-american-elections-yang-weld-column/5877731002/ (accessed June 6, 2021).

48. Edmund Burke, "Speech to the Electors of Bristol," November 3, 1774, in *The Founders' Constitution, The Works of the Right Honourable Edmund Burke* (London: Henry G. Bohn, 1854–1856), vol. 1, chap. 13, document 7, https://press-pubs.uchicago.edu/founders/documents/v1ch13s7.html (accessed June 6, 2021).

Epilogue
The GOP Strikes Back

The whispers began in the summer. Polls showed Glenn Youngkin had narrowed Terry McAuliffe's lead in the Governor's race, with some reporting a slight margin for the former private equity fund millionaire. McAuliffe had won his June primary in a rout but had yet to harness the Democratic energy unleashed during the Trump years. With no record of public service, Youngkin remained difficult to define. He studiously avoided direct linkages to the former President. Trump publicly endorsed the candidate numerous times, but Youngkin rarely mentioned him on the campaign trail. He never asked Trump to campaign with him, even as McAuliffe jokingly offered to buy a plane ticket for the former President to travel to Virginia.

Republicans of all stripes were giddy at the prospects of overturning the Democratic trifecta by defeating the former governor and even retaking control of the House of Delegates. When Youngkin began discussing "election integrity" and "audits," Trump supporters knew he was their man. When he proclaimed he would go "on offense" to prevent abortions in the state,[1] the cultural right joined the effort. And the establishment GOP believed that Youngkin could avoid future entanglements with the former President, even as they realized that any victory would be spun as Trump-generated.

It did not help that some voters felt that Democrats had overreached with some of their policies. While Virginia Democrats increased funding for law enforcement during their tenure, many independents reacted negatively to the "defund the police" mantra that they identified with the national party. McAuliffe initially heralded his plans for the largest increase in educational funding in a generation, but the message was lost in his torrent of anti-Trump ads that flooded the airways. Youngkin began to exploit voter concerns about the schools and perceptions that Democrats were insensitive to parents who wanted involvement in their children's education. In places like Loudoun County, a simmering civil war was being fought over "critical race theory" and the extent to which parents were becoming separated from their children's education. Hence, when McAuliffe's out-of-context statement that parents should not be allowed to interfere with their children's education went viral, Youngkin pounced with a flurry of ads exploiting the gaffe.[2] Between Youngkin's massive spending and his lack of a public record, the attempts to link him to right wing extremism were being deflected. Republicans were seeing their chance, and they were taking full advantage of it.

Into the fall, polls showed a significant increase in the percentage of voters who viewed education as their top issue, rising from 15 percent in September to 24 percent in late October.[3] Election-day exit polling reported that a supermajority of Virginia voters believed parents should have a voice in what schools teach their children.[4] Youngkin's positioning on the issue undermined an element thought key to Democratic victory—suburban women. Two counties where Democrats had gained substantially in recent years illustrated the change. Biden in 2020 had generated a 25-point victory margin in Loudoun County; one year later, McAuliffe could muster only an 11-point spread. Similarly, the Democrats won Chesterfield by seven points in 2020, only to lose it by 11 in 2021.[5] Finally, McAuliffe dramatically underperformed with women. Biden captured this key constituency by twenty-three points, but exit polls indicated that McAuliffe won the group by only six.[6] Education, a uniquely state issue where Democrats had dominated, had been turned against them. As one of my colleagues put it, "Democrats had come to think they owned the votes of suburban women when, in reality, they only had been renting them during the Trump years."

McAuliffe was not helped by Biden's falling poll numbers in the aftermath of the Afghanistan withdrawal, continued anxiety over the Delta covid variant, and the failure of a Democratic Congress to enact a major infrastructure bill. This was not the first time when events in Washington and the national mood affected a Virginia election. While Democratic leader in the Virginia House of Delegates, I witnessed Terry McAuliffe's lead in the 2013 governor's race collapse in the aftermath of the botched rollout of the federal health care exchanges. He won, but only because the campaign ended before the full force of the public's anger could be felt. And while our polling two weeks before that election suggested Democrats could win up to eight House seats, our expectations fell short, and we lost several races by a whisker. Four years later, it was the Republicans' turn to feel the cold wind blowing from DC, as strong anti-Trump sentiment not only vanquished the GOP candidate and produced Governor Ralph Northam's 9-point victory but brought Democrats within a coin toss of parity in the House of Delegates.

Now, it was Youngkin's turn to exploit the national mood. And he took advantage of it.

Virginia Democrats pushed and passed popular initiatives—Medicaid expansion, the ERA, minimum wage increases, gun safety measures, and despite the rhetoric of "defund the police," enhanced funding for law enforcement. But many voters were not focused on what Democrats were doing in Richmond. Instead, they were angry with what Democrats were *not* doing in Washington. Most voters do not become enmeshed in internecine party scrabbles between progressives and moderates. They want results. They were not getting them from DC, and Virginia Democrats felt the blame.

In early October, Democratic party leadership hit the panic button, and attempted a reset built on expanded field operations. Under Democratic leadership, the Commonwealth had just enacted major voting reforms, including a 45-day window for early voting previously unavailable in the state. The party knew where its votes were, and it had 45 days to get them to the polls. But so too did the Republicans. While hammering the theme that Youngkin was "Trump in khakis" appealed to Democratic activists, it also seemed to energize a Republican base who were now using the early voting provisions to their advantage. Early voting was one reason why the Commonwealth saw the largest turnout for a governor's race in recent history—by a lot.[7] Much of the early vote came from reliably red areas across the state. Even as McAuliffe won 600,000 more votes than he recorded in 2013 and 200,000 more than Northam's total in 2017, Republican turnout overwhelmed the Democrats, especially in traditionally red areas, where some increases were greater than 40 percent.[8]

The dynamic of the governor's race eventually affected House contests as well. During late fall, House races showed Democratic delegates expanding their leads, even as they remained within the margin of error. The power of incumbency is always strong, and insiders were beginning to think that House Dems could retain their majority even if McAuliffe lost, a view that ran counter to recent data showing a lessening in ticket-splitting. When the votes were counted, however, the fate of House Democrats was tied to the top of the ticket, and Republicans emerged with a 52–48 margin in the Body.

Elections frequently turn on several factors, none of which are determinative by themselves but in combination, provide the difference. The Washington mood, controversy in the schools, Republican enthusiasm, McAuliffe's gaffe, a decline in the COVID infections, and the effectiveness of Youngkin's campaign were all part of the explanation for the GOP victory. And one should not overlook the decision of Republican leaders to effectively prevent Trump-acolyte Amanda Chase from winning their gubernatorial nomination by devising a "ranked choice voting" system that appeared chaotic at times but ultimately generated a stronger candidate.

WHAT CAN BE LEARNED FROM THE 2021 ELECTION?

First, Virginia remains a political battleground and deeply divided between regions and our respective political tribes. There was little ticket-splitting in Virginia, and that resulted in Democratic losses in close races up and down the ticket. Youngkin's victory was neither a landslide nor a mandate. If the Republican win had occurred 10 years ago, it would have appeared to be just another Republican victory. But the formerly reliable red state has changed in the last two decades—and a GOP win was therefore perceived as a disruptive outlier.

Second, diversity is not destiny. The change in the demographic mix in Virginia has been thought to be a major cause of the rise in Democratic electoral strength in the state, which, prior to 2021, led to victories in fourteen of the last twenty-one statewide elections, wins in every presidential contest since Obama in 2008, and the election of two Democratic U.S. Senators. But this year, it was not decisive. Youngkin made minor inroads in the African American and Hispanic communities, and exit polls suggest that white Virginians accounted for 74 percent of voters, up from 67 percent last year.[9] A majority of them voted for the Republican.

Third, Trump was a factor, but not in the way that was expected. Youngkin was masterful in saying enough to mobilize Trump voters while never explicitly being tied to the former President. In 2017, polling for Virginia House races suggested that our candidates needed to talk about issues besides Trump to win; by 2019, everything was about Trump. In 2021, some of the anti-Trump energy for Virginia Democrats had dissipated, and McAuliffe's efforts to link his opponent to the former President failed to make a difference. In fact, exit polls showed that independents, many of whom were extremely uncomfortable with Trump, broke for Youngkin. The former President attempted to take credit for the GOP wins, but there is little evidence of it.

Since Virginia is viewed as a bellwether state, the Democratic loss was viewed as devastating to the party and its prospects for the midterms. Beyond that, Virginia Democrats were greatly concerned that Republican control would undo key policy initiatives. Barring death or defection, the Virginia Senate would remain in Democratic hands until at least 2023, and it remained unclear how far the Commonwealth would move in a conservative direction. But the Governor's powers are extensive, and his ability to bring change, either through appointments, executive action, or the budget, cannot be overlooked. The next few years will show the degree to which the new Governor will embrace policies pleasing to Trump and his base.

Except for watershed moments, most American elections are pendulum swings around a point that represents the political attitudes of a state or a

Nation. The extent of each swing depends on the candidates, the national mood, unique issues in the campaign, and the composition of the electorate. Recent trends have favored Virginia Democrats, but fortunes can change in a November minute. What the 2021 election portends for our bellwether Commonwealth is a story yet to be written.

November 9, 2021

1. Gregory S. Schneider, "Video Shows Glenn Youngkin Saying He Can't Fully Discuss Abortion or Risk Losing Independent Virginia Voters," *Washington Post*, July 7, 2021. http://www.washingtonpost.com/local/virginia-politics/glenn-young-kin-virginia-abortion-video/2021/07/07/1b551bee-df81-11eb-9f54-7eee10b5fcd2_story.html (accessed November 5, 2021).

2. Shane Goldmacher, "5 Takeaways: How Youngkin's Win Makes Democrats Squirm About 2022," *New York Times*, November 3, 2021, https://www.nytimes.com/live/2021/11/02/us/election-news#election-takeaways (accessed November 4, 2021).

3. Gregory S. Schneider, Laura Vozzella, Karina Elwood, Scott Clement, and Emily Guskin, "Virginia Governor's Race a Toss-up as Election Day Nears, Post-Schar School Poll Finds," *Washington Post*, October 29, 2021, https://www.washingtonpost.com/dc-md-va/2021/10/29/virginia-governors-race-poll/ (accessed November 5, 2021)

4. "Exit Poll Results from the 2021 Election for Virginia Governor," *Washington Post*, November 3, 2021, https://www.washingtonpost.com/elections/interactive/2021/exit-polls-virginia-governor/?itid=lk_inline_manual_21 (accessed November 5, 2021).

5. Geoffrey Skelley, "How Republicans Swept a Bluish State," *FiveThirtyEight*, November 3, 2021, https://fivethirtyeight.com/features/how-republicans-won-the-virginia-governors-race/ (accessed November 4, 2021).

6. Amber Phillips, "Why are Democrats Struggling So Much Politically Right Now ?" *Washington Post*, November 3, 2021, https://www.washingtonpost.com/politics/2021/11/03/why-are-democrats-struggling-politically-so-much-right-now/ (accessed November 5, 2021).

7. Virginia Public Access Project (VPAP), "Record Turnout in Tuesday Election," *VPAP.org*, November 4, 2021, https://www.vpap.org/visuals/visual/2021-election-turnout/ (accessed November 5, 2021).

8. Ted Mellnik, Laris Karklis and Adrian Blanco, "How Youngkin Shifted the Vote Toward Republicans Across Virginia," *Washington Post*, November 3, 2021, https://www.washingtonpost.com/politics/2021/11/03/virginia-votes-shift-democrats-republicans/ (accessed November 5, 2021).

9. "Exit Poll Results From the 2021 Election for Virginia Governor," *Washington Post*, November 3, 2021, https://www.washingtonpost.com/elections/interactive/2021/exit-polls-virginia-governor/ (accessed November 5, 2021).

Bibliography

American Immigration Council. "Fact Sheet: Immigrants in Virginia." *American Immigration Council.* August 6, 2020. https://www.americanimmigrationcouncil. org/research/immigrants-in-virginia (accessed June 5, 2021).

Alston v. School Board of City of Norfolk. 112 F.2d 992 (4th Cir. 1940). https://law. justia.com/cases/federal/appellate-courts/F2/112/992/1498702/ (accessed June 3, 2021).

Atkinson, Frank B. *The Dynamic Dominion: Realignment and the Rise of Two-Party Competition in Virginia, 1945–1980.* 2nd ed. Lanham, MD: Rowman & Littlefield, 2006.

———. *Virginia in the Vanguard: Political Leadership in the 400-Year-Old Cradle of American Democracy, 1981–2006.* Lanham, MD: Rowman & Littlefield, 2006.

Augusta Free Press Staff. "Biscuit Run Grant Pushes State Past Kaine's 400K-acre Conservation Goal." *Augusta Free Press.* January 8, 2020. https://augustafreepress. com/to-conserve-and-protect/ (accessed June 4, 2021).

Bacon, James A. "Virginia's Rural Development Strategy—and Suggestions for Improvement." *Bacon's Rebellion* (blog). November 11, 2019. https://www. baconsrebellion.com/wp/virginias-rural-development-strategy-and-suggestions-for -improvement/ (accessed June 6, 2021).

Bacon, Perry, Jr. "What Republicans and Democrats Are Doing In the States Where They Have Total Power." *FiveThirtyEight, ABC News.* May 28, 2019. https: //fivethirtyeight.com/features/what-republicans-and-democrats-are-doing-in-the -states-where-they-have-total-power/ (accessed June 6, 2021).

Bala, Nila. "Automatic Expungement Plan Would Offer a 'Clean Slate' with Bipartisan Support." *R Street.* July 27, 2020. https://www.rstreet.org/2020/07/27 /automatic-expungement-plan-would-offer-a-clean-slate-with-bipartisan-support/ (accessed June 3, 2021).

Barber, Michael J. "Ideological Donors, Contribution Limits, and the Polarization of American Legislatures." *Journal of Politics* 78, no. 1 (2015): 296–310. https:// www.journals.uchicago.edu/doi/pdf/10.1086/683453 (accessed June 6, 2021)

Barnes, Brian. Review of *Understanding and Teaching American Slavery,* edited by Bethany Jay and Cynthia Lynn Lyerly. *Journal of Southern History* 83, no. 2 (2017): 490–92. https://doi.org/10.1353/soh.2017.0158

Barnes, Catherine A. *Journey from Jim Crow: The Desegregation of Southern Transit.* New York: Columbia University Press, 1983.

Bayh, Evan. "The Exit Interviews: Sen. Evan Bayh." *NBC News.* September 13, 2010. https://www.nbcnews.com/id/wbna39082626 (accessed June 4, 2021).

Bennett, Jared. "Why State Attorneys General Races Are The Next Frontier For Out-Of-State Influence." *Center for Public Integrity.* November 3, 2018. https://publicintegrity.org/politics/state-politics/why-state-attorneys-general-races-are-the-next-frontier-for-out-of-state-influence/ (accessed June 5, 2021).

Bethune-Hill v. Virginia State Bd. of Elections. 326 F. Supp. 3d 128 (E.D. Va. 2018). https://casetext.com/case/bethune-hill-v-va-state-bd-of-elections-6 (accessed June 5, 2021).

Blue Virginia. "Time to Clean Up 'Clean Virginia?'" *Blue Virginia Blog.* July 25, 2020. https://bluevirginia.us/2020/07/time-to-clean-up-clean-virginia (accessed June 4, 2021).

Bostic v. Schaefer. 760 F.3d 352 (4th Cir. 2014). https://casetext.com/case/bostic-v-schaefer (accessed June 4, 2021).

Branch, Muriel, and Dorothy Rice. *Miss Maggie: A Biography of Maggie Lena Walker.* Richmond, VA: Marlborough House, 1984.

Branch, Taylor. *Parting the Waters: America in the King Years, 1954–63.* New York: Simon & Schuster, 1988.

Brandt, Allan M. *The Cigarette Century: The Rise, Fall, and Deadly Persistence of the Product That Defined America.* New York: Basic Books, 2007.

Brennan Center for Justice. "Who Draws the Maps? Legislative and Congressional Redistricting." *Brennan Center.* January 30, 2019. https://www.brennancenter.org/analysis/who-draws-maps-states-redrawing-congressional-and-state-district-lines (accessed June 5, 2021)

Brown v. Board of Education of Topeka. 347 U.S. 483 (1954). https://supreme.justia.com/cases/federal/us/347/483/ (accessed April 22, 2021).

Buckingham, Cheyenne, and Grant Suneson. "Where Is the Best Place to Live in America? All 50 States Ranked." *USA Today.* November 6, 2018. https://www.usatoday.com/story/travel/destinations/2018/11/06/americas-best-states-live-ranked/38375051/ (accessed June 2, 2021), original article published "America's Best States to Live In," *247wallst,* November 2, 2018, https://247wallst.com/special-report/2018/11/02/americas-best-states-to-live-in-3/ (accessed June 2, 2021).

Burke, Edmund. "Speech to the Electors of Bristol," November 3, 1774. In *The Founders' Constitution, The Works of the Right Honourable Edmund Burke,* vol. 1 of 6 vols., chap. 13, document 7. London: Henry G. Bohn, 1854–1856. https://press-pubs.uchicago.edu/founders/documents/v1ch13s7.html (accessed June 6, 2021).

Burnette, Daarel, II. "Does Moving to a Brand New School Building Improve Student Learning?" *Education Week.* April 17, 2019. https://www.edweek.org/education/does-moving-to-a-brand-new-school-building-improve-student-learning/2019/04 (accessed June 6, 2021).

Carney, Timothy P., *Alienated America: While Some Places Thrive While Others Collapse.* New York: Harper Collins, 2019.

Caro, Robert A. *The Years of Lyndon Johnson: The Path to Power*. New York: Alfred A. Knopf, 1982.

Celock, John. "Virginia Ultrasound Bill: Republican Lawmaker Calls Abortion 'Lifestyle Convenience.'" *Huffington Post*. February 16, 2012. https://www.huffpost.com/entry/virginia-ultrasound-bill-republican-abortion-lifestyle-convenience_n_1276799 (accessed June 5, 2021).

Center for Information & Research on Civic Learning and Engagement (CIRCLE), "Virginia Youth Voter Turnout Doubled between 2009 and 2017, Estimates Suggest." *Circle*. November 8, 2017. https://civicyouth.org/virginia-youth-voter-turnout-doubled-between-2009-and-2017-estimates-suggest/ (accessed June 5, 2021).

Chichester, John. "Epilogue: The Virginia Way," In *Governing Virginia*, edited by Anne Marie Morgan and A. R. Pete Giesen Jr., 229–33. Boston, MA: Pearson Learning Solutions, 2012.

Christopher Newport University. Judy Ford Wason Center for Public Policy. "Virginia State Senate Survey." October 28, 2019. https://cnu.edu/wasoncenter/surveys/2019-10-28-va-senate-survey/ (accessed June 6, 2021).

Clabaugh, Jeff. "Northern Virginia Remains the 'King of the Cloud.'" *WTOP News*. September 8, 2020. https://wtop.com/business-finance/2020/09/northern-virginia-remains-the-king-of-the-cloud/ (accessed June 2, 2021).

CNBC.com Staff. "America's Top States for Business 2018." *CNBC*, July 10, 2018. https://www.cnbc.com/2018/07/10/americas-top-states-for-business-2018.html (accessed June 2, 2021).

Cohn, Scott. "Amazon Had It Right: Virginia is America's Top State for Business in 2019." *CNBC*. July 10, 2019, updated July 12, 2019. https://www.cnbc.com/2019/07/09/virginia-is-americas-top-state-for-business-in-2019.html (accessed June 2, 2021).

———. "Amazon Reveals the Truth on Why It Nixed New York and Chose Virginia for Its HQ2." *CNBC*. July 10, 2019. https://www.cnbc.com/2019/07/10/amazon-reveals-the-truth-on-why-it-nixed-ny-and-chose-virginia-for-hq2.html (accessed June 2, 2021).

Committee for Economic Development (CED). Conference Board. "The Future of Work: How America Can Meet the Upskilling Challenge." *Ced.org*. February 2020. https://www.ced.org/solutions-briefs/the-future-of-work-how-america-can-meet-the-upskilling-challenge (accessed June 6, 2021).

Cooper, Elizabeth. "Casting a Wider Net: An Expanding Port of Virginia Considers New Revenue Opportunities." *Virginia Business*, September 3, 2019. https://www.virginiabusiness.com/article/casting-a-wider-net/ (accessed June 6, 2021).

Cournoyer, Caroline. "More State AGs Join Lawsuits Against Trump's Immigration Ban." *Governing*. February 1, 2017. https://www.governing.com/topics/public-justice-safety/tns-state-ags-lawsuits-trump-immigration.html (accessed June 5, 2021).

Dabney, Virginius. *Virginia: The New Dominion*. Garden City, NY: Doubleday, 1971.

Dailey, Jane. *Before Jim Crow: The Politics of Race in Postemancipation Virginia*. Chapel Hill and London: University of North Carolina Press, 2000.

Davis, Sarah B. v. Commonwealth of Virginia. 182 Va. 760 (1944). https://cite.case. law/va/182/760/ (accessed June 3, 2021).

Davis v. County School Board of Prince Edward County. 103 F. Supp. 337 (ED Va. 1952). https://law.justia.com/cases/federal/district-courts/FSupp/103/337/1469032 / (accessed June 1, 2021).

Democratic Political Initiative. "There Are Three Reasons Ralph Northam Might Be Called Coon Man." *Medium.* February 4, 2019. https://medium.com/@ NewsHillbilly/there-are-three-reasons-ralph-northam-might-be-called-coon-man -44b2e82498ae (accessed June 2, 2021).

Dinan, John J. *The Virginia State Constitution.* Westport, CT: Praeger, 2006.

Doleac, Jennifer L. "The Effects of DNA Databases on Crime." *American Economic Journal: Applied Economics* 9, no. 1 (2017): 165–201. https://doi.org/10.1257/ app.20150043

Edds, Margaret. *We Face the Dawn: Oliver Hill, Spottswood Robinson, and the Legal Team That Dismantled Jim Crow.* Charlottesville: University of Virginia Press, 2018.

Edwards, Jeff. "Gun Ownership Mapped: How Many Guns Each State Had in 2017?" *Hunting Mark.* February 18, 2018. https://huntingmark.com/gun-ownership-stats.

Ehrenhalt, Alan. "Will We Ever Slay the Evil Gerrymander? One State Took a Small Step This Week, but We're a Long Way From Eliminating Noncompetitive Districts and Partisan Malfeasance." *Governing.* November 4, 2020. https://www.governing. com/assessments/will-we-ever-slay-the-evil-gerrymander.html (accessed June 5, 2021).

Eide, Stephen. "DE-MUNICIPALIZATION: How Counties and States Can Administer Public Services in Distressed Cities." Report for the Manhattan Institute. July 2019. https://media4.manhattan-institute.org/sites/default/files/R-0719-SE.pdf (accessed June 6, 2021).

Encyclopedia Virginia. 2021. http://www.EncyclopediaVirginia.org.

Epps-Robertson, Candace. "The Race to Erase *Brown v. Board of Education*: The Virginia Way and the Rhetoric of Massive Resistance." *Rhetoric Review* 35, no. 2 (2016): 108–20, https://doi.org/10.1080/07350198.2016.1142812

Family Foundation. "Quote of the Day." March 11, 2010. https://www. familyfoundation.org/blog-posts/tag/Morrissey+Moments (accessed June 4, 2021).

Federal Reserve Bank of St. Louis (FRED). 2021. https://fred.stlouisfed.org.

Fergeson, Larissa Smith. "Oliver W. Hill (1907–2007)." In *Encyclopedia Virginia.* Updated on March 25, 2014. http://www.EncyclopediaVirginia.org/Hill_Oliver_W _1907-2007 (accessed June 3, 2021).

Fiske, Warren. "George Allen's 'Macaca' Moment Enshrined in a Political Manual." *Virginian-Pilot.* June 16, 2007. https://www.pilotonline.com/news/article _9e13d2bd-2bf4-5c37-ad0e-5720a7020036.html (accessed June 4, 2021).

———. "PolitifactVA: Cox Questions Strength of New Marijuana Law." *VPM.* April 26, 2021. https://vpm.org/news/articles/21921/politifactva-cox-questions-strength -of-new-marijuana-law (accessed June 6, 2021).

———. "Terry McAuliffe Is Mostly Right About His Jobs Record." *PolitiFact* (Virginia). December 4, 2018. https://www.politifact.com/virginia/statements

/2018/dec/04/terry-mcauliffe/terry-mcauliffe-mostly-right-about-his-jobs-record/ (accessed June 4, 2021).

————. "Va. Teachers Pay Ranks Last in U.S. Compared to Full-time, Year-round Workers." *PolitiFact* (Virginia). March 22, 2021. https://www.politifact.com/ factchecks/2021/mar/22/terry-mcauliffe/va-teachers-pay-last-compared-full-time -year-round/ (accessed June 6, 2021).

Florida, Richard. *The Rise of the Creative Class: And How It's Transforming Work, Leisure, and Everyday Life*. New York: Basic Books, 2002.

"Former Charlottesville City Council Member Wes Bellamy Rips Del. Ibraheem Samirah: 'This stunt you pulled is exactly what the oppressor always does.'" *Blue Virginia Blog*. September 5, 2020, https://bluevirginia.us/2020/09/former -charlottesville-city-council-member-wes-bellamy-rips-del-ibraheem-samirah-this -stunt-you-pulled-is-exactly-what-the-oppressor-always-does.

Franklin, John Hope, and Alfred A, Moss Jr. *From Slavery to Freedom: A History of Negro Americans*. 6th ed. New York: Alfred A. Knopf, 1988.

Freeman, Douglas Southall. "Virginia: A Gentle Dominion." In *These United States: Portraits of America from the 1920s*, edited by David H. Borus, 374–81. Ithaca, NY: Cornell University Press, 1992.

Geiger, Jacob. "Tim Kaine Says Virginia Named Best Managed State, Best for Business While He Was Governor." *PolitiFact*. April 7, 2011. https://www. politifact.com/factchecks/2011/apr/07/tim-kaine/tim-kaine-says-virginia-named -best-managed-state-b/ (accessed June 4, 2021).

Gentilviso, Chris. "Bob McDonnell Declines Ken Cuccinelli Request for Special Session on Virginia Ethics Reform." *Huffington Post*. August 6, 2013. https://www. huffpost.com/entry/bob-mcdonnell-ken-cuccinellli_n_3710198 (accessed June 5, 2021).

Gentry Locke Attorneys. "State of Play." July 1, 2020. Presentation. https://www. gentrylocke.com/wp-content/uploads/2020/07/Q2-State-of-Play.pdf (accessed June 4, 2021).

Giffords Law Center to Prevent Gun Violence. "Open Carry: Guns in Public." 2018. https://lawcenter.giffords.org/gun-laws/policy-areas/guns-in-public/open-carry/ (accessed June 5, 2021).

Gilliam, George Harrison. "Building a Modern South: Political Economy in Nineteenth-Century Virginia." Unpublished. Ph.D. diss., Corcoran Department of History, University of Virginia, 2013. https://doi.org/10.18130/V39639

Gooden, Susan T., and Samuel L. Myers Jr., eds. "The Fiftieth Anniversary of the Kerner Commission Report." Special issue. *RSF: The Russell Sage Foundation Journal of the Social Sciences* 4, no. 6 (2018). https://www.jstor.org/stable/10.7758 /rsf.4.issue-6

Government Technology. "Report Card Evaluates How States Manage Public Resources." *gt*. March 4, 2008, updated July 27, 2020. https://www.govtech.com /policy-management/Report-Card-Evaluates-How-States-Manage.html (accessed June 2, 2021).

Greenblatt, Alan. "Virginia Scandals Threaten Democrats' High Election Hopes." *Governing*. February 6, 2019. https://www.governing.com/topics/politics/gov

-virginia-governor-northam-fairfax-herring-blackface-assault.html (accessed June 6, 2021).

Green v. County School Board of New Kent County. 391 U.S. 430 (1968). https:// supreme.justia.com/cases/federal/us/391/430/ (accessed June 3, 2021).

Growth4VA. "Virginia Business Higher Education Council Launches Growth4VA Campaign." N.d. https://growth4va.com/2017/09/23/virginia-business-higher -education-council-launches-growth4va-campaign/ (accessed June 6, 2021).

Guttmacher Institute. "Abortion Policy in the Absence of *Roe*." May 18, 2021. https: //www.guttmacher.org/state-policy/explore/abortion-policy-absence-roe (accessed June 5, 2021).

Haas, Lori. "Virginia's New Gun Restrictions Have Been 13 Years in the Making." *Virginia Mercury.* April 16, 2020. https://www.virginiamercury.com/2020/04/16/ virginias-new-gun-restrictions-have-been-13-years-in-the-making/ (accessed June 5, 2021).

Hamby, Peter. "Virginia Governor Scandal: 'That's not the guy we know.'" *CNN Politics.* August 20, 2013. https://www.cnn.com/2013/07/17/politics/mcdonnell -scandal/index.html (accessed June 4, 2021).

Haner, Steve. "Sweet 16 (Tax Bills) Will Cost Virginians Billions." *Bacon's Rebellion* (blog). March 11, 2020. https://www.baconsrebellion.com/wp/sweet-16-tax-bills -will-cost-virginians-billions/ (accessed June 6, 2021).

Hankerson, Mechelle. " Northam Establishes Commission to Examine Racial Inequity in State Laws." *Virginia Mercury.* June 4, 2019. https://www.virginiamercury.com /blog-va/northam-establishes-commission-to-address-racial-inequity/ (accessed June 3, 2021).

———. "What's the Average Teacher Salary in Virginia? Depends Who Does the Math, Lawmakers Find." *Virginia Mercury,* November 20, 2019, https:/ /www.virginiamercury.com/blog-va/whats-the-average-teacher-salary-in-virginia -depends-who-does-the-math-lawmakers-find/ (accessed June 6, 2021).

Harmon, Lauren, Charles Posner, Michele L. Jawando, and Matt Dhaiti. *The Health of State Democracies.* Washington, DC: Center for American Progress Action Fund, 2015._https://www.americanprogressaction.org/issues/courts/reports/2015 /07/07/116570/the-health-of-state-democracies/ (accessed June 2, 2021).

Harrington, Gil, and Jane Lillian Vance. *Murdered Dead and for Good.* Nepal: Vajra Books, 2017.

Harrison v. Day. 200 Va. 439, 106 S.E.2d 636 (1959). https://www.courtlistener.com /opinion/1328174/harrison-v-day/ (accessed June 3, 2021).

Heinemann, Ronald L. *Harry Byrd of Virginia.* Charlottesville: University Press of Virginia, 1996.

Heinemann, Ronald L., John G. Kolp, Anthony S. Parent, Jr., and William G. Shade. *Old Dominion, New Commonwealth: A History of Virginia, 1607–2007.* Charlottesville: University of Virginia Press, 2007.

Hersh, Joshua. "Cuccinelli's War." *New Republic.* March 17, 2011. https:// newrepublic.com/article/85327/cuccinelli-virginia-health-care-tea-party (accessed June 5, 2021).

Hochschild, Arlie Russell. *Strangers in Their Own Land: Anger and Mourning on the American Right*. New York: New Press, 2016.

Howard, A. E. Dick. *Commentaries on the Constitution of Virginia*. 2 vols. Charlottesville: University Press of Virginia, 1974.

Howard, Jacqueline. "The Disparities in How Black and White Men Die in Gun Violence, State by State." *CNN Health*. April 24, 2018. https://www.cnn.com/2018/04/23/health/gun-deaths-in-men-by-state-study/index.html (accessed June 3, 2021).

Howell v. McAuliffe. 292 Va. 320, 788 S.E.2d 706 (2016). https://casetext.com/case/howell-v-mcauliffe-1 (accessed June 4, 2021).

Index Mundi. "Virginia Educational Attainment—Persons 25 Years and Over—Percent Bachelor's Degree or Higher by County." 2014–2018. https://www.indexmundi.com/facts/united-states/quick-facts/virginia/percent-of-people-25-years-and-over-with-bachelors-degree-or-higher#chart (June 5, 2021).

Israel, Josh. "Republican Vows to Bring Near-total Abortion Ban to Virginia." *Thinkprogress*. May 15, 2019. https://thinkprogress.org/virginia-lawmaker-vows-georgia-style-abortion-ban-if-the-gop-controls-wins-the-upcoming-elections-94cfc51628f2/ (accessed June 5, 2021).

James v. Almond. 170 F. Supp. 331 (E.D. Va. 1959). https://law.justia.com/cases/federal/district-courts/FSupp/170/331/2360668/ (accessed June 3, 2021).

Janis, Irving L. *Groupthink: Psychological Studies of Policy Decisions and Fiascoes*. 2nd ed. Boston: Houghton Mifflin, 1982.

Jarvis, Brandon. "Clean Virginia plans to spend $125K against Ayala after Dominion Donation." *Virginia Scope*. June 2, 2021. https://www.virginiascope.com/clean-virginia-plans-to-spend-125k-against-ayala-after-dominion-donation/ (accessed June 9, 2021).

Jay, Bethany, and Cynthia Lynn Lyerly, eds. *Understanding and Teaching American Slavery*. Madison: University of Wisconsin Press, 2016.

Jefferson, Thomas. "Thomas Jefferson's First Inaugural Address." March 4, 1801. *First Amendment Watch, New York University*, edited by Stephen D. Solomon. November 27, 2017. https://firstamendmentwatch.org/thomas-jeffersons-first-inaugural-address/ (accessed June 5, 2021).

Johnson, David E. *Douglas Southall Freeman*. Gretna, LA: Pelican Publishing, 2002.

Johnson, Jeroslyn. "Virginia Passes Law Requiring Universities to Create Scholarships for Descendants of Slaves." *Black Enterprise*. April 3, 2021. https://www.blackenterprise.com/virginia-passes-law-requiring-universities-to-create-scholarships-for-descendants-of-slaves/ (accessed June 3, 2021).

Johnson v. Virginia. 373 U.S. 61 (1963). https://supreme.justia.com/cases/federal/us/373/61/ (accessed June 3, 2021).

Jones, Bradley, "Most Americans Want to Limit Campaign Spending, Say Big Donors Have Greater Political Influence." *Pew Research Center*. May 8, 2018. https://www.pewresearch.org/fact-tank/2018/05/08/most-americans-want-to-limit-campaign-spending-say-big-donors-have-greater-political-influence/ (accessed June 4, 2021).

Jones, Janelle, John Schmitt, and Valerie Wilson. "50 Years after the Kerner Commission: African Americans are Better off in Many Ways but Are Still Disadvantaged by Racial Inequality." *Economic Policy Institute*. Report. February 26, 2018. https://www.epi.org/publication/50-years-after-the-kerner-commission/ (accessed June 3, 2021).

Kaine, Tim. "Transcript of Gov. Tim Kaine's Convocation Remarks." *Virginia Tech*. April 17, 2007. https://www.remembrance.vt.edu/2007/archive/kaine.html (accessed June 4, 2021).

Kelo v. City of New London. 545 U.S. 469 (2005). https://supreme.justia.com/cases/federal/us/545/469/ (accessed April 22, 2021).

Kenneth P. Cuccinelli, II, in his capacity as Attorney General of Virginia v. Rector and Visitors of the University of Virginia. 283 Va. 420, 722 S.E.2d 626 (2012). http://www.courts.state.va.us/opinions/opnscvwp/1102359.pdf (accessed June 5, 2021).

Key, V. O., Jr. *Southern Politics in State and Nation*. New York: Knopf, 1949.

Klein, Ezra. *Why We're Polarized*. Kindle ed. New York: Avid Reader Press/Simon & Schuster, 2020.

Krysan, Maria, and Sarah Moberg. "Trends in Racial Attitudes." August 26, 2016. University of Illinois System, Institute of Government and Public Affairs Race and Inequality Initiative. http://igpa.uillinois.edu/programs/racial-attitudes.

Kusnetz, Nicholas. "Only Three States Score Higher Than D+ in State Integrity Investigation; 11 Flunk." *Center for Public Integrity*. November 23, 2015, updated November 23, 2015. https://publicintegrity.org/state-politics/state-integrity-investigation/only-three-states-score-higher-than-d-in-state-integrity-investigation-11-flunk/ (accessed June 4, 2021).

Lake, Sydney. "Va. Offshore Wind Industry Could Create 5.2K Jobs, Study Finds." *Virginia Business*. September 29, 2020. https://www.virginiabusiness.com/article/va-offshore-wind-industry-could-create-5-2k-jobs-study-finds/ (accessed June 6, 2021).

La Raja, Raymond J., and Brian F. Schaffner. *Campaign Finance and Political Polarization: When Purists Prevail*. Ann Arbor: University of Michigan Press, 2015.

Lee, Lauranett L., and Suzanne Slye. "'The Virginia Way': Race, the 'Lost Cause,' & the Social Influence of Douglas Southall Freeman." University of Richmond Inclusive History Project. January 2021. https://president.richmond.edu/inclusive-history/freeman/report/Douglas-Southall-Freeman-Final-Report-20210216.pdf (accessed June 2, 2021).

Levick, Richard. "Amazon Goes to Virginia: How Long-Term Thinking Won the HQ2 Prize." *Forbes*. April 15, 2019. https://www.forbes.com/sites/richardlevick/2019/04/15/amazon-goes-to-virginia-how-long-term-thinking-won-the-hq2-prize/?sh=3fc23f91264c (accessed June 2, 2021).

Levine, Dan. "Exclusive: As Democratic Attorneys General Target Trump, Republican AGs Target Them." *Reuters*. March 28, 2017. https://www.reuters.com/article/us-usa-politics-republican-ags-exclusive/exclusive-as-democratic-attorneys-general-target-trump-republican-ags-target-them-idUSKBN16Z1A5 (accessed June 5, 2021).

Levine, Sam. "A Record Number of Virginians Have Gotten Their Voting Rights Back, Governor Says." *Huffington Post*. April 28, 2017. https://www.huffpost.com /entry/virginia-voting-rights-restoration_n_59038c64e4b05c39767f4b6e (accessed June 4, 2021).

Lewis, Bob. "Virginia Senate Passes Repeal of Abusive Driver Fees." *Insurance Journal*. February 1, 2008. https://www.insurancejournal.com/news/east/2008/02 /01/86924.htm (accessed June 2, 2021).

Li, Gloria. "Virginia Clean Economy Act Offers Growth, Jobs, and Savings." *Advanced Energy Perspectives* (blog). January 8, 2020. https://blog.aee.net/virginia -clean-economy-act-offers-growth-jobs-and-savings (accessed June 6, 2021).

Library of Virginia. "Questions About Virginia." 2019. https://www.lva.virginia.gov/ faq/va.asp (accessed June 15, 2021).

Lithwick, Dahlia. "Another Virginia Disgrace." May 15, 2012. *Slate*. https://slate. com/news-and-politics/2012/05/tracy-thorne-begland-and-the-virginia-house-of -delegates-the-state-legislature-rejects-the-judicial-nomination-of-a-prosecutor -just-because-hes-gay.html (accessed June 4, 2021).

———. "Virginia's Proposed Ultrasound Law Is an Abomination." *Slate*. February 16, 2012. https://slate.com/human-interest/2012/02/virginia-ultrasound-law-women -who-want-an-abortion-will-be-forcibly-penetrated-for-no-medical-reason.html (accessed June 5, 2021).

Lombard, Hamilton. "Inside the Income Gap for some Black Virginians." University of Virginia, Weldon Cooper Center. *StatChat*. July 31, 2020. http://statchatva.org /2020/07/31/inside-the-income-gap-for-some-black-virginians/ (accessed June 3, 2021).

———. "Since 2010, Household Incomes Have Risen the Most in Rural Virginia," University of Virginia, Weldon Cooper Center, *StatChat*, May 7, 2019, http:// statchatva.org/2019/05/07/since-2010-household-incomes-have-risen-the-most-in -rural-virginia/ (accessed June 4, 2021).

———. "Young Adult Migration Trends in Virginia." University of Virginia, Weldon Cooper Center. StatChat. August 9, 2016. http://statchatva.org/2016/08/09/young -adult-migration-trends-in-virginia/ (accessed June 4, 2021).

Lott, Eric. *Love & Theft: Blackface Minstrelsy and the American Working Class*. 20th Anniversary ed. New York: Oxford University Press, 2013.

Loving v. Virginia. 388 U.S. 1 (1967). https://supreme.justia.com/cases/federal/us/388 /1/ (accessed June 1, 2021).

Lowkell. "Final 2019 Data Show Enormous Amounts of $$$ Poured into Virginia General Assembly Races." *Blue Virginia Blog*. January 19, 2020. https:// bluevirginia.us/2020/01/final-2019-data-show-enormous-amounts-of-poured-in-to -virginia-general-assembly-races (accessed June 4, 2021)

Lumina Foundation. "A Stronger Nation." 2021. https://www.luminafoundation.org/ stronger-nation/report/2021/#state/VA (accessed June 2, 2021).

Marans, Daniel. "Virginia Democrats Score a Surprising Win Against Powerful Utility Monopoly." *Huffington Post*. February 13, 2018. https://www.huffpost. com/entry/virginia-democrats-score-surprising-win-against-utility-monopoly_n _5a8266eae4b0892a0352426d (accessed June 6, 2021)

Marsh, Henry L., III. *The Memoirs of Hon. Henry L. Marsh III, Civil Rights Champion, Public Servant, Lawyer.* Edited by Jonathan K. Stubbs and Danielle Wingfield-Smith. Jonesboro, AR: GrantHouse Publishers, 2018.

Masters, Kate. "In the Final Days of Session, Funding School Construction Remains a Budget Debate." *Virginia Mercury.* March 6, 2020. https://www.virginiamercury.com/2020/03/06/in-the-final-days-of-session-funding-school-construction-is-still-a-budget-debate/ (accessed June 6, 2021).

Masters, Kate, and Ned Oliver. "House, Senate Pass Long-anticipated Immigrants' Rights Bills." *Virginia Mercury.* February 12, 2020. https://www.virginiamercury.com/2020/02/12/house-senate-pass-long-anticipated-immigrants-rights-bills/ (accessed June 5, 2021).

Matray, Margaret. "Del. Rick Morris Says He's Been Vindicated in a Child-cruelty Case. His Wife Threatens to Sue Prosecutor." *Virginian-Pilot.* August 23, 2017. https://pilotonline.com/news/local/crime/article_10711dcb-03a4-52ca-96d5-f7ce164ca6a9.html (accessed June 4, 2021).

Mauger, Craig. "The Cost of Campaigns for the Michigan House Rises . . . Once Again." *Michigan Campaign Finance Network.* March 28, 2019. https://mcfn.org/node/7197/the-cost-of-campaigns-for-the-michigan-house-rises-once-again (accessed June 6, 2021).

Mavredes, Martha S. "Local Government Fiscal Distress Monitoring." Auditor of Public Accounts. Commonwealth of Virginia. June 2019. http://www.apa.virginia.gov/reports/LocalFiscalDistressMonitoring2018.pdf (accessed June 6, 2021).

McCann, Adam. "Most & Least Educated States in America." *WalletHub.* January 20, 2020, updated February 16, 2021. https://wallethub.com/edu/e/most-educated-states/31075/ (accessed June 2, 2021).

McCarthy, Bill. "No, Northam Will Not Cut Off Power, Kill Virginians Who Refuse to Give Up Guns." *Politifact.* January 2, 2020. https://www.politifact.com/facebook-fact-checks/statements/2020/jan/02/facebook-posts/no-northam-will-not-cut-power-kill-virginians-who-/ (accessed June 5, 2021).

McDonnell v. United States. 136 S.Ct. 2355 (2016). https://supreme.justia.com/cases/federal/us/579/15-474/ (accessed June 4, 2021).

McGuireWoods LLP. "Report to Eastern Virginia Medical School." *Eastern Virginia Medical School.* May 21, 2019, 1–55. https://www.evms.edu/media/evms_public/departments/diversity_office/final-evms-report-with-exhibits.pdf (accessed June 2, 2021).

Metcalfe, Trevor. "Hampton Roads Plan to Bring Offshore Wind Supply Chain to Region Gets GO Virginia Funding." *Virginian-Pilot.* September 14, 2020. https://www.pilotonline.com/inside-business/vp-ib-wind-grant-0914-20200914-id6gmqhmmbahjb22xr5vvc4rw4-story.html (accessed June 6, 2021).

Miller, Derek. "Top States for Higher Education – 2019 Edition." *Smart Asset.* March 05, 2019. https://smartasset.com/checking-account/top-states-for-higher-education-2019 (accessed June 2, 2021).

Minchin, Timothy J. "Dan River Mills." In *Encyclopedia Virginia.* Updated on July 8, 2020. http://www.EncyclopediaVirginia.org/Dan_River_Mills (accessed June 4, 2021).

Miranda, Lin-Manuel. "The Room Where It Happens." From "Hamilton: An American Musical." In *Hamilton: The Revolution*, edited by Jeremy McCarter, 186–87. New York: Grand Central Publishing, 2016.

Montemayor, Stacy, Pete Quist, Karl Evers-Hillstrom, and Douglas Weber. "Joint Report Reveals Record Donations in 2020 State and Federal Races." National Institute on Money in Politics. *FollowTheMoney.org*. November 19, 2020. Updated December 22, 2020. https://www.followthemoney.org/research/institute-reports/joint-report-reveals-record-donations-in-2020-state-and-federal-races (accessed June 6, 2021).

Moomaw, Graham. "CBS Calls Lt. Gov. Justin Fairfax's Defamation Suit a Ploy to 'Attack' Accusers." *Virginia Mercury*. November 2, 2019. https://www.virginiamercury.com/2019/11/02/cbs-calls-lt-gov-justin-fairfaxs-defamation-suit-a-ploy-to-attack-accusers/ (accessed June 2, 2021).

———."Defying Early Expectations, Virginia Is Coming Out of the Pandemic Flush with Cash." *Virginia Mercury*. June 17, 2021. https://www.virginiamercury.com/2021/06/17/defying-early-expectations-virginia-is-coming-out-of-the-pandemic-flush-with-cash/ (accessed June 19, 2021).

———. "From Banning Chokeholds to 'Divesting' from Police, Va. Black Caucus Rolls Out Reform Agenda." *Virginia Mercury*. June 24, 2020. https://www.virginiamercury.com/blog-va/from-banning-chokeholds-to-divesting-from-police-va-black-caucus-rolls-out-broad-reform-agenda/ (accessed June 3, 2021).

———. "In Five Weeks, Virginia Democrats Reshape Decades of State Policy." *Virginia Mercury*. February 12, 2020. https://www.virginiamercury.com/2020/02/12/in-five-weeks-virginia-democrats-reshape-decades-of-state-policy/ (accessed June 6, 2021).

———. "A Va. Republican Criticized Democrats in a Tweet. Then They Killed 4 of His Bills." *Virginia Mercury*. February 10, 2020. https://www.virginiamercury.com/blog-va/a-va-republican-criticized-democrats-in-a-tweet-then-they-killed-3-of-his-bills/ (accessed June 5, 2021).

Moomaw, Graham, and Ned Oliver. "Va. Democrats Have Passed Most of Their Gun-control Bills. A Big One is Still Missing." *Virginia Mercury*. January 30, 2020. https://www.virginiamercury.com/2020/01/30/va-democrats-have-passed-most-of-their-gun-control-bills-a-big-one-is-still-missing/ (accessed June 6, 2021).

———. "Virginia Becomes First Southern State to Pass Sweeping LGBTQ Nondiscrimination Bill." *Virginia Mercury*. February 6, 2020. https://www.virginiamercury.com/blog-va/virginia-becomes-first-southern-state-to-pass-sweeping-lgbtq-nondiscrimination-bill/ (accessed June 6, 2021).

Morehouse, Catherine. "Duke, Dominion, Southern won't hit clean energy targets at current pace: Report." *Utility Drive*. March 10, 2020. https://www.utilitydive.com/news/duke-dominion-southern-wont-hit-clean-energy-targets-at-current-pace-re/573769/ (accessed June 6, 2021).

Morgan, Anne Marie, and A. R. Pete Giesen, Jr., eds. *Governing Virginia*. Boston, MA: Pearson Learning Solutions, 2012.

Morgan v. Virginia. 328 U.S. 373 (1946). https://supreme.justia.com/cases/federal/us/328/373/ (accessed June 3, 2021).

Multistate. "2020 Election: State Government Trifectas." December 1, 2020. Presentation. https://s3.amazonaws.com/multistate.us/production/landingpages/ lpmf1up6XCQeO4Ltg/attachment/Deck_%202020%20State%20Elections%20_ %20MultiState%20(6).pdf (accessed June 6, 2021).

Municipal Electric Power Association of Virginia (MEPAV). "Member Utilities." *MEPAV.* 2021. http://www.mepav.org/members-localities/ (accessed June 5, 2021).

Nash, Elizabeth, and Joerg Dreweke. "The U.S. Abortion Rate Continues to Drop: Once Again, State Abortion Restrictions Are Not the Main Driver." *Guttmacher Institute.* September 18, 2019. https://www.guttmacher.org/gpr/2019 /09/us-abortion-rate-continues-drop-once-again-state-abortion-restrictions-are-not -main (accessed June 5, 2021).

National Alcohol and Beverage Control Association. "Alcohol Beverage Control Jurisdictions: A Community Choice." October 2017. https://www.nabca.org/sites/ default/files/assets/publications/statecontrol__w.pdf (accessed June 4, 2021).

National Association of Women Judges (NAWJ). "2019 US State Court Women Judges." *NAWJ.* 2019. https://www.nawj.org/statistics/2019-us-state-court-women -judges (accessed June 4, 2021).

National Conference of State Legislatures (NCSL). "Campaign Contribution Limits: Overview." October 4, 2019, https://www.ncsl.org/research/elections-and -campaigns/campaign-contribution-limits-overview.aspx (accessed June 4, 2021).

———. "Full-and Part-Time Legislatures." June 14, 2017. https://www.ncsl.org /research/about-state-legislatures/full-and-part-time-legislatures.aspx (accessed June 4, 2021).

———. "Public Financing of Campaigns: Overview." February 8, 2019. https: //www.ncsl.org/research/elections-and-campaigns/public-financing-of-campaigns -overview.aspx (accessed June 4, 2021).

———. "State Limits on Contributions to Candidates 2019–2020 Election Cycle." Updated June 2019. https://www.ncsl.org/Portals/1/Documents/Elections/ Contribution-Limits-to-Candidates-2019-2020.pdf?ver=2019-10-02-132802-117 (accessed June 4, 2021).

———. "States Offering Driver's Licenses to Immigrants." February 6, 2020. https://www.ncsl.org/research/immigration/states-offering-driver-s-licenses-to -immigrants.aspx (accessed June 5, 2021).

———. "Undocumented Student Tuition: Overview," March 14, 2019, updated September 19, 2019, http://www.ncsl.org/research/education/undocumented -student-tuition-overview.aspx (accessed June 5, 2021).

National Federation of Independent Business (NFIB) v. Sebelius. 567 U.S. 519 (2012). https://supreme.justia.com/cases/federal/us/567/519/ (accessed June 11, 2021).

National Immigration Law Center (NILC). "State Laws Providing Access to Driver's Licenses or Cards, Regardless of Immigration Status." *NILC.org.* Updated August 2019. https://www.nilc.org/wp-content/uploads/2015/11/drivers-license-access -table.pdf (accessed June 5, 2021).

National League of Cities (NLC). "Principles of Home Rule for the 21st Century." 2020. https://www.nlc.org/wp-content/uploads/2020/02/Home20Rule20Principles 20ReportWEB-2-1.pdf (accessed June 6, 2021).

National Right to Work Committee. 2021. https://nrtwc.org/.

Newport, Frank. "The Presidential Campaign, Policy Issues and the Public." *Gallop*. December 11, 2019. https://news.gallup.com/opinion/polling-matters/269717/ presidential-campaign-policy-issues-public.aspx (accessed June 4, 2021).

Norcross, Eileen, and Olivia Gonzalez. "Ranking the States by Fiscal Condition: 2018 Edition." Mercatus Research, Mercatus Center at George Mason University, Arlington, Virginia. October 2018. https://www.mercatus.org/system/files/norcross -fiscal-rankings-2018-mercatus-research-v1.pdf (accessed June 2, 2021).

Norris, Louise. "Virginia and the ACA's Medicaid Expansion." *Healthinsurance.org*. December 2, 2020. https://www.healthinsurance.org/virginia-medicaid/ (accessed June 6, 2021).

North, Emma. "Population Expected to Shrink in Rural Virginia." *Virginia Mercury*. September 19, 2019. https://www.virginiamercury.com/blog-va/population-is -expected-to-shrink-in-rural-virginia/ (accessed June 4, 2021).

Nuckols, Christina. "McDonnell Rules Kaine Out of Order on Gay-discrimination Ban." *Virginian-Pilot*. February 25, 2006. https://www.pilotonline.com/news/ article_04196d73-5d8d-5f88-a6f4-ec2f83250d06.html (accessed June 2, 2021).

Obergefell v. Hodges. 135 S. Ct. 2584 (2015). https://www.lexisnexis.com/community /casebrief/p/casebrief-obergefell-v-hodges (accessed June 4, 2021).

Old Dominion University. "2017 State of the Commonwealth Report, Center for Economic Analysis and Policy." November 2017. https://www.ceapodu.com/wp -content/uploads/2017/11/SOC-2017-FINAL.pdf (accessed June 6, 2021).

Oliver, Ned. "$15 Minimum Wage, Paid Sick Days Hang in Balance as Democrats Debate Labor Priorities." *Virginia Mercury*. February 18, 2020. https://www. virginiamercury.com/2020/02/18/15-minimum-wage-paid-sick-days-hang-in -balance-as-democrats-debate-labor-priorities/ (accessed June 6, 2021).

———. "Bristol Bigwigs Pump $200,000 into Kirk Cox's PAC Amid Casino Push." *Virginia Mercury*. October 25, 2018. https://www.virginiamercury.com/2018/10 /25/bristol-bigwigs-pump-200000-into-kirk-coxs-pac-amid-casino-push/ (accessed June 5, 2021).

———. "A Kinder, Gentler Todd Gilbert? 'It Depends on the Day and the Issue.'" *Virginia Mercury*. November 19, 2019. https://www.virginiamercury.com/blog-va /a-kinder-gentler-todd-gilbert-it-depends-on-the-day-and-the-issue (accessed June 6, 2021).

———. "Marijuana Will Be Legal in Virginia on July 1. Here's What Is and Isn't Permitted Under the New Law." *Virginia Mercury*. April 7, 2021. https://www. virginiamercury.com/2021/04/07/marijuana-will-be-legal-in-virginia-on-july-1 -heres-what-is-and-isnt-permitted-under-the-new-law/ (accessed June 6, 2021).

———. "A Multi-millionaire Set Out to Counter Dominion. Now He's the State's Biggest Campaign Donor." *Virginia Mercury*. October 21, 2019. https://www. virginiamercury.com/2019/10/21/a-multi-millionaire-set-out-to-counter-dominion -now-hes-the-states-biggest-campaign-donor/ (accessed June 4, 2021).

————. "Pew: Virginia's Payday and Title Loan Laws Among Laxest in the Nation." *Virginia Mercury*. October 10, 2019. https://www.virginiamercury.com/blog-va/pew-virginias-payday-and-title-loan-laws-among-laxest-in-the-nation/ (accessed June 6, 2021).

————. "'A Revolutionary Change': Va. Lawmakers Vote to Reform 224-year -old Jury Sentencing Law." *Virginia Mercury*. October 17, 2020. https://www.virginiamercury.com/2020/10/17/a-revolutionary-change-va-lawmakers-vote-to -reform-224-year-old-jury-sentencing-law/ (accessed June 4, 2021).

————. "Senate Democrats Vote to Increase Minimum Wage to $15, But Only in Northern Virginia." *Virginia Mercury*. February 11, 2020. https://www.virginiamercury.com/blog-va/senate-democrats-vote-to-increase-minimum-wage -to-15-but-only-in-northern-virginia/ (accessed June 6, 2021).

————. "Virginia GOP's Promised Gun-law Study Yields Three-page Report that Makes No Recommendations." *Virginia Mercury*. November 12, 2019. https://www.virginiamercury.com/2019/11/12/virginia-gops-promised-gun-law-study -yields-three-page-report-that-makes-no-recommendations/ (accessed June 6, 2021).

————. "Virginia Lawmakers Get Mixed Reviews on Police Reform Efforts." *Virginia Mercury*. October 20, 2020. https://www.virginiamercury.com/2020/10/20 /virginia-lawmakers-get-mixed-reviews-on-police-reform-efforts/ (accessed June 3, 2021).

————. "Virginia Lawmakers Vote to Repeal Mandatory Ultrasound, Waiting Period for Abortion." *Virginia Mercury*. January 29, 2020. https://www.virginiamercury.com/2020/01/29/virginia-lawmakers-vote-to-repeal-mandatory-ultrasound-waiting -period-for-abortion/ (accessed June 6, 2021).

————. "Why Is a Racist Minstrel Tune Still Recognized in Virginia Code as the 'State Song Emeritus?'" *Virginia Mercury*. February 20, 2019. https://www.virginiamercury.com/2019/02/20/why-is-a-racist-minstrel-tune-still-recognized-in -virginia-code-as-the-state-song-emeritus/ (accessed June 3, 2021).

Oliver, Ned, and Graham Moomaw. "Report: Casinos Could Bring State Millions, But Wouldn't Be Economic Driver Developers Have Pitched." *Virginia Mercury*. November 25, 2019. https://www.virginiamercury.com/2019/11/25/report -legalizing-casino-gambling-sports-betting-could-bring-virginia-367m-in-new-tax -revenue/ (accessed June 6, 2021).

Ortiz, Erik, "Virginia GOP Calls Own Lawmaker's Comments on Confederate Statues 'Idiotic.'" *NBC News*. June 5, 2020. https://www.nbcnews.com/news/us -news/virginia-gop-calls-own-lawmaker-s-comments-confederate-statues-idiotic -n1225806 (accessed June 4, 2021).

Oxfam America. *The Best States to Work Index: A Guide to Labor Policy in US States*. Research Report. Washington, DC: Oxfam America, 2018. https://policy-practice.oxfamamerica.org/static/media/files/Best_States_to_Work_Index.pdf (accessed June 20, 2021).

Pariona, Amber. "Which U.S. States Had the Most Slaves at The Start of The Civil War?" *World Atlas*. September 28, 2018. https://www.worldatlas.com/articles/

which-u-s-states-had-the-most-slaves-at-the-start-of-the-civil-war.html (accessed June 1, 2021).

Paviour, Ben. "Fundraising Doesn't Stop During Virginia's Special Session." *VPM.* August 30, 2020. https://vpm.org/news/articles/16134/fundraising-doesnt-stop -during-virginias-special-session (accessed June 4, 2021).

Pew Charitable Trusts, "3 Steps States Can Take to Strengthen Localities' Fiscal Health: Early Action Can Prevent More Costly Interventions." Pew Fact Sheet. *pewtrusts.org.* June 30, 2020. https://www.pewtrusts.org/en/research-and-analysis /fact-sheets/2020/06/3-steps-states-can-take-to-strengthen-localities-fiscal-health (accessed June 6, 2021).

———. "Rainy Day Funds and State Credit Ratings: How Well-designed Policies and Timely Use Can Protect Against Downgrades."*pewtrusts.org.* May 2017. https:// www.pewtrusts.org/~/media/assets/2017/05/statesfiscalhealth_creditratingsreport. pdf (accessed June 2, 2021).

———. "The State Role in Local Government Financial Distress." *pewtrusts.org.* July 2013. https://www.pewtrusts.org/~/media/assets/2016/04/pew_state_role_in _local_government_financial_distress.pdf (accessed June 6, 2021).

Pew Research Center. "As Economic Concerns Recede, Environmental Protection Rises on the Public's Policy Agenda." February 13, 2020. https://www.people -press.org/2020/02/13/as-economic-concerns-recede-environmental-protection -rises-on-the-publics-policy-agenda/ (accessed June 4, 2021).

Plyler v. Doe. 457 U.S. 202 (1982). https://supreme.justia.com/cases/federal/us/457 /202/ (accessed June 5, 2021).

Pollard, Edward A. *The Lost Cause: A New Southern History of the War of the Confederates.* New York: E. B. Treat, 1866.

Prokop, Andrew. "The Battle Over Medicaid Expansion in 2013 and 2014, Explained." *Vox.* May 12, 2015. https://www.vox.com/2015/1/27/18088994/ medicaid-expansion-explained (accessed June 6, 2021).

Provence, Lisa. "99 Problems That Could Lead to DNA Collection." *Cville.* January 20, 2015. https://www.c-ville.com/99-problems-lead-dna-collection/ (accessed June 5, 2021).\

Publius. "How Tommy Norment Led Republicans Over the Cliff." *Bearing Drift.* November 18, 2019. https://bearingdrift.com/2019/11/18/how-tommy-norment-led -republicans-over-the-cliff/ (accessed June 4, 2021).

Quinnipiac University Poll. "U.S. Voters Oppose Trump Emergency Powers on Wall 2–1 Quinnipiac University National Poll Finds; 86percent Back Democrats' Bill on Gun Background Checks." *Quinnipiac.* March 6, 2019. https://poll.qu.edu/Poll -Release-Legacy?releaseid=2604 (accessed June 5, 2021).

Quinton, Sophie. "Voters Approve Marijuana Measures in Five States." *Pew Stateline.* November 4, 2020. https://www.pewtrusts.org/en/research-and-analysis /blogs/stateline/2020/11/04/voters-approve-marijuana-measures-in-five-states?utm _campaign=2020-11-04+SD&utm_medium=email&utm_source=Pew (accessed June 6, 2021).

Randolph v. Virginia. 374 U.S. 97 (1963). https://supreme.justia.com/cases/federal/us /374/97/ (accessed June 3, 2021).

Roe v. Wade. 410 U.S. 113 (1973). https://supreme.justia.com/cases/federal/us/410 /113/ (accessed June 6, 2021).

Saxman, Chris. "Chris Saxman to Virginia FREE: Interesting Poll and State Rankings." (email newsletter). October 16, 2019. https://files.constantcontact. com/005ceb5f201/f415139e-f39d-4946-a3c0-1b4773b3f3c0.pdf (accessed June 2, 2021).

Schoen Consulting. Memo to Everytown for Gun Safety, "Re: 2019 Virginia General Assembly Polling by Region Summary." *Everytown.* August 21, 2019. https:// everytown.org/documents/2019/08/2019-va-general-assembly-polling.pdf.

Schragger, Richard, and C. Alex Retzloff. "The Failure of Home Rule Reform in Virginia: Race, Localism, and the Constitution of 1971." April 13, 2020, Essays on the Constitution of Virginia, University of Virginia Press, 2021. Virginia Public Law and Legal Theory Research Paper No. 2020–35. https://ssrn.com/abstract =3574765 (accessed June 6, 2021).

Schweitzer, Ally. "Poll: Majority of Virginia Republican Voters Say Biden Did Not Win the Election Legitimately." *dcist.com.* February 23, 2021. https://dcist. com/story/21/02/23/majority-of-virginia-republican-voters-say-biden-did-not-win -election-legitimately/ (accessed June 6, 2021).

Scoble Robert, and Shel Israel. *Age of Context: Mobile, Sensors, Data and the Future of Privacy.* Scotts Valley, CA: CreateSpace, 2006.

Sen, Shonel. "Population Projections Show that Virginia is Aging and Growing More Slowly." University of Virginia, Weldon Cooper Center. *StatChat.* July 1, 2019. http://statchatva.org/2019/07/01/population-projections-show-that-virginia -is-aging-and-growing-more-slowly/ (accessed June 4, 2021).

Shannon, Preston C. "The Evolution of Virginia's State Corporation Commission." *William & Mary Law Review* 14, no. 3 (1973): article 3. https://scholarship.law. wm.edu/wmlr/vol14/iss3/3 (accessed June 5, 2021).

Shelby County v. Holder. 570 U.S. 529 (2013). https://supreme.justia.com/cases/ federal/us/570/529/ (accessed June 5, 2021).

Siegel, Michael, and Claire Boine. *What Are the Most Effective Policies in Reducing Gun Homicides?* Regional Gun Violence Research Consortium Policy Brief. Albany, NY: SUNY Rockefeller Institute of Government, 2019. https://rockinst. org/wp-content/uploads/2019/08/8-13-19-Firearm-Laws-Homicide-Brief.pdf (accessed June 6, 2021).

Silverstein, Ed. " Bristol, Virginia Casino Developers Donate $310,000 to State Political Campaigns." *Casino.org.* October 21, 2019. https://www.casino.org/news /bristol-virginia-casino-developers-donate-310000-to-state-political-campaigns/ (accessed June 5, 2021).

Simkins, Francis Butler, Spotswood Hunnicut, and Sidman P. Poole. *Virginia: History, Government, Geography.* New York: Scribner's, 1957.

Smith, Carl. "Blacks in State Legislatures: A State-by-State Map." *Governing.* January 13, 2021. https://www.governing.com/now/Blacks-in-State-Legislatures -A-State-by-State-Map.html (accessed April 22, 2021).

Smith, J. Douglas. *Managing White Supremacy: Race, Politics, and Citizenship in Jim Crow Virginia.* New ed. Chapel Hill: University of North Carolina Press, 2002.

Sommers, Frank G., and Tana Dineen. *Curing Nuclear Madness: A New-Age Prescription for Personal Action*. Toronto: Methuen, 1984.

Spain, Jack, Jr., "The General Assembly and Local Government: Legislating a Constitution 1969–1970." *University of Richmond Law Review*, 8, no. 3 (1974): article 2, 387–432. http://scholarship.richmond.edu/lawreview/vol8/iss3/2 (accessed June 6, 2021).

St. John, Jeff. "How 4 Top US Utilities Are Grappling with Climate Change and the Energy Transition (or Not)." *Grid Edge*. January 22, 2020. https://www.greentechmedia.com/articles/read/how-4-top-u-s-utilities-are-grappling-with-the-energy-transition (accessed June 5, 2021).

State Council of Higher Education for Virginia (SCHEV). "The Virginia Plan for Higher Education: Annual Report 2019 Summary." January 2021. https://www.schev.edu/index/statewide-strategic-plan/annual-report (accessed June 6, 2021).

State Policy Opportunity Tracker (SPOT). "State Brief: Virginia." 2019. https://spotforcleanenergy.org/state/virginia/ (accessed June 5, 2021).

Stevenson, Bryan. *Just Mercy: A Story of Justice and Redemption*. New York: Spiegel and Grau, 2014.

Suderman, Alan. "For Virginia Tech Parents, New Gun Laws a Long Struggle." *ABC News*. February 23, 2020. https://abcnews.go.com/US/wireStory/virginia-tech-parents-gun-laws-long-struggle-69159946 (accessed June 5, 2021).

Suderman, Alan, and Sarah Rankin. "Virginia Emerges as South's Progressive Leader Under Dems." *AP News*. February 15, 2020. https://apnews.com/55cdfed8d8f1bf661bc94f860a522fd7 (accessed June 6, 2021).

Tartakovsky, Joseph. "Firearm Preemption Laws and What They Mean for Cities." *Municipal Lawyer* 54, no. 5 (2013): 6–9, 30–31. https://www.gibsondunn.com/wp-content/uploads/documents/publications/Tartakovsky-Firearm-Preemption-Laws-ML-09.2013.pdf (accessed June 5, 2021).

Taylor, Jessica. "Cuccinelli Cleared of Wrongdoing in Star Scientific Disclosures." *MSNBC*. September 13, 2013. http://www.msnbc.com/the-daily-rundown/cuccinelli-cleared-wrongdoing-star-scie (accessed June 5, 2021).

Thomas, Jeff. *The Virginia Way: Democracy and Power after 2016*. Charleston, SC: History Press, 2019.

Thomas, Jeffrey. "The Virginia Way, Part 2 – New Threats to Old Powers." *Blue Virginia Blog*. August 2, 2019. https://bluevirginia.us/2019/08/the-virginia-way-part-2-new-threats-to-old-powers (accessed June 5, 2021).

Thomas Jefferson Institute for Public Policy. 2021. https://www.thomasjeffersoninst.org/.

Titus, Jill Ogline. *Brown's Battleground: Students, Segregationists, and the Struggle for Justice in Prince Edward County, Virginia*. Chapel Hill: University of North Carolina Press, 2011.

Tobias, Carl. "Electing Justice Roush to the Supreme Court of Virginia." *Washington & Lee University Law Review Online* 72, no. 2 (2015): article 8._https://scholarlycommons.law.wlu.edu/wlulr-online/vol72/iss2/8

Toscano, David J. *Fighting Gridlock: How States Shape the Nation and Our Lives*. Charlottesville: University of Virginia Press, 2021.

————. "The McDonnell Ethics Scandal: The Governor and Attorney General's Inappropriate Acceptance of Gifts." July 26, 2013. *davidtoscano.com.* https:// davidtoscano.com/general-assembly-2013/the-mcdonnell-ethics-scandal (accessed June 4, 2021).

Trotta, Daniel. "Defiant U.S. Sheriffs Push Gun Sanctuaries, Imitating Liberals on Immigration." *Reuters.* March 4, 2019. https://www.reuters.com/article/us -usa-guns-sanctuary/defiant-us-sheriffs-push-gun-sanctuaries-imitating-liberals-on -immigration-idUSKCN1QL0ZC (accessed June 5, 2021).

Twain, Mark [Samuel Clemens]. *Mark Twain, Selected Writings of an American Skeptic.* Edited by Victor Donyo. Buffalo, NY: Prometheus Books, 1983.

University of Wisconsin Population Health Institute. "Virginia: 2020 County Health Rankings State Report." March 9, 2020. https://www.countyhealthrankings.org/ sites/default/files/media/document/CHR2020_VA_0.pdf (accessed June 6, 2021).

U.S. Bill of Rights. September 25, 1789. *National Archives.* https://www.archives.gov /founding-docs/bill-of-rights (accessed June 8, 2021).

U.S. Bureau of Labor Statistics. "Unemployment Rate in Danville, VA (MSA) [DANV251UR]." Federal Reserve Bank of St. Louis (FRED). https://fred. stlouisfed.org/series/DANV251UR (accessed December 21, 2020).

————. "Unemployment Rate in Danville City, VA [VADANV0URN]." Federal Reserve Bank of St. Louis (FRED). https://fred.stlouisfed.org/series/ VADANV0URN (accessed December 21, 2020).

U.S. Census Bureau. "American Community Survey (ACS)." 2019. https://www. census.gov/programs-surveys/acs/ (accessed June 2, 2021).

————. "Census 2000 PHC-T-4. Ranking Tables for Counties: 1990 and 2000," https://www.census.gov/population/www/cen2000/briefs/phc-t4/tables/tab02.pdf.

————. "Median Household Income (in 2019 Inflation Adjusted Dollars) by County." Prepared by Social Explorer. https://www.socialexplorer.com/17707f1ed3/view (accessed April 25, 2021).

————. "QuickFacts: Chesterfield County, Virginia." July 1, 2019. https://www. census.gov/quickfacts/chesterfieldcountyvirginia (accessed June 3, 2021).

————. "QuickFacts: Fairfax County, Virginia." July 1, 2019. https://www.census. gov/quickfacts/fairfaxcountyvirginia (accessed June 3, 2021).

————. "QuickFacts, Pittsylvania County, Virginia." July 1, 2019. https://www. census.gov/quickfacts/pittsylvaniacountyvirginia (accessed June 4, 2021).

————. "QuickFacts: Prince William County, Virginia." Asian population esti- mate July 1, 2019. http://www.census.gov/quickfacts/princewilliamcountyvirginia (accessed June 3, 2021)

————. "QuickFacts: Virginia." July 1, 2019. http://www.census.gov/quickfacts/va (accessed June 3, 2021).

————. "Population of Chesterfield County, Virginia, Census 2010 and 2000 Interactive Map." *Census Viewer.* http://censusviewer.com/county/VA/Chesterfield (accessed June 3, 2021).

————. "Population of Prince William County, Virginia, Census 2010 and 2000 Interactive Map." *Census Viewer.* http://censusviewer.com/county/VA/Prince %20William (accessed June 3, 2021).

―――. "Resident Population Data: 2010 Census." *U.S. Census 2010.* Archived October 23, 2012. https://web.archive.org/web/20121023151158/http://2010. census.gov/2010census/data/apportionment-pop-text.php (accessed June 3, 2021).

U.S. Congress. *Patient Protection and Affordable Care Act* (ACA) *of 2010.* 124 Stat. 119, Pub. L. 111–148. 111 Cong., 2nd sess. March 23, 2010. https://www.govinfo. gov/app/details/PLAW-111publ148/PLAW-111publ148 (accessed June 9, 2021).

―――. *Voting Rights Act of 1965.* Pub. L. 89–110, 89th Cong., 1st sess. August 6, 1965. https://www.ourdocuments.gov/doc.php?flash=false&doc=100 (accessed June 5, 2021).

U.S. Declaration of Independence. *National Archives.* July 4, 1776. https://www. archives.gov/founding-docs/declaration-transcript (accessed June 8, 2021).

U.S. Department of Education. National Center for Education Statistics. "Educational Attainment of Persons 18 Years Old and Over, by State: Selected Years, 1994 through 2004." https://nces.ed.gov/programs/digest/d05/tables/dt05_011.asp (accessed June 5, 2021).

U.S. Department of Health, Education, and Welfare (HEW). *Vital Statistics of the United States 1967. Volume II–Mortality, Part A.* Washington, DC: GPO, 1969. https://www.cdc.gov/nchs/data/vsus/mort67_2a.pdf (accessed June 2, 2021).

U.S. Immigration and Customs Enforcement (ICE). "Delegation of Immigration Authority Section 287(g)." In *Illegal Immigration Reform and Immigrant Responsibility Act of 1996, Immigration and Nationality Act.* https://www.ice.gov/ identify-and-arrest/287g (accessed June 2, 2021).

U.S. National Archives and Records Administration (NARA). Press Release. "NARA Press Statement on the Equal Rights Amendment." January 8, 2020. https://www. archives.gov/press/press-releases-4 (accessed June 5, 2021).

Vance, J. D. *Hillbilly Elegy: A Memoir of a Family and Culture in Crisis.* New York: Harper Press, 2016.

Varon, Elizabeth A. "UVA and the History of Race: The Lost Cause Through Judge Duke's Eyes." *UVA Today.* September 4, 2019. https://news.virginia.edu/ content/uva-and-history-race-lost-cause-through-judge-dukes-eyes (accessed June 2, 2021).

Vetterkind, Riley. "Record $36 Million Spent on Wisconsin Legislative Races in 2018." *Wisconsin State Journal.* March 6, 2019. https://madison.com/wsj/news/ local/govt-and-politics/record-36-million-spent-on-wisconsin-legislative-races-in -2018/article_48a207c1-a13d-5d97-87b0-6b1dddd029dd.html (accessed June 6, 2021).

Virginia. City of Charlottesville. "Blue Ribbon Commission on Race, Memorials, and Public Spaces." Report to City Council. December 19, 2016. https://www. charlottesville.org/Home/ShowDocument?id=48999.

Virginia. Chesterfield County. "2020 Chesterfield County Election Results." https:// www.chesterfield.gov/802/Election-Results (accessed June 5, 2021).

Virginia. *The Code of Virginia, Volume 1.* Richmond, VA: David Bottom, 1919.

―――. *The Code of Virginia.* Charlottesville, VA: Michie, 1942.

Virginia. Commission on Local Government (CLG). "Report on Annexation Alternatives to the General Assembly of Virginia." Commonwealth of Virginia.

House Document No. 11. November 2018. https://www.dhcd.virginia.gov/sites /default/files/Docx/clg/gena-assem-studies/report-on-annexation-alternatives -housedocument-11.pdf (accessed June 6, 2021).

Virginia. *Constitution of Virginia*, Article IV. Legislature, Section 17. Impeachment. https://law.lis.virginia.gov/constitution/article4/section17/ (accessed June 2, 2021).

———. Article VIII. Education, https://law.lis.virginia.gov/constitutionexpand/ article8/ (accessed June 6, 2021).

Virginia. *The Constitution of Virginia: Report of the Commission on Constitutional Revision to His Excellency, Mills E. Godwin, Jr., Governor of Virginia, the General Assembly of Virginia, and the People of Virginia, January 1, 1969* ("Commission on Constitutional Revision"). Charlottesville, VA: Michie Company, 1969.

Virginia. Department of Education. "Standards of Quality (SOQ) Proposals for Board of Education Consideration." Presented to the Board of Education. October 16, 2019. Presentation. https://www.doe.virginia.gov/boe/meetings/2019/10-oct/item-f -attachment-a.docx (accessed June 6, 2021).

Virginia. Department of Housing and Community Development (DHCD). "Report on Local Vulnerability Analysis." Presented to Commission on Local Government (CLG). Commonwealth of Virginia. July 2020. https://www.dhcd.virginia.gov/sites /default/files/Docx/clg/fiscal-stress/local-vulnerability-report.pdf (accessed June 6, 2021).

Virginia. Fairfax County. "New Demographics Report Reveals Fairfax County Is Growing Older, Richer and More Diverse." Report of Fairfax County, Virginia. February 6, 2020. https://www.fairfaxcounty.gov/news2/new-demographics-report -reveals-fairfax-county-is-growing-older-richer-and-more-diverse/.

Virginia. General Assembly. *Grid Transformation and Security Act of 2018.* Chap. 296, S 966. March 9, 2018. https://lis.virginia.gov/cgi-bin/legp604.exe ?181+ful+CHAP0296+pdf (accessed June 11, 2021).

———. *Virginia Clean Energy Act* (VCEA). HB 1526. April 12. 2020. https://lis. virginia.gov/cgi-bin/legp604.exe?201+sum+HB1526 (accessed June 11, 2021).

———. *Virginia Fraud Against Taxpayers Act* (FATA). § 8.01–216.1, c. 842. 2002. https://law.lis.virginia.gov/vacode/8.01-216.1/ (accessed June 23, 2021).

Virginia House of Delegates v. Bethune-Hill. 587 U. S. ___ (2019). https://www. justice.gov/crt/case-document/virginia-house-delegates-v-bethune-hill-supreme -court-decision (accessed June 5, 2021).

Virginia. House of Delegates Clerks Office. "Advanced Member Search." House of Delegates Demographics, 2010. https://history.house.virginia.gov (accessed June 4, 2021).

Virginia. Joint Legislative Audit and Review Commission (JLARC). "Infrastructure and Regional Incentives." Commission Draft. Report 536. September 14, 2020. http://jlarc.virginia.gov/pdfs/reports/Rpt536.pdfVirginia (accessed June 6, 2021).

———. "Interim Review of the Results of Abusive Driver Fees in Virginia and Other States." Report to Joint Commission on Transportation Accountability. December 5, 2007. http://jlarc.virginia.gov/pdfs/reports/Rpt_2007_driver_fees.pdf (accessed June 2, 2021).

———. "Key Considerations for Marijuana Legalization." JLARC Report 542, November 16, 2020. http://jlarc.virginia.gov/landing-2020-marijuana -legalization.asp (accessed June 6, 2021).

———. "Review of the Tobacco Indemnification and Community Revitalization Commission." Report to the Governor and the General Assembly of Virginia. June 2011. http://jlarc.virginia.gov/pdfs/reports/Rpt412.pdf (accessed June 5, 2021).

———. SB 526 Constitutional Amendment [Marshall-Newman Amendment], April 17, 2006, https://leg1.state.va.us/cgi-bin/legp504.exe?061+sum+SB526 (accessed June 4, 2021).

———. "Technical Report: Impact of Changing the Basis of the BPOL Tax From Gross Receipts to Income." Commission Draft. October 15, 2013. https://www. alexandriava.gov/uploadedFiles/finance/info/JLARC%20BPOL%20report.pdf (accessed June 6, 2021).

———. "Virginia Compared to the Other States." Updated January 16, 2020. http:// jlarc.virginia.gov/va-compared-1.asp (accessed June 2, 2021).

———. "Virginia Compared to the Other States." 2021 Edition. http://jlarc.virginia. gov/pdfs/other/Virginia%20Compared%202021-FULL%20REPORT-FINAL -web.pdf (accessed June 23, 2021).

———. "Virginia's Workforce Development Programs." Report to the Governor and the General Assembly of Virginia. House Document 8 (2015) Commonwealth of Virginia. December 2014. http://jlarc.virginia.gov/pdfs/reports/Rpt463.pdf (accessed June 6, 2021).

Virginia. Legislative Information System (LIS). "HB 1 Unborn Children." November 21, 2011. http://leg1.state.va.us/cgi-bin/legp504.exe?121+sum+HB1 (accessed June 4, 2021).

———. "HB 1639 Human Beings, Preborn." Session 2009. http://lis.virginia.gov/cgi -bin/legp604.exe?ses=091&typ=bil&val=hb1639 (accessed June 4, 2021).

———. "Virginia General Assembly Session, HB 1958." 2019. http://lis.virginia.gov /cgi-bin/legp604.exe?191+sum+HB1958 (accessed June 4, 2021).

———."Virginia General Assembly Session, HB 2732." 2019. http://lis.virginia.gov /cgi-bin/legp604.exe?191+sum+HB2732 (accessed June 4, 2021).

Virginia. Office of Virginia Attorney General. News Release. "Attorney General Herring Sues EPA Over Attacks on Clean Air and Climate Change Efforts." November 15, 2019. https://www.oag.state.va.us/media-center/news-releases /1577-november-15-2019-herring-sues-epa-over-attacks-on-clean-air-and-climate -change-efforts (accessed June 5, 2021).

Virginia. Office of the Governor. Executive Order Number Thirty-Nine (2019): Establishment of the Commission on African American History Education in the Commonwealth. https://www.governor.virginia.gov/media/governorvirginiagov/ executive-actions/EO-39-Establishment-of-the-Commission-on-African-American -History-Education-in-the-Commonwealth.pdf (accessed June 2, 2021).

———. "Governor Northam Delivers State of the Commonwealth Address." Press Release. January 9, 2018. https://www.governor.virginia.gov/newsroom/all -releases/2019/january/headline-837676-en.html (accessed June 2, 2021).

Virginia. Senate. "Points of Personal Privilege." Published 2013. https://www.ncsl. org/documents/irl/PointsofPersonalPrivilege—VASenate2013.pdf.

Virginia. Senate. "Report of the Virginia Metropolitan Areas Study Commission." To the Governor of Virginia and the Members of the General Assembly of Virginia, Hahn Commission. Senate Document No. 16. 1967. Published 1968. https://rga.lis. virginia.gov/?OpenForm (accessed June 6, 2021).

Virginia. State Corporation Commission. "Status Report: Implementation of the Virginia Electric Utility Regulation Act." September 1, 2017. https://www.scc. virginia.gov/comm/reports/2017_veurcomb.pdf (accessed June 6, 2021).

Virginia FREE. "Table 1: Best State for Workers." *vafree.org*. August 23, 2019. https://files.constantcontact.com/005ceb5f201/f415139e-f39d-4946-a3c0 -1b4773b3f3c0.pdf (accessed June 2, 2021).

Virginia Museum of History and Culture. "Civil Rights Movement in Virginia." N.d._https://www.virginiahistory.org/collections-and-resources/virginia-history -explorer/civil-rights-movement-virginia (accessed June 2, 2021).

Virginia Polytechnic Institute and State University [Virginia Tech]. "Mass Shootings at Virginia Tech." April 16, 2007. Report of the Virginia Tech Review Panel Presented to Timothy M. Kaine, Governor Commonwealth of Virginia. August 2007. https://rems.ed.gov/docs/MassShootingsatVirginiaTech.pdf (accessed June 2, 2021). Records available at Library of Virginia. "A Guide to the Records of the Virginia Tech Review Panel, 2007–2009." http://ead.lib.virginia.edu/vivaxtf/view ?docId=lva/vi00999.xml (accessed June 2, 2021).

Virginia Public Access Project (VPAP). "Clark for Delegate—Nadarius, Since 2021" *VAPA.org*, https://www.vpap.org/committees/370874/clark-for-delegate-nadarius/ (accessed June 9, 2021).

———. "Clean Virginia Fund, 2020–2021." *VPAP.org*. https://www.vpap.org/donors /322501-clean-virginia-fund/?start_year=2020&end_year=2021&recip_type=all (accessed June 9, 2021).

———. "Clean Virginia Fund to All Candidates and Committees, 2019." *VPAP.org*. https://www.vpap.org/donors/322501-clean-virginia-fund/?start_year=2019&end _year=2019 (accessed June 4, 2021).

———. "Crossover 2020: A Little Over Half of Bills in the General Assembly Are Still Alive." *VPAP.org*. February 13, 2020. https://www.vpap.org/visuals/visual/ crossover-2020/ (accessed June 6, 2021).

———. "Dick Saslaw, 2018–2019." *VPAP.org*. https://www.vpap.org/candidates /47/donor/120206/?start_year=2018&end_year=2019&contrib_type=all (accessed June 4, 2021).

———. "Dominion Energy in 2020–2021." *VPAP.org*. https://www.vpap.org/donors /120206-dominion-energy/?start_year=2020&end_year=2021&recip_type=all (accessed June 4, 2021).

———. "Dominion Energy to Statewide Candidates 2016–2017." *VPAP.org*. https: //www.vpap.org/donors/120206-dominion-energy/?start_year=2016&end_year =2017&recip_type=statewide_cands (accessed June 4, 2021).

————. "Dominion Energy to Virginia State Legislative Candidates in 2016–2017." *VPAP.org.* https://www.vpap.org/donors/120206-dominion-energy/?start_year =2016&end_year=2017&recip_type=leg_cands (accessed June 4, 2021)
————. "Donations from Retail, Services to All Candidates and Committees, 2020–2021." *VPAP.org.* https://www.vpap.org/money/donors-industry-totals/3/ ?recip_type=all&year=2020 (accessed June 4, 2021).
————. "General Assembly: Legislators." 2019. *VPAP.org.* http://www.vpap.org/ general-assembly/legislators/ (accessed June 4, 2021).
————. "House Democratic Caucus." *VPAP.org.* https://www.vpap.org/committees /147803/top_donors/ (accessed June 4, 2021).
————. "House: General Elections, 2017 and 2019." House of Delegates Campaign Spending. *VAPA.org.* https://www.vpap.org/elections/house/candidates/general/ ?year=2017&competition=all&party_in_power=all (accessed June 6, 2021).
————. "House: General Elections, November 2, 2021," *VAPA.org,* https://www. vpap.org/elections/house/candidates/general/ (accessed June 4, 2021).
————. "House: Historical Trends." *VPAP.org.* 2019. https://www.vpap.org/elections /house/historic/ (accessed June 4, 2021).
————. "House Republican Campaign Committee." *VPAP.org.* https://www.vpap.org /committees/148483/top_donors/ (accessed June 4, 2021).
————. "Lobbying in Virginia." 2020. https://www.vpap.org/lobbying/ (accessed June 5, 2021).
————. "Lobbying: Spending." 2019–2020. https://www.vpap.org/lobbying/ spending/all/?disclosure_period=15 (accessed June 5, 2021).
————. "Montgomery for Delegate—Pamela, All Years / All Filing Periods." *VAPA.org.* https://www.vpap.org/committees/369935/top_donors/ (accessed June 9, 2021).
————. "Similar Bills, Different Fates." *VPAP.org.* February 12, 2020. https://www. vpap.org/visuals/visual/similar-bills-different-fates/ (accessed June 6, 2021).
————. "Spike in Democrat-Sponsored Bills." *VPAP.org.* January 20, 2020. https: //www.vpap.org/visuals/visual/spike-democrat-sponsored-bills/ (accessed June 6, 2021).
————. "S Sonjia Smith, 2020–2021." *VAPA.org,* https://www.vpap.org/donors/3320 -s-sonjia-smith/?start_year=2020&end_year=2021&recip_type=all (accessed June 9, 2021).
————. "Taeb for Senate, All Receipts, All Years/All Filing Periods." 2019. *VPAP.org.* https://www.vpap.org/committees/325331/top_donors/ (accessed June 4, 2021).
————. "Taeb for Senate, 2016–2019." *VPAP.org.* https://www.vpap.org/committees /325331/top_donors/?contrib_type=A&start_year=2016&end_year=2019 (accessed June 4, 2021).
————. "Top Donors, 2020–21." *VPAP.org.* https://www.vpap.org/money/top-donors / (accessed June 4, 2021).
————. "Va League of Conservation Voters to State Candidates in 2016–2017." *VPAP.org.* https://www.vpap.org/donors/148192-va-league-of-conservation-voters /?start_year=2016&end_year=2017&recip_type=all_state_cands (accessed June 4, 2021).

————. "Va Uranium to All Candidates and Committees, All Years." *VPAP.org.* https://www.vpap.org/donors/148831-va-uranium/?start_year=all&end_year=all (accessed June 4, 2021).

Vogelsong, Sarah. "At Senate Panel, a Clash Over the Costs of Shifting Away from Carbon." *Virginia Mercury.* February 9, 2020. https://www.virginiamercury.com /2020/02/09/at-senate-panel-a-clash-over-the-costs-of-shifting-away-from-carbon/ (accessed June 6, 2021).

————. "Governor Signs Bill Making Virginia Council on Environmental Justice Permanent." *Virginia Mercury.* March 20, 2020. https://www.virginiamercury.com /blog-va/governor-signs-bill-making-virginia-council-on-environmental-justice -permanent/ (accessed June 3, 2021).

————. "On Eve of Clean Economy Act Vote, a Split Emerges Among Democrats." *Virginia Mercury.* February 10, 2020. https://www.virginiamercury.com/2020 /02/10/on-eve-of-clean-economy-act-vote-a-split-emerges-among-democrats/ (accessed June 6, 2021).

————. "Virginia Clean Economy Act Clears General Assembly, Aided by Beefed -up Ratepayer Protections." *Virginia Mercury.* March 6, 2020. https://www. virginiamercury.com/2020/03/06/virginia-clean-economy-act-clears-general -assembly-aided-by-beefed-up-ratepayer-protections/ (accessed June 6, 2021).

————. "With New Democratic Leadership, General Assembly Faces Flood of Energy Proposals." *Virginia Mercury.* January 6, 2020. https://www.virginiamercury.com /2020/01/06/with-new-democratic-leadership-general-assembly-faces-flood-of -energy-proposals/ (accessed June 6, 2021).

Walker, Julian. "Redistricting plans are approved [by] General Assembly." *Virginian -Pilot.* April 8, 2011. https://pilotonline.com/news/government/politics/virginia/ article_0887636d-2fd7-5232-b804-166ec05bb4bb.html (accessed June 5, 2021).

Warner, Mark R. "The Sensible Center." In *Beyond the Sausage Factory,* edited by Barnie Day and Becky Dale, 288–89. Lawrenceville, VA: Brunswick, 2005.

Washington, George. "A Decision to Free His Slaves." *George Washington's Mount Vernon.* N.d. https://www.mountvernon.org/george-washington/slavery/ washingtons-1799-will/ (accessed April 22, 2021).

Wehner, Peter. *The Death of Politics: How to Heal Our Frayed Republic After Trump.* New York: Harper One, 2019.

Wilder, L. Douglas. *Son of Virginia: A Life in America's Political Arena.* Guilford, CT: Lyons Press, imprint of Rowman & Littlefield, 2015.

Wilkinson, J. Harvie, III. *Harry Byrd and the Changing Face of Virginia Politics, 1945–1966.* Charlottesville: University Press of Virginia, 1968.

World Population Review. "Danville Population, 2000–2020." 2020. https:// worldpopulationreview.com/us-cities/danville-va-population (accessed June 4, 2021).

————. "GDP by State." 2020. https://worldpopulationreview.com/state-rankings/ gdp-by-state (accessed June 2, 2021).

————. "Educational Attainment by State 2021." 2021. https://worldpopulationreview. com/state-rankings/educational-attainment-by-state (accessed June 5, 2021).

Yancey, Dwayne. *When Hell Froze Over: The Untold Story of Doug Wilder, a Black Politician's Rise to Power in the South.* Dallas, TX: Taylor Publishing, with Roanoke Times, 1988.

Zullo, Robert. "Governor's Office Seeks Legislation to Replace Lee Statue at U.S. Capitol." *Virginia Mercury.* December 23, 2019. https://www.virginiamercury.com /2019/12/23/governors-office-will-push-for-removal-of-lee-statue-at-u-s-capitol/ (accessed June 2, 2021).

Interviews

Robert Brink (former Delegate, Virginia House), by author by telephone, August 15, 2020, November 1, 2020, and January 12, 2021.

Whitt Clement (former Delegate, Virginia House, and lobbyist with Hunton, Andrews, Kurth), interview by author by telephone, November 10, 2020.

Lori Haas, by author by telephone, November 20, 2020.

Don Hall (CEO, VADA), by author by telephone, November 19, 2020.

S. Chris Jones (former Delegate, Virginia House), by author by telephone, October 12, 2020.

Robert F. McDonnell (Governor), by author by telephone and email, January 30, 2020 and January 5, 2021.

Delores McQuinn, by author by telephone, November 18, 2020.

Brian Moran (former Virginia Delegate and Secretary of Public Safety), by author by telephone, March 5, 2020.

Ralph S. Northam (Governor), interview by author in person, Richmond, Virginia, June 14, 2021.

Lisa Smith, by author by telephone November 2, 2020.

William Stanley Jr. (Virginia Senator), interview with author, by telephone, November 15, 2020.

Index

About the Author

David J. Toscano, JD, PhD, served fourteen years in the Virginia House of Delegates until his retirement in 2020, which included seven years as Democratic Leader. Prior to that, he was a Charlottesville City Councilor from 1990 to 2002, and served as Mayor in the mid-1990s. Toscano earned his BA from Colgate University, a PhD in Sociology from Boston College in 1979, and a JD from the University of Virginia School of Law in 1986. He is the author of *Fighting Political Gridlock: How States Shape Our Nation and Our Lives* (Charlottesville: University of Virginia Press, 2021).

CPSIA information can be obtained
at www.ICGtesting.com
Printed in the USA
BVHW031202260922
647986BV00018B/576